All the Rage

All the Rage

THE STORY OF GAY
VISIBILITY IN AMERICA

Suzanna Danuta Walters

THE UNIVERSITY OF CHICAGO PRESS • CHICAGO AND LONDON

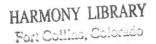

Suzanna Danuta Walters is associate professor of sociology and director of the Women's Studies Program at Georgetown University. She is the author of *Material Girls: Making Sense of Feminist Cultural Theory* and *Lives Together/Worlds Apart: Mothers and Daughters in Popular Culture.*

Portions of chapter 8 were published as "Take My Domestic Partner, Please: Gays and Marriage in the Era of the Visible," in *Queer Families, Queer Politics: Challenging Culture and the State,* edited by Renate Reimann and Mary Bernstein (New York: Columbia University Press, 2001), and are reprinted here by permission.

Portions of chapter 10 were published as "Wedding Bells and Baby Carriages: Heterosexuals Imagine Gay Families, Gay Families Imagine Themselves," in *Lines of Narrative: Psychological Perspectives,* edited by Molly Andrews et al. (New York: Routledge, 2001), and are reprinted here by permission.

The University of Chicago Press, Chicago 60637
The University of Chicago Press, Ltd., London

Library of Congress Cataloging-in-Publication Data
Walters, Suzanna Danuta
    All the rage : the story of gay visibility in America / Suzanna Danuta Walters.
        p.   cm.
    Includes bibliographical references and index.
    ISBN 0-226-87231-9
    1. Homosexuality on television. 2. Homosexuality in motion pictures.
3. Gays in popular culture. 4. Gays—United States—Identity. 5. Gay consumers—
United States. I. Title.
PN1992.8.H64 W35   2001
791.45′653—dc21   2001001665

This book is dedicated to the two most important compañeras in my life, my mother Marianne and my daughter Emma, whose combination of wisdom, commitment, compassion, and humor provide endless joy in the present and expansive hope for the future.

Contents

Acknowledgments

If it takes village to raise a child then it most certainly takes a supportive queer community to birth a book. To continue that unfortunate metaphor, this has been an excruciatingly long gestation. Indeed, there were times I was sure I would never finish it because some new TV show or movie or news bulletin intruded on my sense of finality. Writing this book gave new meaning to the idea of an "unfinished revolution." Thus, my heartiest thanks to all those who midwifed this into light, even though I must assure the reader that—while every effort is in some sense collective—the ideas presented here are mine and I alone am responsible for the good, the bad, and the ugly.

The staff at the University of Chicago Press has been wonderful, from the ebullient Doug Mitchell, whose laudatory comments worked wonders on my ego, to the superb editing and assistance of Russell Harper and Robert Devens, both of whom answered questions (large and small, strange and prosaic) with clarity and alacrity. I must thank the dedicated research assistants who have labored with me over the years on this book. Pedro Briones (researcher/babysitter/activist) was an invaluable help, as was Jamie Poster, who I am convinced will soon make a major contribution to gay studies. I owe you both much. Numerous other students have helped along the way, including Susie Sreedhar and Courtney Frierson. I'd also like to thank my Georgetown students, particularly the delightful and buoyant young women and men of "Representations of Lesbians and Gay Men in Popular Culture" who let me try out these ideas and served as a wonderful resource and sounding board. If they are the future, I'm all for it. The program assistant of the Georgetown Women's Studies Program—Leslie Byers—pitched in when the going got tough and enabled me to finish this work without completely abdicating my other responsibilities. She is invariably smart, capable, helpful, and reassuring. My heartfelt thanks go out to her, and to Carol Gangnath of the Department of Sociology, and Jill Hollingsworth of Lauinger Library. My thanks, too, to Georgetown University for Summer Research Grants, a Junior Faculty Fellowship, and a much needed sabbatical leave that all contributed to the completion of this project. I also want to thank the staff of the Museum of Radio, Television and Film in New York for their eager assistance during a harried visit and the wise and witty crew at Photofest who dutifully dragged out their extensive collection of gay iconography.

The list of colleagues must begin with Josh Gamson, a fairly new friend who fell into my life like some long lost Jewish gay brother. Josh provided always helpful advice, critical readings, and supportive nachas. If only you were a girl, Josh! The members of the Center for the Study of Media and Society project of GLAAD, particularly Catherine Stimpson, Larry Gross, Meg Mortiz, Lisa Henderson, and Rhona Berenstein, have been inspirations in their own work and in the collegiality with which they approach a shared endeavor. Jason Heffner has been enormously supportive and much fun, although we must pledge never to drink martinis together. GLAAD has been a wonderful resource—from their nifty Web site to their wonderful staff. I most especially want to thank the indefatigable Cathy Renna and the resourceful and helpful Jay Plum.

The work of gay scholars is by now a rich and deep treasure trove and—thankfully—numbers too great to list. But some of them have been instrumental—the late Vito Russo, of course, started us all off on this long trek toward a totally gay Hollywood Valhalla, and Larry Gross continues to inspire. Steve Seidman has been both personally supportive and intellectually stimulating in his consistent musings on gay and lesbian identity and politics and, along with Verta Taylor, is one of the few sociologists to bravely cross the disciplinary divides. Michael Warner is always provocative and challenging, and his work has been instrumental in developing my own, as has the work of Michael Bronski. John D'Emilio's historical sensitivity and political economic perspective has helped frame my thoughts as has the groundbreaking work of historians Lillian Faderman, George Chauncey, and Leila Rupp. Barbara Smith's insistent radicalism always adds a much needed reality check to a tendency to be cheerily optimistic. Alisa Solomon has been a tough old political ally whose friendship was forged during the wild antics of "Anonymous Women for Peace" guerilla actions. Another "Anonymous Women" alum continues to inspire—Eve Ensler: one of the few famous people who really deserves her fame. There are too many more gay culture critics than I can even begin to name, but I must put down a few more whose work inspires and incites; Richard Dyer, B. Ruby Rich, Essex Hemphill, Alexander Doty, Constance Penley, Patricia White, Mandy Merck, Judith Mayne, Robin Wood, David Bergman, Isaac Julien, Tania Modleski, and the list goes on.

The women of the feminist poker group (including Valerie Babb, Amy Robinson, Pam Fox, Kim Hall, Elizabeth Velez, Debbie Shore) provided many evenings of unspeakable fun, and the women of the theory study group (including Joan Williams, Leti Volpp, Adrienne Davis, Deborah Tannen, Cindy Aron, Dorothy Ross) proved invariably interesting and a model of sisterly support. My sister Lisa Walters is always there for me, and has pitched in when watching over my daughter and finishing this book became mutually exclusive possibilities. My friend Stanley Aronowitz has always been supportive and a great giver of advice—his lifetime of commitment to social justice is a model for many of us. The work of Ellen Willis fairly crackles with insight and "right-on-ness" and gives cultural journalism a good name. Friend and colleague Molly Andrews, though avowedly heterosexual, is one of the campiest girls I know (remember the gay rodeo in Colorado Springs?). Ara Wilson's sharp mind, cut to the chase commentary, and quick wit continue to enrich my life. Lynn Chancer's idiosyncratic work and equally unusual emotional sensibility keeps a friendship alive. Amy Horowitz—music maven and cultural provocateur—helped me understand the power of patience and has the great gift of knowing how to make a person feel good. I also thank my extended kinship network—including the Levners, the Sreedhars, Barbara Bick, Deborah Shore, and the Brittains.

Marcia Kuntz helped me in ways too numerous to mention, not the least of which has been her watchful and engaged relationship with my daughter. And I'm pleased to say that our tax dollars are hard at work: she proved to be a reliable and helpful source for tracking down legislative arcana and Congressional gossip. We don't see eye to eye on much, but I'm sure we both agree that she has been supportive and caring and infinitely patient.

My faithful and dearest of friends—Annie Gibeau and Diane Lopez— remain the ever-present reminder of what joy a reinvented family can bring to a life. Through the proverbial thick and thin, their support and love is strong and steady. I cherish them both and could not imagine life without them. After twenty years, it only gets better and better.

I thought I was done with mothers and daughters when I finished my first book on that subject. But my wise and witty mother is never far from my thoughts or out of my heart—she is the most gay positive mama a girl could ask for and the most astute judge of the modern moment. She understands the struggle for gay rights not out of some individualized parental love but rather out of her own finely honed sense of justice. She has helped me through the years of work on this book with love, inspiration, careful comments, and lots of childcare. And now that we both revel in the delight that is my daughter Emma, we find that our peculiar story of mother and daughter love extends to another generation. The two of them provide more joy than any one person can rightfully ask for.

Prologue

I think I must have been about 12 or 13 when I first thought I might be gay. I'll never forget the moment I *knew* it to be true, when I kissed a girl for the first time under the stairwell in my school. Like all such kisses, it retrospectively becomes a defining event, although at the time it was simply a thrill. I'll also never forget what it meant to come out, a not-so-sweet sixteen, in what now seems like the medieval 1970s. When I came out, I knew not one other gay teen, although I remember a sensitive boy who avoided my loud coming out like the plague. Now, gay youth groups proliferate and many school systems provide training to staff to alert them to issues of sexual identity. When I came out, I lost many of my high school friends and only found solace with a rather secretive college club. Now, gay teens can meet other gay teens—sometimes even in school-based clubs. Indeed, the Gay, Lesbian and Straight Educational Network (GLSEN) estimates that over seven hundred high school "gay/straight alliances" are registered with the organization, and the numbers continue to grow. When I was a gay teen, harassment was simply what one lived through—the idea of reporting it seemed unimaginable. Now, a young teen in Wisconsin sets a precedent when courts find the school liable for failing to stop anti-gay abuse and awards him close to a million dollars. When I came out, I feared my liberal family would disown me, scorn me, turn away in disgust. Now, kids can refer their folks to PFLAG

(Parents and Friends of Lesbians and Gays) for supportive gay-positive re-education. When I came out, invisibility was taken for granted. I can remember vividly scouring the TV guide for any television program that might give me some indication that I existed, and have only a vague memory of an artsy British broadcast on public TV. I must have watched that every time it was replayed. Now, we have Ellen (and Will and Jack and Carter and Willow . . .). When I came out, I was rushed to a psychiatrist. No one ever suggested that I was healthy. Now, the movement to cure gays again rears its ugly head, but this time it is after all the medical and psychiatric organizations have discredited "reparative therapy" and disavowed the idea of homosexuality as an illness.

When I came out, there were no out gay politicians, no gay studies programs in universities, no advertisements that featured gays, no gay TV stars, few out gay actors, little anti-discrimination legislation, no glossy gay magazines, no gay cruises and few gay festivals. There was no gay chic, no gayby boom, no gay MasterCard. Now, there is all this and more. When I came out, my mother and I both assumed a future without children. Lesbian mother seemed like an oxymoron. Now, we share the care of my daughter and know many gay parents. Then, gay parents routinely hid or lost their kids and few questioned the rightness of this. Now, when a lesbian mom loses her kid, her story becomes a supportive TV Movie of the Week and front page news. When I came out, gay marriage was a contradiction in terms. Now, Congress is so scared it might happen that it enacts legislation to forbid it, free-thinking Vermont gives it a tentative nod, and commitment ceremonies are becoming commonplace.

When I came out, I remember being chased, taunted, spit at. It never occurred to me that I could report this. Now, gay and lesbian anti-violence groups are in most major cities and the inclusion of gays in hate crimes laws moves ahead. When I came out, I ran to the bars because it was the only place I thought I could touch another woman without fearing for my life. Now, that quite justified fear remains of course, but there are plenty of spaces of safety besides the bars and bathhouses. When I came out, I thought homosexuality was the problem. Now, homo*phobia* has been named and declaimed from the byways of small-town America to the grand halls of government. When I came out, I could not help but feel alone, isolated, marginalized. While I knew there was a gay rights movement, the pervasive silence of the larger public world kept me from finding it easily, mired as I was in my overpowering sense of *difference* and aloneness in that difference. Now, that awful closet of isolation and invisibility has been replaced by the wide-open door of public recognition.

Two events, one in 1997 and the other in 1998, dramatically illustrate the new visibility. The coming out of Ellen Morgan on the unevenly successful sitcom *Ellen* was an historic event and in a sense deserved the unprecedented media attention that it garnered. Of course, this televisual fictional event was made juicer and more complicated by the prior coming out of the real life Ellen who plays the character of the same name. Rumors had been circulating for years about DeGeneres's sexuality, and the simultaneous revelation of both the real-life and the fictional Ellen was destined for Hollywood history-making. Indeed, she made the cover of the April 14 *Time* magazine, revealing that, "yep, I'm gay." In addition, she was interviewed by Diane Sawyer on *20/20* (replete with tearful reconciliation with her parents) and put in an appearance on *Oprah* (who also played her therapist on the coming-out episode) the day the episode aired.

There were other television events besides the airing of the actual coming-out episode, because increasingly our mass-mediated cultural world appears as one rebounding, interlocking process rather than a set of discrete objects. In the first place, the show had been airing tongue-in-cheek hints for weeks. Episode after episode included the requisite hints (e.g. Ellen looking in a mirror singing "I feel pretty, oh so pretty. I feel pretty and witty and . . ." ending the song before the word is uttered; or when she is looking at new homes to purchase, she responds to her mother's "where are you?" by popping out of the door and exclaiming "in the closet"). On the talk show circuit, she responded to direct questions about her character's sexuality with coy answers: "The character does find out—and this is where the confusion comes in—that she is Lebanese." On *Good Morning America* she claimed that everything "got totally blown out of proportion. . . .We're adding another character—a guy—and his name is Les Bian."

By the time the actual episode aired, even those most willfully in denial had to admit that Ellen was, indeed, gay. But it did not stop there. In other words, this became a huge and far-reaching media event—no newspaper neglected before-and-after coverage, the news magazines weighed in, and the national gay organizations made this priority number one. The Gay and Lesbian Alliance Against Defamation (GLAAD) sponsored more than fifteen hundred "Come Out with Ellen" home viewing parties, and big-city fundraisers were sponsored by Absolut vodka, replete with celebrity memorabilia including signed scripts from the historic episode and *Ellen* trivia games. GLAAD also fielded thousands of media queries, produced a very popular "Come Out with Ellen" Web page, and served as informal consultants on the coming-out episode (and one of its own—Chastity Bono—even had a guest spot on a later episode).

Protestors showed up at ABC headquarters in Washington, Jerry Falwell referred to her as "Ellen degenerate," a Birmingham Alabama affiliate refused to air the episode, and a Birmingham auditorium was filled to capacity (more than twenty-five hundred people) to witness a direct satellite feed of the episode. A teacher in Alameda was attacked by a parent for discussing the episode in her fifth-grade class (although she was later cleared by the school board and by a state panel), and the network charged twice the normal advertising rates for the episode, and got it. More viewers watched the episode than any other single episode in the history of television, with the exception of the final episode of *M*A*S*H* and the "who shot J.R.?" revelatory episode of *Dallas*. Local stations followed the airing with reports of parties and protests, ancillary commentary on the status of gay life, reports on gays in Hollywood and gays in government. Vice President Al Gore made a speech in October of 1997 to the Hollywood Radio and Television Society where he argued that "when the character Ellen came out, millions of Americans were forced to look at sexual orientation in a more open light." The media coverage even surpassed the Dan Quayle silliness with Murphy Brown. Not long after the coming-out episode, the series was canceled.

If Ellen's coming out was cause to celebrate, then the following year's "gay event" was surely cause to mourn. The 1998 murder of gay University of Wyoming student Matthew Shepard illustrates with sad clarity the state of affairs in the era of visibility. For, of course, death by gay bashing is nothing new. Indeed, there are few gay people who have escaped some form of violence. What was striking was not just the horribleness of the crime, nor that it occurred in these supposedly more liberal times. What *was* astounding to so many was the tidal wave of attention this death garnered. Like the coming-out of Ellen, the murder of Matthew grabbed public attention and shook it by its proverbial ears. On TV news, in magazines and newspapers, in public statements and countless memorials, the death of Matthew Shepard became a flashpoint for gay anger and sympathetic straight grief. While surely Shepard's death was especially ugly (beaten and left tied up on a country road) and his persona especially attractive (nonthreatening, All-American kid from the heartland), that does not wholly explain the depth of the media coverage. In these new times, killing gays still goes on, but it is no longer business as usual. As I joined the mourners on the steps of the Capitol I was struck by the huge presence of the media, politicians crowding to join in, public figures and Hollywood stars weeping at the microphone. Congress joined in the chorus of concern and condemnation. Even the President immediately denounced the incident and named it as a hate crime, using the opportunity to promote stronger legislation in that area. We should never underestimate the significance of an American President speaking out on anti-gay violence. A young gay man's death, which not so very long ago would have been a nonevent, or at best a news story tucked in the back pages, now captivated a nation seeing its sons and daughters with new eyes.

These two events illustrate the confusing and often incomprehensible tenor of the times. We rejoice at breaking down one barrier only to be faced, again, with the ugliness and brutality of another. Ellen comes out, Matthew dies, and the media turns both into iconic events. Ellen gets canceled and Matthew becomes a memory and the parents of both become advocates for equal rights. In the eye of the storm it is sometimes difficult to make out the contours, to see with clarity, to know for sure which way the wind is shifting. Surely, though, we're not in Kansas anymore.

This book is for everyone. It is for the liberal gays, who are now sitting back in wonder at the dawning of a new age, thinking the battles have largely been won. They haven't. Be vigilant. It is for the radical gays, who view with unbridled cynicism these changes, seeing them as solely superficial at best, nefariously co-optive at worst. Relax, there's more to this sea change than homosexuality lite. It is for the conservative gays, who want to slip silently into the night of American society, unnoticed, unseen, unremarked. Forget it guys, keep your suits on but don't ever force our brightly colored tutus back in the closet. It is for the well-meaning heterosexuals, who think an embrace of sameness is the best gays can hope for. It isn't. We cherish our differences. It is for the heterosexuals who didn't even know we existed. Look around you—we are your sons and daughters, husbands and wives, coworkers, bosses, and next-door neighbors. It is for the not so well-meaning straights, who wish fervently that the gay '90s would fade out as a footnote to history. This *is* history. And the new millennium holds hopes and fears as paradoxical as the last.

PART ONE   *It Was the Best of Times, It Was the Worst of Times*

Homosexuality is a sin . . . you should try to show them a way to deal with that problem, just like alcohol . . . or sex addiction . . . or kleptomaniacs.
— Senate Majority Leader Trent Lott on *The Armstrong Williams Show,* June 15, 1998

Being gay, the last time I thought about it, seemed to have nothing to do with the ability to balance a book, fix a broken bone, or change a spark plug.
—former president Bill Clinton addressing the 1997 Human Rights Campaign fundraising gala

On every single kind of question, public opinion toward gay and lesbian people is moving toward acceptance.
—Urvashi Vaid, former director of the Policy Institute of the National Gay and Lesbian Task Force

This sounds like the ultimate homosexual fantasy, that the public is craving leaders who promote and legitimate bizarre sexual acts.
—Robert M. Knight, director of cultural studies for the Family Research Council

One   THE LOVE THAT DARES
TO SPEAK ITS NAME:
THE EXPLOSION OF
GAY VISIBILITY

There is no doubt that gays and lesbians have entered the public consciousness as never before. From cover stories in *Time* and *Newsweek* to TV talk shows and editorials in national and regional newspapers, gays and lesbians have received an unprecedented degree of media attention. Television specials have focused on lesbian communities, lesbian mothers, and the agonies of AIDS. Gay fashion and gay style are featured in glossy magazines. Seven-foot black, gay drag queen RuPaul was the cover girl of the '90s, inspiring both fascination and respect as he entertained millions with his hit songs and videos and entered the public domain with chic ads for high-toned products, tongue-in-cheek cameos in postmodern films, and his own show on VH1.

Where once it seemed as if lesbians and gays never made news, now you can hardly open the *New York Times* or the *Washington Post* (or local papers) without encountering a story with some gay-related theme—from custody suits to anti-discrimination battles, from lesbian activists in Mississippi to proud participants in the Gay Games. Even a cursory search of information data banks such as Lexis-Nexis produces literally thousands of citations, where even five years ago only dozens appeared. In a study of the coverage of gays and lesbians in the news magazines *Time* and *Newsweek* from 1947 to 1997, Lisa Bennett notes that the magazines went from publishing 2 articles in the 1940s, to 21 in the '50s, to

151 in the 1990s. In writing this book, I have been literally overwhelmed by the sheer tonnage of material. "Gayness" has become a favored topic where once it was relegated to either nasty attacks or a culture of avoidance. Popular magazines have glommed on to the new popularity of lesbians and gays, running risqué cover stories such as the one on Grammy winner and open lesbian k.d. lang (replete with sexy photos of lang being shaved by supermodel Cindy Crawford). *Newsweek, Time, Vanity Fair, The New Republic,* and *GQ* are just a few of the publications that have recently produced major stories on bisexual chic, lesbian chic, the rise of gay political power, and gay families, to name just a few. In the January 1994 issue of *Us* magazine, of the top 100 "events" of 1993, "Lesbian Chic" was number 10, "k.d. lang" was number 58, and "Men in Tights" made number 77. In that same issue, a feature story on rock singer Melissa Etheridge focused on her coming out at the gay Triangle Ball during the presidential inauguration. Melissa appeared again on the cover of *Rolling Stone* magazine, draped campily with partner Julie Cypher, two kids, and donor dad David Crosby—touting alternative families.

Superstars are coming out all over—from Martina Navratilova and her parade of glamorous lovers to skirt-wearing, made-up basketball star Dennis Rodman, who proclaims his sexual "openness" to legions of presumably homophobic sports fans. Sitcom cutie Amanda Bearse joins forces with girl-next-door Candace Gingrich and sexy diver Greg Louganis to become spokespeople and poster children for "the cause." That bellwether of popular sensibilities, *People* magazine, regularly includes features and style bits on gay celebrities, lesbian life-partners, and ministers reckoning with their own closets. Even gossip queen Liz Smith outs herself in her best-selling memoir.

Hollywood has hailed the "new queer cinema" as the wave of the future. Gay-themed and gay-produced independent films are carrying away major prizes at reputable film festivals, and the Hollywood mainstream has joined in with a range of gay films, including the hugely popular AIDS drama *Philadelphia* and the drag farce *The Birdcage.* While '80s films like *Desert Hearts* introduced (some) mainstream filmgoers to lesbian sexuality, the hit of 1996—reviewed *everywhere*—was *Go Fish,* an unapologetic and explicit depiction of twenty-something lesbian love in the '90s. Mainstream films are rushing to tilt the image; the gay character (sister, brother, friend) seems to be almost a requirement these days: *Boys on the Side, Home for the Holidays, It's My Party, My Best Friend's Wedding, The Object of My Affection, The Next Best Thing, Four Weddings and a Funeral, Clueless, Priest, Fried Green Tomatoes, Heavenly Creatures, Three of Hearts, Three to Tango, In & Out,* and even the camp send-up of *The Brady*

Bunch (replete with RuPaul as the hip school counselor). There were fourteen gay-related nominations for Academy Awards in 1995, including *Chicks in White Satin,* a film about lesbian weddings, and the year 2000 brought nominations and victories for a small, heartbreaking film about a transgendered youth.

Of course Ellen came out, marking the first time a lead character on a sitcom announced she was gay in prime time. But TV is now filled with gay characters—on high-end dramas such as *E.R.* and *NYPD Blue* and camp cartoons like *The Simpsons.* Gays are witty sidekicks, girls next door, doctors and lawyers, city officials, and teenage experimenters, garnering Emmys, accolades, and great ratings as they invade the family home through the ubiquitous tube.

Cartoon characters are coming out, too. *Doonesbury's* resident hipster Mark realized he was gay, partnered with a conservative buttoned-down Republican, and promptly took on homophobia in the Catholic Church. DC Comics (home of *Superman*) recently introduced a tough lesbian police captain who bravely fights the forces of evil as she balances the needs of lover and child. One of the biggest Broadway hits of recent years—*Angels in America*—is an epic about AIDS, homophobia, and other assorted tribulations of American culture, and its author, the openly gay activist and playwright Tony Kushner, won the Pulitzer Prize. We are in the midst of a gay publishing boom, with substantive advances going to gay authors and gay books hitting the best-seller lists. *Fodor's Guides*—the solemn father-figure of travel advice—has now come out with a guide to "Gay USA." The staid Book of the Month Club has offered a new line of gay and lesbian literature called "Triangle Classics." What's next, a gay *Reader's Digest?*

Advertisers have finally targeted the gay market, and companies like Banana Republic, Gap, Benetton, American Express, and Apple Computer have had gay-toned ads in both gay and straight publications. Even the macho brewmeisters at Budweiser urge readers to realize that "labels are for clothes, not people" and you should "have fun, be yourself, and make it a Bud Light." AT&T initiated a national mail campaign aimed at the lesbian and gay community and Subaru cars are set to target the always ignored lesbian market. You can now get American Express traveler's checks with your same-sex partner, and see Martina Navratilova's schedule on her Apple PowerBook. The Los Angeles Police Department "has used a deeply tanned, chisel-faced model in a wet suit to convey its recruitment messages to readers of a gay magazine called Urban Fitness. 'Not All Out Officers Wear The Same Uniform,' the full-color advertisement proclaims."[1] The furniture superstore IKEA sent shock waves through Madison Avenue with its mild portrayal of a gay male couple buying a dining room table, prompting conservative critics to herald the demise of "family values" in the face of gay interior decorating.

The major gay organizations—the Human Rights Campaign and the National Gay and Lesbian Task Force—have seen an unprecedented rise in memberships and contributions, leading to lavish and expensive fundraisers and benefits that would have been unheard of only a few years earlier. Presidents and vice presidents speak at their gatherings. In addition, new organizations have developed—many around the AIDS crisis (ACT-UP, Queer Nation) but many others geared to electoral politics and governmental lobbying (e.g. Victory Fund, Stonewall Democrats, Log Cabin Republicans). The Gay and Lesbian Alliance Against Defamation grows as a feared watchdog of Hollywood homophobia, receives unprecedented funds from granting agencies, and plays frequent "script consultant" for an increasingly pink Tinseltown. The Stonewall Inn— site of the 1969 riot that many see as the birth of the modern gay rights movement—has received national historic landmark status by the Department of the Interior, a first for a gay-related location.

Family life is not immune from this historic shift. Domestic partnership laws, gay marriages, donor insemination, adoption—all unthinkable a few years ago—are now part of the larger social landscape. Gays are having children in record numbers, and lesbian and gay families have become the subject of docudramas and news articles, feature films and advertising campaigns, forcing their way into the mediascape of "family values." Hundreds of universities, cities, towns, and private businesses (including major corporations such as Apple Computer and Disney) have instituted domestic partnership policies, allowing unmarried couples (both homosexual and heterosexual) to share health benefits, housing rights, and other amenities typically accorded only to married heterosexuals. Even Reform rabbis have agreed to officially sanction same-sex unions, making them the first major religious denomination to do so.

The hallowed halls of academia are slowly filling with the voices and images of the minority still legally outside equal-opportunity laws. Gay studies programs are cropping up at universities around the country. In 1989 the City College of San Francisco established the first department of lesbian and gay studies in the United States, and just one year later the Center for Lesbian and Gay Studies opened at the Graduate Center of the City University of New York. New gay academic journals are popping up all over, many located in such revered sites as Harvard University, and gay alums and gay-friendly corporations are sponsoring college scholarships for out gay kids with good GPAs. Dozens of courses and curricula are being developed in the expectation that lesbian and gay studies, still marginalized in the academy, will soon go the way of at least some of the programs in black and women's studies and be fully integrated into the everyday life of the academy. Prestigious universities such as New York University advertise for administrative positions that serve the "gay, lesbian, bisexual, and transgendered" community, and gay history month is slowly taking a place women's history and black history have already secured.

Everywhere there are gay entrepreneurs, creating flourishing businesses in retailing (selling every form of pink triangle and rainbow accessory!), travel, services, entertainment. There are gay rodeos and gay cruises, gay retirement homes and gay campsites. You can get a gay housecleaner, a gay carpenter, and buy your PC at a gay computer store. If you're planning on renting a car or taking a trip, be sure to use the Los Angeles–based Access Alliance service, which provides discounts to lesbian and gay consumers. And if you're flying, United Airlines wants you to know that they're "helping build a stronger community" with their support of gay and lesbian organizations. If you're moving, be assured that you can hire some nice gay boys and girls to handle your valuables. You can brunch and watch a drag show at any number of restaurants, or just go to New York's Lucky Cheng's for an all-drag dining experience. If you're visiting the City of Brotherly Love, don't forget to check out the wildly popular Gay Bingo night, featuring a cross-dressed campy emcee and benefiting AIDS support services. You can even get advice on lesbian romantic conundrums from Judith Martin's Miss Manners. If your spirit needs replenishment, you can now chill out at "a 22-acre ranch that has been transformed into an ecumenical spiritual retreat for gays and lesbians."[2]

If theme parks rock your world, you can join the gay denizens of Mickey Mouse at the annual gay day at Disney World (100,000 in 1998), or sample the rollercoaster at Virginia's Kings Dominion, which recorded a record 3,000 people for its "gay day" in 1998. If religion is your thing, you can join the hundreds of gay and gay-friendly churches and synagogues around the nation, including the hugely popular Metropolitan Community Church with 314 congregations in 16 countries, totaling a membership of over 50,000.[3] The quadrennial Gay Games have hit the big time, with countries vying for the right to host thousands of gay athletes and onlookers in a combination sports event, cultural festival, and lovefest that rivals Woodstock. 1998's Amsterdam Gay Games brought 15,000 competitors engaging in standard athletic fare as well as the requisite "drag races" and tutu-wearing volleyball games. World famous gay artists and performers entertained thousands, including the Israeli trans-sexual Dana International, whose victory in the Eurovision Song Contest rocked the Middle East.

The first National Lesbian and Gay MasterCard was launched; you can now have a portion of your telephone bill go to lesbian and gay causes through "Community Spirit" (the long-distance calling program "for our community"); and the all-American Miller Brewing Company sponsored Gay Games IV. There is even a gay beer: Triangle Brew. There are camps for kids of lesbians and gay parents, gay retirement communities, and oodles of gay vacation resorts, including a resort for "couples just like us" in "gay and lesbian friendly" St. Croix. And for those who miss their Barbies and Kens, you can get a Billy doll, replete with trendy outfits from hot designers.

Capitalizing both on the new interest in gay and lesbian life and the increasing "outness" of the gay community, gays are not only insisting that mainstream culture "get with the program" and depict gay life in meaningful ways, but have begun to produce their own media, including numerous cable access programs, and slick publications such as *Out* and *Curve,* replete with ads from major corporations and companies. The Gay Television Network (GTN) is set to launch on Dish Satellite Network, featuring talk shows ("Good Morning, Gay America"), music videos, religious services, gay-themed movies, and a cooking show hosted by transvestite Betty Delicious.[4] Gay merchandising firms are proliferating, Gay and Lesbian Business Expos attract hundreds of high-profile companies, and the "gay market" has become the subject of numerous surveys and polls. Proudly displaying themselves *as* gay, these products and services don't hide behind the old brown paper wrapper or lurk in the backrooms of seedy stores.

But if gays seem like the paragons of trendiness, then they are being simultaneously depicted as the very anti-Christ, the sign of a culture in decay, a society in ruins, the perverse eclipse of rational modernity. As religious fundamentalism grows, becomes mainstream and legitimate, so too does hard-edged homophobia. The country's most popular radio talk-show therapist—Dr. Laura Schlessinger—feels few qualms about declaring on her show of December 8, 1998, that "if you're gay or a lesbian, it's a biological error that inhibits you from relating normally to the opposite sex. . . . The error is in your inability to relate sexually, intimately, in a loving way to a member of the opposite sex—it is a biological error." Nevertheless, in another indication of the contradictory nature of the current moment, her hard-edged homophobia was met with even more determined anti-homophobia. Indeed, "even she could not have been prepared for the resistance by gays and feminists that preceded

[the] debut of her new eponymous weekday TV show. Her incendiary views have galvanized anti-hate groups into perhaps the most successful 'education campaign aimed at advertisers'—don't call it a boycott—in talk-show history. Before the television show was ever on the air, potential advertisers were backing out. Even her six-year-old radio show starting taking on water, and 16 percent of the regular advertisers have jumped ship."[5] One can argue that, in a strange way, Dr. Laura's failure was due to an odd combination of gay activism and the absence of gay-bashing on her cleaned-up TV show. While hateful Dr. Laura's power may be on the wane, hate crimes are on the rise—not just in pure numbers but in the severity and brutality of the acts: anti-gay violence rose 127 percent from 1988 to 1993, and in 1998 the FBI reported a 14.3 percent increase from the previous year, even though other serious crimes experienced an overall decline. Since the institution of "don't ask, don't tell," dismissals of lesbian and gay service members have risen precipitously. President Clinton has been called the most pro-gay president, yet he authored this disappointing policy on the military.

In Colorado and Oregon, as in numerous cities and counties, initiatives and referenda have been introduced to deny lesbians and gay men equal rights under the law. Anti-gay referenda are not new, but from 1992 to 1995 they grew exponentially, and they show no signs of abating, jumping from 160 bills affecting gays in state legislatures in 1996 to 472 in 1999. Opposition to gay rights is proving to be a litmus test for Christian "family values" in electoral politics, so that a notoriously "gay-friendly" president pledged his opposition to gay marriage in the name of those self-same "family values." For the right wing, gay rights have emerged as the proverbial line in the sand, prompting a 1998 series of ads promoting the "ex-gay movement" and reparative therapy and making anti-gay state legislation top priority.

(IN)VISIBILITY BLUES

So are these really the *worst* of times? Or is this backlash only a temporary roadblock along the clear path towards true inclusion? If the problem once was perceived as invisibility itself, then how is the problem defined in an era of increased visibility? If the closet was the defining metaphor for gay life in earlier eras, then what do we make of the swinging door that is gay life in the nineties and beyond? It is not that the closet itself has disappeared; many still feel its power and live deeply within its parameters. But it is no longer simply life as we knew it.

Gay life and identity, defined so much by the problems of invisibility, subliminal coding, double entendres and double lives, has now taken on the dubious distinction of public spectacle. Everyone seems to agree that the '90s were gay, but beyond the odes to openness, diversity and "tolerance," few (except on the right of course!) have questioned the value of this almost obsessive fascination with gay life. At first glance, perhaps even after some thought, these stunning changes seem all for the good. And, really, none look back fondly on older times. As a long-time student of the media and an analyst of popular culture, I cannot help but be intrigued by the cacophony of competing images and attitudes, legislation and government decrees. But as a media scholar I also realize that this brave new world demands a rich, textured, and subtle analysis, not simply celebratory high-fives or nostalgic pessimism.

Surely, times *are* better, but I believe there are ways in which this new visibility creates new forms of homophobia (for example, the good marriage-loving, sexless gay vs. the bad, liberationist, promiscuous gay) and lends itself to a false and dangerous substitution of cultural visibility for inclusive citizenship. In many ways, this moment provides us with a picture of a society readily embracing the *images* of gay life but still all too reluctant to embrace the *realities* of gay identities and practices in all their messy and challenging confusion. We may be *seen,* now, but I'm not sure we are *known.*

Then what *are* these new eyes seeing? Are they seeing the richness and complexity of gay life? Or are they becoming glazed over, dimmed by the rush of bright colors? How are we to understand these confusing times? We *are* witnessing an historic moment in American society. These times *are* earth-shattering and exciting, but also deeply confusing, often ambiguous, and paradoxical with a vengeance. It is a *paradox* because the increased visibility of marginalized groups often creates new restrictions and recycles old stereotypes. It is often assumed that increasing visibility is a unmitigated "good thing," inherently promoting awareness and producing sensitivities. Most people believe that the more lesbians and gays are assimilated into the everyday life of American society, the more readily straight people will "understand" and "accept" them. To some extent, I believe this to be true. As an openly gay person I have ample evidence that seeing gays and lesbians in all walks of life helps to shatter old myths and challenge misinformed judgments. I have seen numerous students and colleagues reevaluate their prejudices when faced with a lesbian professor. Indeed, several years ago, when I announced my pregnancy, a colleague's first words were "But I never thought *you* wanted to have a *family!*"—the assumption being, of course, that lesbians and gay men were beyond the realm of family life. While she is not quite on the barricades for gay rights, my everyday presence and that of my daughter has surely made her more aware of the multiple ways of forming family. More recently, a student taking my class on gay and lesbian representations in the media sent me the following note:

> As a heterosexual student here at Georgetown, I must say that I probably learned more in your class than I have in any other class I have taken in my four years here. Before this class, I can't say that I knew very many openly homosexual students, or anything about the issues they deal with on a daily basis. I feel far more informed today on issues important to the gay community than I did on the first day of class in August. I never considered myself homophobic, but as I look back, I see that some of my actions could easily have been construed as such. I think that this course should be recommended to every student at Georgetown, because I know that every person that takes this class would be a better human being for doing so. I just thought that you would appreciate knowing that you and your class have really made a difference in at least one formerly homo-uneducated individual.

So there is some merit, then, in the idea that a simple *closeness* to gay people (through media images, through family relationships, through out gay coworkers, through teachers) creates a familiarity, an ease, that begins to overcome prejudice and irrational fear.

Yet is "getting to know us" a clear and untrammeled route to social change? During the last presidential debating season, the Republican vice presidential candidate (now VP) Dick Cheney (father of lesbian Mary) was applauded for urging us "to do whatever we can to tolerate and accommodate whatever kind of relationships people want to enter into." In this statement, are we witnessing the strange logic of acceptance come home to roost? Is this a more secular version of "love the sinner, hate the sin?" Why does the major gay rights organization take Cheney's acceptance of his daughter (but embrace of anti-gay party platforms) as a sign of change, claiming that he "broke ranks with Bush and the extreme right" even when his love for his lesbian daughter has not altered one iota his support for explicitly anti-gay policies and platforms? Indeed, Cheney is not just applauded for "accepting" his lesbian daughter, but is seen as a "fitting model for this moment," a moment in which "the center is shifting because millions of Dick Cheneys, people in the middle who might prefer not to think about the rights of gays and lesbians, one day see the issue indelibly stamped with the faces of their daughters, sons, neighbors and friends."[6] The "center" then becomes an apt metaphor for "don't ask, don't tell, don't think, don't act," a place to "accept and be tolerant," a place to be compassionate and to love your kid *even* if she is gay. But the center, then, is not a place to challenge unjust laws and unequal treatment. The fact that he doesn't buck his party's abysmal and Draconian stance towards lesbians and gays recedes to the background as his "bravery" in standing by his gay daughter trumps more substantive proposals and initiatives to enable that same daughter to have equal rights with his other, heterosexual, daughter. "Accepting" your gay daughter is no compensation for second-class citizenship and may in fact mask the continued reality of structural exclusion even as it creates the illusion of inclusion (see, even the Republicans have gay kids!).

The simple visibility of gay people and concomitant steps toward assimilation are not, therefore, solely beneficent. We tend to believe the illusion of visibility as progress and this is nowhere more true than when we think of gays, whose lives have been so deeply constructed by denial, avoidance, invisibility, and subterfuge. Indeed, it is hard for me—a child of a different time—to avoid the celebratory glee. To finally see oneself and be *seen* publicly is exhilarating. My heart *does* leap with the joy that public recognition brings. Every time I turn on the TV, flip through a magazine, watch a movie, or listen to politicians I am awed by the new presence of my tribe in civil life.

But is visibility enough? Can it even be a setback? Can visibility be a dead end, or a road to nowhere, or, worse, a deceptively smooth path that can knock us off the course of meaningful change? History has shown us—with horrifying detail—the ways in which forms of bigotry sustain themselves and even grow in the face of public, cultural visibility. No group of Jews were more visible and mainstreamed than German Jews. Rape statistics and sexual harassment claims rise as women become more visible in the public sphere. While there may not be a causal relationship between the two, public visibility has not stopped violence nor ended discrimination. Women's visibility in popular culture has clearly not "led" to real political or social power, although surely it has been a part of the changes wrought by the women's movement. African-Americans are no longer depicted simply as smiling servants or brutal gangsters, yet impoverishment and disenfranchisement continues to grow. The enormous success of *The Cosby Show* in the '80s—which brought middle-class African-Americans into the living rooms of millions of homes around the world—coexisted alongside increased racial discrimination and governmental neglect. Ironically, it was one of the most popular shows in apartheid South Africa! To be *seen,* therefore, is not necessarily to be *known.* Indeed, media saturation of a previously invisible group can perpetuate a new set of pernicious fictions, subduing dissent by touting visibility as the equivalence of knowledge.

And of course, the visibility of any minority group is always tenuous at best. One year's saturation can turn into next year's old news, as the minority group is made "re-invisible" and finds itself truly back to the future. As critic Josh Gamson points out, "It's certainly not hard to find the homo, which is a great relief if you've been mostly invisible at the center of American culture, but somehow I'm not ready to celebrate. After all, not long ago *The Cosby Show* seemed to put the nail in the coffin of all-white TV, and hour-long dramas like *ER* and *NYPD Blue* are as racially integrated as can be, yet this season, as Kweisi Mfume of the National Association for the Advancement of Colored People (NAACP) pointed out to high publicity, the major networks planned their entire lineup of new shows without a single major character of color. . . . It can't hurt to be more visible, for sure, but you can be made to disappear just as abruptly."[7] And Daniel Harris argues that "the concept of visibility . . . assumes that the concrete legal changes that we have failed to realize through conventional methods can be enacted through a more media centered approach,"[8] which often depends on an airbrushing of the blemishes of gay difference.

Visibility is, of course, necessary for equality. It is part of the trajectory of any movement for inclusion and social change. We come to know ourselves and to be known by others through the images and stories of popular culture. There is nothing worse than to live in a society in which the traces of your own existence have been erased or squeezed into a narrow and humiliating set of stereotypes. The power of cultural visibility and memory is potent, and the absence of that public face can crush even the hardiest souls. I remember that so vividly from my own history, and wonder how different things might have been had I and those of my generation seen other gays in some symbolic register. But visibility does not erase stereotypes nor guarantee liberation. In this age of new gay visibility, for example, one of the most popular television characters is the narcissistic, shallow, Cher-loving, boy-chasing, fashion-obsessed, show-tune-singing Jack of *Will & Grace*—a sturdy stereotype if ever there was one. The fact that he is proudly gay and hilariously witty adds no small amount of confusing static to our cultural reception.

Never have we had so many openly gay elected officials, *or* so many anti-gay initiatives. Domestic partnership laws and regulations proliferated just as Congress officially moved to restrict marriage to heterosexuals. A state supreme court rules that the Boy Scouts can't discriminate against gay scoutmasters, the Supreme Court overturns the ruling, and editorials in major papers largely support the right of gays to be scouts. Indeed, "almost six months after the U.S. Supreme Court upheld the Boy Scouts' right to discriminate against Gays, a small but growing number of local governments, school boards, churches synagogues, United Ways, and businesses are cutting—or reducing—their ties to the once universally venerated youth organization,"[9] including seven cities and agencies, fourteen school systems, nine corporate and charitable foundations, ten individual Scout groups, and eight religiously affiliated institutions. As gay religious organizations grow, so do attempts to rein in gay-positive clergy who minister to homosexual congregations. The very fact that churches are wrestling with the issues of gay ordination and inclusion speaks to great change, even as these struggles often end in defeat for gays, such as the recent ban on gay ordinations decreed by the Presbyterian Church.

Contradictions abound. Indeed, within the course of just a few brief weeks in 1996, we saw the Supreme Court issue the strongest pro-gay rights ruling ever (*Romer v. Evans*) *and* Congress proclaim gays ineligible to participate in the institution of marriage (Defense of Marriage Act). Gay weddings abound on TV as they are being denounced in Congress. Ellen comes out on prime time, only to be denounced by the usual right-wing suspects as well as gospel girls Angie and Debbie Winans, who released a song called "Not Natural," rapping that "there were people celebrating and congratulating the new addition to the gay community . . . but just because it's popular doesn't mean it's cool. It's not natural." Gays are at once the sign of social decay *and* the chic flavor of the month.

The age of visibility produces both realities: the hopeful moments of rights and inclusion and the fearful moments of victimization and reaction. Some have argued that the contemporary moment reveals an accepting and positive *cultural* milieu for gays but a retrogressive and excluding *political* environment. Richard Lacayo, for example, claims that "gay politics is more complicated than ever right now because what seems like an irresistible force of cultural change is meeting an immovable object of political resistance. For a long time, lesbians and gays have been defining themselves into the ordinary fabric of life. All the while, conservatives have been field-testing homosexuality as a defining issue for the Republican Party, especially for the next presidential election. This is all happening while Americans generally are drifting toward a bumpy accommodation, making judgements that are intricate, ad hoc and unpredictable."[10] Contra this analysis, I see *both* the cultural shifts and the political shifts as contradictory. Both environments—both the cultural and the political—are captured by the same paradox of visibility and filled with similar contradictions and confusions. The cultural moment is not wholly embracing, nor the political moment wholly rejecting: both realms coexist and interact in an uneasy mix of opportunity and opposition, inclusion and exclusion. I see this period as one of strange and confusing disjunctures and ruptures: disjunctures between gay weddings and the Defense of Marriage Act; between the actual custody case of Sharon Bottoms (in which a Virginia lesbian lost her son to her own mother) and the laudatory TV movie of her life; between the astounding victory for civil unions in Vermont and the crushing blow of anti-gay Proposition 22 in California; between lavish fundraisers and the realities of continued political exclusion.

Certainly culture and politics move at different paces and sometimes it does seem as if the public world of media culture is the real site of dramatic change, becoming a more welcoming place for lesbians and gays. It would be easy to see this time, therefore, as one marked by seismic *cultural* shifts and faltering *political* steps, but that framework is too simple and belies the "uneven development" that characterizes these gay '90s. We all carry with us a belief in a sort of causal connection between cultural visibility and political change, but I am convinced that, more often than not, there is actually a radical *disconnect* between the two. Further, the seemingly obvious signs of cultural change are more complicated than they initially appear. At times, cultural visibility can simply be synonymous with commercial exploitation or with the "de-gaying" of gayness for heterosexual consumption. As gay culture critic Michael Bronski says, these "displays of contained gay culture depend on a context in which homosexuality has little possibility of an authentic, sustained public presence. In this framework they function as an outlet, albeit limited, for gay expression as well as a safe place for the dominant culture to experience pleasure and freedoms."[11] At other times, though, cultural visibility can really push the envelope, bringing complicated and substantive gay identities into public view. And sometimes these cultural images slowly, almost imperceptibly, chip away around the edges of bigotry, never really getting to the core but perhaps revealing it all too clearly.

The same is true for political initiatives—some offer gays inclusion into the heterosexual mainstream at too great a cost, while others go beyond inclusion to shake up politics as usual. The project at hand—the goal of this book—is to identify these disparate moves of visibility so we are better able to understand which forms of visibility are the ones that shake up the world, and which ones just shake us down.

HOMOSEXUALITY LITE: BEYOND GAY CHIC

Far too often, gay access to cultural visibility seems predicated on an acceptance of two possible modes of representation: the exotic but ultimately unthreatening "other" (the cuddly cross-dresser), or gays as really straights after all, the "aren't we all just human beings" position that reduces cultural specificity to a bland sameness that ends up assuming and asserting the desirability of the mainstream. Few seem able to move beyond the cultural preoccupation with gays as "really" just the same as heterosexuals after all. In earlier times, gays were simply depicted as deviants, as aliens from sexual outer space set to wreak havoc on straight ("normal") society. But in these more open times, lesbians and gays are more often represented as "normal" (just like us), or at least as having the same basic social and material needs as heterosexuals.

It is reminiscent of the insidiously racist statements made by whites when they utter such phrases as "But I don't think of you as *black.*" While often well-meaning, these sort of statements indicate the dangers of a thoughtless assimilationism. What kind of life can be lived when it is made "acceptable" by the refusal of its difference, its specificity? What does it mean that the Human Rights Campaign responds to anti-gay "conversion" ads with its own ads claiming, "We are a typical American family, with old roots in the heart of America. . . . We cross-country ski. We're Republicans." Noted gay historian John D'Emilio argues that this new, normalizing visibility "performs the useful function of—and I use this word advisedly—*normalizing* gay as a part of our landscape. Which I think is a good thing. I mean the fact that in the course of your evening's entertainment, heterosexuality is broken, something else intrudes—that is a good thing." [12] Well, yes and no. In an episode of the (now canceled) TV series *Designing Women,* one of the continuing characters meets up with an old friend who turns out to be a lesbian. Her initial—and quite virulent—homophobia is challenged not through an understanding of the variety of human sexuality and cultural difference, but rather through the insistent assertion that they are all alike, gay and straight. The gay woman is never shown in any gay cultural or social context, and is stereotypically "feminized." Indeed, the episode ends with the heterosexual woman "accepting" her lesbian friend because she realizes how alike they really are. So alike that she insists that "if we can get a man on the moon, we can surely get one on you" to her new lesbian friend. Now, it is not to say that lesbians (and gay men) don't come in all styles, and that many "resemble" heterosexuals. But far too often this new visibility and "acceptance" (itself such a problematic term yet one used all too frequently) is predicated on a comparative model: the straight person (or character in a film or TV show) can only "accept" the gay person once he or she has interpreted that person as "just like me."

The flip side of the depiction of gays as straights in (fashionable) sheep's clothing is the depiction of gays as chic arbiters of cutting-edge style. In a culture so relentless in its search for new people and objects to sell in an endlessly omnivorous marketplace, the current fascination with the vicissitudes of "gay style" must surely be greeted with suspicion. It might be fun to see top models and pop stars donning the accouterments of the opposite gender (Madonna in suit and monocle, the faux lesbian scenes of contemporary advertising, Denis Rodman in lipstick and skirt), but this is not to be confused with social acceptance of gender ambiguity. When drag star Lypsinka models for retail chain the Gap, are we to believe gay liberation has been achieved? After all, the very antithesis of drag (gay conservative icon Andrew Sullivan) also modeled for the Gap. How do we understand the relationship between these hip media images and the stubborn persistence of discrimination? These are the best of times *and* the worst of times.

Gay as chic can be used in ways that deflect attention away from more substantive concerns about lesbian and gay civil rights. Lesbian activist and author Sarah Schulman argues that "what we're seeing is the creation of a false public homosexuality that is palatable and containable and that is not authentic. This first happened with AIDS and now it's happening to gay life in general."[13] The straight flirtation with the more "transgressive" aspects of gay culture should not be mistaken for an honest embrace of the varieties of gay life. Indeed, the current hipness of drag among the heterosexual cognoscenti might be more akin to white delight in Amos and Andy and "Stepin Fetchit" than to any substantive engagement with gay culture and homophobia.

RuPaul is himself representative of the ambivalence of this transformation. Seen at an awards ceremony with Milton Berle (who ad-libbed at his expense) and on billboards advertising make-up and liqueurs, RuPaul began as a cult favorite in clubs and dance halls. He is now marketed by record producers and fashion houses as the ultimate crossover drag queen. Like Madonna's public toying with lesbianism, RuPaul's persona has been carefully crafted; he is not so much a drag queen as the image of one. Even his hit video "Supermodel" artfully played on artifice itself—RuPaul posing as the young starlet seeking fame and fortune on New York's fashion runways. RuPaul merged the artificial world of high-fashion modeling with the subculture of vogue balls to create a giddy image of gender-bending camp. Is he the radical gender-bender, forcing straight culture to reckon with the love that dare not speak its name? Or is he rather the harmless side dish for an omnivorous cultural appetite, simply the '90s version of Berle's assuredly heterosexual cross-dresser? Straight people may watch and enjoy RuPaul and then think that they have somehow done their "gay-positive" deed for the day. The cultural visibility of crossing often "crosses out" the cultural visibility of the more mundane and prosaic gender-bending moves, such as lobbying Congress for an end to employment discrimination, or pursuing second-parent adoptions. In other words, it might just do more harm than good.

Our current historical moment seems mired in this ambivalence: are gays the exotic other to be watched voyeuristically from a safe distance, or are gays just June and Ward Cleaver with different haircuts, family friends you can go bowling with and slap on the back? While this new visibility has indeed opened up public awareness and an appreciation of gay and lesbian rights, it has also circumscribed those rights into categories that may themselves become new kinds of "closets." The options appear too limiting: either representation as somehow "other," different from the "average person," or as "the same as you and me" and therefore accepted under that criterion.

And what to say to gays who decline the position of spectacle but who also aren't really interested in being Cleaver clones? Gays ought not need to put a straight face on homosexuality (another form of the closet) in order to be treated as free and equal citizens; indeed, to do so is to implicitly accept the limiting stereotypes that have so plagued gays for years. Gay difference is therefore reduced to sexual choice; if gayness is redefined as fashion statement, all that is left to differentiate gays and straights is the object of sexual desire. Furthermore, gay identity is made legitimate only through assimilation into the dominant heterosexual gestalt.

The real *dangers* of homophobia are too often brushed aside in depictions of generous heterosexuals embracing their gay brethren. And *homophobia* itself is largely depicted as either the brutal acts of narrative outsiders (anonymous gay bashers, ancillary characters) or the automatic response of over-the-top bigots (e.g. the corporate monsters of the film *Philadelphia*). Alternately, when homophobia is (rarely) portrayed within the universe of the main characters, it is seen as the misguided ignorance of basically good-hearted people who will, eventually, see the error of their ways and walk down the path of "tolerance."

Perhaps D'Emilio is right when he suggests that "we are both different and the same, and, while mainstream culture may take care of the same part—which they've never done before—it's sort of up to us to preserve the different part."[14] In the face of an homogenizing culture, a culture that reduces difference to another sexy commodity, a culture that too often uses the metaphor of melting pot rather than tossed salad, this will be hard work indeed.

STRAIGHT FACES

Of course, many gay people *do* want assimilation and nothing more. Indeed, conservatives like Andrew Sullivan have been pushing this line for years, arguing that "before AIDS, gay life—rightly or wrongly—was identified with freedom from responsibility, rather than with its opposite. Gay liberation was most commonly understood as liberation from the constraints of traditional norms, almost as a dispensation that permitted homosexuals the absence of responsibility in return for an acquiescence in second-class citizenship. This was the Faustian bargain of the pre-AIDS closet: straights gave homosexuals a certain amount of freedom; in return, homosexuals gave away their self-respect."[15] For many like Sullivan, self-respect is precisely defined by the toleration of heterosexual society. If a gay person successfully garners that acceptance, he or she can fit in and has "made it."

Of course, there is an important truth to this: obviously gays should not be depicted as freaks and others, as sideshows to the main stage of heterosexual family life. And of course gays are "just like straights" in some important, human ways. We all want to find satisfying relationships, meaningful work, supportive communities. But, like many such well-intentioned discourses, this misses two important points. First, it depends on sameness to argue for equality. When mainstream gays and their straight allies argue for the inclusion of gays because gays are no different from straights, real inclusion can never take place. This is never a smart move, because once those inevitable differences rear their flamboyant heads, the rug is pulled out from under the unsteady furniture of tolerance. As Michael Warner forcefully argues, this normalizing move "merely throws shame on those who stand farther down the ladder of respectability,"[16] gaining respectability for a few at the expense of relegating the "abject" to the nether regions of disenfranchised otherness. And second, the assimilation route eradicates the difference difference makes by rendering invisible the lived experience of being gay in a homophobic culture, an experience that—while not singular certainly—is also not *reducible* to the dominant heterosexual gestalt. One of the positive "fallouts" of discrimination is the forging of community and the development of a concern for others, activism, a culture of responsibility. The response to AIDS is only one example.

Many of the odes to assimilation do ring true—and a return to invisibility and narrow coded stereotypes would be anathema to even the most critical gay activists. But many—both currently and in the past—have celebrated the differences in being gay, and have linked gay struggles for equality with larger agendas of social change and cultural transformation. The new visibility—by focusing so much on gay similarity to "straight" people—can therefore erase and marginalize those who desire something more than mere inclusion in straight society. Nevertheless, as Ellen Willis, director of NYU's Cultural Reporting and Criticism program, points out, "It is a victory to get into the cultural mainstream because this then provides a springboard from which you can always have more radicalism. I don't ultimately believe in cooptation.

I don't really think that's the way it works. I think what happens is that there's a struggle between radical ideas and a more conservative culture and then some kind of usually liberal compromise takes place."[17]

Nowhere is this tension more vivid than in the recent "breaking of bread" between archconservative Jerry Falwell and newly out gay minister Mel White and assorted gay activists and religious figures. Is eating brunch with a man who claims gays an abomination and Teletubby Tinky Winky an undercover agent for kid-hungry gay perverts a sign of changing times, warming hearts, expanding viewpoints? Or is it the sure sign that gay radicalism has breathed its last breath, that the leaders now are more likely to be "people of faith" than "people of the rainbow"? As writer Richard Goldstein asks, "What happens when a leader is more interested in returning to the fold than in breaking the mold? The answer will determine whether the gay movement is about changing straights or accepting their hospitality."[18]

RETHINKING THE RAINBOW

There is surely the potential to turn the current "chic" status of gays into real and substantive political power and social inclusion, and Willis is right in insisting that "there is a certain squeezing the toothpaste out of the tube character of cultural change. It never goes back to where it was before."[19] But there is also the real danger of this period becoming a passing phase, a fleeting moment of flamboyant fun in the rollercoaster ride that is American popular culture. For the "gay '90s" (and beyond) to be meaningful, this new visibility must bring with it substantive social transformations—equal rights legislation, revised domestic partnership and marriage laws, vigorous enforcement of hate crimes, and the opening up of all areas to lesbians and gay men.

The many venues of increased visibility for lesbians and gays can be understood as both opportunity and obstacle—opportunity to secure civil, political, and social rights while at the same time posing the threat of creating new stereotypes, imposing new and equally limiting rules of conduct, convincing gays that they are "accepted" even as they fade into yesterday's news. The gaying of American culture can and should be more than fleeting fashion statement or subcultural suicide. In insisting on visibility without assimilation, the new gay moment can change the table setting themselves, not simply find places already set. Indeed, the very future of American democracy is dependent on these difficult issues: the ability to revel in difference without succumbing to discrimination; the ability to be known but not to be explained away; the ability to be imagined but not to be compared.

Perhaps what we need is something like a "conscious integration" where the play of differences helps to break down stubborn categories while at the same time enhancing substantive civil rights. But this cannot be done at the expense of articulating a difference, a gay culture—or better yet—cultures. Much as Eastern European Jewish life, for example, has always been a part of what we blithely call "American culture," it was important for Jews to both insist on this—their presence everywhere, their implication in all of America—and also to hold on to a distinctiveness "Jewishness," what some call "Yiddishkeit" and others simply know as a vague yet definable gestalt.

It is important to see the gayness in supposedly straight culture, to articulate how gay authors, actors, writers, scientists, and politicians have always been a part of American culture. Increasingly, the lines between gay culture and straight culture are blurred, as gay themes and images enter into the everyday iconography of American society. To see the ever-present queerness in the most prosaic straightness is important to be sure, as it has been for every oppressed minority. Gay iconography and gay discourse have so permeated our culture that there are fewer boundaries and demarcations between "gay" and "straight," creating a "bleeding through" effect. Indeed, there is a healthy and exciting tension between the "gaying of America," in which gay identities and images truly expand our social and cultural lives, and "gay assimilation," in which gay identities and images get lost in the abyss of cultural sameness.

This is not to say that there is one, singular "thing" that *is* gay culture, or that it can even be identified in any coherent way. Nevertheless, the experience of growing up in a world in which your very way of loving is largely illegal and is often deemed immoral, where you possess few legal rights and are constantly in fear of less abstract violations of your personal integrity, where the metaphor that defines your coming of age has to do with a darkened room and the opening or closing of doors, where you *can* hide and thus must choose whether or not to stay locked in that metaphorical closet—these experiences shape collective identities and produce collective cultures. In a culture that deems gay men the ultimate "sissies," we do drag—playing up the artifice of gender and laughing at our own restrictive definitions. The attraction of a doomed Judy Garland and the pathos of an elegant aria speak to a sense of vulnerability. The costumed madness that is Halloween has been appropriated by gays as a place for free expression and gender-bending. In a culture that straight-laces women into limited gender roles, enforcing a kind of femininity that hobbles and narrows, we don boots and t-shirts, attiring ourselves in eclectic mixes of leather and lipstick that aim to please a different group of onlookers. We have created a network of bookstores, restaurants, resorts, coffee shops, support groups, safe houses that *is* community. From the Michigan Womyn's Music Festival to Wigstock in New York's Greenwich Village, from knowing glances and coded clothes to the much-vaunted "gaydar" that gays proudly extol, community has been forged in the presence of violence and endless threats of loss. This was vividly illustrated when the crisis of AIDS hit. Gays took care of their own.

John D'Emilio believes, as do others such as the aforementioned Lacayo, that "there is this interesting disjuncture between what is going on in politics and what is going on in culture and everyday life. In terms of culture . . . *gay* and *lesbian* is becoming increasingly embedded. Whereas politically, even though there is more of the gay and lesbian movement than there was 10 or 15 or 20 years ago, the opposition to gay rights is much more articulate, much more organized and much more on the offensive than it's ever been before. While there are a lot of cultural victories that we have, politically the situation is more challenging than it's ever been. And, while I wish that half of the equation were not true, I actually take tremendous hope from the cultural change that is occurring, because laws can flip flop very easily, whereas the cultural stuff seems to reflect the way Americans are actually living."[20]

This disjuncture could also be read in yet another way, a disjuncture between the everyday life of gay people and the representation of that life in popular culture. While surely it is "better" to be a gay teen coming out now than, say, ten years ago (much less twenty!), it also produces a new sense of frustration and ambiguity. For earlier generations, coming-out stories were marked by the persistence of feelings of aloneness. The refrain you heard over and over was "I thought I was the only one." Indeed, I cannot help but remember my own gay youth, not so very long ago. Then, in the late 1970s, I knew not one single gay teen—and I lived in a large urban center. Then, there were no support groups for gay kids (like SMYAL—Sexual Minority Youth Assistance League, in D.C.) or even physical spaces one could go to for some sense of shared contact. Then, there were the bars and bookshops, perhaps a university group here and there (my own personal savior). Now, gay youth (and adults as well, of course) turn on the TV and see some version of themselves served up for prime-time consumption. While that awful sense of isolation may no longer be the same, it is not at all clear that gay teens really find living life as an openly gay person that much easier or feel that less personally alone, or find it any easier to tell their folks, their schoolmates, their bosses. The media touts gays boldly going to the prom with their same-sex partners, and surely school administrators are more tuned in to homophobia, yet suicide statistics on gay teens remain alarmingly discordant with that of the general population.

Gays are no less vulnerable to anti-gay violence, and still carefully check their behavior in public. Just because Roseanne gets kissed by a woman on TV doesn't mean that a gay person walking down the street is able to feel comfortable holding her lover's hand, much less planting a visible kiss. This disjuncture between lived experience and cultural representation must create an enormous sense of what psychology calls "cognitive dissonance," particularly for young people.

What profound (and new) alienation must be felt when a gay person looks at a gay wedding cheerfully depicted on TV and then has her/his partner studiously ignored at a family gathering. What does it feel like to be depicted as the cutting edge of chic postmodern style as you are getting fired from your job, rejected by your family, and targeted by right-wing activists? These are new problems, surely, for those who came of age in the gay '90s. The gap between new expectations and old realities can produce a postmodern fun house of the soul, as gays live out the paradoxes of our times.

While these times are surely unique, I don't mean to imply that gay cultural life has no history prior to its emergence onto the very public stage of popular culture. Indeed, George Chauncey and others have written convincing histories challenging the prevailing mythology that views Stonewall as the initiating moment of gay culture, thus relegating earlier periods to darkness and invisibility. While it is true that gay "subcultures" have flourished in many times and locales (including the pre-WWII world of balls and saloons in New York that Chauncey so eloquently describes), gay presence in *mass* media has followed a different trajectory. Here, the story of a move from invisibility and stereotyping to relative visibility and more diverse imagery is a fairly accurate narrative. Indeed, for cultural studies, one of the crucial questions concerns the relationship between these subcultures and the mass-produced culture that purports to constitute a sort of national discourse on identity.

Clearly, identity is complicated by this entrance into the "regime of the visible." John D'Emilio has made a compelling argument that links visibility with a kind of internalized oppression. If "gay and lesbian oppression has functioned historically to marginalize us," the internalization of that marginalization produces an "*uncontainable* urge to reproduce marginalization. So that we come out, we come out, we come out. We say 'we are everywhere,' and then when we start to *appear* everywhere we are beset by worries as to the fact that we are appearing everywhere as opposed to saying that the new world in which we're working for change is a world in which there are gay news stories in the paper pretty regularly, and there are gay characters on TV."[21] If we as a society are to go beyond a gay "Martin Luther King Day" or "Year of the Woman," there must be an invigorated concern with changes not only in the *quantity* of representation but in the *quality* as well. It is clearly both inadequate and potentially dangerous to accept the new visibility as an unambiguous sign of real and meaningful social integration, celebration, or even benign acceptance. Indeed, this visibility can lull us into believing that change has really occurred when it is, too often, purely cosmetic and superficial. It is a necessary but not sufficient element of social change. It is the *quality* of this visibility that matters. More *Basic Instincts* or avoided prime-time kisses do not a social transformation make. The complexity and diversity of the gay and lesbian community needs to be *represented,* not promoted as simply heterosexuality with a twist.

In other words, the new visibility *is* here and a return to the old days where the closet ruled is pretty impossible and hardly desirable. Nevertheless, the closet and the gay ghetto are not the only alternatives to the dubious status of public spectacle. This book tries to take us past this impasse and into a "third way," beyond the limiting options of chic accessories or forgotten identities. This third way depends upon an analysis of gay identity as never singular (e.g. "*The* gay experience") but as also never separate from the vicissitudes of commercialization and heterosexual, mainstream culture. The "third way" (beyond the impasse created by the assimilation/ghetto paradigm) can be helpfully imagined by embracing the triangulated sense of "all the rage" (*all the rage* as all the fashion, *all the rage* as gay anger at discrimination and exclusion, and *all the rage* against gay visibility and gay identity itself) and moving beyond it towards what I would call a kind of conscious, conscientious integration, where lesbians and gays are full citizens in a society that is fundamentally altered by their inclusion. The third way facilitates the introduction and analysis of new (gay-inspired) ideas and constructs about fundamental social structures and intimate relationships, to rethink and reimagine marriage, family, partnerships, sexual and gender identity, friendships, love relationships.

How can a culture negotiate an identity that is at once "all the rage" (of fashion, of TV, of pop culture) without displacing and disappearing all the rage of gays still discriminated against, still second-class citizens, still other? A full and complete "conscious integration" of gays into American society means not just an end to the closet, or double standards, or gay stereotypes in popular culture. It means an opening up, a breaking through the tightly drawn wagons of heterosexual assumptions that could, potentially, challenge and expand all our conceptions of family, gender, love, intimacy, sexuality. The paradoxes we are witnessing now (the simultaneous embrace and rejection) are reflections, if you will, of a culture terrified of the potential disruption that full inclusion and integration would provoke. Like the white suburban kids who buy rap CDs yet aren't necessarily anti-racist, the heterosexuals who laugh at *Will & Grace* may dig the aesthetic but avoid the implications. This is the tension that faces us now: how to embrace the new visibility without losing gay uniqueness and gay difference; how to link the explosion of cultural images to a simultaneous explosion of actual gay rights; and, most importantly perhaps, how to make this visibility last, grow, develop, expand so that it becomes not a moment in American history but American history itself.

The dilemma of visibility that I am examining speaks, I think, to a peculiarly American phenomenon. It is by now banal to point out that the United States is unique in its heady mixture of diversity and homogenization; the immigrant experience defines the tension between a commitment to inclusion and a desire to maintain boundaries, between the American sense of "fair play" and the equally American distaste for the "other," between commitments to secular universalism and devout adherence to biblical scripture. The vaunted American melting pot of difference has always walked this precarious line and the contradictions facing gays today are, at least in part, a product of the vexing American inability to resolve the incongruities between its deeply held democratic ethos and its equally deeply held hatred of those different ingredients in that very same melting pot. The anxieties of the current moment (crystallized in the polls that suggest most people support equal civil rights for gays but not equal familial rights) speak to an American desire for "equal rights" that don't alter the status quo, an "inclusion" that doesn't come too close to home, impinge too much on mainstream sovereignty. We've seen this before—work with me, but don't live with me; enter into my government but don't expect me to do the childcare; be seen but be quiet. As Tony Kushner said in his passionate editorial after the death of Matthew Shepard, "We need to see the gay man crucified on the fence," to see the blood and the pain to remind us "that we have lazily misplaced our humanity" and that things like this "shouldn't happen out there to those people, and something should be done. As long as I don't have to do it."[22] The tensions we will see displayed throughout this book are the tensions of a nation caught in a dilemma of its own making and, while different locations express this tension in different ways (TV, for example, has always seemed to me one of the few arenas in which these tensions are at least openly addressed), the explosion of gay visibility is simultaneously the continuation of the American question of whether *democracy in difference* is possible.

These types of dilemmas cannot necessarily be resolved, but they can be *themselves* made visible, opened up for public consumption and lively debate. To see these times as paradoxical and contradictory—with all that implies about the good and the bad—and not simply cause for celebration is an important step in that direction. This book doesn't offer the typical platitudes or exhortations to toe one or another political line, although it takes positions all the time. Embedded in this book is an insistence on critique and exploration, even as the successes seem to make us complacent and the setbacks render us cynical and pessimistic. Much is genuinely exciting about these new times, and much is genuinely cause for concern. There are substantive moments—in TV, in film, in political discourse, in the popular press—when we glimpse exciting possibilities for both gays and straights in the gaying of American culture, possibilities for a reworking of our limited notions of family, sex, love, intimacy, civic life, politics. And, yes, there are also moments when the visibility appears as a smokescreen for continued oppression and discrimination, when it does appear as simply window dressing and eye candy. The work of this book—and the work for us all—is to continue to identify and debate those moments, and in that debate, to begin to articulate futures ever more enriching.

Too much ink has been spilled either simplistically claiming the nineties as one big gay-positive party, or equally simplistically deriding the times as not really a-changin' at all. And too much ink has been spilled in the simplistic debate between assimilation and separatism. The truth is, as always, a bit more complex. By examining in some depth the enormous changes wrought in recent years, we can begin to evaluate the impact: where and when and in what kinds of venues has the new gay visibility helped to reshape a more inclusive culture? And where and when and in what kinds of venues has this new visibility closed down that inclusiveness and instead refashioned gays as hip but expendable? This new historical period cannot be simply boiled down to the narrow terms of positive or negative images, or the equally narrow political debate about assimilation versus separatism. To be finally *seen* is a huge transformation, but vision is never neutral or endlessly open-ended. Who is pointing the spotlight and who is being consigned to the shadows? What nuances of color, gesture, voice are obscured by the glare of the media? What lives are hinted at, finally if obliquely, in the stories of the nineties?

The question is not simply one of realism. I don't think that we can expect or should expect the media to "accurately" reflect the ways real-life lesbians and gays live. Media images are never a direct reflection of lived experience and to ask that of our media culture is to immediately set oneself up for sure disappointment. The real issue is this: in the context of historical invisibility and the emergence of a new openness, what is the vision of gay life and gay identity being projected from the TV screen, from your local multiplex, as you turn the pages of a magazine? And what kinds of beliefs about gays are embedded in those images?

All the Rage throws its net wide, investigating these stories of gay visibility emerging in a culture at once fascinated and unnerved. Each chapter hones in on one site of this cultural and political sea change and, like a many-faceted stone, turns that site around and around to reveal hidden meanings, recurrent themes, sudden sparks of refreshing light. While each chapter has its own integrity, it must be said that overarching motifs emerge, particularly around the specific ways in which the new visibility does or does not lend itself to substantive social change. Of each site we ask the question, Is the rage contained, refashioned, slyly refitted to stitch decorously into the overarching pattern of American culture? Or, alternately, is the rage allowed to *be,* exceeding the strict borders of the marketplace, rubbing just enough the wrong way to cause irritation and disruption? What parts of this visibility allow us—American society—to really see differently and to see difference? And what parts of this visibility make of sight a facile object of exchange, an accessory that makes the acquisition of the garment redundant?

If there is much more in this book on TV than film, it is deliberate. In the first place, I am convinced that TV has become our national cultural meeting place, a site of profound social meaning and effect. While films certainly continue to make their mark on the collective body politic, it is television that—for better or for worse—acts itself out in our daily lives in ways both obvious and incremental. Secondly, I firmly believe that the story of gays on TV is a more complicated, fractured, and ultimately interesting one than its filmic counterpart. This may be counterintuitive, as our society tends to view TV as the awkward bastard cousin of the more "mature" medium of film. But there is no avoiding the reality that this contemporary story of gay visibility has been told more consistently on television than in popular film. While independent, foreign, and crossover films offer complex and challenging images of gays and lesbians,[23] mainstream Hollywood has progressed at a slower pace than many assume. The number of big-budget, wide-release films with substantive gay themes, characters, and content remains alarmingly small, although the numbers of secondary, "incidentally queer" characters has risen dramatically. But TV headlines gays, features gay docudramas and made-for-TV movies, and integrates gay characters into the everyday life of numerous TV series—and into numerous TV-watching families. Heterosexuals can largely avoid gays in choosing their movies for a Saturday night out; it's much more difficult to do that when watching TV, even for the aggressively homophobic channel zapper. As Todd Holland, gay director of the hit new sitcom *Malcolm in the Middle,* argues, "There's less risk on TV, so you have more freedom . . . a gay character in 22 hours [of a television show] . . . is not as important as a gay character in a two-hour movie. You aren't risking your entire box office by having a gay character."[24] When wide-release films cost millions, the lure of the predictable is palpable and often offsets the possibility of gay centrality. While TV is of course more often than not predictable and formulaic, it is telling that the boom in gay visibility has been more significantly located in the everyday, background world of television than in the more aesthetically interesting and "artistic" realm of Hollywood film.

It must also be said that there is a certain encyclopedic quality to this book. When you live amidst such rapid and conspicuous change, it is hard to avoid obsession. The need to catalogue, to note, to remember, to *put it down* is, I think, a trait of the liminal. As a Jew, I grew up with the admonition to *never forget*. While to some this is a glib cliché, to many it carries a potent truth that motivates historians and folklorists and cultural archeologists the world over. It motivates this book, with a twist of course. While we must never forget the history of our oppression and victimization, we must also mark those rare and chaotic moments when all the verities come tumbling down, when we look around us and cannot even begin to reckon with all the *noise*. For these changes are all over the place — in every realm of culture, media, politics, intimate life, workplace dynamics. To name it all, to speak it, to analyze it, to ponder it, to refuse the easy answers, and to live with a little confusion — this is the project of *All the Rage*.

These are the confusing challenges that try postmodern souls, for, at least to the naked eye, these really *do* seem to be the best of times. If the sixties were marked by the civil rights movement and the anti-war struggles, and the seventies by the transformations wrought by the women's movement, and the eighties by the peace and anti-nuclear movements, then this past decade — the gay '90's — was equally sweeping in its reach and historical magnitude. Unlike people of color and women, however, gays are not necessarily or inevitably "visible." Most of the time, difference is not marked on our bodies. We are largely born to and raised by those different from us, are not birthed into a ready-made identity, and must actively seek out and construct a community and identity whose existence is predicated on that seeking. Gays can hide, be overlooked, be mistaken for heterosexual. Thus, for lesbians and gays, issues of visibility and "coming out" are centrally and inextricably linked to the process of acquiring civil rights, in a way I think quite different from other minority groups for whom *mis*representation has often been a more driving concern than simple *re*presentation. The closet is a very specific metaphor, and defines the crisis of a community for whom simply being *visible* can be an act of rebellion.

But for the majority of Americans, gay people *were* invisible or, worse, despised: unseen, avoided, unknown. The '90's burst that all apart and catapulted lesbians and gays into the hearts and homes of everyday Americans. The love that dare not speak its name became the love that would not shut up, proclaiming its right to be *seen* and *heard* from the manicured lawns of suburbia to the tight tenements of our megacities. No one can remain unaffected. As Michelangelo Signorile, one of the current crop of gay pundits, claims, "So many people are openly gay that hiding it has become less necessary, at least in places where coming out doesn't threaten one's safety or job. People used to be embarrassed to be out of the closet and now they're embarrassed to be in. We've come a long way." [25] Indeed we have.

$\mathcal{T}wo$ PRIDE AND PREJUDICE:
THE CHANGING
CONTEXT OF GAY
VISIBILITY

Picture this, if you will. It is inaugural night, a night of celebrations and champagne, dancing and exultant speeches, ballrooms filled with big bands and brightly colored balloons. It takes place every four years, as Americans welcome a new president with all the glitz and kitsch that signifies American popular culture. Yet 1992 was different. As I walked into the bedecked halls of the National Press Club Building, I could feel the excitement in the air. We had made it. In glittering gowns and elegant tuxes, leather vests and kilts, we too danced cheek to cheek, reveling in our newfound legitimacy, enjoying for a rare and glorious moment the feeling of inclusion. After all, *this* President had welcomed us, met with our leaders, spoken at our rallies, courted our campaign dollars, invited us to have a "place at the table" of the new, inclusive American feast he hoped to prepare. We could, legitimately, celebrate him as we celebrated our own coming of age as a movement. We ate delicious hors d'oeuvres, listened deliriously as rock star Melissa Etheridge came out, old folkie Janis Ian joined her, and celebrities mingled with new administration insiders and activists to rejoice in the miracle of the evening: a gay inaugural ball! Unlike the straight balls I went to that evening, this was like a big family gathering. As we walked half dazed through the gyrating crowds of dancers, there were gentle kisses proffered to strangers, admiring remarks made to particularly glamorous revelers, shared tears passed around freely.

As a young girl coming out in the late '70s, I would never have dreamed that one day thousands of gay men and women would be celebrating the election of a "gay-friendly" president. Hope was in the air, you could feel it as you danced around the floor, as you smiled at the stranger who felt the same, as you heard the clear, strong sound of closet doors being snapped open. It was indeed a special night.

THE VISION THING: CLINTON'S WHITE HOUSE

If the culture has shifted queerly, so too has the political world. The administration's "embrace" of the gay and lesbian community has marked gay issues as media friendly and intersects with the growing visibility in the cultural sphere. In a speech to a Hollywood gay group during the early days of his first campaign for president, Bill Clinton opened a door that had never even been cracked before when he said, "I have a vision, and you are a part of it." Unarguably, Bill Clinton was the most pro-gay president in American history. Clinton's gay-positive presidency was marked not only by specific speeches and official acts, but by a baby boomer, '60s man uniquely comfortable with gay life and gay identity. His ease is palpable (analogous, I think, to his ease with communities of color) and created a social and political ambience noticeably warmer than previous regimes.

Not only did he openly and warmly reach out to the gay community during his campaign, but Clinton did more for gay people than any other president. He issued an executive order prohibiting sexual-orientation discrimination in the executive branch. He appointed more openly lesbian and gay people to positions in his government. He removed sexual orientation as a basis for denying security clearances and endorsed the Employment Non-Discrimination Act (ENDA)—the federal bill to prevent private employers from discriminating on the basis of sexual preference. He appointed an AIDS czar and created the position of liaison to the lesbian and gay community. He regularly met with gay officials and leaders (including the unprecedented July 1999 meeting with state and local openly gay and lesbian elected officials in the White House and another meeting in January 2000 with local lesbian and gay community centers in consultation with gay activists and administration officials and Cabinet members), counts openly gay congressman Barney Frank as a trusted adviser, and publicly opposed the anti-gay initiatives in Colorado and Oregon (and applauded the Supreme Court decision upholding the

Colorado Supreme Court overruling of the anti-gay Amendment 2). In an historic move, President Clinton addressed the Human Rights Campaign's annual fundraising gala in 1997, the first time a sitting president formally addressed a gay rights group. And "on January 19, [1999] Bill Clinton became the first president to mention sexual orientation in a state of the union address. 'Discrimination or violence because of race or religion, ancestry or gender, disability or sexual orientation, is wrong and ought to be illegal,' Clinton said. 'Therefore I call upon Congress to make the Employment Non-Discrimination Act and the Hate Crimes Prevention Act the law of the land.'"[1] He even honored the thirtieth anniversary of the Stonewall rebellion by issuing an official proclamation declaring June Gay and Lesbian Pride Month and exhorting the nation "to observe this month with appropriate programs, ceremonies, and activities that celebrate our diversity and to remember throughout the year the gay and lesbian Americans whose many and varied contributions have enriched our national life."[2]

Barney Frank notes that Clinton "has turned the largest employer in the United States—the federal government—into an almost completely gay-friendly place."[3] More open gays and lesbians were members of his administration than ever before in history, including veteran gay activist Virginia Apuzzo, appointed as assistant to the president for administration and management. By some estimates, Clinton appointed over 150 gay and lesbian people during his presidency.[4] After it became clear that an entrenched Republican-controlled Senate wouldn't even vote on the nomination of James Hormel, Clinton made a recess appointment for the philanthropist and former law school dean to be the first openly gay ambassador (to Luxembourg).

Starting with the 1992 campaign, Clinton recognized gays as a vital voting bloc, and the president and first lady were honorary chairs of the display of the AIDS quilt. Clinton has been out front and on record in his condemnation of anti-gay violence. Speaking in California at one of the largest-ever gay political fundraisers (Access Now for Gay and Lesbian Equality), Clinton decried hate crimes and deemed bigotry and hate "America's largest problem." This marked "the first time Clinton, or any other president, has spoken publicly to a gay group outside of Washington."[5]

The list of firsts goes on and on. No president was so accessible and so identified with gay issues and the gay community. And, of course, no president so disappointed that same community, most notably with the gays in the military debacle and his decision to sign the Defense of Marriage Act (DOMA). These acts of betrayal (as they are viewed by many) may reveal much about Clinton, but they also transcend his presidency. The "uneven development" of gay rights is precisely the political context of the new visibility. Indeed, though gays were undoubtedly better off with Clinton, things were also more complicated and marked less by a sense of incremental progress than one of dramatic lurches backwards and forwards.

It is not only the president who embraced gay rights; gay civil rights are now a part of the legislative arena. In June of 1995, even after the conservative onslaught of '94, the Human Rights Campaign Fund released the results of a survey of Congress, indicating that 71 Senators and 234 House members pledged not to discriminate on the basis of sexual orientation. In 1996, the Human Rights Campaign reported that 66 of 100 Senate offices have nondiscrimination policies as do 238 of the 435 House offices. When ENDA came to a vote on the Senate floor in 1996 (as a consolation prize to opponents of DOMA), it received a remarkable 49 votes. In 1998, Democrats (with some Republican support) defeated the Heffley amendment, which would have nullified the president's executive order banning discrimination on the basis of sexual orientation in the federal workplace, and in the summer of 1999, in a further evidence of a post-DOMA, post-Monica sea change, defeated an anti-gay adoption amendment to the D.C. appropriation bill. ENDA was reintroduced in the spring of 1999 with a record 160 originating cosponsors in the House.

More and more open gays are running for office in local, state, and federal elections, supported both by their party machinery (largely Democratic) and powerful new organizations such as the Gay and Lesbian Victory Fund. Five openly gay Democrats ran for Congress in 1998, setting a new record, and Tammy Baldwin became the first out lesbian to be elected to the House of Representatives (as well as Wisconsin's first female member of Congress). The last election season was even pinker, with "more than 200 gay politicians . . . elected across the country on November 7."[6] Out gays are on city councils, state assemblies, school boards, and every other realm of local and state government. Out gay judges sit in courts around the country.

In the 2000 presidential campaign season, Democratic contenders vied for the most gay-friendly position. While Democratic combatants Gore and Bradley refused to endorse same-sex marriage, they both spoke in favor of giving the benefits of marriage to same-sex domestic partners and matched each other one-for-one in efforts to woo the gay vote. Gore even claimed that he would set up a presidential commission to study the marriage issue. Both spoke emphatically for sexual orientation inclusion in hate crimes legislation and for federally legislated job protection for gays and lesbians. Gay groups are targeted, courted, spoken to at meetings, invited to confer with candidates and their handlers, and invoked repeatedly in televised debates.

While the Democratic Party has seen most of the pro-gay action, gay Republicans have been prominently featured in the press, as either brave soldiers or as human paradoxes. Willfully ignoring the explicit homophobia of the GOP, these activists see themselves as shifting both the party and gay politics. The Log Cabin Club—a gay Republican organization—endured the embarrassment of having their donation of $1,000 to the failed presidential campaign of Bob Dole returned, and had but one brief meeting with Bush during his presidential campaign.

Senate Majority Leader Trent Lott's homophobic remarks of June 15, 1998, elicited a vigorous response from all quarters and inspired no small amount of debate within the Republican Party itself, with many "fearing it could make the party appear intolerant and drive out moderates and economic conservatives."[7] Indeed, both Lott's remarks and the impeachment experience combined to put a new spin on explicit homophobia. As the president himself said, perhaps a bit optimistically, "I don't think it will ever be fashionable for people in national life to demonize gays again."[8] Nevertheless, at the same time that Lott's words evoked criticism and concern, the nation witnessed an unprecedented coordination of efforts of Christian conservatives that resulted in a series of full-page ads attacking gays and promoting the idea that homosexuality is a disease that can be cured by "reparative therapy." The Human Rights Campaign responded with a vigorous ad campaign of its own.

Whether as objects of attack or voting blocs to be wooed, gay issues have entered the political mainstream. The presidential election of 1992 catapulted gay issues into the front pages and provided a stark contrast between a candidate actively courting the gay vote, promising substantive changes, and a candidate actively allying himself with a growing anti-gay, Christian conservatism that deemed gay rights the soul of a modern-day Gomorrah. Indeed, the conventions could not have been more of a study in contrasts, with archconservative Patrick Buchanan railing against gay marriages and invoking fears of a culture war while the Democrats provided two openly gay speakers (future White House aide Bob Hattoy and San Francisco city supervisor Roberta Achtenberg) to the speechifying event. The party platforms, as well, were a stunning study in opposites.

It is not that gay political activists had previously been silent, but this time they organized *as gays*—a lavender bloc to be contended with. New organizations such as the Victory Fund, started in 1991, represent a dramatic coming out for gay politics, with gay money funneled to gay candidates. Gay organizations routinely conduct surveys of candidates and incumbents on their stance on gay issues and generally receive thorough responses. And recent studies and polls have begun to define an active and engaged "gay vote" to join already defined minority voting blocs. No doubt about it, gay visibility has not been confined to the cultural arena but has most assuredly made its mark on the political process.

OF SHOWERS, SOAP, AND FOXHOLES:
THE MEDIA AND THE MILITARY

This new visibility of lesbians and gays—and the more open and embracing atmosphere in the White House—raised the ante in gay federal politics and cost Clinton. Gays held out great hope for him and his presidency, and he disappointed in significant ways, none so devastatingly as the gays in the military debacle. He raised the issue himself during the campaign, making a personal promise to discharged lesbian colonel Greta Cammermeyer, and delivered only the unworkable "compromise" of "don't ask, don't tell."

When the whole furor erupted, three students taking my Introduction to Sociology class approached me tentatively and asked for a meeting. All three were in the Navy, getting through nursing school on Navy scholarships. They wanted to talk with me—their openly gay professor—about gays in the military. We talked for over an hour. I listened as they told of the "panel discussions" with their officers, officers who were actively propagating the military commitment to exclusion, officers whom these young women respected and found difficult to confront. Yet they sensed that something was wrong, and had the bravery and intelligence to seek further knowledge. Listening to the misinformation and scare tactics used to get "the troops" in line on this issue was both terrifying and edifying. From the ludicrous flat feet analogy (the armed forces excludes on a number of grounds, like flat feet—so why not gays?) to the HIV red herring, these bright young women were being trained in bigotry. As we talked, I saw both their shame at having believed their superiors, and their commitment to thinking for themselves. They were confused, having to reconcile what they had heard about gay people from their superiors with a teacher they respected and learned from.

I am not surprised at the outpouring of bigotry and hatred that accompanied Clinton's decision to end discrimination in the military. I have not grown to be a thirty-something lesbian in this world without some degree of awareness of the reach of homophobia and sexism. I am, however, surprised at those (including the media) who deemed these battles a waste of the president's "political capital." He was not wrong in expending that capital. The mistake was in giving in when the expense proved too great.

The terrible irony of military men fearing harassment from gays should not be lost on anyone familiar with the recent "Tailhook" scandal, or anyone who has taken a cursory glance at the statistics on sexual violence and sexual harassment. These are overwhelmingly acts committed by heterosexual men. Victims don't undermine morale; perpetrators do. If any fear is justified, it is the fear of gay men and lesbians who face violence every day, not the least in the military. Ask Allen Schindler's or Barry Winchell's parents about the fear their gay sons felt as they were called "fag" and "queer" and then brutally beaten to death (by heterosexual servicemen) simply because of who they were and how they loved.

Yet there was much talk over the opening few months of Bill Clinton's presidency. Many declared it a bumpy beginning, already claiming an administration in crisis (little did they know what was to follow!). The media pundits read the postmortem on an administration not even at the midpoint. Clinton's insistence on pursuing this issue, against all the advice of those who would have him save himself for the "real issues," illustrated his understanding (however insufficiently realized) that gay liberation and the right to live with freedom and dignity is not something extra, something strange, something severed from the everyday life of our society. A healthy democracy is not just evidenced by a high GNP and a low debt. Clinton's pledge to "put Americans back to work," for example, would have meant much less if there had been an asterisk by gays and lesbians, excepting them from the full exercise of that right.

Yet, well-intentioned though he may be, things did not go quite as planned. Only a few months after Clinton's initial announcement that he would fully integrate the armed forces, hopes were dimmed by the months-long "gays in the military" debate. Reversing himself, Clinton conceded to military hard-liners and produced a ludicrous policy that was doomed to fail in theory and in practice.

"Don't ask, don't tell" could not be a more apt metaphor for our confused times. The impossibility of this policy—military "tolerance" of gay service members as long as that identity is kept invisible and is not discussed, much less lived—reinstates the closet and entrenches marginality. It is as if the Army sent out a new jingle just for gays: "be all that you can be" NOT! What was given with one hand seemed to be taken away with the other. And, again, this points to the double-edged quality of many recent events around lesbians and gays. While gays were pleased to have a president take on the sacred cow of the military and demand its accountability to the Constitution, they witnessed a devastating and wrenching backtracking. In the course of the months that followed his initial attempts to remove the ban outright, Clinton's resolve fell apart in the face of strong opposition and his defensiveness about his own military record.

As case after case winds its way through the court system, it is clear that the Supreme Court will one day have to reckon with this issue. Discharges of gays and lesbians from the military have increased 67 percent since 1994[9] and it is apparent to most that the policy not only is illogical but has fostered witch-hunts of post-WWII proportions. Indeed, the policy is so visibly unworkable that even candidates Gore, Bradley, and Hillary Clinton herself repudiated it during the last campaign season, with the president joining in, calling the policy "out of whack" in a December 1999 radio interview with CBS.

Again, we see the paradox at work. For, on the one hand it seems as if we have to claim "sameness" in order to advocate for equality: let us into the army, we want to fight for our country just like you do, we believe in a strong military just like you do. But, on the other hand, a large segment of the gay and lesbian movement has historically been aligned with a politics that challenges the centrality of the military and criticizes its bloated budgets and aggressive international policies. So many of us, myself included, found ourselves in the strange and disconcerting position of arguing for inclusion in an institution which so often seemed antithetical to the very values of peace and nonaggression we held dear. The gay soldier as the icon of gay visibility and inclusion is a strange image to be sure. While gays must, of course, be allowed access to every arena of public life if we are to have a true democracy, we also risk assimilation and the weakening of gay liberation politics if we seek only simple acceptance and inclusion.

This paradox was brought home to me by the controversy surrounding the week-long celebration in New York City of the twenty-fifth anniversary of the 1969 riots precipitated by a raid on a Greenwich Village gay bar. The Stonewall riots are often said to mark the beginning of the modern gay movement, and to commemorate them there was a dance held aboard the USS *Intrepid*, docked in New York Harbor. This dance, entitled "Big Guns," sparked some degree of controversy within the gay community. Are we to see this as a capitulation to American military might—gays boogying on the decks of the very ships that have come to symbolize their own exclusion? Or is this a sly infiltration, a camp send-up of military straightness, an insistence on being all you can be where you are not allowed to be, a parody of the "big guns" that want to exclude gays?

The hysteria that followed hard on Clinton's challenge to the ban on gays in the military was not, in itself, surprising. Yet for many who had been warmed by the sunshine of the new climate of civility, it was chilling indeed to witness the spectacle of military leaders and political pundits lining up to save the armed forces from the scourge of open homosexuality. Radio talk shows fielded calls from irate listeners who feared AIDS, shower attacks, loss of discipline, and the general decline of Western civilization if lesbians and gays were allowed to serve openly. Still, we believed this wall, too, would soon come tumbling down. There seemed reason to hope.

The backlash to Clinton's seemingly simple act to end discrimination is anything but simple. It not only reflects the entrenched powers of homophobia but has—especially in the face of strong gay activism— stirred up new political alliances and surprising supporters. No supporter was more surprising than old-time conservative ideologue Barry Goldwater. In several powerful editorials, Goldwater argued passionately for the removal of the ban on gays in the military and, more recently, for the adoption of federal anti-discrimination legislation. The specter of arch-conservative Goldwater supporting gay rights is yet one more sign of our paradoxical times.

IS THERE A PLACE AT THE TABLE?: PRO-GAY INITIATIVES AND ANTI-GAY REFERENDA

If the gay inaugural ball was a burst of new freedom, then the gays in the military debate was most assuredly a burst bubble. Opportunities appeared only to disappear under the weight of new attacks. Impediments to equality remained intransigent. The gay inaugural ball was particularly glamorous, and the gays in the military debate particularly fractious, yet both are indicative of larger shifts in the visibility of lesbians and gay men in all aspects of our society. While this new media attention has seemed to spawn—or would seem to—a new and growing awareness of gay rights as civil rights, it has also emerged in the midst of a phenomenal backlash against lesbian and gay rights. This backlash did not materialize from thin air. The religious right, increasingly powerful and increasingly influential on both local and federal levels, has been preaching its message of homosexuality as evil aberration for quite some time. In addition, the attack on lesbians and gays emerges in the context of a broader attack against forces of change in general: feminists, pro-choice activists, multiculturalists, environmentalists.

If "Willie Horton" became the scary metaphor of choice in an earlier election, designed to play on white fears of black rapaciousness and immorality, then "family values" has become the metaphor for our times, designed to define the American family in exclusive and demarcated terms, playing on fears of difference of any kind—from single mothers to gay weddings. Finding that the abortion issue was holding less and less sway (after all, every poll consistently shows a strong majority of Americans favoring a woman's right to choose) and that extremist groups like Operation Rescue were not only being rebuffed by clinic defenders but challenged by the courts and public opinion, the Christian right focused instead on the "threat" to family values (or, as Pat Buchanan said in his speech at the Republican convention, the need to wage a "cultural war") posed by an evil and unholy alliance of feminists and gay activists. Lesbians and gays are the last group against whom it is still legal and acceptable to discriminate, publicly denigrate, and socially ostracize, thus making them good targets for a right-wing incensed by their inability to gather more public support.

First, the good news. More than 227 jurisdictions (cities, counties, and states) in the U.S. have passed some form of legislation that bans discrimination based on sexual orientation, and twelve states have some sort of statewide anti-discrimination law. Over twenty states prohibit discrimination in public employment based on sexual orientation. However, thirty states have no statewide protection for gays at all. Nearly a quarter of the U.S. population lives in states banning discrimination on the basis of sexual orientation, but there is still no federal law banning discrimination.[10] Twenty-five states plus the District of Columbia have hate crime laws that include sexual orientation, yet a federal bill remains out of reach. The enormity of the shift should not go unnoticed. As Sean Cahill of NGLTF notes, 20 million people lived with gay rights laws in 1990. Ten years later that number stands at 103 million.[11]

Indeed, "this past year [1998] marked the first time in the movement's history that pro-GLBT [gay, lesbian, bisexual, and transgendered] bills outnumbered anti-GLBT bills. Important legislative gains were made in Missouri, which enacted a hate crimes bill that includes gay, lesbian, bisexual and transgendered people; in New Hampshire, which abolished a ban on same-sex adoption; in Nevada, which enacted a bill banning discrimination in employment against GLBT people in both the public and private sector; and in Rhode Island, which joined other states in enacting legislation allowing people to designate persons other than blood relatives to make funeral arrangements and to dispose of remains following that person's death."[12] Even traditionally conservative states like Kentucky are advancing gay rights ordinances. In 1999, "four local governments have added sexual orientation to their anti-discrimination laws."[13]

Most recently and dramatically, the city of San Francisco passed a new law requiring firms doing business with the city to offer employees domestic partnership benefits. The governor of California recently signed several pieces of new legislation, creating a statewide registry for domestic partners, outlawing harassment of gays in public schools and colleges by making school administrations accountable for combating anti-gay harassment, and strengthening older state laws that ban discrimination against gays in housing and employment.[14] In an effort to introduce an anti-discrimination measure, Maryland governor Parris Glendening initiated an unprecedented series of five hearings held throughout the state to gather testimony about discrimination against gay, lesbian, bisexual, and transgendered people.[15]

Over 100 state and local governments provide health benefits to domestic partners. Four states ban discrimination against gay students in public schools and over 300 colleges and universities have nondiscrimination policies which include sexual orientation (including most of the top national universities and liberal arts colleges). These numbers are increasing daily, with the conservative state of Utah becoming the most recent addition. Of course, none of these kinds of ordinances pass without huge resistance, often in the form of packed halls with praying citizens inveighing against the "homosexual agenda."

When the Human Rights Campaign (HRC) released its 1996 report "The State of the Workplace for Gay and Lesbian Americans: Why Congress Should Pass the Employment Non-Discrimination Act," they revealed that a majority of Fortune 500 companies have included gay and lesbian workers in their nondiscrimination policies, including Reebok, Time-Warner, Quaker Oats. Many provide domestic partner benefits, including Disney, which elicited an (erroneous, as it turned out) prediction from Pat Robertson that central Florida would be hit by a hurricane for its defiance of God's will. Compare this to a 1993 National Gay and Lesbian Task Force survey of the Fortune 1000's policies towards gays, which revealed that "only 98 of the 1000 companies completed the survey; 145 refused and the rest did not respond to letters and phone calls. Of the 98, three-fourths have a nondiscrimination policy covering sexual orientation; a quarter recognize gay employee groups; half include gay issues in diversity training; and five offer domestic partner benefits."[16] The 1996 HRC report also reveals that, in addition, 648 companies have nondiscrimination policies, 313 employers have adopted same-sex domestic partner benefits, and 103 companies have gay and lesbian support groups. A more recent survey by the Buck Consultants found that, of the 1,058 companies surveyed, only 6 percent offer domestic partner benefits. However, 29 percent are considering policy changes to allow benefits for domestic partners.[17] Of course, the absolute numbers are low against 6.8 million private and public employers, but they signal profound changes in the workplace environment. At last count, almost 3,000 private companies, universities/colleges, and state and local governments offer domestic partner coverage.[18]

More and more large, publicly traded companies are instituting domestic partner benefits, none more comprehensively than Coors Brewing Company which, in 1995, "became one of the country's most progressive corporations."[19] Coors has gone further, becoming "one of the select few that pass what socially conscious investors know as 'The Lavender Screen,' a five-tiered 'test' of whether or not a company is truly gay-friendly. To get a perfect score, a company needs to include sexual orientation in its nondiscrimination clause, have a lesbian and gay employees group, sponsor diversity training, offer programs supporting employees with AIDS and HIV, and . . . provide benefits to domestic partners."[20] The irony of Coors—which has endured a boycott by gay activists because of the public anti-gay and racist remarks by Coors family members—becoming the darling of pro-gay business should not be lost on anyone. Indeed, GLAAD found itself in a bit of a quandary when it accepted a $110,000 grant from Coors, inciting criticism from activists who reminded GLAAD of the anti-gay actions of the Coors family itself, which remains somewhat distinct from the brewing company. And in August of 1999, "United, the world's largest airline . . . became the first major U.S. carrier to announce plans to offer domestic partner benefits to Gay employees, prompting American Airlines to follow suit six days later."[21]

In addition, lesbian and gay employee support and resource groups have blossomed in recent years. One of the most active and most media-savvy has been "Digital Queers," a Silicon Valley group that is energetically working to make cyberspace more gay-friendly and to use high-tech methods to activate gay rights. Started in 1991 by Tom Reilly of Super-Mac Technologies, it now has hundreds of members, who collectively have "donated $150,000 in computer hardware, software and services to update the creaky computer system of the National Gay and Lesbian Task Force; trained activists across the country in how to network by modem; launched a project to electronically link more than a half-dozen regional gay and lesbian groups; and brought an awareness of gay issues to the executive suites of Silicon Valley."[22] The high-tech industries, along with the entertainment industry, have been in the forefront of pro-gay policies, "extending health care benefits to the domestic partners of gay and lesbian employees."[23] While this often proceeds fairly quietly, Apple became embroiled in a very public battle with a Texas county who "refused to grant Apple a tax abatement because of its benefits policy—and backed down after the issue became a national news story."[24] Art

Bain, publisher of the New York–based Gay/Lesbian/Bisexual Corporate Letter, said many computer industry leaders are open to gay concerns because they are entrepreneurs who are used to breaking rules and are not bound by convention. "It's an industry with a lot of companies started by people who grew up in the '60s and have liberal social values," he said. "And the competition for talent is probably more extreme than in virtually any other industry, so it doesn't make (economic) sense to discriminate."[25]

Indeed, corporate America seems to be moving fast toward anti-discrimination policies as business-as-usual. Gay workplace issues have clearly taken the forefront: "From a Clinton administration official's call for 'lavender capitalism' to Apple computers elegant soiree under tents, a weekend conference at Stanford University showed many signs that the movement for gay rights in the workplace is reaching critical mass. More than 400 gay and lesbian employees attended the National Gay & Lesbian Task Force's third annual workplace conference, up from 120 in 1991. For the first time, corporations were invited to send human resources personnel, and dozens, including Xerox and MCA, did."[26] Gay leaders such as Melinda Paras, former executive director of the National Gay and Lesbian Task Force (NGLTF), have expressed surprise that "the corporate boardroom is far outpacing the halls of government when it comes to recognition of gays."

At an NGLTF gathering for corporate leaders, there was a sense that the tide was turning, notwithstanding the conservative attacks and boycotts:

> Among the big-name corporations that sent employees to the conference or donated money: Pacific Gas & Electric, AT&T, Chevron, Pacific Bell, Hewlett Packard, Intel, Oracle, Kaiser-Permanente, DHL, United and American Airlines. Conference officials pointed to Xerox Corp. in Stamford, Conn., as a model employer for gays and lesbians. Most recently, Xerox added domestic partnership benefits that include health insurance, bereavement leave, relocation expenses and other policies that mirror the benefits offered heterosexual spouses. Gay employees at Xerox are encouraged to invite their partners to company picnics, or to dinners with top executives.[27]

Now, while these moves are to be heralded, they still remain fairly tentative and are hardly the law of the land. In addition, it is important to remember that changes in corporate policies do not necessarily signal changes in larger social beliefs and ideologies. However, just because most corporations are doing this because it is good business (the costs of providing domestic partner benefits are quite small and the benefits of keeping a healthy, happy, loyal workforce far greater) should not detract from the real effects these corporate policies may have on corporate culture and the larger culture as well. In other words, intent does not have to be purely benevolent for the results to be beneficial.

Now, the bad news. If the nineties will be remembered as the era that brought unprecedented political access and cultural visibility to lesbians and gays, they will also be remembered as the time of vehement gay bashing in the form of a well-organized and well-funded anti–gay rights movement. As one commentator noted, "Gays and lesbians nationwide, fresh off a decade of remarkable advancements, now face a potentially devastating string of political defeats, as anti-homosexual crusaders portray them as the undeserving recipients of special rights rather than minorities entitled to civil rights."[28] This is not to say that anti-gay forces were quiescent prior to the gay '90s, or that gay activism had lain low for all those years. Unfortunately, anti-gay rhetoric and legislative initiatives have a long history and, thankfully, the gay movement was not born yesterday (nor was it simply born in 1969 with the Stonewall riots!).

Indeed, there was a flurry of activity in the late '70s and '80s, the most notorious being Anita Bryant's campaign. While "the issue of equal rights for gays has been in the voting booths since Anita Bryant's 'Save the Children' campaign in Dade County, Fla., in 1977, . . . the current proliferation of initiatives really began in 1992 when groups in Oregon and Colorado gathered enough signatures to put propositions on the ballot asking voters to undo any law that prohibited discrimination against gays. Voters in Oregon said no; voters in Colorado said yes."[29] So, anti-gay referenda are not new, but from 1992 to 1995 they grew exponentially. In 1992, the state of Colorado passed an anti-gay initiative which was found unconstitutional by the Colorado Supreme Court, and the U.S. Supreme Court upheld the state court's ruling. In the same year, Oregon's anti-gay initiative failed, but in 1993 and 1994 the OCA (the Oregon Citizen's Alliance, which organized the anti-gay initiative) managed to pass over twenty-five local anti-gay initiatives, as did many other cities and counties in which rights laws, partnership laws, and anti-discrimination laws were repealed. In 1994, anti-gay initiatives were on the ballot in eight states, and the OCA sponsored similar initiatives in municipalities throughout Oregon and have worked closely with groups in Colorado and Maine and other states to keep momentum on these initiatives. A 1995 attempt in Maine to repeat the Colorado victory was defeated. Georgia's Cobb County became a flashpoint when a resolution condemning the "gay lifestyle" was met with challengers from Atlanta and beyond, promising boycotts, protests, and a "Queer family picnic" in Marietta.

In more recent years, ballot measures have grown and met with mixed success. There were six GLBT-related ballot measures in the November

1998 elections with five losses and only one victory. And the most recent election produced a mix of results as well. The Oregon anti-gay measure (a measure that would have barred public schools and colleges from "encouraging, promoting, or sanctioning" homosexuality) was narrowly defeated but the Maine gay civil rights law was repealed and the Nebraska anti-gay marriage bill—like most introduced in the states—overwhelmingly passed, the first that not only barred civil unions but legislated against domestic partner benefits as well. Anti-sodomy laws still exist in twenty-four states, with ramifications far beyond the occasional criminal case. Sodomy laws have been used by courts and in public discourse to justify discrimination in a variety of other areas. We have seen this most dramatically in the case of Sharon Bottoms, where the courts used the statewide anti-sodomy law to argue that Bottoms was a felon, and that "felons" (sodomites) are not fit parents, thus depriving a lesbian mother of her child.

Now that the Supreme Court has ruled on Colorado's Amendment 2, upholding the state supreme court's finding of unconstitutionality, the future looks less friendly for anti-gay referenda, as Colorado for Family Values executive director Kevin Tebedo himself admitted, when he conceded that "a decision by the largely conservative court upholding the ban would give a green light to countless other jurisdictions where similar bans are likely to be considered. But a decision overturning the ban would 'force this culture to affirm and accept homosexuality.'"[30] While the Supreme Court victory regarding Colorado remains sweet, particularly given the strength of anti-gay forces in that state, it was soon followed by a matching defeat, in the form of Maine's repeal of their statewide antidiscrimination law in February of 1998.

The discourse used by the right wing was nothing short of inspired. A 1993 *Boston Globe* report on anti-gay activism summed it up fairly well:

> "We are not going to recognize homosexuality as a minority classification, or allow any classification like sexual preference to be established in the law," said Lon Mabon, an organizer of antihomosexual rights ballot initiatives in Oregon, Idaho and Washington state. Said Rev. Lou Sheldon, a California activist: "homosexuals are really asking for special rights. They don't qualify." The actions have shaken gay communities in a way not seen since Anita Bryant launched her moral crusade in the 1970s. They come at a time when more gays than ever before are winning public office, and gay rights have been pushed to the forefront by a president intent on championing the cause. In the last several years, in cities and states across America, gays won civil rights legislation with relative ease.[31]

To frame the debate as one of "special rights" evoked images of both American individualism and the black civil rights movement that very effectively turned around a quite simple civil rights issue. Indeed, one of the major issues for gays fighting these attacks has been to deal with the analogy of the civil rights movement. In other words, to what extent do gays need to "look like" other protected groups in order to gain legal protection against discrimination? The anti-gay activists have indeed tried to make common cause (typically to little effect) with civil rights groups by arguing that gays should not be compared to other groups (such as African-Americans) and that to do so is to minimize the "real" pain and suffering caused by racism, and not, therefore, by homophobia.

While generalizations are hard to come by in these confusing times, the courts often support the move towards more equity. In "the nation's highest-profile case challenging the Boy Scouts of America's ban on Gays, the New Jersey Supreme Court ruled August 4 that the organization violated state law when it ousted Dale from his position as assistant scoutmaster because of his sexual orientation."[32] Even though overruled by the Supreme Court, the Boy Scouts case was an important precedent and joins other attempts to challenge the legitimacy of exclusion based on sexual orientation. If the courts were supportive in Colorado and other key gay rights battlegrounds, they have also provided setbacks, such as the Supreme Court decision to not hear a case involving Cincinnati's 1993 amendment banning laws that protect gay people from discrimination,[33] which raises the specter of further challenges to invalidate the positive Colorado ruling.

There has also been considerable backlash against the forward-thinking and pro-gay policies of certain corporations. Companies have faced boycotts and negative publicity when they adopt domestic partner policies or when they are seen to be "aligning" with gay rights. No boycott has been as visible as the boycott of the Walt Disney Company by the Southern Baptist Convention:

> Religious conservatives are turning up the heat on the Walt Disney Co. following last month's vote by the Southern Baptist Convention to boycott the entertainment giant over its gay-friendly employment policies and adult-themed films. The American Family Assn. (AFA), a Christian pressure group that has battled the entertainment industry for years over sex and violence in programming, is throwing its formidable public relations machinery behind the Disney boycott, according to AFA founder Rev. Donald Wildmon.[34]

The AFA also distributed "recorded 'public service announcements' to about 1,100 Christian radio stations, urging listeners to refrain from purchasing Disney products until the company ceases its 'anti-family' activity. One spot declares: 'We must show Disney that families are tired of a place where molesters and lesbians are hired to make films and movies that say it's OK to go against morals and grow up gay.'"[35] Ads and public service announcements were joined by a campaign "asking Southern Baptists to withhold at least $100 million in spending from Disney during the coming year."[36] While much of this action has been criticized, some critics (most notably Jonathan Yardley of the *Washington Post*) have argued that however wrongheaded they may be, the Southern Baptists are to be applauded for at least believing in something (even if it is gay bashing), while the Disney folks have developed a "new attitude toward homosexuality" simply to get "a piece of that action."[37] Attempts by gay groups to place anti-gay-bashing ads in TV and radio have not met with the success of the anti-gay ads placed by the right. When PFLAG (Parents, Families, and Friends of Lesbians and Gays) ran thirty-second TV ads denouncing gay bashing and hate speech in 1995, not only did the Christian right successfully pressure stations to refuse the ads, but both print and radio ads ran into similar problems.[38]

And now the Christian right has moved on to a new terrain, offering compassion and concern to those wayward lesbians and gays "struggling in the homosexual lifestyle." In a series of print and TV ads, Christian conservatives have resurrected the old canard of homosexuality as illness that can be cured. The media barrage presents images of chastened gays, having thrown off the yoke of a sinful lifestyle through "reparative therapy" and born-again religiosity. Here, "former homosexuals" are presented as evidence that gays can and should switch to the heterosexual ball team. Of course, gay groups have responded with their own campaign to reveal the homophobic agenda at the heart of this kinder, gentler attack on gays.

One of the results of the increasing devolution of authority to the states that began with the Reagan Revolution is that while gay activists fight on the federal level for increased civil rights legislation the reality is that each state has increasingly different policies—around hate crimes, employment, housing, domestic partnership, etc. Many of our national gay organizations recognized this, particularly NGLTF, whose 1999 "Equality Begins at Home" campaign focused activism and training on the state and local level.

It is too easy to label these anti-gay initiatives as pure backlash, although they are surely that as well. Susan Faludi brilliantly documented the anti-feminist backlash of the '80s, and her general analysis of the backlash impetus can be applied in this case as well. However, the forces of change and the forces of backlash are occurring *simultaneously*. Unlike the backlash against the women's movement (which really hit full force after the heyday of the '70s movement and during a somewhat low-key moment in movement activism), anti-gay activity coexists uneasily with this increased visibility and pro-gay sentiment.

The crusade against gay and lesbian rights has been matched by an equally vigorous (albeit less well-funded) resistance by gay and lesbian organizations and activists. The major gay organizations—the Human Rights Campaign Fund (now the Human Rights Campaign) and the National Gay and Lesbian Task Force—have seen an unprecedented rise in memberships and contributions, leading to lavish and expensive fundraisers and benefits that would have been unheard of only a few years earlier. A truly massive effort was initiated by these two groups to oppose state and local initiatives, a campaign that included HRC's "Speak Out" program, letter writing, field training by NGLTF organizers for local resistance, lobbying local and federal officials, fundraising, and voter education. Indeed, HRC had its largest budget for the crucial 1994 election year. Other organizations such as People for the American Way, LLDEF (Lambda Legal Defense and Education Fund), and the NAACP got involved as well, contributing time and money to the fight against the referenda. People for the American Way—not previously known for its involvement in gay rights issues—really started to change its focus when the initiatives began. They released a major report in November of 1993 on the "Hostile Climate: A State-by-State Report on Anti-Gay Activity." Many other liberal organizations followed suit, thus getting involved in gay-positive organizing for the first time.

It is a political truism that nothing mobilizes like a full frontal attack. The wave of anti-gay initiatives and referenda provided that impetus, as did the more generalized targeting by the growing and increasingly powerful Christian right. But the growth in gay activism cannot be understood simply as a response to this concerted attack. In many ways, the gay movement—as a social movement for civil rights and equality—had come into its own. The March on Washington in April of 1993 was only one spectacular and dramatic indication of the "coming of age" of the lesbian and gay movement. Not only the largest march ever for lesbian and gay civil rights, it was quite possibly the largest march Washington has ever seen. The city seemed magically transformed into a gay Disneyland as lesbians and gays poured into the district and surrounding areas, taking up public space as never before. Where typically gays closely monitor their behavior for fear of violence or harassment, now friends and lovers proudly held hands, waving brightly colored rainbow flags, wearing t-shirts proclaiming "Nobody knows I'm a lesbian." The march was more than a show of political force and passionate outrage, it was a bold declaration of coming of age and coming out—anecdotes circled endlessly about how the march was the occasion for revelations to parents, friends, coworkers. It is probably no overstatement to claim that thousands now live more open lives than they did prior to that weekend. And this was, importantly, not simply an urban festival. Small towns are beginning to produce the same sorts of gay enclaves once only found in the larger metropolitan areas such as New York and San Francisco. Gay people have—obviously—always existed in small towns and rural regions. But the new visibility and political power of gays has given momentum to the development of real communities in those previously isolated areas, many of whom were represented at the march.

The march too solidified straight support for gay and lesbian rights. For the first time, sizable numbers of heterosexual supporters marched for gay rights and joined the voices calling for an end to discrimination in the armed forces and elsewhere. Where once gay pride marches were truly an all-gay event, now other supportive organizations joined in—from the newly radicalized PFLAG to synagogues, churches, labor unions, civil rights organizations, etc. Straight celebs were lining up (well, perhaps *somewhat* of an exaggeration) to express their solidarity with gay rights. Foregoing the annual treks to tony Aspen (in support of the boycott of Colorado after the victory of the anti-gay Amendment 2) is not exactly the same as storming the barricades, but it was something.

So is it the case, then, that the general public is becoming increasingly more "accepting" of gays? The polls are actually (and unusually, since polls are typically such a dry and ineffectual way of gauging public opinion) interesting here. An August 1998 *New York Times* article cited the results of a poll conducted by Gallup and the Princeton Survey Research Associates for the Pew Research Center. This poll revealed that increasing numbers of people believe homosexuality is something one is born with (13 percent in 1977, 31 percent in 1998) and growing numbers think homosexuals should have equal job opportunities (84 percent as opposed to 56 percent in 1977). But in response to the question "Do you personally believe homosexual behavior is morally wrong or is not morally wrong?" in a June 1997 poll, 59 percent said wrong, 35 percent said not wrong. And in response to another question, "Is it generally a good thing for our society or a bad thing for our society or doesn't make much difference that more gay and lesbian couples are raising children?" 56 percent said it was a bad thing, 6 percent said it was a good thing, 31 percent said it made no difference.[39] Indeed, in survey after survey readers are faced with an interesting contradiction; while there is a high level of national "disapproval" of gays and lesbians, ranging from 50 percent to 77 percent, there is an equally strong belief that discrimination is wrong. Indeed, "American acceptance of gay men and lesbians has swelled substantially in recent years, as has support for their civil rights, but a majority of the population still disapproves of homosexuality, according to a study released on Friday by the National Gay and Lesbian Task Force, an advocacy group based in Washington. But for all the signs of increased tolerance, the report also represented a half-empty glass for gay men and lesbians: It found that though disapproval of homosexuality had dropped by nearly 20 percentage points since its peak of 75 percent in the late 1980's, it was still 56 percent in 1996, the most recent year examined on that question. Also, gay men and lesbians remain one of the least-liked groups in the country, the survey found."[40]

Like the cultural world, the political world presents a complex picture: increased visibility, increased anti-discrimination legislation, increased access to government, yet, simultaneously, increased anti-gay activism and political rhetoric. The right says love the sinner, hate the sin. The general public—in polls and in anecdotal news reporting—seems to be saying much the same thing, urging "tolerance" and nondiscrimination even as it denounces homosexuality as "wrong" and repeatedly rebuilds walls around that tolerance, particularly when it comes to issues of family life.

ACTING UP OR BUTTONING UP:
DEBATING THE GAY NINETIES

How are we to understand these complicated and seemingly contradictory political shifts? There is no question that this is a heightened period for both sides, and gay rights as a form of civil rights struggle has catapulted in the '90's onto the national stage with a fervor and centrality unmatched by any prior time. As one reporter notes, the political climate has shifted generationally, producing a new kind of activist: "No underground society today, gay life is being transformed by a generation that came of age after Stonewall, a progeny that proudly calls itself 'queer.' For this exuberant set, being gay is more than a struggle for acceptance and equal rights: It is a celebration of American pluralism."[41]

As with any minority group, the moment of public visibility marks the beginning of a complex process. The emergence into public view can aid in the process of liberation; surely liberation cannot be won from the space of the crowded closet. Yet the glare of commercial culture can often produce a new kind of invisibility, itself supported by a relentless march toward assimilation. The debates about assimilation are as old as the movement itself. Indeed, every social movement has at some point been faced with similar questions, and the history of the gay movement is no different, with early organizations such as the Mattachine Society and One, Inc., explicitly opting for a '50s-style conformism as they argued for gay inclusion in the postwar dream world. But what *is* new is that these debates are now taking place in full public view, around the water coolers of corporate America, the hallways of university campuses, the barbeque grills of genteel suburbia, and the streets and malls of both urban and rural areas. No longer restricted to closed-door meetings and internecine battles, these internal debates have been irrevocably externalized.

Clearly, the crisis of AIDS bears a large responsibility for this new visibility, forcing America to reckon publicly and explicitly with a population long kept under wraps. As John D'Emilio argues, "What in the '70s and early '80s was a movement of a marginalized minority, through AIDS unfortunately became a community that was dealing with an issue that was now a *national* issue. AIDS posed a public health crisis that . . . had to be looked at. It led to a much higher level of organization and community infrastructure than had existed before [and] forced the establishment—a range of 'mainstream' institutions—into dialogue, whether they wanted to or not, with this newly mobilized community."[42]

This "dialogue" is often acrimonious. Indeed, one needs only to juxtapose Clinton's embrace of the gay community with Pat Buchanan's by now infamous speech at the 1992 Republican National Convention urging his party to wage a "cultural war" against the infidels, headed up by the unholy alliance of feminists and gays. Both the Clinton embrace and the Buchanan attack mark the first time gays are publicly reckoned with *as* a community and as a voting bloc.

Gay writers, thinkers, and activists have of course pondered this moment. The gay community—like every social entity a diverse and contentious bunch—debates internally the merits of different responses to the current onslaught. Openly gay congressman Barney Frank believes that "visibility is the prerequisite for gay bashing. How do you bash somebody you don't know is there?"[43] For Frank, and I would suspect many observers, "homophobia is diminishing greatly and the anti-gay stuff is a product, first of all, of our not hiding anymore and secondly of the frustration of the bigots that we're breaking out of the restraints."[44] More radical gay activists are less sanguine about the visibility, and less trusting of heterosexual goodwill. As lesbian author and activist Sarah Schulman says, "What *has* changed is that *we* have changed. Gay people's level of self-esteem, and their demand on the society is higher than it has ever been. But straight people have not changed. So that's why you have a much higher level of social conflict."[45] For Frank and other liberals, the rise of anti-gay activism is the desperate gasp of a bigotry with a vastly diminished constituency, spurred on by new gay power and activism. Gay *radicals,* on the other hand, see the anti-gay movement as more embedded in the fabric of American culture, not something that will wither away with the brave new forces of tolerance and inclusion.

Numerous gay leaders celebrate the new visibility as a sign that our time has come. Conservative gay activist Bruce Bawer, author of *A Place at the Table* and *Beyond Queer,* exults over the new experience of openness and inclusion, claiming that lesbians and gays will now have a "place at the table" of mainstream American society. Other conservative writers like Andrew Sullivan (former editor of the *New Republic*) point to the AIDS crisis as the catalyst for "social integration" and a "renegotiation of the gay-straight social contract."[46] For Sullivan, the victimization by AIDS pushed straights toward sympathy and "undercut their [gays'] victimization by a culture."[47] Sullivan sees AIDS as "an integrator" in that it allowed the "strong fear of homosexual difference" to be displaced by a nascent humanity.[48] Congressman Frank believes that "the visibility is, in and of itself, cleansing. Because the best antidote to the prejudice is the reality."[49]

Others bemoan the media wave as the surest indication of an assimilation and co-optation that will only bring about banal inclusion and nodding acceptance. Schulman takes a particularly cynical position, arguing that the reliance on visibility as a primary strategy "was very naive, because it was rooted in the idea that if people knew who we were they would not treat us this way. And it has now proven that this was untrue, and that no matter how much they know about us it doesn't seem to change the way they feel about us. This has been a bitter pill to swallow."[50] Urvashi Vaid, former director of the National Gay and Lesbian Task Force and author of the book *Virtual Equality,* argues "that we are mainstreamed at the same instant that we remain marginalized. Some of us have won mainstream legitimacy and access, but most of us struggle with the same issues that our movement has fought to resolve for decades: whether and where to come out, how to overcome gay self-hatred, how to communicate the real truth of our lives to straight people, how to live free from violence, how to make a living and raise a family as openly gay people. The mainstream attention we now receive is proof that the battle has widened, not that it has ended."[51] Some believe, with Schulman, that the "place at the table" is being set by others, and that the invitation to join will come at the loss of our autonomy, independence, and political power.

Many also argue that the place is only set for a few—those who make the cover of magazines as well-heeled, white, bourgeois "chic lesbians," or as brave, clean-cut, white young men in starched Navy uniforms. There will be no place for the drag queens, the effeminate men and butch women, the outrageous and flamboyant, or perhaps even for the everyday, the poor, those of ethnic minority groups. As Vaid says, "The large numbers of gay working-class people, of queers in the hard-working and ever-squeezed middle class, the queers supporting themselves as waiters and retail clerks and hairdressers and computer data entry personnel, as secretaries and factory workers, as low-paid child care workers and teachers, are ignored in the rush to cover the Armani lesbians and the upwardly mobile gay men."[52] Indeed, critics of the new gay visibility such as Daniel Harris argue that "the Good Gay subscribes to many of the same opinions held by conservative Americans,"[53] thus eschewing the more confrontational and challenging aspects of gay historical identity. While it is true that liberation cannot be won by banking solely on the healing powers of assimilation, I remain skeptical of any position that paints with such a broad brush, insisting instead that we pay closer and more detailed attention to the *differences* in representation during this time period.

Not only do gays debate the merits of the new visibility, but they also debate vigorously the methods of response to anti-gay activism. Conservative activists like Bawer argue that we need to "clean up" our movement, demonstrate our sameness with straight society, distance ourselves from the drag queens and leather boys, and claim our rightful place as, simply, American citizens. Like earlier conservative gay writers (I think particularly of Madsen and Kirk's 1989 *After the Ball,* which treads down a similar path of blaming gay activism and sexual expressiveness for homophobia), Bawer believes in putting our best face forward, cutting off heterosexual distaste by offering an image of clean-as-a-whistle gay Girl and Boy Scouts. Of course, this position has old roots in early days of the gay (then called "homophile") movement, when first-time picketers were sternly told to put on their suits and ties (or dresses and pumps) to show America how respectable they really were. The contemporary analogue to that is the success of the largest and most powerful gay group—the Human Rights Campaign Fund. After a rocky history (and complaints that it was male-dominated) the organization hired a corporate suit as its chief, dropped the "Fund" in its title, adopted a spiffy and "nongay" new logo (an "=" sign) marketed a line of "HRC Actionware," and donated money to the Republican Party. Since January 1995, membership has nearly doubled. As one critic pessimistically puts it, "Thirty years after the Stonewall riots against police brutality in New York City launched the modern gay movement, same-sexers are faced with a paradox: As more and more people have come out, and as the commercialization of gay culture and gay images has amplified our visibility, the national movement has become more and more conservative."[54]

Many gays respond to the anti-gay rhetoric (a rhetoric that inveighs against gay "lifestyles" and "choice") with a biological argument, that gayness is "in our genes" in some fundamental way (the same as skin color, beyond our control, something we are born with) and therefore not a behavior or a choice but a compulsion of sorts. And in the early and mid '90s, it seemed that every magazine was touting a "geneticist of the month" proving that we just can't help ourselves. In response to the recent spate of ads and articles on the "reparative therapy" movement to "cure" homosexuals, Andrew Sullivan argues just such a position:

> Then there's the notion that homosexuals "choose" their sexuality. If the literature of reparative therapy teaches anything, it is how deep homosexuality runs in a person's identity, and how enormously difficult it is to alter. Most reparative therapists think sexual orientation is fixed in early development before the age of 18 months or, at the latest, three years. The most prominent psychotherapist in the field, Charles Socarides (whose own son is gay), specifically denies that homosexuality is a choice. What he and other reparative therapists argue, in fact, is something very advantageous to the argument for gay equality: even if homosexuality is not genetic but environmental, it is still involuntary. In other words, homosexuals have as much choice over their sexual orientation as they do over their race or sex.[55]

It should be no surprise that some of the more conservative gay leaders are those that believe in a biological determinant to homosexuality. Rich Tafel, head of the Log Cabin Club, argues as much when he states that "we want to be treated fairly and not lose our jobs just because we happen to be born gay."[56] Many other gay activists, of course, argue a much different position, that we need not claim "compulsion" or biological status in order to have equal rights and equal treatment. In addition, there is great variation among gays as to why and how they are gay; some resolutely believe that they had no say in the matter and find themselves sympathetic to the biological arguments, while others articulate their sexuality along a continuum and argue that sexual identity is not "hardwired" but rather a much more multifaceted and complicated process. It should be no surprise that these same "born with it" gays also tend to be the ones championing an assimilationist cultural and political strategy, while gays who voice a discourse of choice and volition are more wary of a merger with heterosexual culture.

The gay movement is most assuredly at a crossroads. It seems as though every movement has its time, its defining moment in history, its reaching of critical mass. Lesbians and gays are the last group against whom it is still legal to discriminate, and acceptable to publicly denigrate and socially ostracize. In that sense, gay and lesbian civil rights are the new litmus test for an ailing republic. But just what is the gay movement and how should it move? The mainstream media tends to depict the gay movement as a relative monolith, as it does most "minority" groups. But, as people of color have been saying for years, we do not speak with one voice. And, as more and more people come out and join organizations and get involved in some form of gay activism, the diversity of opinion within the gay community can no longer be ignored.

In many ways, the splits are ones that are familiar to anyone involved in social movements: assimilationism vs. separatism, accommodation vs. confrontation, gradualism and reformism vs. revolution and radicalism. But these categories are too glib to describe the complexities of any social movement. Yes, to some extent they do hold. All one has to do is compare our two most well-known and articulate voices (Urvashi Vaid and Andrew Sullivan) in their recent books to get a sense of the differences between Vaid's radical politics of transformation and challenge and Sullivan's conservative, religious assimilationism.

So while there is a general split between a left-leaning gay radicalism and a sort of neoconservative assimilationism, these parallels leave something out. For gays, unlike blacks and women but much more like Jews, can hide. And this is one place where some of the analogies between the black civil rights movement and the gay movement breaks down. For gays, the mark of difference is often invisible. Except for the drag queens and exceedingly "butch" women, gay people really are everywhere and are, by and large, invisible *as gay* unless they name themselves publicly as gay, or are outed. In many ways, this has been a huge hindrance in organizing gays, because a very deliberate kind of volition must take place to initiate a serious social movement and to create the kinds of communities that sustain those movements. The specificity of the closet and the uniqueness of the process of "coming out" marks the lesbian and gay experience as different—at least in part—from the experiences of other demonized groups.

Whether you believe that the losses outweigh the victories or vice versa, what is uncontested is the sheer *amount* of activity that has swirled around lesbians and gays in recent years. What is also uncontested is the paradoxical and confusing nature of this combination of victory and attack that seems to characterize our era. We have come a long way, but the road we are on is a bumpy one, and the trails ahead circuitous and forked. For a long time, the road to change seemed fairly straight (no pun intended). To be seen, respected, known—to live in the fullness of American civitas. Whether couched in terms of equal rights or radical liberation, the gay movement knew that simply moving out of that proverbial space of the closet and into the full light of the public eye was half the battle. Indeed, to simply get recognized as a political constituency appeared unattainable. The recognition publicly and politically of gay identity itself defined the terrain of political visibility. Or so it seemed. Now, our course is not so self-evident, for gays are surely present as visible participants in the political scene and even seen by many as significant players. The "gay vote" is now a phrase that has entered our political lexicon. So what now?

If the political world presents a series of confusions, dramatic leaps forward and equally dramatic retrenchments, then it would seem that the cultural spaces move unquestionably and ceaselessly forward. As more and more gays crop up in TV shows, in films, in ads, and in other forms of cultural life, it seems that our politics are merely lagging behind our culture, or at the very least moving with more awkward and halting steps. But, as the next few sections will illustrate, the cultural world presents similar contradictions and confusions. Here, too, the road is bumpy underneath the appearance of virtual smoothness. The images of gays that leap forth from our TV screens and from our magazines, like the political initiatives that emerge from statehouses, courtrooms, and corporations, shed an uneven light and even create new problems in consigning some gays to the nether reaches of cultural disenfranchisement while their more "acceptable" brethren do indeed find a place at the table. It is to these curious, confusing, exciting, complicated cultural images that we now turn.

PART TWO *A Kiss Is Just a Kiss*

Let's go out and terrify some Baptists.
—Emma Thompson as a guest lesbian on *Ellen*

And we're supposed to admire you because you went to a gay bar? I'm supposed to think you're cool because you have gay friends?
—Nancy from *Roseanne*

I'm **not** gay. Not that there's anything wrong with that.
—*Seinfeld*

Hello everybody, my name is Lea DeLaria, and it's great to be here, because it's the 1990s! It's hip to be queer! I'm a biiiiiggggg dyke!
—Comic Lea DeLaria on *Arsenio Hall*

$\mathcal{Three}$ READY FOR PRIME
TIME? TV COMES OUT
OF THE CLOSET

Television remains the most conspicuous and visible marker of this
new era of lesbian and gay visibility. While much has been made
of the recent wave of gay-themed films, it is really the more prosaic
medium of television that has beamed gay life (or a televisual version of
it) into millions of homes across this country and abroad. Literally hundreds of articles in newspapers and magazines throughout the country
have chronicled the phenomenal explosion of TV visibility for lesbians
and gays, announcing new gay characters every season in a seemingly
unstoppable trend. Web sites and gay papers regularly carry weekly "gay
watches" that alert readers and viewers to gay episodes, gay-themed specials, hidden gay content, and movies with gay characters. Chronicling
the ever-increasing numbers of lesbians and gay men on TV has become
a full-time job.

The new gay visibility on TV is surely a dramatic departure from the
history of the medium. While film has long dealt with gay subjects,
albeit in a stereotyped and "tragic" way, television's "family-focused" format seemed to insist that lesbians and gays were simply not a part of the
families that made up TV audiences. It is one thing to see gays portrayed
at your local art-house movie theater; it is quite another to have them return to your living room week after week, insinuating themselves into the
very fabric of the American home. The intense intimacy of television, its

location amidst the bric-a-brac of family life, provides a particular kind of viewing experience, removed as it is from the pleasurable anonymity of the darkened movie theater. For lesbians and gays to have sprung up in this at once most generic and most personal space is indeed amazing, and disconcerting to many who are used to the television illusion of heterosexual bliss.

NOT ALL IN THE FAMILY: A BRIEF HISTORY OF GAYS IN TV

While it may seem that now even the determined channel-surfer can't escape the lavender menace, it was not always this way. TV's early history—while innovative on any number of levels—avoided the subject of homosexuality as much as it embraced the image of domestic womanhood à la June Cleaver. While gays were featured in a number of news programs and interview formats (the most notorious being the 1967 CBS Reports special where a somber Mike Wallace ponders "the dilemma of the homosexual. Told by the medical profession he is sick, by the law that he's a criminal. Shunned by employers, rejected by heterosexual society. Incapable of a fulfilling relationship with a woman or, for that matter, with a man. At the center of his life, he remains anonymous . . ."), it was not until the 1970s that any substantive depiction of gays occurred on entertainment, "fiction" TV, marked by the 1972 ABC movie *That Certain Summer,* concerning a father coming out to his son. Needless to say, this fairly sympathetic portrayal did not spark a flood of additional programming. While invisibility and avoidance remained the norm in the '70s, depictions of lesbians and gays did pop up occasionally. The pioneering *All in the Family* aired an episode in 1971 featuring a gay football player, and the venerable Dr. Marcus Welby was eager to "cure" a patient suffering from homosexuality in a 1973 episode. Series such as *Family, Police Woman, Hawaii Five-O,* and *Medical Center* included single episodes with gay characters. Even America's sweetheart, Mary Tyler Moore, featured an episode in which unlucky in love Rhoda falls for neighbor Phyllis's gay brother.[1]

This mistaken identity device has proven to be a guaranteed laugh-line, in films as well as TV. We see this trope used in series such as *Alice, Three's Company, WKRP in Cincinnati, Taxi, Kate & Allie, Cheers,* and, more recently, *Friends. Golden Girls* effectively used the mistaken identity theme in a 1986 episode in which a visiting friend of Dorothy falls for Blanche, much to her chagrin. The long-running sitcom *Three's Company* made it into the gay hall of shame by basing an entire series on the supposedly funny ruse of a straight man pretending to be gay in order to keep an apartment with two straight women.

While film tended to be more graphic in its portrayal of vicious stereo-types, sitcoms typically trotted out the swishy, effeminate queen/hair-dresser/interior decorator while TV movies featured the tragic, closeted victim. And who could ever forget the rapist lesbian of the TV movie *Born Innocent* (1974), where schlock-queen Linda Blair began her illustrious career? Gays were generally played for giggles or pathos; occasionally (as in *All in the Family* and *Family*) to make a point about anti-gay bigotry.

The offbeat parody *Soap* contained that anomaly—a swishy yet strangely nonstereotypical, interesting, continuing gay character (played by the then unknown Billy Crystal) in addition to a strong lesbian char-acter (the two eventually raise a child together). This series is surely a standout in a period of relative invisibility, but it was also a series that traded on its wackiness: gay characters were thus figured as not so icon-oclastic additions to a parade of "deviant" outsiders. In other words, the gay character was configured as yet one more member of a deeply dys-functional TV tribe.

Nevertheless, it took the tragedy of the AIDS epidemic to produce any quantifiably meaningful representations of gays and lesbians in televi-sion. Unfortunately, all too often, those early AIDS dramas portrayed ei-ther promiscuous, "deviant" gays who were threats to society or, as in the case of NBC's *An Early Frost* (1985), gays made acceptable to heterosex-ual society through becoming the object of intense pity and sympathy. As television researcher Larry Gross argues, gays generally have been de-picted on TV as either victims or villains; this is nowhere more true than in the representation of gay men with AIDS.[2] But whether victims or vil-lains (and this villain motif has been used to great effect in a number of TV series in which men with AIDS are seen as bottom-feeding snakes who irresponsibly and knowingly spread "the plague"), TV representa-tions of PWAs (People with AIDS) are notable in their refusal to engage the community context of gay men. This absence of gay culture (the vast and intricate networks of friends, lovers, bookstores, coffeehouses, com-munity centers, political clubs, support groups, neighborhoods, that gay people have been creating for years) in representations with gay charac-ters is still with us today. When gay culture is referenced at all, it usually is marked by the more salacious aspects of bars and sex clubs.

The eighties seemed to offer possibilities, yet more often than not disappointed. The medical drama *Heartbeat*—set in a women's clinic and featuring an openly lesbian nurse—was canceled after one season (1988–89). While it raised many hopes, *Heartbeat* persistently margin-alized the lesbian character, infrequently depicting her with her partner and avoiding any political or sexual explicitness. As critic Meg Moritz argues, the inclusion of lesbians and gay men is often a case of "old strategies for new texts" whereby heterosexual dominance and centrality are effectively recuperated. The similarly brief *Love, Sidney* (1981) began in its pilot with a lead gay character who later metamorphosed into a cheery "bachelor." Other series of the late '70s and early '80s contained occasional gay characters: *Barney Miller's* Officer Zitelli comes out toward the end of the series, Chris Cagney of *Cagney and Lacey* had a gorgeous gay next-door neighbor, *Roc* had a gay brother (one of the few depictions of gay African-Americans), *Hooperman* featured a gay cop, and the long-time soap *All My Children* featured a short-lived story about a lesbian doctor. Several others had "one-shot" gay nights, including *Hill Street Blues, St. Elsewhere, Golden Girls, Doctor, Doctor,* etc. The 1984 Showtime series *Brothers* included a major gay character, critically appraised at the time and soon taken off the air.

One popular series of the '80s was notable for its obvious lesbian subtext and its adamant refusal to ever make the subtext visible. In one memorable episode, however, *Kate and Allie* raises the question of its costars' relationship only to thoroughly dismiss the possibility that two women living together with their kids could be lovers. In this episode, Kate and Allie find, much to their horror, that they face eviction because they do not constitute a "family." Posing as lesbian lovers, they effectively manage to keep their apartment, primarily because their landlady reveals *her* lesbianism to them and embraces them into the sisterhood. Chagrined by the ruse, they fess up, reassert their heterosexuality, and keep the apartment.

Another '80s standout was an ABC Movie of the Week entitled *My Two Loves* (cowritten by noted lesbian author Rita Mae Brown!), which featured Mariette Hartley (Gail) as a recently widowed mother of a teen-age daughter who discovers her desire for tight-lipped Lynn Redgrave (Marjorie), even as she maintains her desire for her new lover Ben (best friend of dead hubby). Like most well-meaning liberal representations, homophobia is not so much challenged as depicted as the misinformed stereotypes of well-intentioned neophytes. So Gail's mom spews homophobic bile but is rehabilitated through the requisite "you're still my daughter and I love you no matter what" speech. And the male lover's anger is justified by his "good guy" persona and obvious devotion to the poor widow. Needless to say, the double standard remains strong: no passionate kisses from lover Marjorie, although there is a strange seduction scene consisting of hair washing, hair conditioning, hair combing, and the reading of tabloid trash. While this scene might appear to present lesbian love as a poor substitute for a trip to the local beauty salon, it actually fits in with much of the rest of the movie, which depicts lesbian desire as the "natural" result of girlfriend bonding. So we have the deep girlfriend chats, the shared aerobic classes, the hair washing: Hollywood's' version of Sapphic foreplay. Confused Gail hies off to a shrink, tearfully parts company with both male and female lover, and pledges herself to a future of introspection. The last moment has mother and daughter warmly embracing, hair-washing lesbian sex now fully pushed into the background (although, thankfully, not denounced). Like so many liberal representations, individual actions and desires are radically decontextualized: are these the only two lesbian lovers in the world? Marjorie has recently split off from a long-term lesbian relationship yet seems bereft of other gay people or anything resembling a community. Indeed, Marjorie's stealthy closetedness (and her unhappy demeanor) tend to give credence to Gail's mother's assertion of the misery of gay life. And the possibility of living an open and proud life is resolutely made invisible, as this scene indicates. The day after the first time they are together sexually, Gail and Marjorie meet up at the aerobic studio (not exactly an aphrodisiac for most of us, but clearly a mainstay of this film). Gail reveals to Marjorie that she told Ben she didn't want to see him anymore, but did not reveal that the "other man" was a woman.

> Gail: I have never known what it was like to evade or omit the truth. I
> mean it's not quite like being a liar, but I feel like a liar. Is this what gay
> people feel like?
> Marjorie: Most of us, yeah. Yes it is.

But, devoid of any larger depiction of either gay culture or heterosexual assumptions, this sad reverie makes the viewer want to run as fast as she can from "the life," if all it amounts to is hair washing, sweaty aerobics, and duplicity. The possibility of a nonduplicitous life (and the suggestion that the duplicity is forced by heterosexual dominance) never emerges in this narrative. Thus, the only possible outcome is exactly what we get: a rejection of both lovers in favor of an ambiguous, asexual bisexuality.

However, in the annals of gay TV history, the '80s will be remembered as the *Dynasty* years. Steven Carrington, the handsome, blond hunk and son of series patriarch Blake Carrington, remains one of the most well-known (if not exactly well-loved) gay TV characters. While not in every episode, Steven was a regular, continuing character and was included in plot lines as much as any of Blake and Alexis's wayward children. Stalwartly manly and deeply troubled by his homosexuality, Steven took us on a Hollywood tour of homosexuality: from tortured closet case, to "cured" heterosexual husband, and finally to a vague approximation of gay and proud.

Undoubtedly a breakthrough role, Steven's persistent attempts to "go straight" and the adamant avoidance of any gay milieu or culture mark

Steven of *Dynasty* fame struggles manfully with his shameful and ever-changing sexuality. Courtesy of Photofest.

this show as deeply flawed and compromised. As in many of the series that featured sporadic gay episodes, Steven's presence is always a *problem;* his gayness and his struggle against it and with his family are the totality of his character. Nevertheless, gay audiences put up with Steven's self-loathing because of their love for *Dynasty's* overt campiness. Bars and clubs around the country featured *Dynasty* nights on big-screen TVs, replete with Joan Collins drag queens and Steven clones. If the Reagan years were harsh for gays, *Dynasty*'s camp send-ups of ostentatious wealth and the outrageousness of bitch-extraordinaire Alexis made the series a staple of gay iconography, even as the actually gay character was hardly a role model of self-acceptance and pride.

Clearly, the eighties began to open up the doors for what became the boom in gay representations of the nineties. Nevertheless, this opening door was not without those who would shut it; indeed, "Although recurring gay characters were relatively commonplace on network series during the late 1970s and 1980s—on programs such as 'Dynasty' and 'Soap'—opposition from fundamentalists who complained to advertisers helped reduce their ranks to zero in the spring of 1991."[3] So, historically speaking, we have a move from almost total invisibility (and, when visible, almost total stereotyping) to an increased presence, albeit a flawed, sporadic and episodic one, to a backlash against that increased presence that then paves the way for the more substantive "open door" that we are now witnessing. One commentator, echoing so many others, couldn't help but note that "gay characters and themes are busting out all over in prime time TV on network and cable. Oh God, here come the queers. First it was the blacks, then the Jews, now it's the gays and lesbians. They've made it to prime time, on Fox, Thursdays at 8 P.M. They're on Comedy Central specials at 10 p.m. They're on ABC, Tuesdays at 9 P.M. They're on Melrose Place, they're on L.A. Law. They're everywhere, for cryin' out loud. Well, basically, that's the point. They are everywhere. They're on The Simpsons and Roseanne. They're next to you at work. They're your friends even though you might not know it. They shop at your store."[4]

SAINTS AND SINNERS: APPROACHES TO GAY CHARACTERS

A comparison here can be instructive. No two approaches could be more dissimilar than those of *Roseanne* and *Melrose Place*, since-canceled series that featured gay characters. *Melrose Place* is perhaps the most frustrating for gay viewers, because at the time it was the one (and only) TV series in which a gay character was a "star," one of the original formative members of the central ensemble. The character of Matt (probably the most boring gay man ever cinematically imagined) was introduced alongside the other regulars that populate the twenty-something world set in the steamy apartment complex of "Melrose Place." This highly popular series was marked by its over-the-top sexuality and ever wackier plot lines—from call-girl rings to multiple personality murderers. And many critics complained about Matt's stalwart goodness and sexual purity in the face of endless mate-swapping and increasingly lurid sexual encounters. Still, in the supposedly gay '90s, the gay character can't get kissed, caressed, stroked (much less anything else)—at least not before the cameras. Now, this is not to say that Matt wasn't allowed a social life. And I think this is precisely the dilemma and source of frustration for viewers: Matt had several relationships (with implied sexual contact), yet his sexuality was never allowed to be visible, as was the sexuality of the heterosexual characters. In other words, the double standard is in full force here, as it is throughout most of popular culture, as even its creator recognized when in an interview he conceded "that 'Melrose Place' viewers had been rolling their collective eyes at gay social worker Matt Fielding's stunted development. 'We received hundreds of letters, the writers asking why all the other characters were allowed to have a love life, but not Matt,' he said. 'Straight viewers identify with him as well as gay viewers. They feel he's part of their lives, and they want to know more about him.'"[5]

Yet Matt's lack of sexual expression was only part of the problem. Matt's gayness, like that of so many others in the televisual world, was both everything and nothing as well. And this is the paradox that seems to permeate cultural representations of gays at the current moment. Matt is the "gay character" and most of his story lines revolve in some way around his sexual identity—he is seduced by a self-hating closet case, his Navy lover is discharged and gets AIDS, he is fired by a homophobic boss, etc. Indeed, his story lines so often take him *outside* the world of Melrose Place, in contradistinction to his straight comrades, whose worlds endlessly and obsessively intertwine. This is, of course, the price of tokenism. Since Matt is the only ongoing gay character, and the show is predicated on endless mate-swapping, his exclusion from the everyday world of the soap seems preordained. So poor Matt does not really live in the world of Melrose Place like his costars. Yet neither does he have a real "outside"—a place of gay community, gay friends, gay culture. Indeed, towards the end of his time on the series, Matt finally found a seemingly active gay man for a friend, only to have him turn out to be a calculating operator. Matt is like a floating and fleeting sign of gayness, unsubstantiated by a gay life and disenfranchised by the dominant heterosexual gestalt. He is homeless and ephemeral: the unkissed in a world of endless kissing.

Matt was forever without a love life and certainly without the hot and heavy sexual contact that is *Melrose Place*'s calling card. He was the source of no small amount of sarcasm within the gay community; one of the gay computer networks kept tabs on Matt's unbelievably dismal social life,

Well-adjusted Matt of *Melrose Place* looked good but was oh-so-unlucky in love. Courtesy of Photofest.

pointing out that it will probably be a cold day in hell when Matt finally gets some.

Unlike earlier depictions of tortured gays, unable to live a happy and productive life (I think here of the poor Steven Carrington from soap trash *Dynasty,* forever miserable about his gayness, forever trying to "go straight," forever disappointing his homophobic—but oh-so-manly— father), Matt is not only well-adjusted and "accepting" of his gay identity, he is a devoutly do-gooding social worker (later med student), always coming to the rescue when his more reckless hetero friends are in trouble. But it seems as if Matt must sacrifice his sexuality (which is after all, the raison d'être of the series) in order to move outside of the stereo-typical portrait of gay men. Matt is marked as different not by any at-tachment to gay iconography, gay politics, gay cultural mores, but rather by a saintly asexuality (the simple polar opposite of the earlier depiction of gays as sex-crazed perverts) that is clearly aberrant in a series in which every single character has slept with every single character (of the oppo-site sex). Even when Matt has a (closeted) live-in lover, the most we see are meaningful glances and manly hugs.

At the end of one of the later seasons, Matt was allowed a kiss but the camera avoided the two men and focused instead on the shocked reac-tion of a watching heterosexual friend. When Matt leans over to kiss his newfound love interest goodnight, we see not the meeting of male lips but rather the horrified face of straight heartthrob Billy, witnessing the moment that happens only in the imagination of the gay viewer. The focus then moves not to burgeoning homo love, but instead to shocked hetero unease.

The hit series *Roseanne* walked a different path. *Roseanne* was not only one of the most successful sitcoms in TV history, it was one of the most unusual as well. Roseanne explicitly marks the '60s as her personal point of reference—often through the "sex, drugs, and rock and roll" motif that finds its way into her offbeat and casual approach to parenting. Roseanne challenges the sitcom and TV itself on its most cherished home front: the family domesticom. It really is the grand reversal of the Anderson family in *Father Knows Best,* exposing both the ludicrousness of those earlier images and offering up a representation of family that is at once working class and progressive, sexual and maternal, funny and loving. She expresses quite different ideas about parenting and about work—Roseanne is everything June Cleaver and Margaret Anderson were not, but she is also **not** bourgeois, successful, tailored Claire Huxtable or Murphy Brown. She speaks, in that sense, to the persistent status of women in the workplace as underpaid service workers.

If Murphy Brown is Mary Tyler Moore's daughter of the '90s, then Roseanne curiously has *no* cultural parentage—she is a unique presence in a cultural landscape that has effectively obliterated both her prime signifiers: class and nontraditional-looking women. And, significantly, Roseanne does address these signifiers directly. Her self-consciousness as a working-class woman is vivid and ever present: through jokes about her tacky Christmas decorations or Wonder bread and meatloaf, Roseanne constantly refers to herself and her family as "poor white trash," thus helping to deconstruct the power these stereotypes exert.

Very clearly too, Roseanne challenges many stereotypes about women: the dichotomy between sexuality and motherhood, male images of beauty, motherlove as kind and beneficent and selfless. Her free and raucous sexuality challenge both the ideology of maternity as opposed fundamentally to sexuality and the assumption of fat women as nonsexual. Her weight is clearly there—present in the structure of the sitcom, not avoided or made invisible or lessened. Yet it is also not narratively central—except occasionally. In not making her physical status narratively central, Roseanne challenges in a larger and more inchoate sense the centrality of physical image and beauty for women in general. Her struggles with work, her relationship with her kids and husband, her deep and abiding relationship with her sister—this is the stuff of her life.

In her benign and banal largeness, she de-emphasizes that wh
come to be the marker of "woman-ness": our bodies.

Not content to have a token gay character, *Roseanne*'s cast in
bisexual Nancy Bartlett (Sandra Bernhard) and business partn
(Martin Mull), who was later joined by (and "married" to) partnc. _ _
As if that wasn't enough, Roseanne's mother Bev reveals her (quite latent)
lesbian yearnings, making her the first lesbian grandma in TV history.
She reveals her sexuality through the hilarious Thanksgiving bombshell,
"By the end of my marriage, the only way I could have sex with my hus-
band was if I stopped off at the store and bought myself a Playboy first."

But it was in March of 1994 that the often controversial sitcom
Roseanne caused a social and cultural uproar. On March 1, an episode
labeled "Don't Ask, Don't Tell" was aired. The episode, featuring a kiss
between Roseanne and another woman, caused a stir even before it aired.
The execs at ABC—pressured by right-wing groups—attempted to get
Roseanne to either edit the kiss or cancel the entire episode. Roseanne
stuck by her guns, publicly declared she would switch networks, and
insisted the episode be aired on its originally scheduled date of March 1.
In addition, she spoke out quite openly when suggestions were made
that the kiss was "disgusting," arguing that the real cause for concern
should be centered around the endless depictions of women being raped,
mutilated, and killed every day on prime-time TV. Prior to the episode,
local TV stations and networks alike ran clips from the episode, rehash-
ing the controversy. Op-eds appeared and pundits weighed in. Like the
return of the repressed, TV's fascination with its own discourse produced
a "Challenger"-like effect whereby we saw kiss after kiss as local stations
reported on the event of the evening.

The *Roseanne* episode truly represented a radical departure in its cogent and sustained attack on homophobia and exploration of the shifting
parameters of sexual desire. While commentators predictably focused on
the heretical moment of a prime-time lesbian kiss, they ignored the full
substance of the episode, itself much more challenging than the brief
peck on the lips. Centered around a trip to a gay bar with the regular
character played by Sandra Bernhard and her new girlfriend (played by
guest Mariel Hemingway), the episode both parodied homophobic assumptions and dealt with Roseanne and husband Dan's own reckoning
with their own homophobia.

Like the *Murphy Brown* flap around "family values," the episode took
on significant cultural meaning precisely because of its location within
a culture which is currently curious about gay and lesbian life. In addition, Roseanne's presence as feminist voice against anti-gay bigotry is

The "Don't Ask, Don't Tell" episode of *Roseanne* challenged homophobia and playfully recognized its persistent presence in the heart of suburban America. Courtesy of Photofest.

well-known, and her costars in the episode also have a location in the lesbian world—Bernhard as the (rumored) one-time lover of pop icon Madonna and Hemingway as star of the lesbian-themed film *Personal Best*.

But, like so much of our cultural output, it was a double-edged sword. On the one hand, *Roseanne* took the opportunity to produce an episode that was notable for its unrelenting parody of stereotypes about lesbians and its up-front critique of homophobia. It was truly a pleasure to watch. Yet, the episode was preceded by a "warning" that the show contained "mature sexual themes" and that parental discretion was advised. Of course, the double-standard remains strong and in force: no parental discretion is advised when heterosexuals kiss (much more explicitly, by the way) and when women are systematically raped and terrorized as part of everyday TV fare. (As mentioned above, Roseanne made this point herself in defense of the episode.) Indeed, TV's other recent lesbian kiss made similar waves, and the character was quickly removed from the series. In 1991, *L.A. Law* featured a bisexual character who caused quite a stir when she planted a lesbian kiss on coworker Abby's lips, a network TV first. The kiss between presumably straight lawyer Abby and avowedly bisexual newcomer CJ (lesbian characters tend to either have men's names or androgynous initials) raised quite a ruckus in Hollywood, prompting *L.A. Law* to quickly find a male lover for CJ, and, in short time, remove her from the show altogether.

We are gladdened by the airing of the *Roseanne* episode, but saddened too as it brings home to us, once again, our own marginalization within American society. In addition, however laudable the show was, there is no question that the kiss was only "allowed" because it was purely didactic: no threat was posed to Roseanne's heterosexuality, and the marriage between the heterosexual couple remained firmly in place, whereas the lesbian couple remained peripheral to the narrative of heterosexual understanding and tolerance. Granted, this is better than complete invisibility, but it does point to the endless and inevitable moves of recuperation that accompany even the most minute attempts at substantive critiques of dominant, compulsory heterosexuality.

Nevertheless, this episode is worth examining closely, as it is one of the few televisual moments in which homophobia and heterosexism are challenged head-on, and in which the cultural and social context of gay lives are not edited out. Indeed, the famous kiss episode was marked by its substantive and deep investigation of homophobia. Significantly, instead of playing the gayness for laughs (as is so often the case), what becomes the object of mockery is homophobia itself. So often, when homophobia is depicted at all it is the acts of anonymous and ruthless bigots—people who are generally not central to the abiding narrative and who are not characters we are otherwise urged to identify with and admire. In *Melrose Place,* Matt's fellow apartment dwellers seem blithely unperturbed by his gayness. The homophobia (when it is shown at all) comes from outside of the TV universe—from anonymous bosses, angry-faced gay bashers, recalcitrant parents. But Roseanne dares to show the homophobic heart of darkness of middle America. After Roseanne is kissed by Nancy's new girlfriend Sharon while partying it up at a gay bar, she is anxious and upset, unable to articulate her discomfort (is it homophobia? attraction? regret?) but also eager to assert her hipness. By having America's fave working class liberal muddle over her own reaction to sexual difference, Roseanne goes where few have gone before and, in doing so, advances the dialogue to a new place. She also explicitly and directly addresses these dilemmas in the discussion between characters. When Nancy challenges her—"And we're supposed to admire you because you went to a gay bar? I'm supposed to think you're cool because you have gay friends?"—Roseanne allows the show to name the phenomenon of "lesbian chic" and critique it at the same time. She is eager to assert her hipness—"Hey, I like that Snoopy Dog Dog"—but that very eagerness exposes her own discomfort with homosexuality. Later on, when she is in bed with Dan and describing the situation at the bar, Rosie realizes that he is getting turned on by the thought of lesbian sexuality. But when Roseanne turns the tables and starts talking about "men rubbing their hard bodies together," Dan immediately turns off, allowing the audience to witness the ways in which gay sexuality has figured in the sexual imagination of heterosexual men.

This is not to say that Roseanne doesn't indulge in stereotypes too (all TV does and the tough women at the bar are no exception), but that she goes far beyond the stereotypes to reckon more substantively with homophobia itself. Her sister Jackie is openly uncomfortable and wary at the bar, yet also expresses regret later that she was not "hit on," exposing the attraction/repulsion dynamic that is so definitive of straight interactions with gays. And stereotypes *are* broken down as well, particularly when Jackie's belief that her pregnancy marks her as unequivocally heterosexual is challenged by the presence of a very pregnant lesbian in the bar. Similarly, Leon, Roseanne's gay coworker, is as different from *Dynasty*'s Matt as possible. A somewhat dumpy, middle-aged man with a longtime companion and a permanent antagonism with Roseanne, Leon is a difficult, uptight, controlling boss. While Matt's gayness needed to be rendered visible through the prism of his saintliness, Leon is just another nasty boss who happens to be gay. Yet his gayness doesn't disappear (indeed, there's a wonderful moment when he learns Roseanne is going to the bar and he marvels at seeing her among "his people"). But what is significant is that his gayness is not so much the subject as is the persistence and manifestations of homophobia in the straight characters.

What marks *Roseanne* out as different is that gays are not simply token signs of cultural hipness and "diversity," but are rather integrated into the life of the sitcom. *Roseanne* has done what is seemingly so simple but has proved to be close to impossible: to depict lesbians and gays as both same *and* different, as being part of the both the dominant culture in which they emerged as well as the more marginalized culture inhabited by their gayness. Although one of the two continuing gay characters left before the final season (Sandra Bernhard's bisexual Nancy), *Roseanne* still had a strong gay presence with the recurring character of Leon.

Another example of a more challenging depiction of gays on TV can be found in the critically acclaimed animated series *The Simpsons*. It should come as no surprise that the series, notable for its offbeat parody of family life and for its sarcastic challenge to TV sentimentalism, should produce a "gay episode" that directly takes on stereotypes and employs them even as it foregrounds their patent silliness. The episode was directed by John Waters (with his voice as the outré antique dealer), a well-known gay director famous for such camp classics as *Pink Flamingos*. In this episode, we witness full-blown heterosexual panic, as *echt*-patriarch Homer Simpson confronts his demons in the form of the "antique" col-

Homer's homophobia gets a kick in the pants from a campy gay antique dealer. Courtesy of Photofest.

lector and all around bon vivant, John. After finding themselves short on cash (due to son Bart's explosion of the hot water heater), they head off to a store called "Cockamamie's" to sell what they think is an heirloom but which John informs them is a liquor bottle purchased with green stamps. John quickly befriends the family, and Homer in particular, until Homer is apprized of his sexual preference by his more attuned spouse Marge ("John is a ho-mo-sexual"). The episode then proceeds down a

Roseanne-like path, reveling in its uncovering of stereotypes at the same time that it uses them to full effect. Homer freaks out, angry at being fooled ("You know me Marge. I like my beer cold, my TV loud, and my homosexuals fla-aming . . .") even though the depiction of John is anything but oblique.

As John introduces the rest of the Simpson clan to the joys of camp and star gossip, Homer goes into full-blown panic mode. Fearing son Bart is gay, dad Homer ousts John from the family ("I resent you people using that word [queer]. That's *our* word for making fun of *you*. We *need* it. Well, I'm taking back that word and I'm taking back my son."). In the quest to make a man of little Bart, Homer takes him on a tour of hetero-sexuality—from sexy billboards (he makes Bart sit in front of a highway billboard all day) to macho steel mills. Of course, the steel mill turns out to be gay, with disco dancing hardbodies hilariously upending both hetero stereotypes of wimpy fags and gay stereotypes of macho clones. In a last-ditch effort, Homer takes Bart out hunting and ends up being rescued from irate reindeer by gay John and his remote-controlled Santa robot. Sardonic to the end, Homer does get enlightened but he doesn't have the last word ("Well Homer, I won your respect and all I had to do was save your life. Now if every gay man could just do the same, you'd be set."). The episode ends with young Bart in the back seat of the car, questioning his own sexuality ("He thinks I'm gay?") as the disco beat resumes.

Like *Roseanne* (and like so little of our cultural output), this episode delves into the familial heart of homophobia and upends not just stereo-types but the supposedly solid ground of heterosexual desire. These innovative episodes are not out to make homosexuality accessible and assimilable, they are not designed to make heterosexuals feel less threatened and to make gays feel more "accepted." Both *Roseanne* and *The Simpsons* deal hilariously with the strange mix of fear and fascination, desire and disgust that marks heterosexual engagement with the vision of the homo-sexual. Roseanne's husband gets turned on by the thought of lesbian sexuality, but turned off by the thought of his brothers boogying to-gether. Homer dances gaily with newfound buddy John, until his hetero-sexual panic sets in and he rushes off to the gun store. Roseanne declares her hipness and gay positivity then freaks out at a casual same-sex kiss. These types of representations, while not perfect, go into the belly of the beast. The gay characters are not the problems to be solved here, nor is homophobia the vaguely vile emotions of outside agitators. *Heterosexual leads* are here the problems: it is *their* discomfort, homophobia, bigotry that must be confronted.

"THROUGH NO FAULT OF THEIR OWN":
DOCUMENTING THE GAY '90s

One would think that documentary TV would provide a more complex rendering of gay life, one replete with "real" people and their complicated identities. But gays and lesbians have suffered the same paradoxical fate in the nonfiction realm of TV culture. Many of these documentaries (on lesbians in Northampton, MA; anti-gay referenda in Colorado Springs; AIDS; gays in the military) are produced in the context of shows such as *20/20, PrimeTime Live* and other tabloid news shows, themselves proliferating in recent years. While these documentaries are often quite evenhanded and even forthright in their condemnation of overt homophobia, they go out of their way to assert gay "sameness." Both the documentaries on lesbians in Northampton and anti-gay activities in Colorado Springs focused on gay people who insistently proclaimed their affinity with straight society. From churchgoing lesbians to gardening gay couples, the documentaries "normalized" gay life and stressed that gays want to just be "accepted" and left alone to marry, raise children, go to church, and sit by the fire and grow old with each other. Many gay people do want these very things and nothing more. As John D'Emilio says, "A normalized visibility in the mainstream speaks to the heart and soul of some gay men and lesbians . . . I'd much rather deal with this world than the old world."[6] But that is only part of the picture of gay life, and a part that asks nothing of heterosexuals but a sort of downcast "tolerance."

In February of 1993 NBC produced a documentary entitled *The Gay 90's: Sex, Power, and Influence,* hosted by Maria Shriver. This program is representative of a great deal of programming in recent years, programming that is liberal and "accepting" of lesbians and gays, even as it creates revisionist histories and narratives of gay life that present troubling arguments. While ostensibly a "fair" piece about gay life and politics in the "gay '90s" this program manages to construct a very particular narrative. Maria Shriver opens with a whistle-stop tour through a (heterosexual) version of gay history. The "Stonewall era" of the '70s is characterized by "an in-your-face sexuality that frightened straight America. The images of flamboyant gays and lesbians engaged in promiscuous sex— the infamous bathhouses—all this indelibly seared the consciousness and led to a severe backlash." Leaving aside for the moment her conflation of "lesbian" and "gay" (women weren't exactly regulars at the bathhouses), Shriver more perniciously constructs a history that blames lesbians and gays for bringing on the backlash by their "excessive" behavior.

In the context of recent attacks against gay men for "bringing AIDS on themselves," this message is particularly frightening. She then segues from the images of partying, seminude men to the emaciated body of a PWA—"In the end, it was AIDS that forced them to save themselves. They changed their habits, they changed their image, they changed their tactics." Save ourselves from what? The implication here is not that gay people rallied around each other to deal with AIDS, but rather that gays themselves needed saving *as gays,* and that it was the disease that made us "clean up our act." She continues to move to the current moment, "Now, in the 90s, they're rich, they're influential, and for the first time they see a future that's different from their past." Not only does this indulge in the myth that gays are richer than the "general population" (a myth that has been refuted by more than one demographer), but it helps to create the illusion of a linear and progressive movement from wanton self-destruction through devastating disease ending up at a place of wealth and influence.

This fictional history is framed by the same "normalizing" impulse that accompanies much of popular culture: "Gays and lesbians say they just want what most of the rest of us want—health and happiness, a good job, a loving spouse, and more and more to be moms and dads, raising kids, going to the Little League games and the PTA. Who are these men and women? Well, they're not the stereotypes of bad movies or scare speeches. They are your neighbors, your classmates, your colleagues. You know them, but don't always know that they're gay. Tonight we're going to see what it means to be gay or lesbian. Some of it might be unsettling. Some of it might be moving." Now, of course, there is always much truth in this normalizing discourse—and who could deny that many people want those very things? But, like the Moyers documentary on Colorado Springs and Amendment 2, the normalizing discourse can easily slip into a kind of fracturing of the gay community into good gays (those who feel they are "born with it," those who are in a "committed couple," those who go to church, those who have kids, those who have weddings, those who want acceptance) and bad gays (those who celebrate their preference as a *choice,* those who prefer multiple partners, those who criticize the nuclear family, those who are atheists, those who want radical social change).

In the Moyers documentary, the gay counterparts to the anti-gay evangelicals were primarily two couples who were either attending church or gardening. Indeed, a great deal of time was spent on the religious faith of the lesbian couple and on the long-term commitment between the two men. Now clearly, this can be a good strategy: by normalizing gays and showing them to live lives that look like everyone else's one can challenge the kind of bigotry that fastens itself to a heightening of difference. But this approach can also have a downside. The narrative counterpart to these two attractive and benevolent gay couples was the constant reintroduction of the infamous videotape *The Gay Agenda* that the Christian right has been circulating for some time. Indeed, one of the interviewees was finally forced to denounce the images depicted on the tape (taken from gay pride parades and showing seminude men, sexualized dancing, phallic images, s-m gear, etc.) in order to press his case for inclusion and equality. While criticism of the images is neither here nor there (and since when has any group had an identical and shared ideology or set of practices?), I fear that it can easily play into the hands of those who would profit by the good gay/bad gay separation. In both the Colorado piece and the Shriver special, it is long-term couples who are featured, weddings that are viewed, and domestic chores that are witnessed. How many scenes of cooking and gardening do we need to see to prove the point that gays are human too? These images of domestic couples—couples not angrily attacking homophobia but winningly pleading for acceptance ("If straight people just got to know me . . .") are always framed by their putative opposite: gays boogying in bars, parading on the street, demonstrating, kissing in public. Even the *Frontline* piece on the murder of Billy Jack Gaither ("Assault on Gay America: The Life and Death of Billy Jack") focused on what a "regular guy" Billy Jack was, thus making his murderers seem even more ominous and homophobic. But one can't help but wonder about the other murders—the murders of the transvestites, hookers, "in your face" gay folk whose deaths are not only invisible but never serve as the catalysts for good-hearted liberalism (e.g. *Frontline*) to challenge homophobia. Thus this normalizing strategy, while successful in humanizing gays for a straight audience, has a tough trade-off that can push other gays further into the margins.

Even after-school series for kids have included gay subject matter, most notably an HBO special on a lesbian couple attending their prom. An unusually well-done program, which prompted response in other media, it was based on the true story of Heidi Leiter and girlfriend Missy Peters and their quest to attend Leiter's senior prom. Even before the TV special, Leiter and Peters had become the media toast of the town, prompting numerous articles in newspapers and popular magazines and the requisite appearances on the talk-show circuit. In the *Washington Post* follow-up story that accompanied the airing of the HBO special, the emphasis was on the *normalcy* of the couple—after all, they were just like any other young kids in love—except that they were two women. As the article says, "They simply wanted to lead their life together as any other couple would. As any *heterosexual* couple could." The author, interviewing the couple, says that "in school, as elsewhere, Leiter insists that they be treated as male-female couples are." Again, we have a failure of imagination here, where equality can only be posited as sameness. To be treated with respect, in this framework, means to have the gay relationship itself turned into a benign version of heterosexuality.

Or there is the 1996 PBS documentary *Whose Family? Whose Values?* produced as part of the *Citizen's '96* series in which the host puts the spotlight on Rockford, Illinois, a town that "matches the nation statistic for statistic." Amidst the standard array of families (single parent, dual income, black, white, stay-at home mothers, working mothers, etc.) we have the by now requisite lesbian couple with children. The story on the gay moms opens in a Catholic Church where one of their sons is taking his first communion. The religiosity of the family is stressed, from scenes of dinnertime prayers to interviews with the "accepting" priest (whose acceptance is based both on their religiosity and on his belief that they can't help themselves, that their lesbianism is biologically determined), and the couple is eager to express their normality, saying fervently that "families like ours are the same as any other family," noting the two kids, dog and cat, two cars, and, importantly, two parents.

Unfortunately, gay people themselves have been both willing and unwitting participants in this media construction of the good/bad divide. Public television aired two specials—*Homophobia in the Workplace* and *Growing Up Gay*—that were essentially taped sessions of gay "diversity trainer" Brian McNaught's dog and pony show, complete with thoughtful audience. While these specials therefore lack the pizzaz and glitz of the infotainment programs, such as those of Moyers and Shriver, they are indicative of the same kind of ideological positioning. Without all the accompanying visuals, McNaught engages in basically the same move of normalization: gays are just like everyone else—and so are people who are "uncomfortable" with homosexuality. In normalizing *homosexuality,* McNaught also normalizes *homophobia* through a discourse that locates heterosexuals as really just good folks with good intentions but led astray by simple ignorance. McNaught toes the same liberal line that we have seen over and over again: just get to know me, he pleads, and I'm sure you'll come to "accept" me. For these liberals, ignorance is the enemy. Therefore, countering homophobia is like a PR campaign: we put our best face forward and pitch our story straight and we'll be tolerated. It is significant that—in arguing for his liberal line—McNaught vociferously invokes a biological argument for gayness: we can't help ourselves: "Gay people don't choose their orientation. None of us choose our orientation. Our orientations are *internal* feelings of attraction. Our feelings result from factors over which we have no control. We don't choose our genetic background. We don't choose what hormones we're getting from our mothers in the womb. Nobody believes that people choose orientation except for people who are trying to confuse other people about this. You can't change your orientation." Indeed, at one point he even says "through no fault of their own"! in describing gay identity, implicitly arguing for heterosexual "tolerance" of the gay "compulsion." This absolutist stand asserting the biological basis of homosexuality is itself problematic, for the research is hardly that definitive. But, more importantly, I am concerned about the ways in which this kind of biological argument fits into a larger conceptualization of gay identity and facilitates a particular argument of "acceptance" and "tolerance" rather than an argument for freedom, pride, and liberation. In so doing, homophobia turns into a benign bewilderment, an unease, that belies its viciousness and deliberateness. By letting homophobic behavior off the hook (as McNaught says, "it's ok to look away"), homophobia thrives, particularly under the surface of polite behavior.

But, one may ask, is this not actually the case? Isn't homophobia just misunderstanding, reasonable revulsion, well-intentioned anxiety? Well, no. Homophobia, like its cousins racism and sexism, is not quite so benign. Granted, many people who voice homophobic statements are surely not vicious gay bashers and can learn the errors of their ways. However, homophobia is a deep and abiding bigotry, much in the same way that misogyny and racism are deeply embedded in our culture. Indeed, many have argued—forcefully—that hatred of gays is deeply connected to hatred of women and institutional sexism. If this is the case— if homophobia can be understood to be as pernicious and deeply felt as racism or sexism—then to present it as simply misguided befuddlement ("what do they do in bed anyway?") is actually to miss the point, and to miss it in a potentially dangerous way. If television makes visible *homosexuals,* but never really makes visible *homophobia,* it is only presenting a very small and skewed part of the puzzle. Homosexuality can only be understood as a problem if the heterosexual majority constructs it that way. But what you mostly see on television is the "problem" of homosexuality without the cause. Homosexuality is not an intrinsic problem, any more than heterosexuality is. What is a problem is irrational and vehement bigotry. But if TV only shows us *homosexuality* as a problem, it participates in the erasure of the real problem of *homophobia.* When homophobia is only evidenced as overt gay bashing, it is like depicting racism solely as cross-burning. Cross-burning is awful and vivid evidence of racism, but it is surely true that the more long lasting, pernicious forms of racism are the everyday acts of denial and dehumanization that occur with banal frequency. When Matt on *Melrose Place* gets gay bashed or fired by his boss (a monster homophobe much like those depicted in the film *Philadelphia*), we do see homophobia at work, yet we do so in the form of nasty outsiders who themselves have little identity. Even when Matt wrestles with his homophobic parents, the resolution is quick and easy (deathbed "forgiveness") and, again, these characters remain outside of the everyday world of the series. What is far more interesting—and promising—is the examination of homophobia inside the world of the series, embodied in beloved characters. This is some of what we begin to get as the televisual gay '90s comes into its own.

Four   DOSSIER ON *ELLEN*

Yes, gays are finally cropping up all over TV-land. But what gays, in what ways? Still, no gay character holds a series, even though they are significant secondary characters in a number of prime-time shows. Every other group has been deemed worthy to headline their own show: we've had single mothers and single fathers, blacks, Hispanics, Asians, working-class and upper-class, Jewish and Gentile, nuclear and reconstructed. Even animals carry shows. But not gays. Until Ellen. Steven Carrington broke barriers and Roseanne raised the ire of the right and Matt of Melrose became the gay poster boy, but no television event has so rocked both Hollywood and mainstream America as the much-hyped coming out of sitcom star Ellen DeGeneres. The show debuted as "These Friends of Mine" in March 1994 and had a mixed ratings history prior to the coming-out episode. While the media swirl around this event seemed a bit hyperbolic, this *was* an historic event. While gays have been more and more visible on TV, particularly in recent years, they had still to headline a show. *Entertainment Weekly* commissioned a poll that revealed respondents to be almost split on the question of whether they would allow kids to watch a TV show with a gay lead. Forty-four percent said that the trend toward more gay characters on TV is bad; but 72 percent claimed they would not be personally offended if a lead character was gay.[1]

The Ellen phenomenon was groundbreaking, but more complicated than it initially appears. In the television show, public discourse, audience responses, and critics' analyses, we see an interesting mixture of benign intent, radicalizing change, rabid homophobia and—perhaps the most dominant trend—the emergence of a new liberalism around gay identity and gay life. The *Oprah* show that preceded the coming-out episode exhibited perfectly this classic liberalism at work. Not only does Oprah herself—with all good intentions of course—voice this discourse ("They [the bigots] don't understand that, to the greatest extent, gay people want the same thing everybody else wants . . ."), but Ellen begins her coming-out process with a "can't we all just get along" quest for understanding and acceptance. Indeed, when Oprah asks her about the seemingly awful moment in which her father and stepmother kicked her out of the house after she came out to them (so that she wouldn't "influence" her young stepsisters), Ellen displays not anger but pained understanding: "I understand people not understanding. I'm fine with that." She essentially repeats this line when confronted by the requisite Christian conservative family seated in the front row. In response to their accusation of the evil of "choosing sin," Ellen joins the chorus of "it's not a choice" biological determinists. When lover Anne Heche joins her on Oprah, she can't quite bring herself to make physical contact with her, although Anne keeps repeatedly reaching out. Ellen's discomfort is palpable.

Now what is so interesting is not Ellen's liberalism (most people do believe that acceptance and tolerance are the roads to equality) but rather how she has so deeply transformed from someone simply voicing the timid plea for acceptance (accept me for who I am) to someone who forthrightly and unambiguously called the networks on their homophobia when her show was canceled. Like it or not, when she came out, Ellen became a spokesperson and became a target of the right: she gained a community and gained an understanding of the vehemence of institutionalized discrimination. Not only did Ellen herself obviously get her proverbial consciousness raised, but her mother joined her, becoming the first heterosexual spokesperson for the Human Rights Campaign, speaking at rallies against anti-gay referenda (such as the one in Maine in 1998) and making endless public service announcements and public appearances.

Yet Ellen was adamant that this was a position she never wanted. When she spoke with a reporter for *Time* she mused about how she "watched . . . Melissa [Etheridge] come out, and she became 'the lesbian rock star.' I never wanted to be 'the lesbian actress.' I never wanted to be the spokesperson for the gay community. Ever. I did it for my own truth."[2] At the beginning of this process, Ellen set herself up as the girl next door who happens to be gay, and girls next door don't get mad. Others chimed in, arguing that "if Ellen does make the historic switch of teams . . . she'd be the perfect character to make homosexuality acceptable. So likable, so adorable, so nonthreatening."[3] When asked by *Time* if she was angry that others in the entertainment industry remained in the closet, Ellen replied that she didn't "care what X or Y does. I didn't do it to make a political statement. I did it selfishly for myself and because I thought it was a great thing for the show, which desperately needed a point of view. If other people come out, that's fine. I mean, it would be great if for no other reason than just to show the diversity, so it's not just the extremes. Because unfortunately those are the people who get the most attention on the news. You know, when you see the parades and you see dykes on bikes or these men dressed as women. I don't want to come off like I'm attacking them—the whole point of what I'm doing is acceptance of everybody's differences."[4] How could she possibly maintain the individualistic, naive posture she initially took? Bombarded by the right, lionized by gays, both Ellen and her show took on a more radical hue.

So how was the actual episode handled? On the one hand, it was both warm and witty, depicting for a national television audience that bracing and tumultuous moment of sexual awakening and self-recognition known as coming out. We see Ellen in full-blown panic, resisting the thought of her gayness and then embracing it with trepidation and joy. Her recognition of her lesbianism gets sparked by two linked events; the reemergence of an old boyfriend (Richard) who shows a renewed interest in her, and the introduction to her old boyfriend's boss (Susan), a lanky blonde lesbian who sends Ellen into panicked denial and, finally, abject adoration. Susan and Ellen hit it off immediately, exhibiting identical behaviors and quirks, but Ellen gets terrified when Susan comes out to her, assuming Ellen's gayness as well. Ellen's anger at Susan's assumption prompts much swaggering denial (which, ironically, has the effect of macho, butch posturing) and accusations that "it's not enough for you to be gay, you've got to recruit others!" When Susan replies, "I'll just have to call National Headquarters and tell them I lost you. Damn! Just one more and I would have gotten that toaster oven!" Ellen assures her that she doesn't get her "gay humor" and puts off no "gay vibe" whatsoever.

Next thing you know, Ellen rushes into Richard's hotel room to "show [you] who's gay," to little avail of course, as we soon find out. While this plays up the stereotypes of recruiting homosexuals and tweaks the panicked defense, it also falls perilously close to acceding to them. While the panic rings true, must we always frame lesbian desire as inevitably, irrevocably linked to the absence of heterosexual desire? While her failure to have sex with Richard is comical ("I'm sorry Richard, this has never

Ellen announces her newfound sexuality to the object of her affection—and an airport of onlookers. Courtesy of Photofest.

happened to me before . . .") it also frames her desire for the woman, a desire desexualized and reworked as the meeting of like souls who "click," as her therapist (Oprah) names it.

Now that the hoopla over Ellen DeGeneres's double-dip coming out (both in TV-land and in that space we sometimes call "real life") has dissipated, it is time for some sober reflection on the multiple meanings of Ellenicity: you go girlfriend! But seriously, I thought I would be the last to sing Ellen's praises, critical as I was of the odes to assimilation and anxious cries of "can't we all just get along" that accompanied the dramatic coming-out episode and its media effluvia. While certainly this was a historic event, marking the first time an openly gay character emerged to headline a series, I was annoyed at the glib assumption that this new visibility necessarily signaled a significant shift in political power and civil rights for lesbians and gays. Let us not forget that for all the media popularity of lesbians and gays, recent years have also brought us more troublesome attention, including the odious Defense of Marriage Act, a rise in anti-gay hate crimes, and a continuing wave of anti-gay referenda. Gays may be the new niche-marketing phenomenon, but that doesn't stop the power and presence of active homophobia—in the family, the workplace, the streets, the government. And Ellen's own assertion of a naive girl next door who just *happened* to be gay furthered the dubious cultural project of depicting gays as "just like straights" (with a twist of course). Indeed, I was the proverbial wet blanket at the Ellen party, cynically chiding her refusal of gay pride and her couching of lesbian desire within a stereotypical discourse of the rejection of men. While others clapped and cheered, I maintained my stern demeanor. Needless to say, that is one party I won't be invited to again.

So imagine my surprise to find myself joining in with cheers and accolades for Miss Ellen. After several irritating episodes in which Ellen (a) can't seem to figure out the great mystery of lesbian love and (b) keeps kissing men to prove she likes women, I was thrilled to see the series develop into that which Ellen herself has vehemently asserted it wasn't: a *gay sitcom*. After much fumbling about, Ellen got herself a nice girlfriend, replete with wise-beyond-her-years daughter and no small amount of gay pride. But, more to the point, Ellen's gayness was not relegated to that Hollywood land of fashion statement and lifestyle choice or, alternately, despair and degradation. In a world so adamantly structured around heterosexuality, sexual identity *does* matter and Ellen's refusal to allow her gayness to slink into the background is a step in the right direction. Don't get me wrong, her constant reiteration of the "but I'm just me" litany of liberal sameness was still tiresome but was now at least partially challenged by a sitcom that actually had lesbian stories and lesbian lives represented, not just lesbian photo ops and chic accouterments as token asides to diversity. We witnessed not just the climactic moment of "coming out," but the more mundane and prosaic process of reckoning with the homophobia (and love) of friends and employers, confronting parents with the truth they so desperately don't want to hear, and negotiating the changing and turbulent terrain of gay identity in a postmodern world. Indeed, the follow-ups to the initial coming-out episode focused— at times painfully—on the aftereffects of announcing the unexpected. As old friends freak out in shared dressing rooms and buddy bosses reveal their homophobic hearts, Ellen finds herself having to confront and reconfront her own worst fears. True, she often responds to heterosexual fear and distaste with assurances that she is still "the same old Ellen" and wants nothing more than "acceptance for who she is," but these episodes also reinforce the ongoing nature of coming out and the ongoing realities of anti-gay practices, even in this new world of "fashionable" lesbians. Ellen even quits her job at the bookstore when boss Ed nixes Audrey's quirky display of lesbiana and, to add insult to injury, refuses to have Ellen babysit his kids.

Toward the end of the series, we actually witnessed an entire episode of lesbian "first time" sex, as Ellen uneasily and with great humor joined literal hands with the love that dare not speak its name. Indeed, the cancellation of the series seems precisely based on a kind of homophobia that Ellen herself naively dismissed. She was an acceptable homo when she promised tearfully (in interview after interview) that she just wanted to be the girl next door, and that the series would never foreground her gayness, quite to the contrary she repeatedly stated. But, the show *did* become a gay sitcom and that was clearly unacceptable. Ellen rightfully claimed homophobia when informed of the cancellation, but I would argue that it was a quite specific form of homophobia. Ellen was not canceled simply because she depicted homosexuality, but because she refused to be then re-closeted, to relegate her gayness to the "been there, done that" realm. She even threatened to quit the show if the TV-14 warning wasn't lifted and made humorous references to the continued harassment by ABC (she aired ads for the show calling it "Ellen Kisses a Girl and Makes the Network Very Nervous").

After the event, the media fever subsided somewhat, only to be ignited again by ABC's insistence on placing a warning at the beginning of the show, sparked by an episode in which Ellen kisses her best (and heterosexual) friend Paige. In addition, there was a great deal of post-coming-out commentary and speculation. Would the show fizzle now that the deed was done? How could she sustain the intense excitement? And, from the right, a fear that the show would become precisely what it did: a gay sitcom. Tom Knott of the *Washington Times* says that "Ellen DeGeneres has become one of the most annoying people in America. She has evolved into a one-note celebrity. This is the note: She's gay." [5] He then goes on a full-blown diatribe, comparing her to woman-biting sports commentator Marv Albert, bemoaning her "false" victim status, and arguing that the networks were right to put a warning label on when she kisses another woman. Keith Marder of the *Daily News of Los Angeles* is more interesting, in that he first chides Ellen for not being gay enough and then for being too gay:

> Ellen DeGeneres, who made history in April by becoming the first openly gay lead character on a sitcom, has said that she does not want to kiss a woman on her television series *Ellen*. In tonight's . . . season premiere, her character, Ellen Morgan, not only abstains from woman-to-woman contact, she soul-kisses a man. . . . The episode, in which Ellen doubts her new-found sexuality, finds the first openly gay lead character on a sitcom falling for an old boyfriend before realizing it was just a 22-minute phase. There is no doubt that Ellen is more comfortable and her show is funnier since her epiphany. But, the problem now is the show is far less accessible. There are too many lesbian in-jokes and references to the character's sexuality. [6]

And the venerable *TV Guide* gives "Cheers to Ellen's classy coming-out soiree—and to ABC for hosting the event. . . . The great part of the April 30 'Puppy Episode,' as the hour was titled, is that it isn't at all polemical. Ellen's discovery was really about identity, not sexuality—and guess what?—it turns out she's just as endearingly clumsy and self-conscious as a lesbian as she ever was as a hetero."[7] So much for vive la différence!

But, despite Chastity Bono's misquoted criticism of Ellen for being "too gay," most (both gay and straight) have strongly supported the development of the series: "After Ellen DeGeneres made history last season, when she became prime time's first declared lesbian star and earned record ratings in the process, the question for her producers was an obvious one: how could they sustain the momentum? The answer this season has been a new 'Ellen,' which is almost entirely about being gay in America. The result has made some heterosexuals queasy ('Can't she do a show that isn't about being a lesbian?'). But gay viewers are nearly unanimous, and plenty of heterosexuals agree with them, in the opinion that a candid 'Ellen' is much funnier than her confused and closeted predecessor, something critics have been saying in recent months as well."[8] The reaction of the gay community (and the gay press in particular) over the post-coming-out direction of the show clearly illustrates one of the central divides within the community—a divide between gays anxious to assert their sameness with straight culture and society and gays eager to foreground the specificity of gay culture and gay identity. So we have writers for the *Washington Blade* stating that "most people are quick to point out when commenting on the show that Gay characters are capable of embodying universal themes, and that Ellen still speaks to a general audience even though its main character is a Lesbian."[9] Indeed, while the gay press was quick to defend Ellen against all attacks, it often did so on the grounds of the "normalness" of the sitcom, for example that it was sometimes funny, sometimes not, like all sitcoms. This quest for some kind of a notion of universality, a notion that never questions the centrality and normality of *heterosexuality,* was the dominant theme with the so-called "liberal" press. Keith Marder of the *Daily News of Los Angeles* writes that "viewers would be much better served if the show evolves past the point that her entire universe revolves around her sexuality. . . . Perhaps when that happens, and once Ellen Morgan gets through her initial awkward stage, which is realistic, she will settle into her normal life, and being a gay woman living in America will be only a part of her personality."[10] This kind of statement seems fair enough at first glance, for it is certainly true that sexual identity is not the axis around which all life turns. However, what this misses is the double standard buried in this liberal offering: when have we ever heard a TV commentator urging *Melrose Place* or *Mad About You* to stop having life revolve around the *heterosexuality* of *their* characters?

On the other hand, many commentators were pleased that the show went "from being about drinking cappuccino in a bookstore to being about a life," illustrating the "the night-and-day difference between a self-loathing closet case and someone who has finally achieved true self-esteem. She is now living a full, three-dimensional life as opposed to being the really obnoxious cardboard cutout that she was before. And here's the big news: she's stopped stuttering!'"[11] Charles Kaiser is right on the money when he further argues that not only has "the show become funnier, it has also become more political, giving America more information about the ins and outs of gay life than it has ever received regularly in prime time before."[12]

A wonderful example is provided by the series of episodes tracing the growing relationship between Ellen, her new girlfriend, and her girlfriend's daughter. Television viewers thus gained entree into the realities of gay family life, a life not simply "the same" as that of heterosexuals. Indeed, the canny daughter quite matter-of-factly states that she was "conceived by artificial insemination. My mom picked my dad out of a catalogue. I was created in a lab." Importantly, we not only see the daughter's ease with her mother's sexuality, but the contrasting unease of Ellen, still reluctant to be known and seen as a lesbian.

Later on in that same episode, Ellen mistakes the daughter's distance for discomfort with their relationship, while it is in fact the opposite. Unlike the halfway-out-of-the closet Ellen, this kid of the '90s is disturbed not by the homosexuality but by Ellen's refusal to be open. "You wouldn't even kiss her good night in front of your own house," she yells at an amazed Ellen. "Are you ashamed of being gay?" Ellen tries to explain, saying, "When I was raised, gay people weren't supposed to show affection in public," to which the daughter responds, "Boy, were you raised in the old days!" But Ellen gets her consciousness raised by the brash young girl, and ends the episode by clasping hands with her lover inside a crowded elevator.

Ellen's introduction to the daughter is paralleled with the introduction of the lover to Ellen's parents, creating an interesting scenario in which the younger generation chastises Ellen for her self-hatred while the older generation struggles even to say the word "lesbian." The linkage between the two stories is not only the theme of introduction and generational difference, but illustrates Ellen's discomfort with her own lesbianism and her difficulty in showing affection to her female lover. Ellen thus manages to reckon both with internalized homophobia (something rarely shown in the mass media and, if shown at all, rendered simply as self-loathing) and the homophobia of heterosexuals, or at least their discomfort and unease.

Other episodes focused on the ups and downs of relationships, and gently insist on how the realities of homophobia (and the concomitant tentativeness of Ellen) impinge on intimacy, such as when the two women go away for their first vacation and are forced to reckon with a recalcitrant hotel clerk who offers them twin beds. In that same episode, the tensions of new relationships are always informed by the particular realities of gay existence. So when the bickering couple attempt to reconcile (at Waterworld no less), Ellen makes her way over to her girlfriend by telling a distraught mother and child "we're lesbians," after which she says to Laurie, "The trick is to get the bigotry to work for ya." Or in another funny episode, Ellen rushes to the hospital after Laurie is in an accident and immediately reveals her sexuality to another woman in the waiting area ("I'm gay. It's my girlfriend . . ."), who turns out to be Laurie's ex (and is played by Anne Heche). As Ellen tries to see Laurie, she is told "only immediate family" until Laurie herself requests her presence, along with that of her daughter. The two march in together.

While a gay community doesn't exactly emerge on the series, snatches of gay life, fleeting moments of vivid gay signifiers push out through the sitcom veneer to speak to a gay audience eager to see something more than straight with a twist. After Ellen reluctantly comes out to her friends ("I for one think it's super!" says resident ditz but lesbian-savvy Audrey), they take her to a lesbian coffeehouse (the real "Little Frieda's" in LA) where k.d. lang warbles a tuneless ode to womanpower and friend Joe assures them all that "it's very fashionable to be lesbian now."[13] Later, when Ellen spies her attractive mortgage broker at a restaurant, they confirm each other's orientation through a discussion of an article in a copy of the *Advocate* that is placed strategically on the table. While Ellen's nervousness is grating—and her straight friend's coaching somewhat humiliating—she does manage to get a date with her and take matters into her own hands and direct her own desires. In yet another episode, after a brief break-up between Ellen and Laurie, the girls (Ellen, Paige, and Audrey) pack up an RV and head to San Francisco for Womanfest, where signifiers of lesbian life abound—from astrology tables to the Indigo Girls and Elizabeth Birch of HRC hawking her wares in the background. Even Ellen's mom has a cameo. And, perhaps unintentionally, the series hints at the ever-present jokes about commitment-hungry lesbians (Q: what does a lesbian bring on a second date? A: a U-Haul) by having an entire episode center around a one-month anniversary between Ellen and Laurie in which tensions surface about the prospect of living together.

Or in yet another episode, Laurie is forced to reckon with her homophobic family when her long-estranged father dies and she agonizes over whether or not to attend the funeral. The two women even discuss the problematics of lesbian visibility: while Ellen wants to support her at the funeral, they also recognize the need for Laurie herself to make peace with the situation. Thus, the series moved from the flashy moment of coming out to the far more interesting (and more challenging) intricacies of negotiating same-sex love in a heterosexual world.

In another episode (a memorable one with Emma Thompson guesting as Emma Thompson), Ellen even engages in a sort of metacommentary on her own public outing. While at a party with friend Paige, Ellen catches Emma in a passionate kiss with another woman. Thus begins a hilarious episode in which Ellen manages to become Emma's personal assistant for the two weeks in which she is shooting a film for Paige's studio. Thrilled to have her as a role model, Emma returns the favor by admiring Ellen's bravery and openness and deciding to come out at an awards ceremony. Grabbing another martini and attired in a ludicrous tiara, Thompson tilts her head and exclaims, "Let's go out and terrify some Baptists." But upon some urging from Paige, Ellen tries to dissuade her, informing her of all the digging that will go on into her past. A scared and soused Thompson reveals a far more disturbing secret, her American ancestry, and lapses into a Midwestern drawl, "I can't come out to the world tonight. I can face telling them that I'm gay. You know Hollywood people can deal with that. But there is no Dayton chic." When Sean Penn turns up on video at the awards ceremony and, invoking Thompson's deep honesty, reveals his own homosexuality ("scene-stealing bastard"), the wind is taken out of Emma's sails. Later, Ellen meets up with her at a restaurant, where she is happily waiting tables following the inevitable tabloid outing. Not only is the episode one of the funniest, but it takes on Ellen's attackers (the Baptists) and reveals the inevitability of the opening of closet doors. It names the risks of revelation and visibility and even shows the costs (no more Jane Austen roles for Thompson!) but revels in the freedom of an openly gay life.

On a more troublesome note, however, Ellen's embrace of her lesbian identity and sexuality is initially viewed through her confused interaction with an old boyfriend. While out on a double date with hetero buds Paige and Spencer, Ellen is turned-off by the beautiful but exceedingly dim woman they set her up with. Finding that the restaurant owner is old boyfriend Dan, she comes out to him only to find herself spending more and more time with him and questioning her new (and sexually untested) identity as a lesbian. While her confusion produces much humor (her cousin Spence, catching her in a kiss with Dan, exclaims in horror "What the hell kind of a lesbian are you?") and no small amount of educational insight in the form of a conversation with gay friend Peter who discourses on the variabilities of human desire, it still feels grating

In the world of pop culture, lesbian love must be preceded by the requisite rejection of heterosexual desire. Here, Ellen tries boys to be sure she likes girls. Courtesy of Photofest.

that a lesbian must confirm her *homosexual* desire first through a rejection of *heterosexual* desire. Her forays into intimacy with Dan, juvenile as they are, are presented as the confirmation of her lesbianism: she feels nothing sexually for him. Just as in the coming-out episode, when her lesbian awareness is first filtered through scenes of heterosexual panic (where she throws herself on another old boyfriend), lesbian identity is depicted simultaneously as really just the same as heterosexuality ("I'm the same old Ellen . . .") *and* as the absence of heterosexual desire. And the first same-sex kiss on the show occurs between Ellen and her heterosexual best friend Paige, when they pretend to be lovers in order to get Ellen out of an awkward situation. The road to lesbianism, it seems, is paved with heterosexual kisses.

Coming out never looked so easy—Ellen's parents find enlightenment and gay-positive energy in a community center support group presided over by a helpful Chastity Bono. Courtesy of Photofest.

The road to lesbianism is also paved with parents who take to the barricades with alacrity. When Ellen comes out to her parents (in a very funny scene at a Chinese restaurant that she picks for its gay waiter), she is first rebuffed by their rejection and dismay, particularly that of her father, whose discomfort is palpable and who desires nothing more than complete silence (the better to play with his train set). But quicker than you can say "gay pride," both parents have embraced their daughter, albeit with the usual unease over sexuality and language. Ellen's mom reluctantly joins her at a gay community center rap session (led by Chastity Bono!) and her hurt turns into anger at the more virulent homophobia of the other parents. As a bigot dad stands up and begins to stalk away, turning to Ellen with anger ("Why should your mother accept this? It's wrong. It's sick. And you're sick . . ."), Ellen's mom quickly stands up to him in defiance, telling him in no uncertain terms that "she is not sick. . . . I love her and I don't want to lose her." In the meantime, during the bigoted dad's harangue, Ellen's recalcitrant father has walked in and witnessed the scene. He stalks into the meeting declaring, "You tell 'em Lois. She's here, she's queer. Get used to it," and joins the mother and daughter in a warm hug ("I read that on a bumper sticker," he tells them proudly).

While I am reluctant to call any televisual moment a "watershed event," it does seem clear that the Ellen hoopla opened doors previously cut off. And it is also clear, and must be stated time and time again for the hopeless cynics among us, that having openly gay and successful and "happy" folks on TV can and does alter the life course of many gay Americans, as this caller to Larry King live noted when she called in to a program on "homosexuality in television" to say, "I'm 14, and I'm a lesbian, and I would just like to thank Chastity Bono—and Ellen and Betty DeGeneres, because I think they personally have saved my life, because I knew I was gay before I even heard of Ellen, but without role models like them, I would have killed myself."[14] Indeed, we cannot and should not downplay the significance of this event and the way it surely must have enabled more people to emerge from their own closets, as in the case of this anonymous chat-line writer: "Ellen's decision to come out has indeed spurred me to tiptoe out of my own closet. I plan to tell my parents this weekend. I didn't want to wait anymore, but needed a push."[15] Clearly the coming out of Ellen spurred many to do the same, but it also provided those already out with a new and culturally legitimated sense of *presence:* whether or not you liked the show, or thought it funny, or thought it tedious, the vision of some sort of gay life being depicted in prime time was exhilarating; as another e-mailer relates: "Seeing her out in the world also means that I can finally have an opportunity on network TV to see someone who vaguely reflects my life."[16] And, as many have argued, perhaps a "weekly glimpse at a fictitious lesbian life may prove to be even more effective as an agent of social change than the birth of another advocate."[17] For not only does the presence of a character you have welcomed into your home challenge one's notion of family, of normal life, of happiness, but the personalization of television articulates well with our highly individualized culture. Sure, Ellen came out to millions on an impersonal mass medium, but the structure of this mass media is to personalize everything so that this unreal character comes to be for many a trusted friend, a real person coming out to us individually.

The cancellation of the series and the network (and, presumably, viewer) unease with gay *life* (rather than just gay characters) should make us wary of embracing the Ellen phenomenon as more path-breaking than it really was. Even typically timid Ellen herself admitted on *Entertainment Tonight* that "I'm gay, the character's gay, that's the problem everyone has with the show. It's just too controversial. Nobody wants to deal with it." One of the most fascinating aspects of this whole phenomenon has been Ellen's own transformation from self-professed apolitical girl next door to activist and advocate. In an interview on *PrimeTime Live* with Diane Sawyer after the cancellation of the series, she is asked about this change and responds that, indeed, "I grew up. Because when I talked with you last year I didn't even realize the internal homophobia, and the shame that I was still dealing with."

We all grew up. For after the euphoria settled down, business as usual seemed to reassert itself. Surely, it is true, gays are not invisible anymore and the fight is no longer centered around simple access to cultural representation. The coming-out episode—like other "firsts"—broke down barriers that may never again be firmly rebuilt. But it is also clearly true that double standards and heterosexual unease are still firmly in place, as the cancellation of *Ellen* sadly reveals. Indeed, the show really *did* become too gay, revealing that a gayness not in the background, not fully assimilated, not willing to slink off, is always *too gay*.

Five   ALL GAY, ALL THE TIME

T he *Ellen* event stands out, surely, as a defining moment in the
      history of gay and lesbian cultural visibility. Nonetheless, there
      is much more to recount and examine. Indeed, the gossipy but
indispensable *Entertainment Weekly* produced not one but two special
issues devoted to "gay entertainment" in which they asked the burning
question "Is your TV set gay?"[1] An October 24, 2000, edition of the
National Examiner screams "TV goes gay crazy!" and "They're brain-
washing America!" Here we indeed have an evil gay conspiracy, revealing a television world "overrun by gay themes, gay characters and gay
plot lines [where] gay producers, directors and writers are running the
show."[2] Ominously run by a Velvet Mafia and Ellen's mom, "The people
behind our nightly diet of network and cable television programming
have a gay agenda."[3] And the 2000 Emmys were the gayest ever. Not only
did *Will & Grace* pick up the best comedy award, and best supporting
actor and actress, but gayness pervaded the event, from jokes about host
Garry Shandling's dubious sexuality to awards and speeches, highlighted
by the "this gives a new meaning to the phrase 'acceptance speech'" by
the cocreator of *Will & Grace.*

   While the '80s and early '90s introduced ongoing gay characters to the
viewing public, they were mostly introduced as problems to be either

overcome or accepted, but problems nonetheless. Most importantly, gays were rarely depicted as anything more than single-episode "issues of the week" to be dealt with and, ultimately, forgotten. Certainly it is only *very* recently that gays have entered into the world of television on an everyday level, although there have been several TV movies over the years. While television of the mid and late '90s was not exactly the gay Gomorrah that right-wing media mavens claim, the explosion in recent years *has* been exponential. It did not begin right away, but by "1995 . . . gay came to stay on prime-time television. Finally, gayness wasn't just a verboten titillation anymore. Suddenly, gayness was cool. Although gay characters still weren't allowed to connect physically in prime time, homosexuality became a topic deemed safe, sanctioned and wide open for discussion on series old and new."[4]

It's not that obvious and dangerous stereotypes simply disappeared into that great land of late-night reruns, but that they are no longer unacknowledged business as usual. GLAAD regularly tracks the movement of representations through its weekly "GLAADAlert," which notes particularly egregious examples of killer queers or desperate bull dykes (and the welcome "good" examples too) and serves as a reminder that plainly bigoted images are hardly a thing of the past. Even in this new era the images are hardly overwhelmingly "positive." The term "queer" is still bandied about, lesbians and gays are still objects of derision, and the perverse killer queen still crops up occasionally in prime-time cop shows. And PBS provoked a wave of censorship when it aired Armistead Maupin's *Tales of the City*—a funny slice of life miniseries circa 1976 San Francisco. Not only was a hullabaloo raised by conservative activists—causing PBS to offer two versions of the film, an uncut version and one edited to remove certain language and sexuality—but Maupin had tried for years to get it produced: fifteen to be exact. And, when it finally *was* produced, it took British money to get it going. Passionate kisses abounded on *Tales*, but PBS has always treaded where Hollywood never would.

Yet it is surely impossible to think of this period without marveling at the proliferation of gay images in television. Primed by the path-breaking *Soap* and urged on by the more formulaic *Dynasty,* gay characters have begun to emerge as continuing, regular characters on series and sitcoms. Until recently, you could count on the fingers of one hand the gay characters on TV; now they are seemingly everywhere. A February 18, 1997, issue of the *Advocate* identified twenty-two recurring explicitly gay characters on TV, and GLAAD announced that the 1997–98 season featured a record thirty gay, lesbian, and bisexual characters—a 23 percent increase from the previous season. The numbers are currently down a bit (seventeen recurring or leading characters for the 1999–2000 season and about the same for the 2000–2001 season), but no one is really complaining. True, few series maintain regular gay characters, but many have aired episodes unthinkable a few years ago. *Coach, Designing Women, Picket Fences, The Mommies, The Simpsons, Beverly Hills 90210, Sisters, Law & Order, Grace under Fire, Seinfeld, Murder One, Frasier, ER, NYPD Blue, Weber, Just Shoot Me, The Practice,* and others have all had episodes with gay characters or dealing with the issues of homophobia and homosexuality. Even the critically acclaimed Washington drama *The West Wing* featured a episode in which the president (played as a feisty liberal by Martin Sheen) excoriates a thinly veiled Dr. Laura character for her "tight-ass conservatism." Indeed, there are very few shows that now abjure the almost obligatory "gay episode."

Clearly, the most important shift is in the form of continuing characters, for it is only when gays are depicted every week, as part of the ensemble "family" of the series or sitcom, that they even present the opportunity for a true "cultural reckoning." It is important to differentiate between the increasingly common "one-shot deal," where a gay character plays center stage for a single episode, and the rise of the ongoing, continuing gay character on television. Dozens of series and sitcoms have featured gay characters and gay themes. But only a very few series have included regular, continuing gay characters. In many ways, the one-shot deals are easier to analyze. Because it is not necessary to envelop these fleeting gay characters in the context of the particular TV worlds they enter, these episodes often appear as fairly progressive "gay nights" that primarily seem to serve the function of presenting a sort of liberal humanist "can't we all just get along?" argument for "tolerance." We see these episodes frequently now, as when the serious, critically appraised drama *Picket Fences* featured an evening in which the lead couple's young teenage daughter is kissed by another girl and begins to question her own sexuality, or when *The Practice's* Jimmy Berluti's mom comes out to him and asks him to take her marriage case to court, forcing retro Jimmy to rethink his ideas of love and sex. Of course, the inevitably campy *Love Boat: The Next Wave,* featured gay men joining the romantic waters and honeymooning couples.

These one-nighters can be merely comic relief, as when straight characters are mistaken for gay (*Seinfeld, Frasier, Friends*) or old (presumably heterosexual) family friends are found hanging out at the local gay watering hole (*Grace under Fire*). *Seinfeld's* hilarious send-up of heterosexual panic hit the mark when Jerry and George are mistaken for gay and are equally anxious to assert their heterosexuality and their hipness. As a college reporter accidentally overhears them pretending to be gay, she approaches them in Jerry's apartment, much to their chagrin:

> Jerry: We're not gay! Not that there's anything wrong with that.
> George: No, of course not.
> Jerry: I mean, it's fine if that's who you are.
> George: Absolutely.
> Jerry: I mean, I have many gay friends.
> George: My father's gay.

These mistaken-identity themes, while often eventually about the re-assertion of the heterosexuality of the character in question, also serve another function. At times, they can point to a blurring of lines between hetero and homo, a questioning of the surety with which we know some-one's sexuality. Indeed, when Frasier is mistaken for gay by an attractive new male station manager, the obvious "queer" sensibility of the sitcom is openly teased. When Frasier finally figures it out, he is astounded: "Well, what on earth could have made him think that I'm interested in him? All I did was ask him if he was attached, and then we talked about the theater and men's fashions—oh my god!" In letting his suitor know the truth, more mockery is made of the fey sensibility of the series and its stars:

> Frasier: It never even occurred to me that you might be gay.
> Tom (the suitor): Well it never even occurred to me that you might be straight.
> Frasier: Thank you.
> Tom (as he goes to leave): So does this mean your Dad's not gay either?
> Frasier: No, Dad's not gay.
> Tom: But Niles—come on!

But these are only moments, and the gay intrusion remains just that and the familiar world is typically reassembled. To introduce a gay char-acter into the rich and textured lives of a sitcom world or into the narra-tive morass of a nighttime or daytime soap, however, is to open up a new door altogether. And this is where the '90s really comes into its own. Continuing characters (either regular or semiregular) include the very fey and campy gay couple on *Ellen* (Peter and Barrett); the lesbian moms on *Friends;* and music teacher Ross on *Party of Five,* who made TV history by adopting a baby (Mitchell Anderson, who plays Ross, also came out at a 1996 GLAAD event). Rhonda cropped up as the sister of lead Leo on the short-lived *Relativity,* and even had a brief, but passionate, lesbian kiss. Michael Boatman plays Carter Heywood—a sharp black gay activist (and mayor's liaison to the gay community) on the Michael J. Fox (later

Charlie Sheen) vehicle *Spin City,* introducing one of the first gay African-Americans to prime time. While Carter is unusually well-integrated into the script, his gayness seems generally to serve the purpose of providing the hip foil to his Neanderthal male colleagues.

The depiction of John Irvin (the administrative aide on *NYPD Blue,* played by Bill Brochtrup) is of a proudly gay, fey, sweet guy dealing in a nonchalant sort of way with the casual homophobia of the precinct room. In addition to aide John, *NYPD Blue* featured another semiregular gay character: the lesbian cop Abby Sullivan, whose ongoing plot line included her request to befuddled colleague Medavoy to donate his sperm. Abby gets pregnant, only to have her lover killed by a psycho ex. The relationship between "daddy" Medavoy and lesbian mom Sullivan could develop in interesting ways, although it seems to have been placed on a back burner. Paul Buchman's sister Debbie came out on the extremely popular *Mad About You,* and her gynecologist lover Joan charmed their mother and delivered Jamie's baby at the end of one of the last seasons of this long-running show. On *Homicide,* Detective Tim Bayliss (Kyle Secor) investigates the murder of a gay man and begins to question his own sexuality. Dr. Maggie Doyle is a semiregular lesbian doc on *ER,* and the show also features the recurring role of gay nurse Yosh Takata, the only gay Asian-American on TV, and there are two gay docs on rival *Chicago Hope.* Sister Stacey is macho Don Johnson's dyke kid sister on *Nash Bridges,* the unnamed but regularly seen waiter on *Cybill* was clearly gay, and the hot new Borg, Seven of Nine, on *Star Trek: Voyager* is rumored to be a lesbian from outer space. But that may just be wishful thinking.

Sisters had a continuing lesbian character whose artificial insemination and subsequent custody battle (shades of the real-life Virginia case) figured prominently. The animated series on Comedy Central, *South Park*—noted for its offbeat depiction of a group of foul-mouthed, violent children—features the noxious Mr. Garrison, a self-hating closet case who has a campy hand puppet named Mr. Hat. Another episode featured "'Big Gay Al,' a stereotypical Gay man whose mission is to provide an ark for all the Gay pets who have been turned away from their owners."[5] Big Gay Al's Animal Sanctuary is "the one place where gay animals can really be themselves" and Stan's pink bandanna–wearing dog Sparky finds his pooch bathhouse of the soul. Along the way, Big Gay Al teaches the dimwits of South Park the evils of homophobia through history ("It's the oppressors! Christians and Republicans and Nazis, oh my!"), and, finally, nasty Mr. Garrison learns to love his "gay side" and comes out, puppet in hand. Even *The Simpsons* have weird Waylon Smithers, though he clings to his cartoonish closet, and a recurring animated segment on *Saturday*

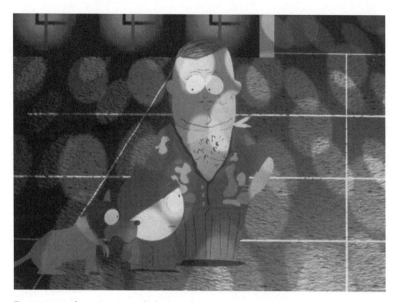

Even cartoon characters are pinkish these days, none more delightfully than Big Gay Al of *South Park* nurturing the poochy love that dares not bark its name. Courtesy of Photofest.

Night Live features "The Ambiguously Gay Duo," the campiest super-heroes ever to hit TV-land, who make perfectly plain the homoerotic subtext of such putatively straight superheroes as Batman and Robin.

Insipid and resolutely sexist *Veronica's Closet* featured an "is he or isn't he" situation in the fey and witty character of Joshua, Veronica's as-sistant. A short-lived series of 1995, *The Pursuit of Happiness,* featured a gay lawyer who worked against stereotype: six and a half feet tall, foot-ball buff, sleazy personal injury shark lawyer. Another brief series— *Daddy's Girls*—starred Harvey Fierstein as a gay designer at the fashion firm owned by lead Dudley Moore (who is raising three daughters alone). Yet another failed series, *The Crew,* featured a gay airline steward, and the short-lived ABC comedy *Oh, Grow Up* featured Ford, who left his wife and moved in with old friends upon realizing he is gay.

1998 also brought us *Will & Grace,* a gay man/straight woman riff on Hepburn/Tracy sophistication, replete with campy gay sidekick. Like many recent films, *Will & Grace* depicts the gay man as best girlfriend and confidant to his heterosexual female soulmate. He may be funny and witty and compassionate, but he also poses no sexual threat or distur-bance to the heterosexual status quo. And he is joined by his campy friend Jack, his subcultural doppelganger who gets all the good lines. While Will is out and kind of proud, he certainly has none of the active sexual life of best buddy Grace, and few other gay friends aside from his object of derision, Jack.

The insipid but popular *Drew Carey Show* includes a heterosexual cross-dresser; in *Wasteland,* we have closeted gay soap star Russell; the animated sitcom *Mission Hill* includes an elderly gay couple. *Suddenly Susan* has a gay mailroom clerk and *The Profiler* includes a gay computer geek. On Spanish TV network Telemundo, a popular sitcom, *Los Beltran,* features a committed gay couple. The controversial FOX series *Action* had several gay characters—one the closeted (and apparently extremely well-endowed) *über*producer who married the former wife of the lead Peter Dragon (played by Jay Mohr). In one episode, presumably straight Peter Dragon appears to receive oral love from a gay actor. Fox's new sci-fi series *Dark Angel* features a lesbian character named "Original Cindy," and the cantankerous Dr. Weaver on *ER* looks to be heading for some Sapphic satisfaction with a gorgeous blonde psychiatrist. And we can never forget Xena, tough warrior hero with tender girl-warrior-in-training at her side. Xena has inspired lesbians everywhere and has cultivated (with no small amount of help from the lesbian writers) a huge lesbian fan following who have little trouble reading the not-so-hidden subtext. The Xena fans are by now notorious, holding Xena nights (replete with big-screen TVs) at lesbian clubs like Meow Mix in New York and embarking on Xena tours and cruises, adorned in full warrior regalia. Led by openly gay producer Liz Friedman, the show actively cultivates a "reading between the lines" by presenting endless scenes of intimacy between tough-girl Xena and her lip-quivering ingénue sidekick Gabrielle. The Xena Web sites are a hilarious testament to the ability of gay people to read gay desire into even the thinnest of narratives, imagining love affairs and passions that defy the heterosexuality of the explicit plot.

The world of adolescent sexuality, long a no-fly zone for homosex, has now been infiltrated. The teen hit *Dawson's Creek* features series regular Jack McPhee dealing with his sexuality and wrestling with anti-gay acts in his high school. Even the macho, endlessly adolescent Steve of *Beverly Hill 90210* reckoned with the realization of his mother's lesbianism. On *Felicity,* our heroine plays a gay-positive college kid, standing beside her gay boss as he faces deportation and finds love, and the high school witches Willow and Tara on *Buffy the Vampire Slayer* began a lesbian romance. Beside the music teacher, the teen drama *Party of Five* featured a lesbian English teacher who temporarily sparked the desire of one of the leads.

There are gay characters on cable shows, including *Oz, Rude Awakening, Sex and the City,* and *Beggars and Choosers,* and Comedy Central has had several specials ("Out There") featuring gay comedians. In 1996, an

With passionate embraces, double entendres, and sisterly support, how could *Xena's* warrior women *not* become lesbian icons? Courtesy of Photofest.

original Showtime series called *Bedtime* was produced which included a lesbian couple in its "diverse" take on the lives and loves of four pairs, and that same cable station produced the memorable series *Brothers,* which had a strong continuing gay lead, and *Linc,* which included a black lesbian character, a military woman no less! Hip straight leads tend to have sympathetic and hip gay friends these days, including Jackie, Billie's (Sherilyn Fenn's) friend on Showtime's *Rude Awakening,* and Stanford, Carrie's (Sarah Jessica Parker's) buddy on *Sex and the City.* And the Independent Film Channel—a cable network that reaches around 30 million—kicked off its Valentine's Day marathon with a four-film collection of gay- and lesbian-themed movies and the Sundance Channel runs gay films in conjunction with Gay Pride Month.[6]

Daytime soap operas have lagged behind, but recently have introduced continuing gay characters and gone beyond the tragic AIDS sufferer or the closeted queen to deal more straightforwardly with homophobia and the problems of coming out. Popular teacher Michael Delaney on *All My Children* came out in 1995 and was soon followed by a gay student and a doctor lover, although all three were eventually written out of the show. Continuing gay story lines are conspicuously absent, but fall 2000 finally brought relief in the form of *All My Children's* Bianca Montgomery (Eden Riegel), recovering anorexic and daughter of the many married and mucho glamorous Erica Kane (Susan Lucci), coming out to friends and family alike. Needless to say, glam mom Erica doesn't take well to Bianca's confession, attempting to find the right man for her or, failing that, scaring off the local pierced and disheveled lesbian who has befriended Bianca.

Gay docudramas seem to be popular these days, most notably with the star-studded adaptation of Randy Shilts's history of the AIDS epidemic, *And the Band Played On,* and the equally star-studded tribute to deposed lesbian colonel Margarethe Cammermyer, *Serving in Silence.* But, like the travails which kept *Tales of the City* from a speedy airing, these projects languished for years, only to finally reach full velocity when a star signed on (e.g. Richard Gere for the Shilts docudrama). Bonnie Bedilia put in a moving performance as the mother of gay-bashed, murdered sailor Allen Schindler in Lifetime's production of *Any Mother's Son,* and cable TV now regularly includes specials on gay-related themes, including *Common Ground, It's a Girl Thing, What Makes a Family,* and *If These Walls Could Talk 2.* Of course, MTV's unctuous series *The Real World* included several young gay people over the course of numerous seasons—including a brash young lesbian, and AIDS activist and educator Pedro Zamora, whose commitment ceremony and death from AIDS figured significantly.[7]

Talk shows are a story in themselves (and none has told the story with such insight as sociologist Joshua Gamson in his book *Freaks Talk Back*). A week doesn't go by without the trash talk shows (and, to a lesser extent, their more "legit" counterparts) weighing in on various gay-related subjects—from issues of coming out in the workplace, to gay husbands, to transsexuals and the rights of lesbian mothers.

Former nighttime superhost Arsenio Hall featured out lesbian comedian Lea DeLaria on his show, not once, but several times. DeLaria's career has taken off since then; she does guest spots on sitcoms and serials, where formally she was restricted to the gay performance ghettos of Provincetown and the Lower East Side of New York. Even the Home Shopping Network has gotten into the act, featuring Ellen's mom hawking her book *Love, Ellen: A Mother/Daughter Journey* and promoting coming to terms with gay progeny.

A note of caution is necessary: While many critics predicted a gay takeover of prime time following the hoo-hah of *Ellen,* a recent survey by GLAAD revealed that "gay or lesbian characters represent just 2% of the 540 lead or supporting roles on ABC, CBS, NBC, Fox, WB, UPN and original cable series for the fall season. Only one is a lead role (Eric McCormack's Will on NBC's 'Will & Grace'); eight are supporting and all but one (Michael Boatman's Carter on ABC's 'Spin City') are white men."[8] As Josh Gamson points out, "It can't hurt to be more visible, for sure, but on television you can be made to disappear just as abruptly."[9] Nevertheless, the sheer numbers of gay characters on television *is* astonishing, particularly when placed in the context of the picture but ten short years ago. The trend towards ever more "gay episodes" as well as an increase in supporting and recurring characters continues. Popular series seem unable to overlook periodic forays into the murky waters of gay life.

SON OF ELLEN: GAY NEWS IS OLD NEWS

I'm not sure if we'll see dozens of TV programs with a gay headliner, but we will—and have—seen more and more programs which fairly successfully integrate lesbians and gays (more often gay men than women) into the fictional world of the series. A good example of this integration is *Spin City*. While an innocuously formulaic show about an addled mayor and his neurotic, overachieving right-hand man, it nonetheless integrates the gay character Carter with a degree of ease atypical until quite recently. Carter's gayness is neither ogled exotica or a "problem" to be solved, but rather central to his identity without being the sum of it. In a delightful episode, the Michael J. Fox character (Mike) learns that his macho childhood buddy (now a sailor) is gay. The revelation is compounded by Mike's jealousy over the affair his friend has with Carter, who is obviously smitten with the dashing sailor. While Mike wrestles with his homophobia (and is told he *is* homophobic by his rather fey psychiatrist), he seems more jealous of his friend's interest in Carter than his revelation of sexual identity. The shocked reaction is clearly presented as the *heterosexual's* problem, and one that the gay man refuses to take on as his own. At the end, after jealous Mike has managed to pull a few strings and have his friend shipped out earlier than planned (thus breaking poor Carter's heart), he arranges a gay replay of the scene from the film *An Officer and a Gentleman* in which a dashing and uniformed Richard Gere comes into the workplace of stunned Debra Winger, sweeping her into his arms and carrying her off. As his office-mates stand around clapping and Mike engineers the boom box, Carter is carried off by his sailor and a renewed Mike wins back the affections of friend *and* colleague. While I laughed heartily at this episode, and was struck by the easy integration of the gay characters into the everyday life of the sitcom, I was also struck by the centrality of *heterosexuality* to homosexuality. Gayness is seen through the eyes of confused heterosexuals, struggling with their own reactions and feelings. While I applaud the attempts to reckon with heterosexual fears and homophobia, I am afraid that this focus can further marginalize gay people, set them aside as *vehicles* for straight enlightenment, much in the way that people of color serve as *avenues* for white understandings of race. Why must Mike bring the two men together and engineer the dramatic reunion? It implies, perhaps unwittingly but surely with effect on the viewers, that gay people aren't capable of rendering their own lives meaningful, of acting with and for each other to make things *happen*.

Much as depictions of gay weddings can turn out to be more concerned with a heterosexual concept of matchmaking, these images can exclude even as they seem to so diligently include. And this is, perhaps, what made *Ellen* so different and what alienated the network: Ellen as gay was not solely seen and understood through the eyes of heterosexuals eager to counter their own fears. The series implicated Ellen in a larger world of gay people, with other gay characters, lovers, gay spaces, and even gay in-jokes. In other words, the series decentered heterosexuality and centered homosexuality, now no longer satisfied with being the object of heterosexual curiosity.

Nevertheless, it remains true that Carter is assuredly one of the most truly integrated gay characters on television. His gayness is neither invisible nor the site of all of his action and identity as a character. Significantly, he comes to the series already out. In other words, since "coming out" was eliminated from his narrative "meaning" to the series, the series is able to explore gay identity and life outside the single cataclysmic moment, a moment that almost always involves heterosexual unease, fear, and rejection, and therefore still allows for the centering of heterosexuality to homosexual emergence. When gay characters don't emerge in a singular moment of coming out, they are necessarily more integrated into the gestalt of the series. Because "coming out" does present a before and after, it presents itself as a "problem"—for those coming out, for their friends, for their family, for the plot itself. In sitcoms like *Spin City* and *Will & Grace,* gayness begins at the beginning. It is a *subject*, certainly, but not a *topic* that is framed by coming-out stories.

For example, several episodes have featured Carter in relationships, and not always as an opportunity for his heterosexual series-mates to freak out. Indeed, one interesting episode featured Carter involved with another black man, this one a boxer who feels he must maintain a mean, hetero demeanor in order to succeed in the ring. Embarrassed when Carter brings him a present at the gym, he talks the macho talk, only to whisper to Carter, "It's all part of the show sweetie." Carter displays his confusion with boxer Bennett's performance of the closet and accidentally blows his cover when he yells "your face, your beautiful face" after seeing him get hit in the ring. His attempt to recover ("I mean, how you gonna nail all them chicks now dude?") doesn't work, and Bennett finds himself outed. This intraracial romance (and how often do we see two handsome black men paired as romantic partners?) was paralleled by the budding romance of the white mayor and his black secretary, and another story line which featured lead Mike's attempt to hide his relationship with Nicky, his coworker. While homosexuality and heterosexuality are shown in interaction and intersection, homosexuality is not reduced here to either exotica or simply a gay twist on straight identity and sexuality. The answer to the mayor's image problem (sex outside of marriage) and the boxer's image problem (fighters can't be gay) is resolved through a fake romance between the secretary and the boxer, ending in a kiss for the TV cameras that sends both Carter and the Mayor rushing anxiously to confront their lovers. The gay man also gets his comeuppance against resident bigot Stuart, who taunts him endlessly ("Oh my god, it's a gay boxer . . .") and ends up being kissed *and* knocked out.

While *Spin City*'s gay character has received little attention (and that in itself is interesting—is it racism? Lack of controversy? And how to explain the relative absence of Carter fan activity? While Ellen and Will and Jack and others have numerous fan sites on the Internet, poor Carter is left relatively unexplored . . .), *Dawson's Creek,* written by out gay writer Kevin Williamson, introduced a gay teen into the soap opera world of the WB hit and was an immediate cultural "moment." Jack McPhee plays a newcomer to the town, who comes out in the form of a tortured poem read aloud in his high school English class. While Jack faces bigotry and harassment from homophobic schoolmates (including a Christian fundamentalist) and his militaristic father, he also receives love and support from the central characters, particularly his girlfriend Joey. While initially denying his gayness, Jack comes out and faces harassment at school ("fag" written on his locker, copies of the poem pasted all over the school) and at home with the distant and disapproving father. Jack finally admits the truth of the poem, comes out to family and friends, and is supported by now ex-girlfriend and male friends alike. Even the religious granny chastises the fundamentalist student for his lack of compassion.

Whatever one thinks about the representation of Jack on *Dawson's,* one thing remains true. In the post-*Ellen* world, the televisual coming out of a character (and the simultaneous coming out of the writer of the character) elicited hardly a ripple, although, "Outside the Wilmington, N.C., set of 'Dawson's Creek,' more than 30 teenagers carry placards reading 'Hollywood: No More Homo Promo' and 'Don't Hollyweird Me' to protest a 16-year-old gay character on the show." [10]

> The response was virtual silence. No loud protests from outraged church or conservative groups. No, 'Yep, I'm Gay!' magazine cover. No celebrities treating it as a crusade. No ponderous essays about what it means to soci-

ety. Nothing. No one cold have missed it when Ellen DeGeneres and her character 'Ellen' came out two years ago. So it may be her most lasting legacy that on 'Dawson's Creek,' a provocative gay story line in a popular teenage drama series is causing barely a ripple.[11]

Like the *Ally McBeal* kiss, and like the relatively untroubled success of *Will & Grace,* the emergence of a gay character is no longer an immediate call to arms, or an obvious flashpoint for right-wing ranting. This can only be for the good, and a sign that, however problematic, the fallout from Ellenmania includes a more easy move into everyday visibility. Nevertheless, it also remains true that double standards continue to plague these gay characters. As critic Ken Perkins asks, "Once that sweet-faced Jack (Kerr Smith) irons out the wrinkles of his hormonal angst, isn't the exploration of sexual territory next? After all, Dawson's Creek remains a sweaty, hormonal playground. And that would be the true test of how much America has changed and grown and become accepting of gay and lesbian relationships."[12] He goes on to argue that "gay and lesbian characters in broadcast network series are said to have graduated from rare exception, but to what—comedic novelty? Take a close look at the 20 or so gay characters (most played by straight actors) on weekly series. Few are in dramas, fewer are sexual, and none, if they're men, affectionately embrace."[13]

WHEN FAIRY MET SALLY

The no-kiss rule seems to apply to the hit series *Will & Grace.* While a show that does not shirk from the subject, it has been plagued by the usual double standards and asexuality of the gay male character, prompting many to note the irony of a single, handsome, gay lawyer unable to get a date on a Saturday night (or any other night for that matter). Both characters are on the rebound from failed relationships, yet Grace manages to have romantic entanglements with no small amount of snogging, while Will seems perpetually in mourning for his old lover, Michael. In one episode, Grace gets anxious over Will and Michael's impending anniversary and arranges for a distracting weekend in the country with friends Jack and Karen. But the distractions are only provided for Grace, as she meets up with a hunky old boyfriend and they proceed to embark on a passionate fling, leaving Will only with the memories of his old lover. One fears, then, that the "no big deal" attitude vis-à-vis gay characters on TV is dependent on a form of representation that largely keeps gays closeted in a tokenized, asexual, largely heterosexual world. While there are endless references to gay identity and gay desire (e.g. one episode featured a scene in which Will reveals his childhood birthday fantasies by saying, "I really loved cowboys. Still do by the way," to which Grace says, "You don't have to tell me. I've seen the magazines . . ."), it's almost as if the *referencing* of gayness becomes the substitute for a fully lived gay *life*.

Is *Will & Grace* so popular (and so uncontroversial) because of the gay boy/straight girl pas de deux at its heart? Are gay male characters rendered palatable by serving as best girlfriend to the wild and wacky (and sexual) straight women they befriend? Surely this has been a trend in film—from *My Best Friend's Wedding* to *As Good as It Gets* to *The Object of My Affection*. As one savvy reviewer writes: "Gay men and straight women are to the '90s what Oscar and Felix were to the '70s. They're certainly the dream odd couple for nervous networks. On one hand, there's enough gayness to grab some hipster cred and lots of Oscar Wilde-ish repartee. On the other, the straight gal keeps the scripts from drifting into Joe Six-Pack—alienating *Ellen* territory." [14]

Of course, the gay man/straight woman duo effectively excludes lesbians from the brave new world of sexless camaraderie. And their situation becomes itself the site for sitcom ha-has, such as the episode when both of them fall for a handsome new guy in the building, and their confusion about his sexuality provokes discussion about "gaydar" from friend Jack. Or there is the episode in which their friendship is perceived by Grace to be the impediment to her own sexual engagement on the heterosexual front, prompting them to move into separate apartments.

The series also includes a supporting gay character who, along with the other supporting character of Karen (fag hag extraordinaire), manages to steal the show episode after episode. Jack is Will's too-gay alter ego: the narcissistic, witty, bitchy, ice-skater loving, clothes horse, workout queen who ogles men endlessly but never is deemed serious enough for a real relationship. If Will doesn't get any because he's too good, Jack doesn't get any because he's too bad. If Will is the hardworking, boy scout attorney, making gays safe for middle America through his resolute sameness and blandness, his asexuality, his ordinariness, then Jack makes gays safe for middle America through his outrageousness, his snappy repartee. It might be easy to see Will as the perfectly integrated gay man (straight with a twist) and Jack as his opposite, the snap queen girlfriend who lives *la vida loca*. But it seems to me that both are integrationist images (not that there's anything wrong with that). If Will is the perfectly integrated gay man through his recognizability to straights (like them and one of them), then Jack is also perfectly integrated through his recognizability as the charming, narcissistic, witty, flitty fag next door. Neither one of them seems to live in any political gay world—AIDS has been excised, as has any sense of a gay community outside of the bars mentioned frequently but rarely shown. Indeed, the writers have been clear that their success depends on making the characters likable, not political. As David Mutchnick, cocreator of the show, makes clear, "It's our *lack* of an agenda that's helped make the show a success. We never sit down and say, 'okay, how can we teach the world about gay marriage?' The minute we start doing that, we fail."[15]

One episode, however, did feature a tongue-in-cheek story about an avoided gay television kiss. As Grace and the boys settle back to watch the first prime-time gay kiss ("one giant step for man on mankind"), the fictional TV show not so fictionally avoids showing the liplock, much to Jack's frustration and Will's bemusement. While Jack gets agitated, Will gets cynical and passive, until Jack goads him into challenging the execs at NBC studio headquarters. After they are given the brush-off by the (gay) man at the studio, Jack accosts Al Roker, weatherman extraordinaire for the *Today Show,* and announces his beef with the studio. As Jack asks Al "how long am I going to have to wait until I can see two gay men kiss on network television?" Will impulsively grabs Jack ("Not as long as you'd think . . .") and gives him a big kiss. While tongue-in-cheek and a witty snipe at network wussiness, Will's motivation to finally help Jack seems premised more on his friendship than on any stated political position. And this was their one foray into the political arena, their one reckoning with institutional homophobia!

Political issues generally seem to enter in the form of the coming-out story, as when Jack (presumably out to the world) finally must come out to his mother, and the trio engage in some touching discourse that begins to depict their relationship in more complicated ways, urging Jack to finally speak with his mother. In another episode, Will's supposedly perfect father comes into town to receive an award from his employers. Even though he assiduously attempts to keep them away, Will and Grace surprise him at the dinner, mistaking his homophobia for self-deprecating modesty. It turns out that Dad has told everyone that Will is straight (and married to Grace) in order to avoid the embarrassment of having a gay son. While Will is furious, and mystified given his conception of his dad as wholly accepting, he comes to realize—in a father/son bathroom talk—that he's "just a man." His dad, clearly stricken, receives the award and immediately announces to the assembled throngs, "My son's gay. He's a proud gay man and . . . I'm I'm a proud father of a proud gay man." This becomes the entree into a long evening of Dad's stand-up routine ("Will, you're here, you're queer, and I love you . . . dear. I love my gay son everybody."). Like the *Ellen* episode where parental homophobia is quickly overcome though a public declaration of solidarity (indeed, the scenes are amazingly similar, although the homophobia is more explicit and articulated in the *Ellen* episode), the ease of the resolution belies the painful realities of anti-gay exclusion. Once again, homophobia is named in order to be trivialized and easily dismissed.

However, this familial reconciliation is paralleled with another story concerning Jack and his despair over his unknown father (it turns out that his mother had a one-nighter with a stranger). Desiring to cheer him up, fag hag Karen secretly hires a detective to locate his biological father and sets up a mysterious meeting between the two men. While the two men flirt at the coffee shop, Karen bursts in and reveals that "he's your daddy" ("not yet" winks Jack). When it gets through to Jack he's understandably upset ("Oh my god I hit on my Dad . . ."), only to find out that the cute "daddy" is no daddy at all but another gay man who has tickets to the Backstreet Boys—and off they go. This playfulness with family and sexuality does, I think, undercut the too neat resolution of the Will/Dad familial embrace and inject a fluidity into the program that nibbles away at the overt double standard.

Indeed, in another episode, Will and Jack get invited to what they anticipate will be a hot and sexy weekend of fun in the Hamptons with old running buddies Joe and Larry. Much to their amazement (and Jack's disgust), Joe and Larry have become parents and the "party" is a big baby fest instead of the babe fest that they anticipated. As they drive home, Will becomes despondent over his inability to care for the child, and Jack reassures him by telling him what a great "dad" he's been to him all these years. But gay wit will out, and the episode ends not with maudlin paeans to parenthood, but by a gentle queering of the family:

Will: Want to stop for ice cream?
Jack: Nah.
Will: Want to go to a bar and look at hot guys?
Jack: I love you daddy.

In a later episode, the crew heads up to Vermont for the wedding of the papas, and, rather than focus on the "political" text (the wedding), the episode becomes much more about the complicated reinventions of family between Will and Grace, rendering the gayness of the wedding surprisingly ordinary and unremarked.

For all its wit and occasional foray into community, the world of *Will & Grace* is a world of well-dressed white gay men in which both lesbians and gays of color are introduced fleetingly and as objects of derision. In one episode, Will enlists Jack's help to conduct a "gay sensitivity training" workshop for the police. The lesbian couple who join in the training are both old-time, dumpy, flannel-shirted stereotypes and the objects of derision from Jack's acid tongue. In another episode, we see an Asian man accompany Jack out of the bedroom (when he is living with Will) only to be used in the most old-fashioned sitcom style as laugh line ("look how funny he talks!")

In more recent episodes it does seem that Will is being more fully developed. We do see him going out on dates, yet not only are those dates chaste but they still seem to happen at the behest of others. Grace's mother fixes him up (upsetting Grace, who is used to her mother meddling in *her* life), Will's boss fixes him up, and Jack presents him with the occasional sailor. But Will has yet to enact his own sexual, gay identity. Indeed, when we do see him in a rare proactive moment, it is a humiliating one where he mistakes his old boyfriend's friendliness as romantic re-interest.

The series then, is a puzzle. Dabbling in double standards yet indubitably gay. Apolitical yet surreptitiously aware. Familial yet hedonistic. Gay male centered yet with two of the strongest female characters on TV. Devoid of larger community yet assuredly not tokenized. As critic Andrew Holleran notes, "Will & Grace is sort of astonishing to anyone who came out in the 70's . . . it's hard to believe what's being referred to, much less said, on the small screen. . . . The expectation was that a gay sitcom would be gay—and my concern was that the gay subject would be, in the end, rather thin and one-note—but if it wasn't gay, what would it be? Just a sitcom. And why worry? It *was* just a sitcom. But it wasn't; it was *our* gay sitcom, fearless and tacky and lewd."[16] And, through it all, very funny.

IT'S HIP TO BE SQUARE: THE NEW HOMOPHOBIA ON TV

It *is* good news to see more gay characters and gay issues on TV, and the shift from invisibility to relative profusion has been extraordinary and has prompted groups like the NAACP to comment on the relative paucity of ethnic minority images in comparison with images of gays. Indeed, there were more gay characters featured in the 1999 fall season than all other minorities combined, prompting one critic to opine, "Oh, to be young, beautiful, musically gifted, gay but definitely not happy and certainly not black."[17] But Gamson makes the important point that, while numbers are important and tokenization always has negative repercussions, playing "the head count strategy" can be problematic, pitting one group against another in a manner that inevitably produces oversimplification and competition.[18]

But why has there been such a rapid increase for gays? One argument for the increase of gay characters on TV is the simple one that many writers and directors and producers in Hollywood are gay (e.g. Max Mutchnick, who writes for Will & Grace, Kevin Williamson, who created Dawson's Creek), are more likely to be out these days, and are more likely to have powerful straight allies in Hollywood who share their concerns. Therefore, more gay writers = more gay characters. That is often the response to the perplexing lack of representation of African-Americans, Asians, and Latinos in TV: there are very few minorities in high levels in the industry. Yet if that formula were followed, it would stand to reason that we would see a cavalcade of Jewish characters on TV, as many writers, directors, and producers are Jewish. While there have been notable exceptions (Molly Goldberg in the early days and Jerry Seinfeld and Paul Reiser in the contemporary period), identifiable Jews are often as invisible as many other minority groups. Critic Josh Gamson pays cautious heed to the insider argument that claims invisibility and stereotypes can be rectified if only we had more (name your pick: blacks, gays, Hispanics) in the industry in decision making positions. But this position, too, has problems. It has always been the case that writers "write outside their experience" and the assumptions of some direct "correlation between industry personnel and broadcast imagery"[19] is too simple and narrow a view of how meanings get produced even as it may push the industry to take new notice of absences and stereotypes.

The reasons for the outpouring of gay images and the simultaneous retreat on images of other minorities has to do, it seems to me, with the difficulty in assimilating (and therefore making less threatening) minority groups whose "difference" is visible. For a whole host of reasons, including the ability to "pass" and simultaneously the ability to be chic and exotic, gays have been easier to assimilate into mainstream television. While TV tends to ghettoize African-Americans into specific time slots and all-black sitcoms on black-identified networks, no such strategy exists for gays, who only find a home in a presumably all-straight television world. Perhaps it's just the "natural" trajectory of cultural inclusion and we will someday see gays facing the same situation as African-Americans are currently, dealing with all-gay sitcoms in gay-identified networks and decreasing gay visibility in the prime-time mainstream. But somehow, I don't think so, because the possibilities for assimilation are not simply identical for all minority groups, and the ease of integrating gays into prime time says much about that difference.

And in some senses, whether the motivation is financial (tapping into the gay market, creating controversy to raise interest and sales) or political (some on the right have even suggested that there is a "pro-gay" cabal operating in Hollywood) is irrelevant. Yet, as I have repeatedly warned, it would be foolhardy to see these changes as signaling a fundamental ideological shift in American perceptions of homosexuality or even a real shift in the *content* of gay representations. As noted, the vexing problem of double standards continues, where the sexuality of gay characters on TV is roped off, leaving heterosexuals to have more complex lives and loves. In a piece on NPR's *All Things Considered,* commentator Andrea Bernstein accurately portrayed the current dilemma facing gays watching themselves on TV:

> In mainstream TV and in the movies, finally, gay people exist and that's a big step forward. Some people think it's a good thing that television is showing us holding down jobs, going on dates, playing cards, having babies and not focusing on all that sex stuff. After all, many people think our whole lives revolve around sex. I suppose if I had to choose, I'd rather the mass media show all the mundane aspects of our lives and leave the rest up to the imagination. But why should we have to choose? Heterosexuals get to wait tables, host radio talk shows, raise families and still have sex. Americans are so used to sex on TV and the movies, that presenting homosexuals as sexless beings makes us seem like freaks. Now that the purveyors of prime-time TV have decided that a gay character or two livens up almost any show, and that America has responded, for the most part, with a collective yawn, it's time for Hollywood and the networks to take on a new challenge—presenting us as full, three-dimensional human beings with the same worries, concerns and desires as everyone else. When Mariel Hemingway seduces Morgan Fairchild right into the bedroom, I'll be watching.[20]

It's also important to reiterate again and again that it is not the case that "gay and lesbian plotlines are taking over the airwaves. Although both GLAAD and conservative groups trumpet 'more than 25' gay characters in prime time, there are really only seven who appear regularly in sitcoms and drama series on the six networks. (The rest exist, but they are 'recurring' and may or may not return.) That's out of over 600 regular characters on more than 85 prime-time network series."[21] But in this new era of "tolerance," homophobia in public realms such as TV more often appears in ambiguous form, hidden under a veneer of liberal acceptance. Homophobia can now often take the form of network acquiescence to right-wing pressure to "tone down" gay content or remove it altogether. Indeed, as Tom Hopkins notes:

> Long after gays began appearing on TV, sponsors' fear of viewer boycotts continues to make broadcasters reluctant to depict gay relationships

honestly and openly. When *L.A. Law* featured a kiss between two women attorneys in 1991, advertisers bailed out. Darren Star's casting of a gay regular on *Melrose Place* was encouraging, but Fielding (Doug Savant) has languished in subplot hell—a sad reminder that it's OK for us to see a gay man, but not OK for us to see him in a flesh-and-blood, loving relationship with another man. No network has demonstrated much courage in this regard: ABC barred *thirtysomething* from showing two men in bed together. CBS barred *Picket Fences* from showing two teenage girls kissing. NBC barred *Quantum Leap* from dealing with a gay teenager contemplating suicide. Fox snipped an offending kiss between a homosexual played by Eric Stoltz and a heterosexual (Randy Quaid) in last year's movie, *Roommates*. Roseanne has opened some doors, introducing the gay restaurant boss (Martin Mull) and the lesbian friend (Sandra Bernhard) who introduced another lesbian friend (Hemingway)—but when that BIG KISS came, all we saw was the back of Hemingway's head.[22]

While too much can be made of this, the kiss has come to symbolize the point of no return, that which normalizes gays as it refuses invisibility, challenging their status as perpetual outsiders. Commentators did not hesitate to point out the double standard so clearly embodied in the reluctance to depict even the most tepid gay sexuality. As Frank Bruni, writing in the *Arizona Republic,* says, "As popular television shows and movies slouch toward greater inclusion of sympathetic gay characters, the step they seem most reluctant to take is the candid portrayal of same-sex desire or intimacy."[23] The obvious absence of a juicy kiss has been noted by even the most obtuse commentators as the clear double standard that it is, and as a ploy ("will they or won't they," back and forth leaks and hints) to boost ratings by creating controversy.

But even the addition of a kiss seems filled with contradictions. For so many, "putting same-sex kisses on-screen—and giving those kisses to respectable, appealing characters in unremarkable settings—is a vital step toward full acceptance of gays in society at large. Unlike bizarre scenes of gays in strange underground bars, which movies have seldom hesitated to show, a simple kiss affirms not how different gays and lesbians are to everyone else, but how similar."[24] Here again, though, the kiss is offered up as "evidence" of gay similarity to straight people, and is made legitimate by that very comparison. The right to have a sexuality can only be understood *as a right* to the extent that it is fused into the heterosexual framework.

While the avoided kiss may be a crime of omission, outright censorship and advertiser pressure is a crime of commission, practices that remain even in this more "open" era. The infamous 1989 *thirtysomething* episode suffered from a one-million-dollar sponsor pullout and was not rerun. Other series, most notably *Roseanne,* have been threatened with similar advertiser defections. The Christian Coalition, Family Defense Council, Traditional Values Coalition, Family Research Council, and other right-wing pressure groups regularly fire off angry letters to the networks and incite boycotts and advertiser withdrawals. When *Serving in Silence* (the story of gay colonel Margarethe Cammermyer) was set to air in 1995 on NBC, the Family Defense Council weighed in with threats of an advertising boycott, focusing specifically on the kiss. Chairman Howard Hurwitz argued that "the great majority of people in the country don't want to see this kind of stuff on TV . . . it's utterly unacceptable. If they don't cut it out, we will contact the advertisers in an effort to get them to withdraw their advertising."[25] And, often, particular episodes with gay themes mysteriously end up being pulled from syndication, such as an episode of *Frasier* which featured a spoof of a Dr. Laura–like character.[26]

However, it does seem clear that advertiser defections are really the secondary phenomenon; advertisers are generally not pulling out (when they do) of their own accord, but are facing serious and sustained pressure from right-wing groups and Christian family values activists. Gay-themed shows seem to pull in a substantial market share, so profit-minded advertisers often think diversity is good business and are eager to create both a frisson of controversy (which often stimulates sales) and tap into the gay market, along with other niche-marketed populations. But as the right wing has increasingly seen lesbians and gays as the fault line of an eroding society and central combatants in the "culture war," the pressure on advertisers, networks, writers, producers, directors, stars, is great. Indeed, even in this time of supposed openness, there are very few openly gay producers, directors, writers, stars. And it is still very difficult to get a gay-themed program produced, and when they are produced they face attacks by the right, balking advertisers, and zealous censors. In an article arguing that the gay '90s are really more of a closeted '90s, Steve Weinstein flies in the face of the common wisdom which asserts a powerful and substantive shift toward more open and diverse depiction of gays on TV. Writing in 1991 (before *Melrose Place* and *Roseanne*), Weinstein details the advertiser hesitancy and producer avoidance that has helped fuel a return to the closet. Weinstein concludes that right-wing pressure on networks and on advertisers has had the effect of nixing most gay content early on in the production process. Protests from right-wing groups persist unabated, although perhaps with less overt success. Every new gay character, every gay-themed episode, every movie of the week brings letters, pickets, pressure. Piqued by the proliferation of "positive" gay images, conservatives like the Rev. Louis Sheldon, head of the Orange County–based Traditional Values Coalition, make endless statements claiming that "'homosexuals should not be portrayed at all on TV.'" Sympathetic gay role models confuse viewers, he argues, and "if young males need to identify with someone, they should identify with Clint Eastwood."[27]

If this seems like a narrative of a past we have since transcended, it remains true that there is still backlash from some viewers, as Joss Whedon, the writer of *Buffy the Vampire Slayer,* found out when he started a lesbian relationship between witches Willow and Tara. Not only did he get concerned admonitions from WB (no kissing!), but fans registered their hostility on the Web site. Whedon made it clear in an interview with David Bianculli on NPR's *Fresh Air* program that the network "obviously has issues" with the newly minted lesbian relationship between witches Tara and Willow. "They don't want any kissing—that's one thing they've stipulated," he adds.[28] On the program's official Web site, Whedon railed at the homophobic postings that followed Willow's foray into witchy lesbian love and also made the case that the censors prohibitions against even the remotest sexual display (e.g. kissing) made him a better writer by forcing him to be creative.

For most reporting on the gay boom in TV, this visibility is only good news. Commentators do often point out the double standards and continuance of stereotypes, while insisting on the inevitably happy outcome of the march of assimilation and integration. There are exceptions, and a surprising number of reporters have gone further, endeavoring a more substantive critique of the current "boom" in gay images. Critic Frederick Biddle notes that "network TV's prime-time treatment of homosexuals remains a tentative, anachronistic premise, gay neither in the traditional sense nor in that of the with-it '90s. It is, at best, where it was in depicting black Americans circa 1963."[29] Biddle argues that "gay characters' main purpose often is to vex main characters. The woes of Ross, the puppy-dog-cute loser-in-love of NBC's 'Friends,' originate in his divorce from his first wife, Carol, who put him down for another woman. When not thus victimized, heterosexual characters get belly laughs (and catch comic hell in their fictional worlds) by being mistaken for gay because they socialize with gay friends."[30]

Even when suspicious of the new visibility, most do see a trend toward more multidimensional characters, noting that "the new wave of gays on television features fully formed characters whose sexuality may not be their most defining facet. Ellen DeGeneres clearly paved the way for a new era and more evolved ways of thinking about gays and lesbians, on TV and in life. Ellen Morgan has many characteristics—funny, loyal, neurotic—and viewers understand her gayness is not the defining characteristic."[31]

TV columnist John Goodman (no relation to the actor) may be right when he argues that "being played as the buffoon or mocked openly may be the new issue du jour."[32] The brief moment of what has been dismissed as "political correctness" (i.e. treating gays with respect and dignity) is now over. If gays are now a regular part of the visual landscape, then they too can be mocked and "dissed." As gay critic Richard Goldstein claims, "The culture of casual bigotry should be seen as a nostalgia for the way things used to be, an attempt to restore the old racial and sexual order. It's backlash politics in the guise of entertainment."[33] Gay jokes, which seemed a thing of the past (along with blanket invisibility), now seem back in, as Goodman catalogues in the 1999 fall season, where he observed pilots filled with gay jokes. Indeed, the short-lived John Goodman sitcom (in which Goodman starred as a gay man returning to his home town) played on the laughs garnered from the Archie Bunkerish epithets hurled by John's homophobic dad. And gay *Survivor* winner Richard Hatch explains to the viewers of CBS's *The Early Show* that fellow contestant Rudy's constant references to him as "queer" mean nothing because "Rudy is a kind and honest and straightforward guy." This is not to say that these are the only kinds of images available on TV. But, more and more, and particularly in shows that position themselves as "hip," the new homophobia takes the form of a "gloves off" approach that many mistakenly see as the true sign of inclusion and integration.

Indeed, as one commentator notes, "throughout prime time, gay characters are cropping up as the late-'90s version of the requisite 'wacky neighbor' of sitcom convention. They're there for quirky comic relief. In a couple of sitcoms this fall, viewers will see characters who seem gay but are actually 'in denial.' UPN's 'Head Over Heels' borrows Patrick Bristow from 'Ellen' to play 'a sardonic, frustrated romance counselor who has taken a vow of celibacy.' NBC's 'Veronica's Closet' offers Wallace Langham ('The Larry Sanders Show') as the loyal assistant 'who faces a sexual identity crisis.' In both cases, homosexuality is a running gag."[34]

Still others seem to feel that gay TV is just one big ho-hum now and "that's because today, in 2000 A.D. (After DeGeneres), gay characters are so common on television, so unexotic, that their sexual orientation has become all but invisible to most viewers."[35] In this version of events, gays have—with a few caveats—achieved "acceptance," so that "like blacks and single moms before them, [they] are now allowed to be every bit as boring (or smart or stupid or ruthless or whatever) as anybody else on TV."[36] Of course, that ignores the ghettoization of blacks on TV, the almost complete invisibility of other racial/ethnic minorities (of *any* sexual preference), and the continuation of double standards for gays. In this story, Hollywood becomes the champion of change, bravely pushing the envelope of acceptability as a reluctant society lags behinds, "championing gay rights in much the same way it fostered civil rights in the 1960s and 1970s, when it tried to change America's hearts and minds about race by presenting more positive black characters on its shows."[37] Thus the *addition* of gay characters becomes, by default, the *championing* of gay rights. But depicting gay *characters,* as I have argued throughout this book, is not in itself a televised argument for gay *rights.* As sociologist and TV critic Josh Gamson points out, "TV visibility may be a necessity and a pleasure, but it guarantees nothing more than itself."[38]

And, still, for all the talk of the diversity of gay characters, noticeably absent are gays of color and sexually nonconformist folks, such as transgendered people. With the exception of *Spin City,* gays of color have been and remain largely invisible, particularly when it comes to continuing or recurring characters. One early, contentious, exception was Fox's *In Living Color,* a multiracial variety show featuring the "Men on Film" skit with two black gay queens prancing through films reviews. This skit invoked much controversy. Many found it hilarious and parodic while others, like the late filmmaker Marlon Riggs, felt that it came closer to caricature than camp and perpetuated "a notion that black gay men are sissies, ineffectual, ineffective, womanish in a way that signifies inferiority."[39] But there is little else that lies between dapper and witty (and mostly dateless) Carter and the swishy film boys of "Men on Film," although the teen hit *Felicity* does have a continuing Hispanic gay character. Lesbians of color are simply not represented at all, although there was one episode of the since canceled *Livin' Single* in which an old college friend comes out and announces her plans to marry another woman. Indeed, the whiteness of gay TV has prompted out director and writer Paris Barclay to call for "the gay African-American action hero, the Latina lesbian who balances career with lover, the transgendered person who is not the butt of jokes. Somewhere in the Land Where Television is Made, we are only slightly visible—and then woefully out of focus . . . Lesbian, gay, bisexual, and transgendered people of color who look and act like anyone we know. We have sat by, apparently content with the queeny, quipping white males who pop in for humorous asides on quite a few sitcoms or the occasional sardonic transvestite or the 'Surprise!' lesbian or the one black gay man (who at least has a political consciousness) on *Spin City.* . . . Now it's time for the Second Wave."[40]

While that "second wave" has most assuredly not arrived, we did finally get a TV movie featuring an African-American gay man who is a devout pianist for the church by day and a career drag queen by night. *Holiday Heart* starred Ving Rhames as the big- (and broken-) hearted Holiday, who rescues a teenage girl and her drug-addicted, battered mom and attempts to form a family with them, only to be sidelined by the mother's return to drugs. While *Holiday Heart* is a touching soap opera of redemption, the African-American gay character (like his counterparts in films such as *To Wong Foo, Thanks for Everything, Julie Newmar*) is not only desexualized but primarily oriented towards the needs of others. While the interesting and implausible ending challenges a bit (after the mother is killed by drug dealers, Holiday raises the girl with the help of the mother's good-hearted and paternal drug dealer ex-lover), the resounding image we are left with is a Mammy for the millennium—a maternal/confidant black figure who cares for others and wallows in her/his romantic memories of past (but unseen) loves.

If gays of color are mostly invisible in both the ghettoized world of WB and Fox and the white gay world of prime-time big networks, then transgendered people—of any ethnicity—are shown (if at all) as sites of humor and befuddled alarm. In *Drew Carey,* the cross-dressing brother is proud but assuredly heterosexual. In an episode of *Just Shoot Me,* Dennis's best friend emerges after years only to be, surprise, a woman— a beautiful, buxom blonde no less! More laughs, especially as Dennis falls for Bert/Brandy only to be rebuffed. In *Ally McBeal,* a transgendered client serves as erotic interest that mingles with horror, and the horror wins out as attracted lawyer Mark rejects Cindy and she becomes the butt of jokes culminating in coworker Fish's obsessive gargling after a kiss.

Indeed, no series has so delved into the strange heart of the heterosexual at once disgusted by and desirous of gay sexuality as *Ally McBeal.* This new, millennial reckoning with homosexuality emerges most perniciously—and paradoxically—in sites such as this, where hip young professionals give free rein to fears and fantasies, and give free rein to a homophobia newly acceptable because it is enacted by those who wear the mantle of liberal acceptance. In one particularly complicated episode, wacky and winsome Ally and conniving and forthright Ling confess an attraction to one another. You really know you've hit prime time when Ally McBeal, anorexic post-feminist icon of the end of the millennium (and the end of feminism?), ponders the love that dare not speak its name. The episode opens with Ally—finger dreamily in mouth—staring off into space as Ling watches intently from across the table. Later, Ling approaches her and wonders whether she has ever kissed a woman. Flustered Ally agrees to go out with Ling and then confides to best girlfriend Renee that "gay women, for whatever reason, love me. They're attracted to me." Ally also confesses her desire, but not without the proviso of generic heterosexual disgust: "As a general rule," she says to Renee, "the idea of kissing another woman grosses me out. Ick. But sometimes the idea of kissing *certain* women doesn't gross me out. It's not like I'm

attracted to them but the idea of kissing them isn't . . . I don't know . . .
repulsive." Relieved as we are that Ally isn't wholly overcome by disgust,
the episode proceeds next to the restaurant, where the two nervous
women have drinks after dinner. If the assertion of disgust wasn't explicit
enough, this scene proceeds with the relieved women revealing that, as
Ling says, "what I really want out of a relationship, at the end of the day,
is a penis." Ally agrees wholeheartedly and then the girls move to fulfill
yet another heterosexist male fantasy by displaying some hot girl-on-girl
action on the dance floor, replete with avid male onlookers.

But little Ally's "curiosity" is still unsated, and the requisite kiss comes
in the next scene, when the girls go at it "just to see what it's like." Of
course, Ling reveals that it "didn't suck" and they continue smooching in
the office as the camera fades out. Just to make sure we are clear that our
heroines are assuredly heterosexual (but oh so curious!), they confront
each other the next day with more revelations about that "missing ingre-
dient you need for the tingle" and the anonymous penis once again rears
its persistent head.

In this hip late-'90s series, lesbian desire is reduced to fetishistic curiosity, to fantastical dreams (the plot is paired with another about
coworker Nell's fantasy of being spanked), to display for male delecta-
tion, to displaced desire for the real thing. What does it mean that the
sexiest, longest, tonguiest television kiss between two women occurs in
this context? Between two women anxious to prove their own heterosexuality? Between two women who declaim with ease their repugnance at
the thought of lesbian desire? Between two women who can't say enough
how much they love men and their appendages? Perhaps this episode
speaks with forked tongue, displaying a most obvious homophobia at the
same time that it protests a bit too much. While a noxious show to watch,
it also reveals a bit more than it should about the fragile state of heterosexual love, about the frantic defenses put up against its homosexual
doppelganger, about the desperation to place homosexuality back where
it belongs—in dreams, in bars, in male fantasies, in that nook marked
sideline to the real show. If we watch too closely we just may see the
frayed stitching being slowly pulled apart.

AND NOW FOR SOMETHING COMPLETELY DIFFERENT

That stitching was positively *yanked* apart by the new and controversial
series on Showtime, *Queer as Folk*. Preceded by the most expensive marketing campaign "ever aimed by a mainstream market at gay audiences
and probably the most elaborate ever with gay themes aimed at mainstream audiences,"[41] *Queer as Folk*'s $10 million was the largest ever

spent for a Showtime series and included massive outreach to gay audiences through aggressive niche marketing. It paid off with high Nielsen ratings and sustained viewer interest. Adapted from the successful (and grittier) British series of the same name, this series is indeed a groundbreaker, on at least two fronts. If gays on TV (and in mainstream film) have too often been relegated to the token roles of sidekick, accessory, neighbor, on view for heterosexuals within a largely heterosexual world, here gays are the only show in town, "the first series in which all the primary characters are gay or lesbian."[42] Not only are all the main characters gay (and straight characters relegated to the outsider role), but *Queer as Folk* breaks through that other stubborn double standard by displaying active and explicit gay sexuality. Two of the primary complaints about gay representations on TV—that gays are tokens, isolated from other gay people, and that gays are desexualized, denied the pleasures of the flesh—have thus been challenged by a series that wears it pathbreaking identity proudly on its sleeve. As Josh Gamson says, "On 'Queer as Folk,' straight people are the visitors . . . and the gay folks get to be sexual. That is, strangely, a kind of progress."[43]

Centered on a group of gay male friends (and one lesbian couple) who live in Pittsburgh, *Queer as Folk* intends to take the viewer boldly where few heteros have gone before—into the world of bars, backrooms, gyms, drugs, and casual sex that defines the existence of this particular group of youngish men. The gang consists of the sweet-faced and boyish Michael (who narrates and holds a torch for his best friend Brian, the rakish and predatory "center" of the series); Justin, a teenage boy discovering his sexuality (and in love with heartless Brian); Ted, a slightly older accountant burdened by his banal looks (and in love with Michael); and Emmet, a queeny designer who gets the good lines. Rounding out the cast are the lesbian couple Lindsey and Melanie, one of whom gives birth to a child with the help of Brian's sperm, and Michael's aggressively gay-positive Mom, played by Sharon Gless.

While some reviewers have commented on the unidimensionality of the characters and the stilted dialogue, most have been positively glowing in their rush to knight *Queer as Folk* as double-standard dragon slayers for the new gay visibility. Reviews invariably attest to the "breakthrough" quality of the series and the "refreshing" way in which it allows entree into an "honest" and "shocking" portrayal of gay male sexuality. True enough, I suppose. As Nancy Franklin notes in a review in the *New Yorker,* "This is the first dramatic series to show, without apology, and without sitcommy evasion, what many straight people don't want to think about: that gay people have sex lives."[44] Perhaps this is just a case of "gay soaps can be as bad as straight ones," and we should leave it at

The boys of *Queer as Folk* break down the old sexual double standard only to shore up thin scripts, flaccid acting, and tedious sexism. Courtesy of Photofest.

that, applaud its breaking down of barriers and hope for more nuance in the future. Putting aside the poor writing and tepid acting, I'm still bothered by the rush to view this as unproblematically honest and truthful, as (finally!) a straightforward rendering of the lives and loves of (some) gay men, as if the *absence* of stereotypes (asexual, victims, tortured, self-loathing) implies the *presence* of complexity. Sure enough, many people live aimless and empty lives where politics, family, friends, ideas are an afterthought to the burning quest for sexual pleasure and old-style disco dancing. And while I applaud the breakthrough quality of its depiction of sexuality, *Queer as Folk* seems to substitute sexuality for community and to imply that gay sexual expression means an absolute erasure of everything else. Work is shown only to lead up to sex (Brian seems to seduce every client in his high-priced ad firm). But, most disturbingly to me, gay community and gay friendships—which have provided such creative and vivid alternatives to the standard familial couplings of American heterosexuals—are here made newly invisible. While these folks are meant to be longtime friends—particularly Brian and Michael—we get no depiction of genuine care, concern, knowledge, engagement. Indeed, Brian shows his respect for best buddy Michael by giving a backseat blow job to a boy while Michael drives, and by having sex with that same boy in Michael's old room at his Mom's house, as Mom and Mikey wait patiently downstairs. And while the sex is refreshingly visible and vibrant, it remains curiously unpleasurable. While the search for sex is the raison d'être of the show, the pleasure in getting it seems strangely muted. At least the women in HBO's *Sex and the City* (the series most comparable to *Queer as Folk*) seem to enjoy their escapades. No one (with the notable exception of teen Justin, who, along with his newly enlightened mother is one of the more complicated characters) seems happy or even grounded in any meaningful way, hinting at the old canard that gays are stunted and narcissistic, if not self-loathing.

Now, clearly, Brian is our classic ne'er do well, our (lovable?) scamp, our Peter Pan in leather chaps and Hugo Boss, although I agree with critic Matthew Gilbert in wondering "why the men in 'QAF' are so powerfully drawn to such a tedious vampire who tosses off simplistic lines like 'I don't believe in love.'"[45] But even the good boy Michael (and *this* gay everyman hero is closeted!) exhibits only the most tepid emotional connection to his gang; when friend Ted lies near death in a coma he manages some grub for his mom but tears and major anguish seem out of the question. Brian, of course, responds by screwing the nurse as Ted emerges from his coma. And if this is a community, it is curiously place-less. While the British series capitalized on its gritty urban environment (most assiduously *not* London), this is a Pittsburgh without any distinguishing markers, where people of color are invisible (except as laughable, non-English-speaking hookers) and city life antiseptic and disengaged.

And the potential for a compelling depiction of alternative gay families is lost in the nails on the chalkboard rendering of the lesbian couple who, curiously, decide to have a baby with Brian—a thoroughly rancid person who just happens to be despised by a member of the couple. As one critic notes, "that Brian has an abundance of cute genes seems to matter more to Lindsay than coming to an agreement with her partner about the most important decision of their lives."[46] Not only does this make lesbians out to be really stupid ("Hey honey, thought I'd get pregnant by an irresponsible, sexist, and vile man whom you hate. Hope you don't mind!") but it renders the whole (gay) concept of a "family of choice" ridiculous. Much has been made of feckless Brian's growing domesticity as he begins to ponder fatherhood. But he never actually cares for the child, and even has the chutzpah to disrupt the baby's bris in an ostentatious act of caring. He treats the mother (another old friend and past lover whom he supposedly adores) with deep disrespect and callous disregard, yet we are clearly meant to feel warm fuzzies in the scene in which Brian is shown sleeping with the baby on his manly chest. And how different is this? A woman (gay or straight) holding a baby is not even worthy of notice; for men this is the domestic equivalent of the money shot. The lesbians are there—like women in so many films and TV shows—to serve as nutritional supplements to the main course of male (this time gay male) sexuality and life. So far, their relationship has no history, no story, no meaning other than their battle over Brian. Surely they are more sexual than most lesbians we see on TV, but just as surely this is a boys' own story and the girls are, like in heterosexual boys stories, incidental. And just how queer is that?

CODA ONE: A TALE OF TWO TALES

In the beginning of this new millennium, two hotly hyped, made-for-cable specials premiered—one on Showtime and the other on HBO. While one might have conjectured that these airings would be the opportunity for cultural overload, à la *Ellen,* it is a sign of the changing times that these specials received hype but little hoopla, either in the form of censorship or celebration. Both programs featured well-known writers, directors, and actors, including Ellen DeGeneres. Both garnered no small amount of critical praise and occasioned larger discussion on gay representations in the media. Both followed similar three-part formats, tracing the changes in social attitudes toward homosexuality through several historical periods as they enact themselves on a single small town (in the Showtime special) or on a single small house (in the HBO special). And both share a typical narrative conceit: the forward march of history means a 2000 fairly free of homophobia, where gay weddings and gay mommies are warmly welcomed by an all-embracing public. In the Showtime special (*Common Ground*), the year 2000 brings us a gay wedding, replete with gay wedding planners, lesbian cake bakers, and cold feet. While the protesters are there—in the form of a ragtag group of ex-military guys—even the curmudgeonly father comes around in the end to bless the nuptials. In the HBO movie (*If These Walls Could Talk 2,* sequel to a 1996 special), the millennial moment is represented by a happily integrated lesbian couple planning their insemination. While references are made to intolerant adoption agencies and a world that "doesn't understand," the couple proceed as if they believed the media fiction of a gay new world.

This ideology was voiced by Anne Heche—the writer and director of the "2000" segment of the HBO special and DeGeneres's former partner—in an interview on *Larry King Live.* When King wonders whether these sorts of representations actually change the people who view them,

If These Walls Could Talk . . . they would say: Sharon and Ellen, sorry, but the world ain't one big gay-positive parenting party! Courtesy of Photofest.

Heche argues that "the intent is to bring familiarity and what that familiarity means to me is when we start to understand that we're all based in the same human emotion. We have the same emotions as any other couple. And that to me is what some of the people who have seen it have come to me and said. Like, I get it, I'm starting to get it. You love the same way I love, you argue the same way I argue." Or, as Sharon Stone (along with DeGeneres one of the actors in that segment) says, "ultimately, it's a universal story." In an interview with Phil Rosenthal of the *Chicago Sun-Times,* both DeGeneres and Stone reiterate this theme of universality, with DeGeneres saying, "I learned that I'm exactly like a straight woman, but I don't have sex with a man. We're kind of the same."[47] This brave gay world is white, bourgeois, coupled, familial, and familiar.

The HBO trilogy repeats the format of its 1996 predecessor, which focused on the subject of abortion and how this issue played out in the lives of successive groups of women residing in the same house over a period of several decades. An intriguing device, this structure should allow for a kind of historical complexity and depth rarely found in mainstream television. And while the first segment, set in the early '60s and starring Vanessa Redgrave, captures the sense of the closet and its repercussions, the other segments are either historically confused or historically vacant. The second segment attempts to play out the tensions in the early '70s between a burgeoning women's movement and the lesbians within it and outside it. Unquestionably the sexiest of the three, it enacts this tension without any substantive attempt to explain it, so that the butch, working-class outsider becomes simply a "self-determined woman" in pop psychology parlance.

Common Ground has a somewhat wider time frame, with the first story set in 1954, the second in 1974, and the last in 2000. Unlike the other HBO special, this one participates in the erasure of gay sexuality by having only the remotest hints of warmth between gay lovers. And, unlike the HBO film, this one centers itself on not only the town, but on the person of a continuing character named Johnny Burroughs—played in the last two parts by Eric Stoltz—who functions as a sort of Greek chorus, moving from rejection to embrace. While homophobia is certainly shown, the emphasis is on the "common ground" between gays and straights. Both films should be lauded for depicting the violent realities of homophobia and the pain of the closet, for showing the rejections of families and peers, and the desire for connection with other gays. But the HBO special was intimate and sexual, focusing less on "tolerant" or "intolerant" straights than on gay lives and loves, while the Showtime film insistently focused on heterosexual response and reaction, and even further centralized straights by honing in on the patriotic heterosexual man as "everyman" coming to terms with changing times. These two films, then, are both similar and different. Similar, in that they refuse an examination of the continued presence of virulent homophobia and whitewash the contemporary by depicting it as one big gay-friendly theme park. Different, in that one treats gay identities through the prism of straight "coming-to-tolerance" narratives (or, alternately, coming-out struggles), and the other respects gay identities enough to think there is merit in the stories they have to tell.

CODA TWO: THE REAL *REAL* WORLD

In one of the funnier episodes of *Ellen,* cousin Spence gets knocked out by pesticide in a grocery store and dreams of a gay world, a world populated by gay stores, gay groceries, and gay dominance, in which heterosexuality finds itself on the outside looking in, marginalized by an all-powerful gayness. In this dream sequence, Harvey Fierstein emerges to announce: "Submitted for your approval. An alternate universe. Where straight people are the minority and gay people are calling the shots. Ellen Morgan and Spence Kovac have just crossed over into the nicest part of the Twilight Zone, where we've already begun renovations and are raising property values like you wouldn't believe." In this gay twilight zone, the homos venture down to Straight Town to ogle the congregated hets with their bad art, absence of rhythm, and Barcaloungers. It's an old device, to reverse or invert social reality to point out to those on top what it feels like to be on the bottom.

In my more fanciful millennial visions, I like to imagine turning on the TV on a Wednesday evening and hunkering down for a night of viewing which includes a sitcom chronicling the chaotic household of a lesbian single mother bravely raising her kids, surrounded by assorted ex-lovers, friendly gay uncles, confused but engaged grandparents, and wacky heterosexual neighbors. Later, I'd switch to *Law and Order: Hate Crimes Unit,* where gay and straight cops and DAs sternly work to rid our cities and towns of bigoted acts of anti-gay violence. In between, I'd see commercials with gay couples purchasing cars and clothes, gay teens frolicking at the local McDonald's, gay dads struggling to get little Sally's soccer clothes their whitest white, and single dykes chugging brews at the local watering hole. The handsome, blow-dried anchor on the nightly news would banter with his coanchor about the irksome ways of his longtime companion Jason, and late-night talk show host Lea DeLaria would feature the Five Lesbian Brothers as the house comedy troupe. *Days of Our Gay Lives* would follow the intersecting lives and loves of a small community in San Francisco, led by the conniving and ruthless Mr. Bruce, scion of a wealthy family and CEO of a fashion empire, and talk show *über*mama Rosie would open her show with self-deprecating barbs aimed at her closeted past. My daughter would veg out on Saturday-morning cartoons featuring the silly antics of an interspecies coterie focused on a collection of genderless anteaters, merrily growing up and learning love in a communal household.

To some, these fantasies seem terrifyingly real, promising a scary world of gay pervasiveness. To others, these fantasies seem depressingly out-of-reach, revealing the absence of real integration and representation. But imagining a cultural field *radically* different is a must for marginalized groups as utopian fantasizing. These imaginings add an important corrective and reality check for a world in which a few gay characters seems like an avalanche and one gay smooch appears to many as the sign of a kiss-in of epic proportions. The '90s has ushered gays into the family living room via the omniscient tube, but has done so in a way that continues to refuse and avoid gay identity. In making gays palatable to the TV-consuming culture—to the denizens of Ricki Lake and soap operas and sexy yarns—gays have been made invisible in a new way, confined to the roles of straight wannabes or exotic "others." There are the brave and rare exceptions—images of gays that are rich, specific, and varied—but too often gays are trapped in the twin roles of heterosexual look-alikes or deviant outsiders. The intimacy of television proves a rare stage to play out American anxieties—about sex, about class, about race, about gender—and as such it is, in my mind, the site of the most interesting attempts to reckon with the anxiety of sexual difference. In that reckoning, we see the anxiety at work—containing, curtailing, dumbing down, roping off. But in seeing the anxiety, and having it brought into our living rooms, television provides opportunities to move beyond and through the vexing contest between sameness and difference.

PART THREE *Coming Soon to a Theater Near You*

Gosh, I really love you guys.
—Andy Beckett (Tom Hanks) to his family
in *Philadelphia*

Fuck you and fuck Barbra Streisand.
—the jilted fiancée of outed Howard Brackett
(Kevin Kline) in *In & Out*

Six

HIDING, DYING, AND
DRESSING-UP

We tend to think of film as a more "progressive" medium than TV, one step ahead of its slightly outré cousin in exploring the relevant social topics of the day. Yet, in many ways, mainstream Hollywood filmmaking has always been more reluctant to openly and nonstereotypically engage with gay subjects and gay characters. These last years have brought welcome changes, even if those changes have been compromised by both a coyness around gay subject matter and an increasing exploitation of gay life.

THE WAY WE NEVER WERE: A BRIEF HISTORY

The representation of gays in film has a long history, amply documented by the late film historian Vito Russo in his groundbreaking book *The Celluloid Closet*. More often than not, lesbians and gays have been depicted in coded terms, their identity hidden from mainstream viewing and knowable only to the astute (often gay) filmgoer. Otherwise, gays entered the silver screen as tortured, self-loathing creatures of an exotic and dangerous subculture. From prison matrons out to seduce the unjustly incarcerated innocents to limp-wristed dandies plotting government overthrows and familial unrest, the depiction of gays and lesbians was characterized by a plethora of outlandish stereotypes. The other option was a kind of willful and rampant invisibility. Life was indeed often nasty, brutish, and short for the celluloid homosexual.

This is not to say that gay people were completely absent. Here and there a film emerges which actually has a relatively open gay character. But most of those openly gay characters were depicted with all the venom of the times—as mincing and menacing "sissies," as malevolent and preying bull dykes, as tormented spies. So we have the bitter bull dyke of *The Killing of Sister George* and the fey murderers of Hitchcock's *The Rope*. Or the anguished Shirley MacLaine of *The Children's Hour* who kills herself rather than live with the love that dare not speak its name. Or the endless parade of bloodsucking vampires. Or the lesbians murdered and/or married by heterosexual men. Or another suicide in Otto Preminger's *Advise and Consent*. The parade of gays who are killed is almost as long as the parade of gay killers. Gay characters that were clearly marked as gay usually had to die, often to enable the "real" heterosexuals to get on with business (often the business of marriage). As film critic Richard Corliss writes,

> American films—like America itself—have typically treated gays as a joke or a curse. Homosexuality was described as a disease, a mental illness, the most mortal of sins. Its carriers were monsters or, the luckier ones, martyrs. . . . Mostly homosexuals have had nonperson status in movies. What a destiny, in movies or in life: to be either reviled or invisible. Briefly, in the early '30s, gays were familiar screen types: 'pansies' (often played by Franklin Pangborn) for comic relief and, more heroically, bisexual heroines (incarnated by Garbo and Dietrich) who looked thrillingly glamorous in their tuxedos and bachelor togs.[1]

In the context of this Hollywood history of stereotype and invisibility, reading between the lines—or against the grain—often produced richer and more varied images than those to be found in the explicit portrayals of lesbians and gay men—the psychopaths and killers, the mean old dykes and frustrated "spinsters." Russo's book—and the recent film version—beautifully documents these hidden meanings, and argues that they were a product both of a population desperate to see itself represented as well as of writers and directors (such as Gore Vidal) who could only get by the censors through an elaborate and circuitous process of encoding gay content. Gays have always found ways to "read queerly" in a culture that seems to be fixated on either neglect or stereotype.

For many lesbians and gays, representation was something you *created*. Because gays were largely invisible (in other words, not explicitly gay or spoken of as gay), avid filmgoers found ways to read between the lines, and—if need be—to "rewrite" scripts, characters, cinematic moments to create a space for themselves; indeed, "film became a form of 'found' propaganda that the homosexual ransacked for inspiring messages, reconstituting the refuse of popular culture into an energizing force."[2] We witness this process of "reading queerly" when lesbians moon over Marlene Dietrich in *Morocco,* sighing at her tuxedoed kiss of another woman even as she finally walks into the desert in pursuit of her man. And in the famous—not very coded—scene in *Spartacus* (indeed, any scene in *Spartacus* seems over the top homoerotic!) when a young and sultry Tony Curtis is queried as to his preference for oysters or eels. Tough women in cowboy gear (Joan Crawford and Mercedes McCambridge in *Johnny Guitar*), regal women without men (*Queen Christina*), and schoolmarms and their adoring charges (*Maedchen in Uniform*) became icons for lesbian viewers, while sensitive boys in adolescent rebellion (Sal Mineo and James Dean in *Rebel without a Cause*) became icons for gay men, themselves mostly closeted and fearful. Pre-gay-liberation cinema abounds with hidden meaning and coded messages, as well as rampant stereotypes.

The recent release of the film version of *The Celluloid Closet* vividly illustrates the ways in which gayness was "read into" films endlessly, by gay men and lesbians whose exclusion from the central world of the cinema provided only more additional evidence of second-class status. Receiving universal applause, this film charts both the obvious and more hidden images of gays in Hollywood film. Its release during these transformative times is telling, holding open to public view the embarrassing history of Hollywood homophobia. Clearly, lesbians and gays no longer have to face a cinema of invisibility or even a cinema of coded and hidden meanings. Gays are explicitly visible and present in a way that has never before been even imagined. As film critic David Ansen notes,

> According to Hollywood, homosexuality officially did not exist between the years 1934 and 1961. During those 27 years, the Motion Picture Production Code saw to it that any depiction of 'sex perversion' was banished from the screen. Is it any wonder that the love that dare not speak its name has, lately, been hollering from the rooftops? At the recent Sundance Film Festival in Utah, lesbian characters were so ubiquitous on screen that gay film critic Ruby Rich quipped, 'We're this year's Jack Russell terriers.' And this was less than an hour away from Salt Lake City, where, before passing anti-gay legislation, the Utah Senate met secretly to watch a lurid anti-gay propaganda film.[3]

Indeed, the release of the long-awaited (and ten years in the making) *Celluloid Closet* became the opportunity for no small amount of reflection on the history of gays in film and on the current situation as well. Literally hundreds of reviews and review essays emerged commenting favorably (to a one) on the film but also going further to indict Hollywood for its refusal to openly, actively, and nonstereotypically engage with lesbians and gays as cinematic characters.

One of the most interesting aspects of the "explosion" of gay films in the '90s is not the films themselves, but the varied and engaged commentary on them. Newspapers, magazines, industry journals, and newsletters regularly report on the dilemmas of depicting homosexuality in the cinema and publish quite stinging denunciations of Hollywood homophobia. Mainstream publications such as *Time* and *Newsweek* have published numerous critical pieces condemning the rampant homophobia and self-censorship of Hollywood film executives and urging more nuanced, diverse portrayals of lesbian and gay life.

The attention to gays as a mis- and underrepresented minority marks a shift for the popular press, a shift perhaps more important than the relatively few gay-related films actually made during this supposed gay boom. This new focus on Hollywood's reluctance to treat gay subject matter with depth and dignity has also focused new attention on gay filmmakers and the independent film industry as a point of comparison.

Certainly, gays have been present in film before the '90s. The development of a political and open gay movement in the late '60s and early '70s forced some degree of representation out of a reluctant Hollywood. *The Boys in the Band* (1970) was probably the first full-scale, fully gay-themed film, adapted from the off-Broadway play of the same name. Filled with self-deprecating wit and truckloads of self-hatred, it was nevertheless a breakthrough film and in some ways the end of an era—depicting a kind of stereotyped, witty, bitchy, nonpolitical gay man that was to be radically challenged by the Stonewall events the prior year and their aftermath. Two other films are considered "breakthrough" films: "mainstream" Hollywood movies that sympathetically and quite forthrightly placed gay relationships on center stage. Both those films, *Making Love* (starring Harry Hamlin and Michael Ontkean) and *Desert Hearts,* were not exactly boffo box-office-wise. Indeed, *Making Love* was a dismal failure and was difficult to make, as one male star after another turned down the opportunity to "play gay" and reports of horrified hetero audiences storming out of theaters kept box-office sales down. Other films periodically entered the fray, including John Sayles's quirky *Lianna,* and the awful jock-drama *Personal Best,* but very few seemed to make a mark on the broader cultural imagination, although gay audiences flocked to these failed films. Indeed, *Personal Best* has become a sort of legend in the lesbian community (even Ellen is heard to utter "I never should have watched *Personal Best*" in the famous coming-out episode) and lesbian viewers have been quick to construct alternative endings to the "lesbian finds true love with a sexist man" theme of the overt narrative. Even Harvey Fierstein's odious film version of his Broadway hit *Torch Song Trilogy* came and went rather quickly. In films in which there were explicitly gay characters, they were often either saved from their homosexuality by true love of the opposite sex (*Personal Best*), killed/stalked/beaten (*Cruising*), or filled with self-hatred and internalized homophobia (*Boys in the Band*).

There are some notable pre-gay '90s exceptions to the endless parade of comic swishes and mannish tough girls. Al Pacino's star turn as the gay bank robber/lover of a pre-op transsexual in the brilliant *Dog Day Afternoon* and William Hurt's Oscar-winning role as the imprisoned gay cinephile in *Kiss of the Spider Woman* were thoughtful, complex, rich depictions of gay identity, although many critics (Russo included) found *Dog Day* a "freak show." Smaller, independent and foreign films such as *Prick Up Your Ears, My Beautiful Launderette,* and *Parting Glances* were also notable exceptions.

While gay-themed films and gay characters are not exactly filling the multiplex movie malls of American suburbia, there does appear to be a marked increase in the numbers of films containing gay characters. A "critical mass" has developed, so that gay-themed films no longer exist as rare and financially risky outposts in the barren desert of heterosexual romance, but rather begin to refer to each other, to construct a "genre" or a group of films that engage actively in a dialogue with other mainstream entertainment. In an era of newly acquired visibility, the depiction of gays is not simply hidden or circuitous or restricted to a few choice stereotypes, although to say that there is an "outpouring" would be an overstatement.

It is curious—and revealing—that the very existence of *any* openly gay-themed films immediately produces breathless reports on the overwhelming tide of gay life that is flooding American cinema. Still, they are only a handful. Still, gays are mostly present as secondary "others" (what I discuss below as the "incidental queer") and are hardly the fully developed, fully sexual, fully human characters that gays have been clamoring for for years. And still, most representations of gays emerge from the independent film industry, and either then make a "cross-over" or are picked up for mainstream distribution.

Many attribute the rise of gay-themed films to the power of the pocketbook. Niche marketing has become commonplace, as TV, cable, print media, and film increasingly seek to tap into and even create specific audiences for specific "products." As lesbian chic and trendy drag queens emerge into the commercial world, the marketing of gay images to both gays and straights becomes good business. So, clearly, one can understand the recent "emergence" of gay films not necessarily as a sign of greater "acceptance" or even of the assimilation of gay life into visual culture, but rather as an aspect of the commodification of just about everything. In that sense—gay films as good business—this becomes less of an epoch-shifting trend and more of a consumer marketing moment (and thus possibly less lasting).

Many of these films are not only being marketed to a gay audience but are clearly being marketed to a straight audience as well. A *New York Times* article discussed the recent bumper crop of gay-themed films and raised the issue of marketing gay films to a straight audience. The author of the piece, Howard Feinstein, details the transformation from an early-'80s Hollywood that produced the flop *Making Love* to the '90s surge of successful gay-themed films such as *Philadelphia*. As he reviews the numerous gay-themed films then in production (including *Jeffrey; To Wong Foo, Thanks for Everything, Julie Newmar; Falsettos; The Mayor of Castro Street*), Feinstein reveals the paradoxes inherent in contemporary culture. Should these new films be marketed as "gay," risking the loss of a heterosexual audience? Or should a broad appeal be sought, downplaying the gay aspects of a film and shooting for box-office payoffs?

In searching for that "broad market," stereotypes of gays and lesbians are often invoked. Regarding the movie *Priscilla, Queen of the Desert*, Feinstein quotes the head of Gramercy Films, who asserts, "It's not a gay picture. It's not about gay love. There's no sex in it. The last thing I want to do is ghettoize it. There is nothing that you'll see in the materials that we create that is necessarily gay." The trajectory here is telling: a gay picture is seen as one that has gay sex in it, implying that gay life is solely marked by sexual practices. Is a film "heterosexual" only when there is a heterosexual sex scene? The film president is eager to distance himself from the "gay ghetto," but, in doing so, he invokes stereotypes that help to keep gays ghettoized.

There is no question, though, that things are opening up. Nevertheless, as in TV, it would be naive to believe that both overt and—more generally—covert censorship doesn't still exist. There is no longer a production code that specifically rules certain images out of existence. However, Hollywood's seeming embrace of gay themes is both cautious and limited. One critic interviews several filmmakers, including the writer-director Randal Kleiser, who argues that a kind of self-censorship becomes the preferable mode in this changing but cautious climate: "'There were never any suggestions from the distributor (MGM/United Artists) about cutting scenes,' Kleiser says of *It's My Party*, which stars Eric Roberts as the dying host and Gregory Harrison as his film maker ex-lover. 'But I myself took out an early love scene that showed the two men in bed together. I didn't want to preach to the converted. I wanted to grab people that might not stay if they saw a scene like that.'"[4] Jonathan Demme and other "sympathetic" filmmakers have been heard to utter similar statements, balancing an honest and well-rounded depiction of gay identity with the desire to reach a heterosexual audience presumably uneasy with any depiction of gay sexuality.

There is now a large and active and engaged gay movement that assiduously examines Hollywood's images of gays and rapidly responds to those thought to be gratuitously stereotypical or violent or otherwise reprehensible. The work of a group like GLAAD (the Gay and Lesbian Alliance Against Defamation) cannot be overestimated; its very existence changes the representational frame, as does the presence of a gay community and culture that is out and proud. If, in the early days of Hollywood films, anti-gay images abounded but could not be challenged because of the pervasive culture of invisibility and the firmness of the closet door, now these images (which of course still exist) are challenged vigorously and aggressively by a gay political community that can name itself and thus engage with the more public naming that is Hollywood entertainment. Thus, the kind of outright and explicit homophobia that characterized earlier Hollywood images is no longer everyday business, which is not to say that homophobic images do not still exist. But— and this is a point I am trying to make throughout this book—homophobia *itself* changes and mutates and transforms in the presence of a culture of the visible. It is surely different to produce films in an era of gay visibility.

THE *PHILADELPHIA* STORY

No film so illustrates the "paradox of visibility" as the 1993 hit film *Philadelphia*, about a young lawyer battling both AIDS and a homophobic law firm. The film, an enormous mainstream success garnering an Oscar for lead Tom Hanks, provoked no small amount of controversy in the gay press and among gay activists. Deliberately marketed as a "straight" film about AIDS, *Philadelphia* chose the path of least resistance in its attempt to reach a heterosexual audience. As much as *Philadelphia* might have been groundbreaking (and it was to some extent), Hollywood had waited almost fifteen years to make a film about AIDS. The gay man was played by heterosexual star Tom Hanks, his male lover was marginalized (and played by another straight man, heartthrob Antonio Banderas), and the film portrayed its villains and heroes in black-and-white terms: the homophobic corporate lawyers vs. the loving and accepting family members. Not only did this ring false to many gays (it is often in our families that we experience the most hatred and abandonment), but the absence of any gay culture or gay politics was annoying to many filmgoers. Gay activist and author Larry Kramer wrote a vitriolic "review" of *Philadelphia* that excoriated it on every possible grounds. Kramer, a playwright and AIDS activists, first criticizes Hollywood for waiting so long to make a film about AIDS, and then finally making a film that "doesn't have anything to do with the AIDS I know, or with the gay world I know. It doesn't bear any truthful resemblance to the life, world and universe I live in."[5] Kramer harshly dumps on the movie from every angle, taking apart its black-and-white portrayal of brave gays and their homophobic counterparts, lashing out at the medical and legal inaccuracies (was there no other lawyer Andy could find? What about all the gay legal organizations and AIDS advocacy groups?), and calling the leading man an "utter cipher" who doesn't seem to have any beliefs, values, opinions at all. More than anything, Kramer is furious at the film for completely ignoring the role of the government in evading, denying, and generally avoiding meaningfully dealing with this crisis. And he rejects the "old chestnut" that middle America would not go to a serious, thoughtful film about AIDS, thus rejecting too the "lowest common denominator" thesis that seems to govern much of entertainment decision-making.

The Advocate, a national gay weekly, criticized the film for its pandering to stereotypes and its patronizing attitude toward gays. Many reviewers—both gay and straight—have argued that the film, for all its good intentions, still desexualized homosexuality. Andy and his lover Miguel are never shown displaying physical intimacy (except for a brief dance at Halloween), even when the heterosexual couple are given such moments. Clearly, this is no accident. Indeed, bedroom scenes were shot and then cut in the service of mainstreaming. The directors made a choice: this was to be a film about AIDS (and to a lesser extent about homophobia) that wanted to attract a middle-America, "unhip" audience. The casting of Tom Hanks is significant, as he himself wryly noted when interviewed for *The Celluloid Closet.* Boy-next-door Tom Hanks would be the perfect actor to make homosexuality safe, accessible, and unthreatening. *Philadelphia* envisioned a desexualized, apolitical gay man as sympathy point, and a homophobic lawyer as point of identification.

Significantly, the controversy stretched beyond the gay community and the gay press. In discussing the phenomenal success of the movie, *Time* film critic Richard Corliss notes Kramer's attack and points out that "among homosexuals all over the country, the film was stoking an agitated debate. Their central questions: Is the movie accurate? Is it good for gays? And does its success mean a more gay-friendly cinema—one that admits to the existence and humanity of this besieged minority?"[6]

In *Philadelphia,* gay martyrs find common cause with recalcitrant bigoted lawyers, but little common life with other gays. Courtesy of Photofest.

And herein is the dilemma. In producing a film that featured non-gay actors (and that carefully avoided the complex world of gay culture), this film was able to reach and perhaps enlighten a straight audience as to the horrors both of AIDS and of homophobia. But in doing so—in humanizing the gay character and rendering him more an Everyman who happens to be gay than a gay man—the film runs the risk of assimilating to the point of absorption. Too often, a sympathetic gay character is made somehow "not gay" in order to be watched by millions of heterosexual viewers. This is reminiscent of the charges levied against *The Cosby Show*—that its phenomenal success was dependent on the invisibility of black culture. If *The Cosby Show* was *Father Knows Best* in blackface, is *Philadelphia* perhaps *Inherit the Wind* in drag? Or is it rather the breakthrough film of the decade—the first blockbuster film that sympathetically portrayed a gay man? For, surely, the film did break new ground. The gay man was neither simpering villain nor swishing object of amusement. In other words, he was not a stereotype (although he *did* have a fondness for opera). And homophobia was addressed and certainly depicted as "wrong" if not substantively challenged. Gay men with AIDS—so typically either portrayed as wasted martyrs or as reckless sex fiends—are here portrayed with both dignity and agency—not the passive victims of a disease but actors in their own complex lives. But what is lost when sympathy towards a gay person with AIDS is predicated on a depoliticization and a desexualization that renders both the gayness and the disease almost *too* generic and universal? Are viewers given a cathartic moment of identification and empathy that carefully avoids any self-examination or even any examination of the homophobia of others?

And what of these presumably heterosexual viewers (for obviously the film was aimed at a straight audience)? Viewers are clearly meant to see themselves not in Andy, the dying gay man, but in Joe Miller (Denzel Washington), the straight lawyer who reluctantly takes the case. The sympathy of the audience is transported through the identification with the initially homophobic and AIDS-paranoid Joe, as he moves into understanding as a champion of Andy's case. So viewers can gain "understanding" of a gay man through an experiential identification with a homophobic straight man, thus avoiding a more challenging (and unnerving) identification with the gay man himself.

CROSS-DRESSING FOR SUCCESS

If brave gay martyrs emerged as heroes of the nineties, then cross-dressing, straight-talking drag queens emerged as our national Dear Abbys—providing sassy but affectionate insight into the vicissitudes of heterosexual romance. It is telling that the recent boom in gay-themed films should so gratuitously feature cross-dressing as the metaphor of choice. Filmmaker Jeffrey Friedman (*The Celluloid Closet*) claims that "it certainly seems that America loves drag queens."

As Friedman and others have noted, the curious cultural fascination with drag and cross-dressing does not necessarily entail a challenge to traditional definitions of gender. Indeed, it is striking that the most commercially popular film about drag starred two hypermacho action heroes (*To Wong Foo, Thanks for Everything, Julie Newmar,* starring Patrick Swayze and Wesley Snipes), whose endless interviews tirelessly asserted their stalwart heterosexuality as well as their newfound sensitivity to "difference." As in one of the other recent drag hits—the Nichols and May film revival of the '70s breakthrough *La Cage aux Folles*—male drag performers are presented as nonthreatening homebodies at heart, family gals who desire nothing less (or more) than the reconstitution of heterosexual bliss. In *To Wong Foo,* and also in *The Birdcage* (the story of a gay couple who run a drag club and the wacky confusion caused when their son announces his engagement to the daughter of a right-wing senator), gay men are desexualized through drag (*homo* but not *sexual*), and are primarily oriented towards uniting young heterosexual lovers. In the process, they gently tickle stereotypes, and ridicule bigotry. Fair enough. But at what cost? *The Birdcage* appears to put a gay twist on family values, depicting the gay male couple as the everloving parents in the face of right-wing "family values" yahoos. But the "can't we all just get along?"

liberalism is constructed on the bent backs of gay fathers (proving their love through self-abnegation and denial), and the arrogant shoulders of straight sons (proving their privilege through requesting the denial). The gay family may indeed be the only decent one in this film, yet its members are required to dissimulate, lie, and hurt each other in their quest for heterosexual "acceptance." And, strangely, the gay couple are not at all updated from the original 1978 version: "Old swish stereotypes to begin with, they make even less sociological sense in South Beach two decades later. Babyboomers Armand and Albert behave in the queenly, asexual style of an older generation of gay men. Of course we know the real reason for this: two men kissing is a box-office no-no."[7]

Indeed, even the straight press read the success of *The Birdcage* ($18.2 million in its first weekend) less as "evidence that old-fashioned Hollywood liberalism has staged a remarkable comeback" and more as "an indication of the popularity of comedy in general and Robin Williams in particular."[8] Anne Thompson, of *Entertainment Weekly* magazine, argued that "the success of 'Birdcage' is less a public affirmation of the gay lifestyle than the quest for a good laugh . . . it's entirely unthreatening. It's one of the great reassuring gay comedies.'"[9] Richard Corliss writes that "this gently supportive comedy about gays, a sweet parable of family values, is no more threatening to mainstream American sensibilities than the pro-Indian Pocahontas. Maybe once a year, a big studio trots out a big picture with similarly sympathetic gay characters in leading roles: *To Wong Foo, Thanks for Everything, Julie Newmar* last year, *Philadelphia* before that. Is this enough to constitute enlightenment?"[10] While "the film is bold enough to propose the integration of gays—and by extension of anyone 'different' . . . this may be a part of Hollywood's continuing reluctance to confront the issue. As exotics—drag queens or dying swans—gays are fine fodder for movies. But Hollywood sees little need to show that the vast majority of gays are ordinary, reasonably complicated people. They are the folks who work next to you at the steel press or in the sales office."[11] And the reconciliation at the end (between the gay couple and the heterosexual homophobic couple) is predicated on a desexualization of the gay couple and a merger of hetero and homo in the wacky and wonderful world of drag.

To Wong Foo, Thanks for Everything, Julie Newmar, follows our cross-dressing entourage on a cross-country road trip gone bad, as drag divas Noxeema Jackson and Vida Boheme pick up drag diva wannabe Chi Chi Rodriguez and head off to Vegas for a big ball. On the way, they get accosted by a nasty cop, bop him on the head, and, thinking he is dead, hit the road—only to have their convertible break down plump in a middle-American small town, replete with off-beat residents and rough youth.

In *To Wong Foo,* the men are even more desexualized than in *The Birdcage* and are also primarily engaged in the reconstitution of heterosexual romance. The older and wiser drag queens Vida and Noxeema (played by Patrick Swayze and Wesley Snipes) become the tough-love parents to drag ingénue Chi Chi (played by John Leguizamo). But their tough love entails encouraging Chi Chi to relinquish the hold he has on a good-hearted country bumpkin in order to unite said bumpkin with an appropriate young woman. Chi Chi becomes fully accepted into the "family" only when he proves his mettle by denying his own sexual and emotional needs and desires. Of course, the other characters are equally de-gayed and de-sexualized, or rather this is gayness depicted solely as fashion statement.

By plumping the drag queens down in Middle America, the film intends to both use the exotica and contain it simultaneously. For it is the exotica that provides the narrative movement: how will the townsfolk respond to the queens in their midst? Yet the difference is contained on multiple levels; first, by desexualizing the men, and second by assimilating them fairly easily into the gestalt of the town. Homophobia is almost completely invisible, although it begins as a motivating factor. A few townsfolk are initially hostile but by film's end they are partying with the queens, protecting them from the farcical forces of the law, and clearly better people for their encounter with "the other."

As in so much of contemporary popular culture, homophobia itself is downplayed or isolated, never depicted as the insidious, ever-present, life-threatening reality that it is. Homophobia is reduced to small-minded bigotry, bigotry that can be cured by a personal encounter with a gay person (or a de-gayed drag queen). Indeed, the end of the film reiterates the opening drag show, first confined to an all-gay ball, now opened up to the accepting heterosexual world. The heterosexuals save the homosexuals by associating themselves with them ("I'm a drag queen," says one elderly woman to the cop who comes to arrest them). The resonance with a seemingly more serious film such as *Philadelphia* is striking. Homophobia is depoliticized and decontextualized by reducing it to the bigotry and/or ignorance that results from simply not knowing any gay people personally. Just get to know me, these films seem to say, and you will surely "accept" me.

In films and in popular culture generally, drag becomes a safe and circuitous way of dealing with gay subjects without having to reckon with the homophobia of heterosexual society. As *Tales of the City* writer Armistead Maupin says, "We're back to a time when the sissy is acceptable again. I'm not sure if that's progress. My dream is to see gays in our infinite variety, including sissies. I just resent the way Hollywood cur-

In *To Wong Foo, Thanks for Everything, Julie Newmar,* drag queens are a girl's best friend and a town's redemption, showing the clear path to love and acceptance through self-abnegating desexualization. Courtesy of Photofest.

rently implies homosexuality is about what one wears, not what one feels. I'm not against the current wave of drag movies, every one of them delivers a message about compassion and humanity. But until they're done in a way that really deals about [*sic*] what people hate about homosexuality, the physicality of same-sex affection, they'll feel more like exploitation than honest examinations of human lives."[12] Or, as Jeffrey Friedman notes, "America loves drag queens, they're nonthreatening, amusing clowns because they're nonsexual. Hollywood gay characters are allowed to be like normal people as long as they don't have a sex life. It's particularly ironic to take sexuality away from a gay character when that's what defines us."[13] Surprisingly, even mainstream film critics and culture vultures voiced criticism about the recent embrace of drag. David Ansen, writing about gay films for *Newsweek,* argues that "Hollywood has embraced cross-dressing as the safest way to pitch gayness to a mass audience. Drag queens are the cinema's favorite naughty pets, harmless if not quite housebroken."[14]

IS IT MY PARTY?: AMONG THE OTHERS

If Hollywood consistently depicts gays as witty, happy adjuncts to a blissfully unexamined heterosexual life, it has also now begun to show gays as having other gay friends, a community even, existing for each other and not just for the amusement of hetero buddies. Typically, it has only been in independent films that gays have existed as anything other than tokens, but that is now beginning to change. Of course, dramas about AIDS signify heavily here, for it is difficult (although *Philadelphia* certainly attempted it!) to portray the crisis of AIDS without in some fashion reckoning with a gay cultural and social context. *Longtime Companion* was one of the first, followed by *It's My Party, Jeffrey, Love! Valour! Compassion!* and others. These films are interesting, in that they give us an intimation of what Hollywood imagines gay *life* to be, not simply what Hollywood imagines a gay *character* to be. Many of these films are refreshing and encouraging in that they finally offer up gays who partner, gays who are single, gays who cruise; gays who have deep and lasting friendships with other gays. Indeed, to see a community of some kind being depicted is a huge move away from the tokenism that inevitably marginalizes gays as it subtly reasserts the centrality of heterosexuals to both heterosexual and gay life.[15]

Nevertheless, it is telling that the "gay life" films (the mainstream ones, not necessarily the independent films) almost to a one center around AIDS. Is it that Hollywood cannot imagine gays having an autonomous culture and community that is not in crisis? Would that be *too* normal? While the AIDS dramas are sympathetic and certainly endeavor to enlighten and tug the heartstrings, isn't it also true that the very *difference* of a life-threatening illness must always set them apart? So, in some sense, gay community as such is not being shown at all, but rather the community of AIDS sufferers and their caretakers.

One of the best is one the earliest, *Longtime Companion,* made in 1991 and one of the first mainstream attempts to deal with the AIDS crisis and, most importantly, to situate the crisis in the context of gay male life. While a moving and gentle film, *Longtime Companion* is relentlessly "positive" in its depiction of handsome, white, bourgeois gay men bravely fighting an ominous disease, replete with scenes of a luxurious and decadent Fire Island idyll. There is, however, a wonderful scene in this film, where the group is gathered to watch the first gay kiss on TV between two male soap stars, one of whom figures in the group. As they watch the kiss, they begin to comment on their new status as chic and fashionable even as the crisis of AIDS looms large and as straights watch in horror/disbelief as storefront TVs broadcast the "gay kiss." Nonetheless, for all the tunnel vision of its white and upper-class view of gay life, we do see gay men living with and loving each other, rather than living lives centered around heterosexuals. And we even witness the realities of gay political activism when uptight lawyers are seen volunteering at New York's Gay Men's Health Crisis and changing the diapers of ill friends.

Love! Valour! Compassion! is the 1997 answer to *Longtime Companion,* moving with a group of gay male friends through the trajectory of their lives and the trajectory of the virus as it hones in on this particular group. Updated for the late nineties with a more multicultural cast (albeit tokenized) and more obvious gay wit, this film does—like its earlier counterpart—place the viewer in an assuredly gay world.

In *It's My Party,* a hunky AIDS-sufferer played by Eric Roberts gathers his friends and ex-lovers around him for a final celebration before he kills himself. Friends and family gather, rekindling old loves and reawakening old hurts. Like the discourse around *The Birdcage,* the buzz about this film included the usual odes to diversity. A CNN story featured Nathan Lane of *Birdcage,* Tamra King of GLAAD, and Gregory Harrison of *It's My Party,* who argued that "this film is about issues that are much more eternal and much bigger than that—like dignity, grace, closure, friendship, and family."[16]

A more recent version of the gay buddy movie, *The Broken Hearts Club,* premiered at gay film festivals and then segued into mainstream release in the fall of 2000. Like its TV counterpart *Queer as Folk, The Broken Hearts Club* broke ground by depicting a group of gay friends and abjuring the token and asexual roles typically reserved for gays. But, like *Queer as Folk, Broken Hearts* does so in a way that renders these friendships empty and meaningless, reveling in the "friends as family" mystique while denuding it of any substantive intimacy or engagement. Indeed, when the mother-hen figure of the film (played by *Frasier* dad John Mahoney) dies, this supposedly tight-knit group of friends don't even know the name of his longtime partner. These films and TV shows traffic in glib types (the sexy slut, the young neophyte, the queen), none more

In these gay-life movies, all the gays are men, all of them have nice houses, and most of them are white. Courtesy of Photofest.

offensive than the token black gay queen who is played for over-the-top laughs or (like his counterparts in other gay buddy films such as *Love! Valour! Compassion!*) ogled as oversexualized fetish objects.

One of the things that characterizes these few feature films that actually delve into some semblance of gay life is that they have all been fairly abject failures. While these "gay life" movies may seem to be the ultimate crossover successes, they do miserably at the box office compared to those films in which gays are depicted as witty, incidental, asexual accessories to heterosexual plotlines. *Jeffrey, Love! Valour! Compassion!, Go Fish, The Broken Hearts Club, High Art,* and others have all grossed well under $5 million while films such as *My Best Friend's Wedding* grossed over $125 million and *As Good as It Gets* grossed over $145 million. These are not films that registered on the cultural body politic. They

Jeffrey is too buff, too sexy, too gay. Courtesy of Photofest.

didn't make a dent in our national consciousness. Now, clearly, this is not because of the subject of AIDS. Hollywood loves a good tragedy, and the phenomenal success of *Philadelphia* indicates that tear-jerking heterosexuals on the way to consciousness is good box office. So why did all these other films fail so spectacularly?

Jeffrey, by all accounts, *should* have been a big success. Written by hot gay writer Paul Rudnick (who scored big with the infinitely more acceptable *In & Out*), *Jeffrey* tells the story of a young man in New York whose fear of AIDS and what it has done to the pleasures of sex impels him to swear off sex indefinitely. With lots of direct address, witty urbane humor, and nonrealistic Greek choruses imploring Jeffrey to have sex, this film has charm and no small amount of daring in its satirizing of both gay and straight responses to AIDS. But the failure of the film surely must rest on its resolute gayness, its refusal to see Jeffrey's dilemma through the eyes of heterosexuals, its insistence on a broadly gay world, where every waiter and caterer and jock is a wink away from Christopher Street.

Not only do gay men live in a gay world here, but they actively desire as well. We watch as agonized Jeffrey gazes longingly at the ample crotch of his object of desire, a hunk of a bartender who happens to be HIV+. We hear the dish and snap of gay men cruising each other during a memorial service. What we see of heterosexuals is minimal—they are do-gooding socialites at a hoedown for AIDS or befuddled moms marching with their pre-op sons at Pride or grossed out teenagers positioned as the audience of *Jeffrey* viewing a same-sex kiss.

Heterosexuals in *Jeffrey* play the outsiders to a rich and somewhat varied (although still resolutely white and male) gay life that includes a stylish interior decorator (played with aplomb by Patrick Stewart of *Star Trek* fame), his lower-class *Cats* boyfriend, and a desperately horny, show-tune-enamored gay priest played by Nathan Lane. While not exactly a cross-section of gay difference, the film does show moments of political savvy, as when the gay patrol group "the pink panthers" shows its face, or during a gay-bashing scene, or at a Pride march. But the ribald *Jeffrey*, replete with well-known actors, high production values, and established writers, failed at the box office, alongside the other "gay life" films. These failures reveal the limits of liberal tolerance. Gays are good box office when they are sick, but alone. Gays are good box office when they are coming out, but not when they are already there. Gays are good box office when they primarily relate to heterosexuals, not to each other. Even the films we will examine next promote their liberal agenda of "tolerance" through an often subtle reworking of gay identity that renders it asexual, passive, and deeply alone.

Seven   OUT IS IN: LIBERAL
NARRATIVES FOR
THE NINETIES

While drag queens and dying victims still serve as popular icons in the Hollywood imagination, the visual field continues to transform. As the AIDS crisis became routinized and a part of the background of American culture and drag became domesticated, Hollywood films edged a bit further in their continual quest to represent "gayness." While undoubtedly the major form of representation is what I discuss below as the "incidental queer," gays have come to figure more centrally in the prominent plots and relationships that make up mainstream films.

But, of course, we must remember that at the same time that these liberal narratives of gay inclusion are being proffered by Hollywood, more dangerous illiberal narratives of the gay threat are being offered by an increasingly hostile segment of our political culture. It is easy to look at the proliferation of these liberal "gay-positive" films and feel assured that they signal a fundamental shift in the cultural body politic. To a certain extent, of course, they do. But these liberal films of gay goodness are played out in the same cultural milieu that brings us the Defense of Marriage Act and the California Knight Initiative.

One of the more interesting aspects of nineties images of lesbians and gays is the way in which, quite often, gays have come to figure as the sites upon which large moral and ethical issues of good and evil, justice and decency get played out. If gays no longer serve quite so easily as the signs of cultural decadence or social unrest or threats to the family, then they are strangely situated as the space of the reconstitution of family life (*The Object of My Affection*) or individual identity. It is refreshing to see gay characters as decent, loving human beings who are not homicidal serial killers, suicidal losers, or angst-ridden closet cases. Yet the introduction of the "good gay" in film, like in television, often depends on a desexualization and loss of community. Heterosexual characters can be valorous, brave, noble without being stripped of passion and desire. In other words, the emergence of the new good gay reveals to us both how far we have come (gays are no longer the easy and obvious choice for villain) and how steadfastly double standards still prevail.

In *As Good as It Gets*, obsessive-compulsive writer and all-around meanie Jack Nicholson gets "saved" by the love of a good woman *and* the friendship of a good fag. The traditional romantic story line of curmudgeonly antisocial man given humanity by the warm and down-to-earth *über*mama is updated now to use the victimized homosexual to educate and humanize the arrogant straight man. To be fair, the performance by Greg Kinnear as the mugged and abandoned gay artist is rich and textured, and he is allowed more than the typical "incidental queer" in his thorough integration into the plot. But it is a plot that, like so many integrations, is not really his own. Romantic love is not his to have, and while he is a sympathetic character, he largely serves as an agent for others' desires and developments: primarily to humanize homophobic Jack and nudge him toward his love for the saintly Helen Hunt. He is confidant to both the macho, neurotic bigot and the sainted waitress, who reciprocate by taking him in when he is brutalized. His gay friends, at least the few we do see, clearly abandon him, so that he has no recourse but the brutal and homophobic stranger next door whose heart of gold he helps uncover (with the waitress of course). While outwardly a warm-hearted tale of mutual aid and friendship, upon closer examination films such as these reveal a gay character unable to act for himself, unable to maintain relationships with other gays, unable to do anything other than support floundering heterosexual love.

In *& Out*, a successful comedy starring Kevin Kline, perfectly exemplifies this liberal mode. Inspired by the "real-life" Oscar moment of Tom Hanks in which he thanks his gay teacher for inspiring him to play the role of the lawyer with AIDS in *Philadelphia,* this film tells the story of Howard Brackett, beloved high-school English teacher in Anytown, Indiana, whose movie-star protégé Cameron (campily played by Matt Dillon) "outs" him on Oscar night. Performed in high comic mode (and with hilarious "scenes" from the fictional Oscar-winning film *To Serve and*

Protect) the film is a feel-good, funny skewering of stereotypes, uniting family and friends in support of the beleaguered and confused Howard, now faced with soul-searching on the eve of his wedding to fellow teacher and former fat girl, Emily. Like so many of these recent well-meaning films, the gay character provides an opportunity for others to confront their own closets. There is an hysterical scene after Howard has come out at the altar in which a group of elderly women in full wedding regalia are sitting around amidst the detritus of the abandoned wedding, speaking of their own hidden stories, from revelations of stolen cookie receipts to husbands with three testicles. That gay honesty can inspire others to be more open is not in itself a problem. And the insistence that the problems of the gay closet have "universal" parallels in other forms of dissimulation is important as a corrective to our vexing inability to see gay rights as similar to other civil rights issues. However, what can and does often get lost here is the specificity of the closet and of the repercussions entailed in disavowing it. Making connections between forms of discrimination and patterns of denial is important, but need not be done at the expense of reckoning with the specific nature of homophobia and the unique experience of the closet.

The film also creates a vision of a fundamentally embracing and accepting public, one not seriously challenged by the revelation of homosexuality. While students cringe and the weasely principal acts unprincipled, all come around in the end in a love-fest finale of heteros and homos dancing to the disco beat . . . at the "wedding" of Howard's parents that has replaced the aborted one of Howard and Emily. In the pivotal scene that occurs after Howard has come out at the altar, he slips onto the stage at the high school graduation after having been fired by the weasel principal, and witnesses his award as "teacher of the year" summarily passed on to another. While he sits by—ostracized and on the sidelines—hetero but artistic protégé Cameron marches into the school and leads the students and townies in a rousing gay rendition of "Ich bin ein Berliner" (I am a Berliner—from Kennedy's 1963 speech at the Berlin Wall). As student after student gets up to declare their gayness in the face of the principal's bigotry, they are joined by Howard's parents, brother, the fire fighters, the local barber, until the entire auditorium is "coming out" in solidarity with their benighted and bemused hero. While it is gratifying to see the support and entirely appropriate in this feel-good flick, the film creates a false sense of solidarity. I can't help but think of the real-life lesbians terrorized by their small-town compatriots in Ovett, Mississippi, who received no such local support.

In addition, all the gay person has to do is "be honest about himself" and the more active work of challenging homophobia can be done by heterosexual comrades. Howard remains passive throughout, even urging everyone to sit down once the show of solidarity begins. He gets kissed by a man (Tom Selleck as a slick but adorable gay reporter) and obviously enjoys it but doesn't himself do any kissing. His gayness is the simple absence of heterosexual desire (why won't he sleep with his fiancée?) and the presence of "obvious" signs (tidiness, disco fever dancing feet, sensitivity, literateness). While the film is witty enough to send up and embrace gay stereotypes (English-teaching, neat-dressing, Streisand-loving, disco-dancing, girl-avoiding) and challenge heteromasculinity (in full panic mode, Howard takes to listening to "Exploring Your Masculinity" audiotapes, which insist on crotch-grabbing and flannel shirts as ultimate signs of real man status—"At all costs, avoid rhythm, grace, and pleasure . . ."), it also embraces a kind of liberalism that disempowers gay activism and promotes a naive and illusory vision of small-town togetherness.

In & Out does the same thing Wong Foo does in having the small-town folks transformed from roughneck bigots to swishing mimics of homosexual men. The focus is on the ease with which bigots can be transformed and learn the errors of their ways, making homophobia fairly benign. Also, in both films, the moment of transformation is signified by the claiming of homosexuality by the hetero small towners. Straights, it seems, can only fight homophobia by joining homosexuality. It also aligns with the narrative of Philadelphia, which centers the anti-discrimination rhetoric around the workplace, avoiding the more contentious issues of discrimination found in familial issues and rights. Like Philadelphia, it functions as an all-American "'right to work' narrative in which a homosexual is fired from a job for his orientation and is later shown to be a valuable contributor to the country and his profession."[1] And, like Philadelphia, this film was hyped as a breakthrough, primarily because of the kiss between Selleck and Kline. As Neal Karlen reports, though, the film "does little to correlate gayness to gay sex" and "seems no more subversive than a rerun of 'Spartacus,' and its core resembles the Hollywood screwball schmaltz of Preston Sturges or Frank Capra far more than any overt work of sexual politics."[2]

Other films with the same liberal tenor are more courageous. I think here particularly of a film like Flawless, starring Robert DeNiro as a played-out macho ex-cop living in the same building with drag artiste Rusty, played brilliantly by Philip Seymour Hoffman. While a formulaic film with a contrived plot, it differs from its cross-dressing for success predecessors by its insistence on depicting the gay man as having a life, having a community, and certainly uninterested in the arduous and thankless task of educating the curmudgeonly bigot. Indeed, when the DeNiro char-

In & Out is the perfect liberal film for the '90s, gently exploiting stereotypes and promoting "acceptance" while giving all the brave lines to enlightened heterosexuals. Courtesy of Photofest.

acter yells homophobic epithets at his loud gay neighbors, Rusty yells right back, telling him precisely where to shove his homophobic thoughts. So Hoffman's character is not simply a desexualized, exoticized conduit for straight awareness, but rather a complex gay man with confused desires, serious politics, and a strong strain of chutzpah.

While the bigot does come around to a friendship with the drag queen, it is he who must pursue the rapprochement. Importantly, and

The challenging politics of *Flawless* were lost in a thin plot and wayward directing. Courtesy of Photofest.

unlike in so many of the films we have been discussing, the gay man is shown here in a *context,* a context that not only includes other gay friends but includes several scenes at the New York Lesbian and Gay Community Center, scenes in which the politics of gay resistance vs. the politics of gay assimilation are played out quite explicitly.

INCIDENTALLY QUEER

While films with a centrally gay theme have grown in recent years, even more striking is the rise of what I call the "incidental queer." These are characters who are inserted into the film in order to exhibit a certain hipness but who are insignificant as anything *other* than signs of hipness and, further, signs of the hipness of the lead character. Incidental queers have always popped up now and again in films, mostly for either comic relief (the effete decorators of older films and their '90s counterparts in films such as *Father of the Bride*), or for terror effect (such as the lesbian vampires in *The Hunger*). And there are certainly examples of serious and substantive "incidental queers" whose gayness is neither all consuming nor avoided. I think here of a film such as *Silkwood,* in which Cher's lesbian character is integrated into the main story.

But, more recently, the comic or evil incidental queer has given way to the incidental queer as hip accessory. Like with television, gays here are being used—to a certain extent—to add a certain up-to-date cachet of hipness to the film. So Alicia Silverstone's character Cher in *Clueless* mistakenly falls for a moody guy until he is revealed to be a "disco-dancing, Oscar Wilde-reading, friend of Dorothy." The old friends in *Four Weddings and a Funeral* include a gay couple, perfectly integrated into the rubric of the thin plot yet absent of any gay identity or sexuality. The British *Big Chill*-ish *Peter's Friends* includes a gay man, who similarly seems alone in the heterosexual world. Or, more problematically, the incidentally queer character serves to add a frisson of authenticity ("real life") to the more narratively central heterosexual characters, as in *Four Weddings and Funeral* or *Clueless* or even the surprise British hit of 1997 *The Full Monty*. Even the very hetero Adam Sandler vehicle *Big Daddy* featured two lawyer friends of the Sandler character who turn out to be gay and share an on-screen smooch.

Harvey Feirstein seems always ready to play these roles, from the gay brother of cross-dressing hetero Robin Williams in *Mrs. Doubtfire* to the gay decorator on Showtime's *Common Ground*. Or we have the lesbian daughter of one of the avenging ex-wives in *The First Wives Club* and the lesbian bank robber of *Set It Off*. In the first, the gay person is clearly introduced for comic value and hipness, allowing the befuddled but open-minded mom to venture forth into the happening lesbian world with her equally game friends; in the second, the gay person is much more integrated into the narrative and issues of homophobia are more forthrightly dealt with. Nevertheless, the film trades in obvious stereotypes, depicting a butch/femme couple that are almost a parody, providing brief moments of soft-porn voyeurism for her heterosexual comrades in arms.

Whoopie Goldberg plays another incidental queer in the road movie *Boys on the Side*. Here, Goldberg's lesbian character is, as usual, denied any sort of a romantic or sexual life, while her heterosexual comrades romp all over the place. Goldberg's character serves two functions—as accomplice to heterosexual romance and as site for a merging of discourses of female friendship with lesbian sexuality. One thing that marks out these incidental queers from, say, a more thoroughly integrated model of gay identity, is that these gay characters rarely seem to have other gay people to love and socialize with. Typically, the incidental queer finds him or herself located almost entirely in a world filled with heterosexual couples and their desires and their longings. They are the "gay friends" who have no gay friends of their own.

In addition, the incidental queer often serves to unite heterosexual couples, or to provide solace to heterosexuals suffering from the slings and arrows of wayward affections. Incidental queers can be used very deliberately in the service of heterosexual reunion. In Jody Foster's *Home for*

Queen Latifah (*Set It Off*) gets fetishized as a butch lesbian bank robber, Whoopie Goldberg (*Boys on the Side*) gets leaned on as a never-gets-laid lesbian, and Rupert Everett (*My Best Friend's Wedding*) begins his filmic reign as best girlfriend. Courtesy of Photofest.

the Holidays, the gay brother comes home with a handsome young man, conspicuously not the partner he lives with. His sister mistakenly assumes he is his lover, only to find out he is straight and perfect for her. The gay man loses a love interest (and his real lover is only shown in flashbacks) and the heterosexual woman gains a male lover. The Julia Roberts vehicle *My Best Friend's Wedding* features Julia's witty and charming gay sidekick (played by the witty and charming Rupert Everett), who pretends to be her lover in a (pathetic) attempt to win over her best friend, who is about

to be married to another woman. Incidental queers, such as this one, are often a girl's best friend, shown to be the one man a woman can talk to, confide in, cuddle, and go shopping with—all at the same time. Often, the self-directed desires of these incidental queers are nonexistent. Instead, they serve the function of confidant to the central heterosexual characters, helping them negotiate their relationships, relationships that are more often than not given the significance of physical contact.

Significantly, lesbians rarely figure in this "best buddy" mode of incidental queers. It is precisely the stereotypical image of gay men as charming, relational shopaholics that makes the confidant role work—indeed, we have endless books, articles, TV shows, and films in which the gay man serves as a straight woman's best girlfriend, sharing in trips to the stores, beauty tips, and boytalk. But the image of lesbians as hostile, decidedly uncharming, man-hating meanies exempts them from being anyone's sidekick. This means, therefore, that if incidental queers have become the main way Hollywood integrates gays, lesbians are made even more invisible because of their putative inability to fulfill the sidekick role.

The incidental queer can also emerge in less benign ways. Certainly, outright homophobic and offensive portrayals of lesbians and gay men have not disappeared in this new epoch, much as they might be under attack and criticized by even the mainstream press. Several films emerged in the early '90s which produced heated demonstrations, protests, counterprotests, and debates. *Basic Instinct, The Silence of the Lambs,* and *JFK*—all produced in the same year—became targets of intense media scrutiny and gay activism because of their depiction of gays. In *Basic Instinct,* lesbians are shown as ruthless psycho killers, and bisexuality is presented as a turn-on for the "real show" of heterosexuality. *JFK,* director Oliver Stone's ambitious revisiting of the Kennedy assassination and cover-up, includes a strange conjured-up sequence somehow linking S-M gay villains to the death of Kennedy. Both these films have been roundly condemned by the gay press and many in the mainstream press as well. *Silence of the Lambs,* however, is a somewhat more complicated case. A taut and riveting thriller made by progressive and avowedly pro-gay director Jonathan Demme, *Silence of the Lambs* was condemned by many for its depiction of the serial killer "Buffalo Bill" as a transsexual whose killing was motivated by his desire to be in "another skin." Yet the film starred Jodie Foster, herself a powerful female star and one "known" to be gay (although officially in the closet). The role of Clarice Starling was one of the most self-directed, nonsexualized, powerful female roles that Hollywood has produced in years. In addition, director Demme publicly and explicitly denied any homophobic motivation, arguing instead that the character of Buffalo Bill is not gay at all, but rather simply crazy. In a dossier on the film in the *Village Voice,* many feminist critics took issue with the gay critique of the film, arguing instead that the focus should be on the uniqueness of Foster's portrayal as powerful heroine, not on the relatively minor status of the killer.

On the one hand, the rise of the incidental queer could be read as a heartening sign, an indication of the full implication of gay people in the everyday lives of Americans, or at least those lives as fantasized by Hollywood producers. In and of itself, the token gay could be seen as progressive—gays are not introduced to filmgoers as special "themes of the week," but rather begin to pop up in all the places gays do pop up. Which is to say, everywhere. And some of these "incidental queers" are truly integrated rather than simply dropped in for hip value. I think here of an otherwise annoying film of 1998—*Your Friends and Neighbors*—in which a series of frustrated couples and their dismal affairs includes a lesbian duo, as vacuous and uninspired as their heterosexual counterparts. Or there is the black comedy *Election* where a lesbian teen runs for school president against her football star brother who has stolen her girlfriend. The hipster film *Go* features a gay male couple whose relationship angst is neither heterosexualized nor exoticized. The Clintonesque *Primary Colors* features a gun-toting, just out of a mental hospital, old '60s lesbian who, interestingly, serves as the moral center of the narrative. While wacky and ultimately suicidal, she is also the one with both cojones and integrity in a film in which everybody is an operator. *Being John Malkovich*—a bizarre and funny film about a nerdy puppeteer who finds a portal to actor John Malkovich's brain—features a gender-bending scenario of male-embodied lesbian lust, as the puppeteer's mousy wife finds passion with another woman through her colonization of Malkovich's brain and body. Spike Lee's *Summer of Sam*—ostensibly about the serial killer known as Son of Sam who terrorized New Yorkers in the 1977—features Ritchie as the neighborhood punk rocker who leads a double life as a gay hustler and dancer and another man who serves as the "fag in the hood" and is a taunted but beloved object of derision. Both representations are complex and interesting.

In the edgy hit *American Beauty,* the gay couple (Jim and Jim) are the only "normal" people in a film filled with seriously disturbed heterosexuals and nuclear families. The abusive, ex-military dad next door is a wacko closet case whose desires break out in murderous rage, thus indicting the repressions of enforced heterosexuality and revealing the darkness at the heart of suburban familialism. The gay couple jog blithely along with their lives while infantile heterosexuals and murderous and closeted homosexuals run amok. Gayness here can serve both the function of moral barometer (the one normal couple are the gay guys next door, carrying their welcome basket to the dysfunctional hets) and the site of immoral psychosis as the repressed military-nut-next-door gives in to all his wildest fantasies. Written by openly gay writer Alan Ball, *American Beauty* was an Oscar triumph, garnering awards for best picture, best screenplay, and best actor (Kevin Spacey). While heralded as a dark and deep look at the underbelly of American suburbia and the costs of an unlived life, *American Beauty* trades on both misogyny (the stereotypical shrewish wife as bête noire of masculine identity) and a strange obsession with homosexuality to make its points. As media critic Larry Gross asks, "How does a film that gives us yet another murderous closet case manage to win the Best Oscar from an officially gay-friendly Motion Picture Academy?"[3]

Which is not to say that killer queers are always a bad thing. It's up for grabs—in this film and in others—as to the interpretation of the murdering men. Is the pain of the closet, the cost of duplicity, being depicted? Is homophobia and self-hatred the cause of the violence? Or is it perhaps a bit more muddied, linking repressed homosexual desires with a kind of generalized anger and bigotry that propels antisocial behavior? *The Talented Mr. Ripley,* another film that raised these issues, also raised the ire of some who saw in the lead character yet another example of Hollywood's fondness for conniving killer queers. It features newly minted matinee idol Matt Damon as the sociopathic and charming murderer whose homosexuality is both integral and unspoken, and his image revives 1950s-era stereotypes of the vicious, narcissistic queer whose class aspirations are as devious as their perverse sexual desires. On the other hand, he is a curiously likable anti-hero, a working-class gender nonconformist whose murderous ways can be understood to be produced, at least in part, by the frustrating inequities of class and sexual hierarchies. It doesn't hurt that the men he kills are odious and offensive in their high-flying assumption of bourgeois privilege. This film, along with other, smaller films featuring not-so-likeable gays (*High Art, Swoon, The Opposite of Sex*) prove that the alternative to "negative stereotypes" need not always be saintly asexuals, and that the "incidental queer" can, at times, be more complex and central to the very structure of the film.

Yet upon closer examination it seems that—with a few notable exceptions—these gay characters are meant to serve less as subjects in their own right, and more as mirrors of the main characters and main plots. Like other minorities, gays are now part of the imagination of Hollywood image doctors but—like other minorities—find themselves token signs of hip authenticity. Many believe that this is the first step, that the token becomes the couple, becomes the family, becomes the community. But history shows us otherwise. The price of tokenism is often exclusion from more substantive representations. Tokenism oftentimes begets more tokenism. Or, worse perhaps, today's included tokens can be tomorrow's invisible minorities. Because incidental queers are so often ancillary to the central narrative, so often serve as conduits and confidants for heterosexual romance, and are so rarely shown in anything but singles or pairs, they can disappear as surely as they seem now to flit across the screen at every turn.

These walk-ons, small parts, and tokens can be seen as a "realistic" sign of a new awareness that gays really are everywhere, but placed against the backdrop of the larger representational field these incidental queers are more troubling. Because these token gays thrive and are loved at the box office while at the same time the gays that are not incidental but invested in relationships within a gay community (*Jeffrey,* etc.) are ignored, one can't help but be suspicious. It reminds me of the Christian right's claim to hate the sin but love the sinner. Individual gays, isolated from the "sin" of gay community and politics and sexuality, can be loved by the pop culture consumers. But place those same gays in any larger gay world and gay community, and the twin dangers of sex and politics rear their uncomfortable heads.

JUST ANOTHER PRETTY GIRL?: LESBIAN CHIC IN MAINSTREAM FILM

The problems of representing gays are compounded when homophobia meets sexism. The relationship of lesbians to the cinematic has always been complex and more deeply coded by invisibility than that of gay men. Simply put, the cultural stereotypes of lesbians are not that funny. While gay men—in the guise of the sissy or the dandy—have served as camp fodder for an overtly campy medium, gay women have been much more firmly located in the Freudian realms of pathology and deviance. Men without women have been depicted in all kinds of ways (indeed, the Western is built on a celebration of male homosociality), not all of them threatening to the status quo of heterosexuality and patriarchy. But women without men, well, that's another story. If *heterosexual* women without men (single mothers, "career women," outlaws) have been punished for their errant ways, then we can imagine the cinematic treatment of *homosexual* women without men.[4] Yet "lesbian chic" was a watchword of the '90s—we were told by critics and pundits everywhere that lesbians are hot, happening, and boffo box office. As one reviewer notes, "Call this the year of Lesbian Cinema and you won't be far off track. It's only February and the movie horizon is already dotted with films by, about and for lesbians—everything from lesbian coming-out yarns to a lesbian-noir thriller with killer chicks in leather. Last month at the Sundance Film Festival in Utah there were 10 films—including shorts—featuring lesbian stories or significant lesbian characters."[5]

As stories on lesbian chic and oh-so-wacky cross-dressers hit the newsstands, the tendency to coin new stereotypes emerges. If lesbians were previously depicted (if at all) as flannel-shirted, overweight, hairy-legged, "man-haters," then they are now being envisioned as the ultimate

'90s party girl—perfectly coifed and nattily attired, either enjoying the benefits of corporate culture or standard-bearers for a world-weary Gen-X hipness. Lesbians may be chic in the media-concocted public imagination, but in popular film it also appears that they are either vicious killers or (worse, I think) misguided souls ready to be rescued from a life of Sapphic sorrow by rough and ready men. In *Three of Hearts*, the lesbian couple break up and, when one hires a gigolo to win back the other, the woman finds herself in love with the man. In *Fried Green Tomatoes*, the obviously intimate relationship between the two women is made ambiguous and, as if that weren't bad enough, one tragically dies off.

If we are now not merely struggling against the twin forces of a simple invisibility or stereotyping, what is actually out there for lesbians in popular film? Given the heady combination of sexism and homophobia, it should come as no surprise that gayness in films has more often than not been a male endeavor. There have been dozens of recent films with gay male characters—both major and minor. But there are still comparatively few lesbian characters popping up on the silver screen, although television and the music industry have provided many more venues for lesbian visibility. Lesbian sex maven and roving pundit Susie Bright echoes many when she says, "I guess I'm yearning for more grown-up movies about lesbians . . . that aren't coming-out-of-the-closet stories, like 'Desert Hearts' (1985) or 'Personal Best' (1982) or some tired retread of 'The Story of O.'" Commenting on mainstream cinema, Bright adds that "the gay male image is much further along. You have gay characters that appear on screen who are already gay, and it's not discussed how they got that way. They just are and they have a whole set of concerns and they have a life."[6]

The brouhaha over the 1992 hit *Basic Instinct* illustrates a great deal both about Hollywood's increasing fascination with lesbianism and the growing clout of the gay movement. The film—in which lesbians and bisexual women are depicted as evil seducers and vicious murderers—ignited gay activists who staged a series of visible and creative protests both during the filming and at selected movie theaters around the country. Like so many larger than life media events, this controversy sparked discussion in the popular press about the depiction of lesbians in film. A piece in *Glamour* magazine illustrates once again the paradox of visibility. On the one had, this is a good piece, discussing Hollywood's "lesbiphobia" and bemoaning the stereotyping of lesbians as either "The Psychos, like *Basic Instinct*'s jealous voyeur Roxy, who murdered her young brother and tries to run over her girlfriend's lover (Michael Douglas), or . . . The Invisible, like Ruth and Idgie of *Fried Green Tomatoes*, who are so in love, they function as married, yet whether they are lovers is left ambiguous."[7] But the *Glamour* author, like so many others, insists on the assimilationist path as that desired by most lesbians: "Real-life lesbians want movie characters who are just like everyone else except that they happen to be lesbians."[8] Much too much, it seems to me, was made over the film. For in many ways, Sharon Stone's character was a classic noire femme fatale—updated for the gay '90s. She lured men into her intriguing web of confusion with her sexuality and mystery, now this time coded as "bisexual." In many ways, then, this film could fit under the "incidental gays" regime as well as the more traditional gays as exotic and sick killers.

So what now? What happens to representations of lesbians in an age that declares our identities chic while at the same time unable to assume full citizenship and civil rights? Two films of 1996 illustrate the stark options offered the lesbian character and the lesbian filmgoer in this age of lesbian chic. On the one hand, we have *Chasing Amy,* a Gen-X male angst/slacker film in which a male lead falls in love with a lesbian. And on the other hand, we have *Bound,* a neo-noir thriller featuring a butch-femme duo on the lam with loot from the mob. While seemingly on opposite sides of the spectrum, both films, I think, construct an image of the lesbian subject that is predicated on a narrowing of lesbian culture and politics.

While I find both these films problematic, it also must be said that both films do point to a somewhat different strategy of imagery in this new cultural and political scene. For lesbians here are not the signifiers for infantile, delayed development or exotic otherness or pathological evil. They aren't murdered in the end, they don't (at least in a straightforward and simple way) get rescued by male heterosexuals, and they aren't secondary to a more significant discourse of heterosexual familialism. They aren't hypersexualized nor are they pathetically desexualized. Indeed, in *Bound* we are treated to a fairly explicit portrayal of lesbian sexuality, coached by none other than Susie Bright. And yes, it is significant that the women don't get either killed off or redeemed by heterosexuality, but instead, in the case of *Bound,* drive off into the twilight together, content with each other and with the money they stole from the nasty mob men, or in the case of *Chasing Amy,* apparently resume lesbian relationships after a heterosexual hiatus. So this is progress. Virulent and explicit homophobic stereotyping is not the order of the day in popular media, which doesn't mean, of course, that homophobia hasn't taken on new and perhaps more perplexing forms, such as asserting gay sameness to heterosexuals, or touting an ideology of liberal assimilation. So this is not to say that these hip films don't signify. I think now, however, they signify precisely both cinematic hipness (white lesbian characters serving a similar function for male heterosexual directors as black heterosexual men serve for the likes of Quentin Tarantino) and a broader cultural hipness.

In both films, however, lesbian culture as something larger than individual lives or couples crops up only to be a site of stereotypical scariness (*Bound*) or stereotypical man-hating bitchiness (*Chasing Amy*). In *Bound*, we have ex-con Corky (Gina Gershon) trying to pick up a woman in a seedy bar replete with tough-talking gals and underworld ambience, the antithesis of the lipstick lesbians portrayed in independent films such as *Bar Girls*. In *Chasing Amy*, other lesbians are introduced more often but in equally disturbing ways. On one hand, they are anonymous, nameless, speechless objects of desire or curiosity, performing for the het boys and the lead lesbian as well. In addition, *Chasing Amy* presents us with an almost vicious depiction of man-hating dykes condemning their newly hetero sister, dismissing her love for Holden with a snide "another one bites the dust" comment. Now this is not to say that lesbians—like any marginalized group—may not react negatively when a member of that group goes outside the group bounds. Or that some lesbian bars aren't seedy and predatory. The point, however, is that while individual lesbian characters may now have some range and depth and narrative engagement, lesbian culture is still depicted (if depicted at all) in the narrowest and most stereotypical of ways. So, in both films, lesbian communities emerge briefly, only to be firmly repressed through an all too familiar depiction of an unsavory demimonde or a catty, unsympathetic coffee klatch of man-hating dykes. The lead lesbians then are freed from any complex negotiation with other lesbians and can get on with the business of beating the gangsters at their own game or joining the hetero club at theirs.

In an interesting reversal, it is *Bound*, which is less "about" lesbianism, that unabashedly centralizes the lesbian relationship. In contrast, *Chasing Amy* is explicitly a boy's fantasy movie about girls who like girls. A film about twenty-something cartoonist Holden, his homophobic best friend Banky (who may or may not be in love with him), and the lesbian Alyssa who is the object of Holden's affection, this film instantiates an ideology of lesbian identity that is at once unapologetic and regressive. In its explicit discussion (but not portrayals) of lesbian desire and sexual practice, this film positions itself as hip consciousness-raiser, teaching the uncomfortable audience and Holden alike that lesbians can "discourse sex" as good as the next guy, challenging the dominant mystifications of lesbian sex as hand-holding cuddles. If that was the mythology of '70s dykes, the new mythology (wrought by such films and contributed to—of course—by lesbian sex activists) is that lesbians are signifiers for a new polymorphous perversity, once solely the province of their gay brothers.

Yet in this film which has the most sustained and explicit *discourse* of lesbian sexuality ever in popular movies, actual lesbian relationships are largely invisible. Alyssa's lesbianism is thus figured *through* her growing attraction to a man or through two classically voyeuristic scenes in which she makes out with a speechless woman, much to the fascination and distaste of Banky and Holden.

Lesbianism is here figured as liberal homage to diversity, as in the conversation Alyssa has with Holden after they become lovers. He asks why she wants *him,* given her self-definition as gay. She responds that, when she started becoming attracted to him she "put a ceiling on that because you were a guy, until I remembered why I opened that door to women in the first place: to not limit the likelihood of finding that one person to complement me completely. I got here on my own terms." So lesbianism is not proactive desire *for* women, but desire *not* to limit, *not* to fall into the accepted status quo, not to be like everyone else, in true Gen-X rebel without a clue fashion. And while Banky's homophobic claim that Alyssa just needs some "deep dicking" to bring her to the hetero side is depicted as the pathetic rant of a juvenile man afraid of his own desires, the fact is girl does fall for boy and the only real display of intimacy we see is certainly heterosexual.

Bound, too, plays on the Gen-X aesthetic both through its hip neo-noir look as well as its depiction of the masculine, boyish, boxer-short wearing, tattooed, pouty, tough dyke looking like a low-rent Calvin Klein ad. To have lesbian lovers central to such a typically male-defined genre is potentially disruptive, yet their relationship is so schematic and vacuous that their lesbianism emerges not as the site of a radical subjectivity, but rather as a lame attempt to inject a frisson of controversy and allure (à la *Basic Instinct*) into a derivative and *Pulp Fiction*esque film formula. Their highly stylized butch-femme dance is played almost to the point of parody, yet ends up formulating this kind of interaction as mere windowdressing, the insubstantial gloss on an essential sameness, as they indicate in their final words to each other as they drive off with the money, to the effect of "we're not so different after all."

In *Chasing Amy,* not only are we presented with a real live lesbian (or is she a bisexual?), but we get a rare appearance by a snap queen black gay man, who portrays Hooper, a comic-book writer and friend of Banky and Holden who poses as a black radical gun-toting caricature in order to sell his work. He figures as the incidental queer here, as the witty moral barometer for Holden when he is freaking out over Alyssa's past. He gets to play with the straight white boys, but where are his friends, his lovers, his community? And why on earth is he friends with such nerdy white bigots?

If lesbians are hip and happening in these types of recent films, they are also still homicidal in others. Films such as *Fun, Heavenly Creatures, Butterfly Kiss,* and *Sister My Sister* depicted lesbian love (or a version of it) as so out of control that murderous mayhem soon follows. Unlike later independent films such as *The Incredibly True Adventures* and *Go Fish,* adolescent lesbian love in these films is anything but happy-go-lucky, as our heroines turn their often unacknowledged passions against other women, killing mothers, employers, friends.

AMOUR FOU: STAR-CROSSED LOVERS
AND MISPLACED AFFECTIONS

Another popular genre of recent years is the story of star-crossed lovers, or rather, wannabe partners whose sexual orientations are at odds. Numerous films have depicted triangles of all sorts or a heterosexual falling for a homosexual, or vice versa. It seems to me that this is Hollywood's way of reckoning with the hetero/homo divide and envisioning a love that crosses bounds, that knows no limits. It also spices up the tired genres of heterosexual romance and melodrama, adding a "third term" that raises the stakes for the would-be lovers. Obviously, this structure can also allow for an actual engagement with gay and lesbian sexuality and identity and, importantly, a reckoning with the interaction between hetero and homo worlds and desires. Too often, of course, heterosexuality wins out—not simply as the denouement of the film but also as that which is given more narrative weight and centrality. One indication of the meaningfulness of recent changes in representations can be reflected in the extent to which homosexuality is envisioned as secondary, subsidiary to the main machinations of heterosexual romance. In other words, does boy get girl in the end? In the 1993 film *Three of Hearts,* lesbian love runs a distant second to passionate romantic heterosexuality. In this film, we find lesbian lovers Connie and Ellen stereotypically butch/femme and stereotypically devoid of any visible signs of affection. As "real lesbian" Connie gets dumped by Grace Kelly look-a-like Ellen, the plot begins to be set for the reassertion of heterosexuality. Befriending a hunky, heart-of-gold, high-end male prostitute (hetero of course), Connie hatches a plot to have said hooker Joe (played by William Baldwin) seduce Ellen and break her heart, enabling Connie to come in and pick up the pieces. Of course, hooker and glam gal fall in love, the nefarious plot is revealed, and the film ends with the lesbian and the reformed boy toy plotting how to win the girl back . . . for the man.

In this film, lesbianism cannot win. Pretty girls like Ellen are not real lesbians, but rather brokenhearted babes seduced by the nurturing arms of trusty lesbians. Throughout the film, we are told repeatedly that Ellen met Connie after she was hurt by a male lover. This theme of lesbian desire as reactive to heterosexual disappointment is repeated, as Connie and Joe hatch the plot to bring the girls back together on the premise that brokenhearted Ellen would then (and only then?) return to "the life." But true heterosexual love trumps all, and even the best laid (and most homophobic) plans are quashed in the face of the "real thing." While at least the film doesn't end with the hetero couple going off into the sunset together, it certainly does diminish the seriousness of lesbian love and firmly reassert the centrality of the heterosexual romantic couple. And the "real lesbian" in the film gets curiously constructed as a boy's best buddy; her desexualization allows her to become the confidante and helpmate to love-struck hunks, turning her loss into nothing more then the vehicle for heterosexual reunion.

In the similarly themed (and similarly titled) *Threesome* (starring yet another Baldwin boy, this one the greasier Stephen), three college kids find themselves caught in a quintessentially hip '90s triangle. Lara Flynn Boyle's Alex moves into a dorm room occupied by the opposites Eddie and Stuart. Eddie, who narrates the film, is neat and intellectual yet befriends his sex-obsessed, sloppy, beer-swilling "dude" of a roommate. The buddy bonding is broken when the girl intrudes, and falls for "sexually ambivalent" Eddie who falls for macho Stuart who falls for Alex. Thus a triangle is born. After Eddie reveals his ambivalence to the lusty Alex, they become fast friends. But when Alex realizes little Eddie has yet to have sex with anyone (male or female) she is delighted: "Then you're not gay. You're a blank slate. I'll mold you into a heterosexual with my bare hands." Alas, Eddie's desire for Stuart grows and his lack of interest in the increasingly frustrated Alex grows as well. Finally, Stuart confronts him with his knowledge that Eddie has been "checking out my butt":

> Stuart: Are you a homo?
> Eddie: Fuck off.
> Stuart: It's ok if you are. It doesn't bother me. I'm secure enough in my own sexuality to not feel threatened by it. I have a very hip attitude about this sort of thing. . . . It's ok if you look at my butt.

Eddie runs off (he's always running off from anything sexual) but the three begin to deal with their complicated situation, which gets even more complicated as they all fail at "outside" encounters and eventually have the inevitable threesome, also inevitably focused on the girl. On the way to the threesome, Alex sleeps with both men, only confirming Eddie's homosexuality. What is interesting about this generally insipid film is that on the one hand the double standard is alive and well as Eddie never is shown doing anything more than gazing lovingly at Stuart's butt or touching said butt during the threesome. But, on the other hand, the homosexuality is not really highlighted or rendered a "problem of the week"; this is not a coming-out story and Eddie's incipient homosexuality is presented as just one more facet of the "essential" college experience of deep and fumbling friendships. It merely adds a sort of '90s twist to a fairly formulaic story of college hijinks and identity development.

But these films of misplaced affections and hetero/homo interactions get much more interesting when *Chasing Amy*'s doppelganger is the popular, less Gen-X, and infinitely more complicated *Object of My Affection*. While in many ways an annoying and cloying film about a young heterosexual woman (Nina) who falls in love with her openly gay best friend (George), this film takes an unusual turn. The film opens by setting the gay man and the heterosexual woman up as well-paired opposites—both young, attractive, socially concerned (he's a committed first-grade teacher, she's a counselor at a community center). Both have difficult partners, he a self-important, preening English professor and she a loudmouth, rough-at-the-edges lawyer. George and Nina "meet cute" at a party and, after George is unceremoniously dumped by the suave professor, he moves in with Nina. A temporary stay becomes an abiding friendship, and the scenes of their growing affection mirror those clichéd Hollywood montages of young lovers falling for each other, sans the sex but with a certain amount of physical intimacy.

When Nina becomes pregnant, she articulates her desire to raise the child with George and not her lover Vince because, as she says, "he's not home to me. You are." While George is resistant to the idea and more than a little conservative in his conceptualization of family ("You should be with the father of your child . . ."), Nina insists that "we can make this up for ourselves. None of the old rules apply." The film goes on to give qualified credence to her insistent plea for constructing families of choice. When George inevitably comes around, he displaces Vince, who seems unable to handle this arrangement. Now, while this initially seems like a cop-out (one man displacing another as "father"), actually the ending pushes the envelope a bit, bringing Vince back into the picture without simultaneously displacing George.

While dramatic tension is produced through an interrupted sexual encounter between Nina and George and George's subsequent involvement with a man, the film manages to paint a quite unusual portrait of family life. However, as one critic noted: "Despite all its winking and flirting, the film is rather demure. It is, after all, aimed at the mainstream audiences who embraced gay characters in 'My Best Friend's Wedding,'

The Baldwin boys have a thing for threesomes (*Threesome*), and for gallantly rescuing wayward women from the perils of lesbian love (*Three of Hearts*). Courtesy of Photofest.

'In & Out,' and 'The Birdcage.' At one point, Aniston [Nina] and Rudd [George] are on the brink of unbuckling when they are saved by Ma Bell: A sexy-sounding guy (Amo Gulinello) is on the phone for him. It's a predictable turn of events, but it salvages the movie's remaining believ-ability and the characters' credibility. Rudd doesn't turn into a happy hetero."[9]

What is different about this film is that, in the first place, the gay man is proudly gay and uninterested in a "conversion." And the gay man is not denied a life or a sexuality and is, importantly, not writhing in the sea of self-discovery. Indeed, the aborted tryst is an unwelcome and awkward (if not wholly believable) intrusion into the narrative; while we believe Nina's love for George is complicated, an audience would be hard-pressed to buy their nonchalant attitude both during and after the encounter.

While her insistence that "things can't stay the same" upholds the untenability of their alternative union, it is not then replaced with a more traditional structure, but rather by a complicated and expansive formation of family that includes her new lover (a handsome African-American policeman), Vince, George, his lover Paul, and the older gay man whose desire for Paul gets sublimated into the role of witty fey uncle. The final scene is quite amazing, depicting an alternative family life that would make Gary Bauer's minimal hair stand on end, as the assembled throngs (along with Nina's stepsister and husband) sit in the audience kvelling over the singing talents of the beloved daughter, now a first-grade student at the new cooperative school that George runs. Nevertheless, like so many liberal movies of the time, the refusal to reckon with homophobia that seems to accompany even the most timid reckonings with homosexuality makes this an uneven film: "As the movie's designated liberal spokesperson, [Alan] Alda also points out that homosexuality 'is a valid choice.' No doubt millions of gay men and lesbians will be relieved to find this out. Alda's is the kind of line and 'The Object of My Affection' is exactly the kind of movie 'Seinfeld's' creators had in mind when they came up with the rejoinder, 'Not that there's anything wrong with that.' If that's the case, why bother to say so in the first place?" [10]

The newest entree into the gay man/straight woman category is the film *The Next Best Thing*, starring Madonna and Rupert Everett as best friends whose one night of drunken sex leads to years of shared parenting. Like its earlier counterpart, *The Object of My Affection*, it seeks to use the gay man/straight woman couple as both poignant comedy and vehicle for the reconstruction of family life. Forgetting for a moment the miscasting of Madonna in a role that requires more depth, *The Next Best Thing* argues that—while heterosexual relationships are pivotal—they are not definitive of familial ties and emotional commitments. Like its predecessor, familial relationships are tangled, untangled, and retangled to form new paradigms of intimacy and community. While heterosexual relationships always intrude (both women in both films meet men who then become third parents in their complicated family), they do not push aside either gay identity or the relationship forged between the gay man and the straight woman.

While *The Object of My Affection* completely disappeared the gay community in its race to unpack the confusions of the mismatched duo, at least *The Next Best Thing* pictures its male gay character as having some other gay friends, albeit in the form of old queens and dying buddies. But, as film critic Manohla Dargis argues in one of the few favorable reviews of the film, "*The Next Best Thing* takes two motifs from the earlier movie—the romantically challenged single woman and her supportive, single gay friend—and pushes those types past badinage and fabulousness into something like real life. The result is a genre hybrid that draws on the women's picture, romantic comedy and gay film, but with a critical new twist: *The Next Best Thing* may be the first Hollywood movie about a gay man that could be classified as 'post-identity.' Mr. Everett's character is neither playing a neutered homosexual nor is he coming to terms with his sexuality; rather, he's a loving parent in a world that insists that fathers are men who only sleep with women. That gives the film politics."[11] Like *Object,* this film dares to imagine a world beyond the nuclear family, beyond the couple, beyond the isolated individual. Indeed, the relationship between the gay man and straight woman in both films is far more intimate and interesting than the clichés that pass for intimacy between the heterosexual couples. While not perfect films by any stretch of the imagination, they do push beyond the simple paradigms where gays are straights in better clothes or exotic freaks of nature. In these films, the dike begins to crack just a bit, allowing alternative visions of family, of love, of intimacy to seep in. While the cuteness factor (gay man/straight woman as witty pair) does irritate, it also does provide for a displacement of the heterosexual couple and the nuclear family as the centerpiece around which all our meals take place. The true test of whether these family dramas can really break new ground will come when the cuteness recedes and other more unnerving prospects emerge. I can imagine a version of *The Next Best Thing* in which the displacement becomes more pronounced through depictions of lesbians cavorting with their straight but feminist sisters, or multigenerational parenting that breaks down on gender and age and sexual lines. But that's my movie.

Other, smaller films engage this theme. *Love and Death in Long Island* and *Gods and Monsters* both depict fading, anachronistic older men besotted with studly younger (and presumably heterosexual) hunks. Still others, like 1999's ridiculous *Three to Tango,* feature mistaken-identity themes, which of course leads to much hilarity as the "really" straight

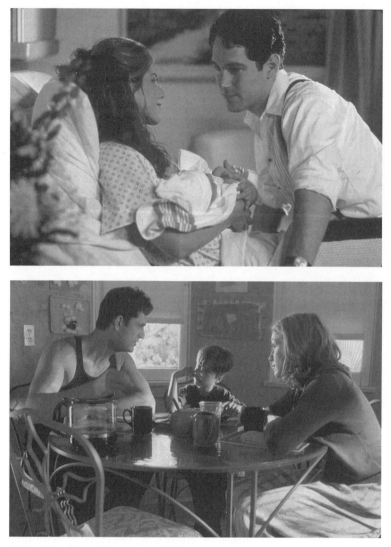

Weak acting, awkward directing, and Madonna's strange accent don't stop these two films (*The Object of My Affection* and *The Next Best Thing*) from interesting forays into the complexities of constructing alternative families. Courtesy of Photofest.

man "pretends" to "act gay" but is forever frustrated by his true masculine desire to win the girl's hand. Indulging in stereotypes and sending them up as well, films such as this appear liberated but are actually predicated on the horror of the "really" heterosexual man at the thought of being perceived as gay, even as the heterosexual man becomes educated in diversity by film's end.

Of course when one enters the world of independent film,[12] the story becomes quite different. Alternative and independent filmmaking has always provided a wider and more engaging range of images of lesbians and gays. I cannot begin to do this vast world of rich and textured films justice here (another book perhaps!) but I would be remiss not to comment on the substantive difference in gay-produced films made for a largely gay market. Now, many of these films actually do find a crossover audience, either by being picked up by commercial distributors or simply by virtue of critical acclaim. They also provide an important point of comparison—both for straight audiences and for critics—as to the depiction of gay identity. While few generalizations can be made about the independent gay films (and this in itself says volumes about the diversity of representation here), one thing that always strikes me is that, freed from the need to make homosexuality accessible through its engagement with heterosexuality, gay-produced independent or "small" films often construct a narrative in which gay lives have their own integrity, their own community, their own mise en scène apart from the Hollywood necessity to see queer lives through a straight lens.

I think here particularly of films such as *Go Fish,* which captured a slice of lesbian life without ever insisting on either boring stereotypes or pandering to a heterosexual audience. This film, perhaps more than any other gay independent of recent vintage, attracted enormous attention from both the gay and straight press, particularly after it was picked up by a large distributor and shown in art houses around the country. The success of *Go Fish* provided access for its director, Rose Troche, whose second film was a big-budget feature (*Bedrooms and Hallways*) that featured no lesbians and whose gay male lead ends up in bed with his old girlfriend. Or the other lesbian independent that garnered a great deal of press—*The Incredibly True Adventures of Two Girls in Love*—which not only depicted an interracial lesbian high school romance, but placed one of the lead characters in a lesbian family context.

Indeed, it is telling that independent and foreign films feature lesbians and lesbian culture much more than mainstream films, which tend to focus on gay men. And, tellingly, unlike the mainstream films, these films don't fall into simple categories—they evade easy classification. We have films as different as the Canadian film *When Night Is Falling,* which depicts lesbian romance against the dual backgrounds of Catholic education and eroticized circus arts. Or the ironic comedy *French Twist,* which simply adds lesbianism to the stew of the traditional French farce; or *Better Than Chocolate,* the slim but sexy story of (more) young girls in love.

The Incredibly True Adventures of Two Girls in Love, Go Fish, and Boys Don't Cry broke rules and spoke directly and unapologetically to gay audiences—and heterosexuals *still* came to see! Courtesy of Photofest.

While many independent gay films never gain a distributor and are primarily seen in gay festivals, many—such as those mentioned above—find larger gay audiences and straight audiences through the more established sites of art and foreign film houses. Indeed, the world of independent film seems permeated with gay themes and gay-focused films, particularly as the film circuit continues to grow and independent filmmakers gain access through established venues such as the Sundance Festival. Other films such as *Swoon; The Living End; Poison; Paris Is Burning; The Adventures of Priscilla, Queen of the Desert; Priest;, The Opposite of Sex; The Sum of Us; High Art;* and the films of Derek Jarman have had critical success within the gay community and, to a lesser extent, with straight audiences.

In the early nineties, gay-themed films permeated the independent market, with crossover successes like *The Wedding Banquet, Farewell My Concubine,* and *Orlando.* It is obvious to even the casual observer that independent and foreign films often have a texture, a richness, a range that box-office-focused Hollywood films never even try to attain. Occasionally, these smaller films manage to reach out to the larger cultural imagination and touch many with their complicated portrayals of gay life and gay identity.

I think especially here of a film like *Boys Don't Cry,* which managed to win a Golden Globe and Academy Award for its star Hilary Swank, in

her portrayal of Brandon Teena, the transgendered youth raped and murdered by two men who discover that he is "really" a woman. Or the heartbreaking tale of a little French boy in *Ma Vie en Rose* whose love of fantasy and desire to wear clothes destined for the opposite sex provokes
complicated reactions in friends and family. Others, such as *Stonewall*
from 1995, situate personal narratives within a vivid and complicated social and political history, combining postmodern artistry with agitprop
storytelling.

There is no question that these independent films (and there are so many others) move beyond the paradigms discussed thus far. Queers are not incidental here, but narrators of their own lives and invested in a vast and rich world of gay politics amid the realities of heterosexual hegemony. And, certainly, gays are not sideshow freaks or signs of token hipness or afterthoughts. This is not true just for gays of course. Any social group finds itself more complexly represented when outside the strictures of bottom-line commercial image-making. One trip to a feminist film festival provides ample evidence of the range of images available to those whose inclination and ability leads them to such sites.

But most of the world doesn't see these images. As successful as a crossover film like *Go Fish* was, it doesn't compare to the audiences garnered for even the most tepid Hollywood production. These other images *do* stand as examples of what can be visualized when the reigning tropes of sameness and difference are ignored in favor of a rich social and political and sexual world. And these independent films should serve both as reprimand and as warning: reprimand to Hollywood for remaining still so stuck in these narrow frames, and warning to gays themselves not to think that the price of visibility is always banal cooptation or paternalistic tolerance. Both the independent films and these few Hollywood ones that hint at destabilizations and challenges, that dethrone heterosexuality, hearth, and home as the frames through which gay life and gay love is imagined, offer representations beyond the simply formulaic models that all too often characterize the new gay visibility. As with their television counterparts, this new gay visibility in film breaks through when it imagines gay people as living and loving in a world filled with other gays and with complicated (not just "tolerant") straights, with politics, with community, with sex and desire, where gays act on their own behalf and narrate their own lives, lives in which being gay is both everything and nothing. At the same time.

PART FOUR *In the Family Way*

Is it worth being boring for a blender? Gay marriage:
You might as well be straight.
—found on postcards and posters throughout New
York, produced by DAM! (Dyke Action Machine!)

Just a thought. How soon before expectant parents
tell their friends: "It's twins. A boy and a girl. They're
going to be gay. We're calling them Michelangelo
and Martina. We've painted the nursery lavender."
—Sir Ian McKellen in the *Guardian*

The civilizing influence of family values, with
or without children, ultimately may be the best
argument for same-sex marriage.
—William Eskridge, Jr., *The Case for Same-Sex
Marriage*

Eight   WEDDING BELL BLUES: IMAGINING MARRIAGE

Into this strange register of the visible enters the sound bite-ish "gay marriage debate," a debate played out in the pages of gay journals but also played out on our TV sets, in glossy mainstream magazines, in prime-time news specials, in legal argumentation, in everyday talk. Gay marriage has wreaked havoc on the public imagination. Indeed, the peculiarly public display that is the marriage ritual emphasizes the centrality of the visible to marriage, in a way that domestic partnerships or even commitment ceremonies can never quite manifest. Weddings are highly commercialized public signs;[1] it is no accident that this imagery has captivated public imagination, pushing aside the more mundane and everyday images of lesbian and gay life by making visible that which we cannot have.

Gay marriage has certainly dominated recent political debates, and more than enough ink has been spilled by both the gay and straight press arguing for—or against—marriage rights for lesbians and gays. Here too, much contradiction abounds. When it looked as if Hawaii would grant married status to gay couples, Congress moved to pass the Defense of Marriage Act, designed to overrule state laws. When Vermont succeeded in creating the closest thing to gay marriage (civil unions), angry Vermonters and their supporters began an anti–civil union campaign, targeting elected representatives who had supported the case and

fomenting a "Take Back Vermont" anti-gay populism. All over the nation, state statutes prohibiting the possibility of gay marriages proliferate (at last count, twenty-nine states had enacted anti-gay marriage laws), just as commitment ceremonies, weddings, and associated public rituals grow and are sanctioned by gay religious organizations (the Metropolitan Community Church) and runaway pastors alike. A *legal* same-sex wedding even took place in the fall of 2000 between a lesbian couple in which one of the women was transgendered and thus, for legal purposes, a man. Indeed, gays themselves have contributed to the marriage frenzy, devoting huge resources to legal battles and cultural initiatives, such as the National Freedom to Marry Day, held in February of 1998, which included a Marriage Resolution filled with institutional and personal signatures. Gay wedding announcements are a staple of reporting now in the gay press, independent documentaries focus on "chicks in white satin," and an online wedding between Gay Financial Network mogul Jeffrey Newman and his partner Jeffrey Parker occurred on October 16, 1999, and was Web cast to many on Out.com and officiated by celeb rabbi Charles Lippman.

For many heterosexuals, gay marriage is the sure sign of the coming apocalypse and, as right-wing pundit William Bennett asserts, "would be the most radical step ever taken in the deconstruction of society's most important institution." The language of pollution could not be more vivid, as gay marriages are depicted as taking us down a slippery slope that includes bestiality, incestuous unions, and polygamy. Often couched in family-values rhetoric, heterosexuals depict gay couples as demeaning the institution of marriage and threatening the very fabric of the American family by demanding access to such a "sacred" backbone of American society.

Because the right has used this as a "wedge" issue in recent elections, gays have to some extent been forced to fight on this turf, responding to right-wing hysteria with assurances of shared "family values" and reverence for traditional marriage. So mainstream and conservative gays assert the centrality of marriage and pledge their commitment to maintaining its traditions, arguing that "legal gay marriage would be the stamp of approval from mainstream American society."[2] It is difficult to hear the more radical gay voices, those that would say to Bennett and his ilk: "Would that it were so! Forward deconstruction! Onward challenge! Hi ho revision!" In this truncated battle, the complicated and difficult politics of marriage evaporates in a sea of assimilationist paeans to divine coupledom.

Of course, gays themselves have debated the issue vociferously and many, particularly lesbian activists, strongly argue against marriage as the route to social change, charging instead that marriage is an inherently patriarchal institution that will only serve to further distance gays from the dream of a transformed body politic. For if marriage itself reinforces structural inequalities within families, it also "privileges" state-regulated long-term pairing over other forms of intimacy and connectedness. Many in the gay movement—like their counterparts in the women's movement—have been critical of marriage not only for its gender inequity and history of violence, but for the ways in which it contributes to a *devaluing* of other ways of being sexual, loving and nurturing.[3] Perhaps, as one critic argues, "we might be better off seeking . . . civic and legal supports for different kinds of families that can address the emotional, physical and financial obligations of contemporary life."[4] If gays succeed in sanctifying the couple as the primary social unit (the one that gets financial and legal benefits), does that help to set up a hierarchy of intimacy that replicates the heterosexual one, rather than challenging or altering it? Gay marriage might grant visibility and "acceptance" to gay marrieds, but it will not necessarily challenge homophobia or the nuclear family. Indeed, it might demonize nonmarried gays as the "bad gays" (uncivilized, promiscuous, irresponsible) while reluctantly embracing the "good gays" who settle down and get married.

But the internal debate within the gay movement rarely gets media coverage. Indeed, if one believed the press, all gays want marriage and—given that right—will lay down their swords and pick up the keys to the family SUV. The press coverage of gay marriage has been huge, and—by and large—amazingly evenhanded and generally supportive even as it adopts that curious liberal tone that grants a sort of benign legitimacy to anti-marriage advocates. While editorials rail against gay marriage (and some support it) and anti-gay activists are given voice, so are the voices of gays who desire marriage and advocate for legal recognition.

The public face of gay marriage tells primarily three stories. The first—told by conservative gay pundits like Andrew Sullivan, Jonathan Rauch, and William Eskridge—is that gays should be allowed to marry because it would tame them (particularly those nasty, overly sexual, promiscuous, bathhouse-visiting men) and thus bring gays more fully into mainstream, normative culture. The second—told by more liberal lesbians—is that gays should be allowed to marry because it would free marriage from its patriarchal and narrow history. In this story, "same-sex marriage is a breathtakingly subversive idea . . . allowing two people of the same sex to marry shifts that institution's message."[5] The third story is told by well-meaning heterosexuals who argue that to deny gays access to marriage is discrimination, plain and simple, although they often use the selling point of story number one to reach out to the skeptics.

And now that the debate has settled on the state of Vermont, it has been narratively turned into a homespun family drama, pitting down-to-earth farming folk against the rabble-rousing outsiders who would usurp their way of life. Anti–civil union proponents are described as populist and independent, angered more at the state intrusion than at the gay thematic. As one sign-painting stalwart says, her signs aren't "meant to bash anybody" but merely to object to "the way the government takes more control."[6] Now, the civil union supporters come off well too. They are portrayed as earnest lovebirds who want simply to be left alone to live their lives in peace, love, and equality. In this rendering, the anti-gay activists come off as legitimate and honorable, not bigoted and homophobic. Marriage segregationists are never spoken of *as that,* in the way we might now expect reporting about unreconstructed Southerners who rail against intermarriage or "the mixing of the races." The coverage of the gay marriage debate is yet one more indication of an "official" popular culture that is no longer explicitly homophobic but that still treats homophobia as the *legitimate* disgust of good-minded people whose religious and moral beliefs ground their revulsion.

GOING TO THE CHAPEL: MEDIA VOWS

Inevitably, this political and legislative issue has also seeped into the fictional worlds of our films and TV shows, where we find gay weddings and commitment ceremonies becoming a part of our cultural landscape, even as it moves tumultuously through the courts and legislative bodies of our cities and states. At once sign of the most public challenge and most humiliating defeat, gay marriage serves as one of the most contradictory of public images. The images of gay marriage that show up in popular culture—on network series, in the news, in films, in tabloid articles—challenge gays and straights alike to reckon with the very meaning of gay identity. The depiction of gays participating in one of the most valorized social institutions presents a heightened site to watch these issues of sameness/difference play out in our cultural life. Depictions of gay weddings shock with their imagery: two grooms atop the wedding cake, two brides under the chuppah. At the same time, they soothe with their vision of liberal inclusion, portraying earnest gay couples whose desires for the socially legitimate display of "commitment" and "family" are no different than their heterosexual counterparts. It is no accident that gay marriage has captivated the gay movement, even as it debates internally the political savvy in arguing for marriage rights.[7]

The mutually determining relationship between politics and culture means that, inevitably, the debates over gay marriage will turn up in fictional spaces. Gay weddings have appeared on numerous series, including *Friends* (with Candace Gingrich, the lesbian half-sister of Republican standard-bearer Newt, playing the lesbian minister), and the since-canceled *Northern Exposure* and *Roseanne*. For all the obvious newness of these representations, most have forgone the taboo gay kiss and presented gay marriage ceremonies as cuddly, desexualized mirrors of the more familiar heterosexual ritual. Notably absent are the odes to same-sex love and the revisions of traditional vows that most assuredly accompany many gay commitment ceremonies. The *Friends* wedding—while carefully sensitive—went out of its way to portray the gay wedding as an exact replica of its heterosexual counterpart, only with two bridal gowns. Out comic Lea DeLaria, who had a cameo in the lesbian wedding on *Friends,* complains: "They needed at least 30 or 40 more fat dykes in tuxedos. All those thin, perfectly coiffed girls in Laura Ashley prints—what kind of a lesbian wedding is that? And no one played softball afterwards?"[8] With Victorian wedding gowns, elegant floral arrangements, and tasteful musical accompaniment, these women walked down the aisle on the arms of men, one in full military garb to further the imagery of inclusion. Many critics, however, laud the move as an indication of full assimilation, as does this critic:

> With nearly 32 million acquaintances in attendance, Carol and Susan, two lesbian characters, were married on Thursday on the NBC comedy 'Friends.' The presiding minister was played by Candace Gingrich, whose brother presides over the House of Representatives. During any other television season, it would have been the same-sex wedding of the year. This

season, it was more like the same-sex wedding of the month. In December, the gay characters Leon and Scott were married on 'Roseanne' on ABC. And only two weeks ago, on the NBC comedy 'Mad About You,' the main character's sister, Debbie, professed her love for Joan. So it is not hard to imagine more commitment-ceremony bells in the future. A same-sex wedding might have provoked rebellion among network affiliates not too many years ago, but NBC reported that only two—KJAC in Port Arthur, Tex., and WLIO in Lima, Ohio—had decided that the 'Friends' episode was 'not appropriate' for their viewers. On the other hand, 212 affiliates chose to broadcast the segment. In other words, the biggest news about the wedding on 'Friends' was that it was almost not news at all."[9]

The *Friends* episode focused much more on the heterosexual response to the gay environment than on the gay participants themselves. Indeed, the gay wedding was framed by a secondary plot line concerning the impending divorce of a character's traditional mom, implicitly linking heterosexuality and homosexuality in a liberal scenario of sameness. In an interview with Jim Moret on CNN's *Showbiz Today,* Candace Gingrich speaks of her role as the lesbian minister administering the marriage vows to Susan and Carol on *Friends:* "People that tune in are going to find out that it's really not much different from other people's weddings. That's one of the things that I love the most about 'Friends' is that it's an accurate representation of gay and lesbian America. You know, we're in committed relationships, we want to celebrate those relationships, and we can be parents."[10]

It is interesting to note that in three of the major "gay weddings" handled on TV, it is a heterosexual character who brings the nervous and fighting homosexual couple together when the nuptials are threatened. In *Friends, Northern Exposure,* and even the more innovative *Roseanne,* one of the series regulars has a "heart-to-heart" with one member of the bickering gay couple and convinces them to go through with the planned wedding. Often, it is the character who is most resistant to the wedding (ex-husband Ross in *Friends* and rich town leader Maurice in *Northern Exposure*). This strange pattern is not, I'm afraid, merely coincidental. Rather, the confidential tête-à-tête between gay outsider and heterosexual insider renders not only homosexuality but *homophobia* benign and palatable. The appalled Maurice, who complains about these "tutti fruttis" ruining the very concept of marriage by engaging in a same-sex version of it, becomes not a bigoted homophobe but rather a befuddled and ultimately good-hearted traditionalist. In the *Friends* wedding, Carol rushes to the gang on wedding eve when trouble hits in the form of a fight with fiancée Susan. It seems that Carol's folks are not coming to the wedding and Carol, in her sadness, thinks perhaps they should call it off. But ex Ross comes through and saves the day:

> Ross: Look, do you love her? And you don't have to be too emphatic about this.
> Carol: Of course I do.
> Ross: Well, then that's it. And if George and Adelaide can't accept that, then to hell with them. Look, if my parents didn't want me to marry you, no way that would have stopped me. Look, this is your wedding. Do it.

Both lesbians are thus voiceless, and it takes the wise words of an enlightened heterosexual—comparing it to his own experience—to set the world right. Indeed, the last image is of *Ross* and Susan dancing together at the wedding. The straight characters get reformed and redeemed through their expertise in prewedding cold feet, thereby avoiding reckoning with their previously impregnable homophobia. This redemption, alongside the approving and supportive stance of all the other heterosexual characters, allows the shows to avoid dealing with the actual homophobia that erupts at the thought of a gay wedding. And the gay characters get "redeemed" by participation in the very familiar ritual of "cold feet."

In this scenario, straight people know more about family, life, relationships and are needed to pass that knowledge on to their floundering gay brethren. The implication here is that gays are simply not knowledgeable about the "real-life" issues of forming families, making commitments, raising kids.[11] Not only does this infantilize them, but it reintroduces an old canard about homosexuals as childlike, immature, unformed versions of heterosexuals. This backlash scenario argues to "accept" homosexuals, but not as full-fledged people who can handle their own lives.

In addition, there is a certain amount of hubris at the specter of the straight homophobe playing Dear Abby to the jittery gay person. Do these gay people on TV never have *any* gay friends to consult in their various travails? Isolation and assimilation are often the price of tokenism. But at least the *Cosby* family had each other. Gay people on TV appear to have sprung full blown from the Zeus's head of heterosexuality. The social, political, and cultural context that "births" gay people gives way to the fiction of the fully formed fag, parented by bravely reconstructed heterosexuals. Homophobia is reduced to ignorance, bewilderment, and discomfort. In the television land of gay life, the perpetrators of homophobia (aside from the obvious gay bashers) are not *offenders* but are basically good-hearted souls whose liberal inclinations win out in the end.

Gay weddings (here on *Roseanne* and *Friends*) figure large in the televisual imagination—an easy place to strike a blow against homophobia without challenging heterosexual privilege. Courtesy of Photofest.

Like the other gay weddings on TV, the wedding on *The Practice* serves more to "educate" the skeptical heterosexual than to elaborate any substantive gay reinvention of marriage. In this early episode of the acclaimed law series, which features Michael Badalucco as Jimmy Berluti, the working-class, Catholic novice lawyer, Berluti's widowed mom surprises him by coming out and asking him to petition the court for a marriage license for herself and her female partner. The episode is framed by a number of other plot lines. In one, indeed the one that opens the episode, Jimmy is seen—to the horror of his colleagues—producing a television advertisement in which he attempts to drum up business by speaking to the down and out Everyman: "Think nobody will fight for you? You're just a *grunt. I'm* a grunt. There's a lawyer out there for you. It's me. Just dial 555-GRNT." The ad gets results—the law office and adjoining halls become crowded with "freaks"—an old woman walking around holding a birdcage, a gospel group that wants to sing in a synagogue, a blind guy . . . and Jimmy's lesbian mom. In addition, another plot develops in which legal eagle Eugene has a crisis of conscience over his methods of destroying the integrity of rape victims in order to win acquittals for his clients. So the coming out and the wedding are framed by discourses of strangeness but also by a troubled discourse of "fighting for the little guy" and the dilemmas of conscience.

Mom comes out to Jimmy at the same moment that she asks him to be her lawyer, thus conflating the coming-out story with the marriage story. Indeed, the marriage story here ends up serving the coming-out story: all the mom really wants is for her son to accept her, and arguing the case to the judge provides that avenue and that evidence.

Jimmy—the ultimate Everyman—is at first both uninformed and upset, wondering if his mom is "dual-sexual or . . . the other?" When she begins to enlighten him, to explain to him that she is, in fact, gay, and that her marriage was a lie because "that's what women of my generation did. We married men. It didn't matter whether you were heterosexual or not," his anger and disgust comes to the fore: "Is that what killed him?" Later on, she gets to the point: "We love each other. We want to be recognized as a couple," and he responds with revulsion, saying, "I got to be honest Ma. I think it's . . . sick, disgusting." But like all major characters, Jimmy's homophobia gets quickly turned around, and by the end of the episode, he's not only making a passionate defense of gay marriage to the judge but throwing the couple an impromptu wedding in the law offices, replete with gospel singers, a religious figure, and bemused smiles.

While Jimmy's defense of gay marriage is righteous, both the judge and the opposing council are given equal legitimacy. The judge is initially described as "liberal," and his remarks at the end ("I'm willing to tolerate homosexuality, I'm just not ready to *encourage* it . . .") have by now become the standard argument that gives credence to second-class citizenship and reframes equality as an issue of "tolerance." Even supposedly open-mined lead character Bobby only smiles with amusement when Jimmy rants and raves about how the coming out is worse than being told his mother was dead. No argument from Bobby (the persistent moral voice of the show), but rather that benign and bemused smile that implicitly grants a level of legitimacy to homophobic ranting that would never be allowed with other forms of explicit bigotry.

Interestingly, sexuality enters into the picture in a curious way. While the opposing counsel quotes gay conservative Andrew Sullivan in support of his argument that gays can't be "faithful" ("a homosexual union requires a greater understanding of the *need* for extra marital outlets"), Jimmy picks up on that to opine that "she understands what commitment to family means." While he calls the judge on the double standard ("that crack about gay people being promiscuous and not understanding fidelity, what's that if not blatant bigotry? If we said that about blacks or some other race, you would have pounced on him, but you let it go about homosexuals. Shame on you . . ."), he also makes it clear that he "hate[s] the fact that my mother's a lesbian" even while he claims that he's "never been more proud of her." But what is he proud of? Her self-sacrifice for him ("when does the time come for me?"), her desire to continue her "family values" by marrying? So is this a liberal version of hating the sin and loving the sinner? And what of this "sinner?" Has she no voice? Her only voice is in attempting to counter his revulsion ("That's not the way I raised you . . .") and recounting her life of sacrifice. By episode's end, the "grunt" has indeed shown how he "fights for you." The earlier language of hatred, revulsion, disgust are now forgotten, set aside in the blissful reunion of mother and son brought about by the wedding ceremony. As his coworkers look on tolerantly, he embraces this mother whose sexuality disgusts him.

In the episode of *The Practice,* a newly enlightened heterosexual became the advocate of gay marriage, but in an episode of the highly acclaimed *West Wing,* already enlightened heterosexuals (staffer Josh and President Bartlet) find themselves facing off against a gay Republican Congressman who supports the anti-gay "Marriage Recognition Act" (i.e. the Defense of Marriage Act). In this episode, out Republican Matt Skinner (played by out actor Charley Lang) finds himself the point man on the bill and sets out to assure a victory by arguing with liberal staffer Josh, who finds it amazing that a gay man supports an anti-gay bill. While assuredly anti-homophobic (the series is noted for its liberal politics), it also legitimizes the congressman's position by having him assert a standard argument to the effect that being gay is not the totality of his being and therefore shouldn't govern his political decision-making, given that he agrees with "90% of the Republican agenda."

Contrast this delusional neoliberalism with the realities of anti-gay politics. The same year that witnessed ratings-successful gay weddings on TV also saw the U.S. Congress overwhelmingly support an anti-gay marriage bill—and a putatively "pro-gay" president sign it. Television abounds with gay weddings while our elected officials rail against it (and state after state votes to restrict marriage to heterosexuals), and polls suggest most Americans agree with the officials and not with the television shows they watch so assiduously. For the religious right, gay marriage is most assuredly the proverbial line in the sand; banning it keeps heterosexuals safe from the invading hordes of gay barbarians eager to say their "I do's" in the Chapel of Love. A full-page ad by the Family Research Council in the *Washington Post* quite explicitly locates marriage as the glue that holds society together—and that keeps out the undesirables. Above a picture of a crumbling wedding cake, the ad encapsulates the "family values" rhetoric and reveals its political heritage: "The institution of marriage was built to last . . . It was made in heaven . . . Recognized by the state . . . Sanctioned by faith and honored by the community. It has gone hand-in-hand with the rise of civilization. Marriage has survived Marxism. Outlasted Free Love. Outlived Woodstock. Toughed-out the Playboy philosophy. Even endured radical feminism." Opponents of gay marriage link the supposed evils of same-sex love to all the other supposed evils of a secular humanist society—the ogre of sixties-style sex, drugs, and rock 'n' roll meets up with the shibboleth of radical feminism encounters the Godzilla of gay marriage.

IS THAT ALL THERE IS?: GAY AMBIVALENCE

If the liberal popular culture depicts gay weddings as cheerfully hetero we-are-the-world assimilation, and straight homophobes depict them as the satanic rituals of secular humanism run amok, then how are gays themselves representing this contested institution? While there is no measurable correlation between desire to marry and desire to assimilate, testimonies and anecdotal evidence suggest that many gays who desire marriage ceremonies are precisely those gays who are most interested in showing straight America that they are just the same as them. A piece in the *Washington Post* entitled "Every Girl's Dream" describes the ceremony of two women ("On this Untraditional Wedding Day, the Traditional Jitters and the Traditional Tears"). Like all of these narratives of gay mimesis, the article draws you in by describing the couple the morning before the wedding (like any other couple) then hits you with the bombshell: "Angela is a bride. So is her fiancee."[12] Parents comment on how it is "just like a regular wedding"[13] and bride Elise expresses her desire to do it exactly like the "real people." The "brides" observe a vow of celibacy the week prior to the "wedding" and the whole event is recounted in loving and supportive detail. While filtered through the (presumably heterosexual) journalistic gaze, the words of the women themselves betrays an investment in mainstream conceptualizations of marriage, family, coupling. Is the dream of a seamless inclusion really so foolproof?

In particular, the gay marriage advocates are often the more religious members of the community and more anxious to assert the absolute validity of long-term "commitments" over other forms of loving. As Mr. Linfoot, the minister at Grace Fellowship Church says, "'We in the gay community need to be more serious about our relationships. With Don and myself being very public in our church, we felt it was important that we make ourselves an example; that is, to make a commitment and to live by it.'"[14] In similar, more academic pieces by noted gay writers such as Andrew Sullivan, William Eskridge, and others, this theme of gays "overcoming" their wild wanton ways and settling down to the "mature" life of marriage is offered as sop to straights who fear that gays will bring their difference into the marital union. Indeed, even more popular journalistic screeds on gay marriage—typically by gay men—argue that far from spreading homosexual licentiousness, gay marriage will help curtail "the bathhouses and wanton sex of gay San Francisco or New York in the 1970s" and tie men down into mortgage-paying units which we all know "is a very good thing, especially as compared to the closet-gay culture of furtive sex with innumerable partners in parks and bathhouses."[15] Jonathan Rauch's argument for gay marriage, like Sullivan's, thus invokes quite explicitly the most conservative doctrines on sexuality (it should be monogamous and in the context of a marriage) and family (two parents are always preferable), and insists that gays must marry (and are to be pitied and scorned if not) if given the option, thus setting up a very explicit hierarchy that privileges marriage as "better than other ways of living."[16]

There is no doubt that many gay people—in constructing ceremonies of commitment—try very hard to find ways to render them differently. Because of their very nature, gay ceremonies have a variety and diversity not often witnessed in heterosexual ceremonies, and many writers have chronicled the "ceremonies of the heart" that gays have been creating for years. In Ellen Lewin's thoughtful and fascinating tour of lesbian and gay commitment ceremonies,[17] she rightly stresses the often uneasy mixture of the traditional with the "queer" in the formation of these ceremonies, the mixing of genres and ideologies implying a sort of postmodern pastiche of gender-bending imagery. Clearly, alternative forms of family exist and many lesbians and gays are parenting and partnering in ways that challenge traditional models of family and intimacy. There are commitment ceremonies that are campy and expansive, inviting in old lovers, extended fictive kin, dear friends to celebrate new ways of being in the world. There are ways of parenting that resist traditional gendering, that enmesh children in an extended network of care, that encourage choice, that are uninterested in the comparison to heterosexual life. But difference rarely has a voice, or is muted and pushed aside in the rush up the matrimonial altar. The desire to mimic heterosexual pairings is strong (and understandable, given the relative invisibility of alternative forms of loving), as evidenced by "Sandy Berthlot and Doris Wertz [who] exchanged vows six years ago Tuesday. Ms. Berthlot proposed at the top of Flagpole Hill. 'I got down on my knees right in front of the Buick,' she says. 'She was sitting on the hood. I can't believe how corny I was. But I told her I wanted her and I to be an us.'"[18] Indeed, even pro-gay heterosexuals get into the sameness act, as does this PFLAG mom in responding to Ann Landers' refusal to condone gay marriages. "Our gay children," she says, "can develop healthy self-esteem and move into relationships that mirror the commitment of heterosexual couples. First comes love, then comes marriage—having one's relationship recognized by society is the next logical step."[19]

I went to a lesbian wedding recently in which it was absolutely impossible to tell the difference, except for the presence of two women in front of the rabbi. Traditional wedding gowns were worn, matching bridesmaid outfits for the bridesmaids (and what a sexist concept to begin with!), men and women on separate sides with only the men holding the chuppah. Not one speaker mentioned the lesbianism of the couple, no one spoke of the illegality of their union, no one mentioned the gay movement. No gay rights songs were sung, no alternative words recited, no gay liturgy on display. Forgotten, unmentioned, was the absence of certain parents who refused to show up. It was, in fact, one of the most traditional weddings I have ever attended, completely obliterating the possibility of reinvention. But, for this couple and I would guess for many, this was in fact the end point. To *not* do it any differently, to *un*mark ourselves, to slip ever so silently into the bright light of assimilation was seen as the new space of freedom: a place where gay weddings *are* no different. The straight people attending the ceremony were no less celebratory than the gays, and all seemed to view a "gay wedding" as inherently radical. The depictions of wedding ceremonies in the mainstream press are similarly laudatory, applauding gays for their bravery and often explicitly exulting in gay desire to "settle down" and get married.

Perhaps one of the reasons *not* to have same-sex weddings is that attendance lets the attendees off the hook. For many heterosexuals, attending a gay wedding becomes their fist in the air against homophobia, their magnanimous moment of "acceptance." At the gay weddings I have attended (admittedly few, as one might imagine!), heterosexual attendees seem to positively glow in their newfound bravery and inclusiveness, patting themselves on the back for participating in this daring thing called a "gay wedding." Like Dorothy, whose ruby slippers make her immune from the attacks of bad witches, I fear these heterosexuals feel themselves similarly immune from accusations of homophobia as they—just this once—embrace their gay sisters and brothers in the illusion of inclusion that marriage offers.

Gay weddings are still, of course, the site for humor, as evidenced by the remarks between Chandler and Joey during the *Friends* ceremony. As they survey the scene in the wedding hall Joey remarks that "it just seems so futile. You know, all these women and, nothing. I feel like Superman without my powers. I have my cape and yet cannot fly." And laughs keep cropping us as Chandler repeatedly hits on an obviously disinterested woman ("I shouldn't even bother coming up with a line, right?") only to end the entire episode with this bon mot, "Alright, look, penis-shmenis, we're all people," as the object of his affection stalks off. Nevertheless, these days gay weddings are more often than not the place where heterosexual ambivalence is addressed and homophobia redressed. The Showtime special *Common Ground* is a perfect example of the confusion and ambivalence embedded in the marriage debate. Set in the small town of Homer, Connecticut, the film weaves together three distinct stories set in the 1950s, the 1970s, and the year 2000. Centered figuratively around the town square ("common ground") and endlessly symbolized by the flag being carefully raised, lowered, and folded up by the narrator—a heterosexual man who moves from childhood through middle age and is the only constant in the film—the narrative offers supposedly representative snapshots of different historical periods as they impact on gay identity. The final segment—written by gay actor and playwright Harvey Fierstein—centers on the wedding of two men (wittily named Amos and Andy) and the response of the town and, most specifically, Amos's father.

The significance of having a wedding as the final scene reiterates the liberal theme of inevitable progress. The previous segments take us through the brutal 1950s, where a young woman is discharged from the Army for suspicion of homosexuality and rejected by family and community and forced to leave the town, to the more mixed response of the changing 1970s where a young gay teen comes out, is brutalized by his peers, but finds support and solace in a gay teacher. In the first segment, gay identity is itself unclear; the young woman isn't sure but hies off to New York to find out. In the second segment, coming out is itself the theme—as both boy and teacher come to terms with their identities; indeed, identity itself emerges. In the final segment, gay *identity* is a non-issue; the wedding ceremony symbolizes the full integration of gays into American society.

While in many ways a typically assimilationist and celebratory drama about the wonderful changes wrought in the last decade, *Common Ground* also offers up—in this last segment—a more complicated and nuanced portrayal of a gay movement uneasy with assimilation, unsure of how to proceed in these new times. As groom Amos runs off on his wedding day to mope in a tree house, he is met by his troubled father— in full uniform—who has helped organize his veterans' group to protest the impending nuptials. As the father and son watch the action unfolding below them, they begin to wrestle with their relationship and shared discomfort with the wedding. While the father's homophobia is revealed, the son refuses an apologetic or pleading position: no desperate desire for "acceptance" here. The scene turns when the father realizes that his son has "wedding day jitters." Pinching his cheeks and suddenly warm and animated, he finds it "cute" and "wonderful" because "this is one of those father-son things I was sure I'd missed out on." When the son attempts to brush him off, Dad continues to pursue: "Listen, it's normal, perfectly normal. I had 'em too. Ahh son, look at you, you're normal." At first glance, then, this seems like those other television moments we've seen, where the bigoted hetero comes around to an "acceptance" of the wedding through the act of shared sympathy with the gay person's wedding day jitters. To a certain extent, this scene is no different from those, bringing father and son together through the fiction of shared experience. And, indeed, the son does come down from the tree house to get married and his father does join the family and well-wishers at the ceremony. All ends well.

But this liberal message of sameness is complicated by the dialogue that ensues. Amos refuses the simple turn of events that interprets his jitters as indistinguishable from hetero wedding angst:

> Amos: Dad, I've worked my whole life to prove that I'm as good as any-
> body else is, and what happened? I've turned out just like everybody
> else. I mean, I'm a gay man in a heterosexual world and that hardly
> seems to matter anymore.
> Dad: You've lost me now . . .

Amos: I've been in a monogamous relationship longer than 83% of American marriages. Our house is paid off. I own my own business, we have two cars, a pickup truck, Andy's on a second career. We've been to Disneyland—twice—Disney World three times. We did Eurodisney for our fifteenth anniversary! Think about this: Congress passes a law against gays getting married and *we* are having our wedding ceremony at a *community* center, thrown by a town committee with the blessings of the town fathers.

Dad: With protestors, give yourself a little credit.

Amos: Dad, this is a town of 27,000 people. If that's all the outrage they can muster it's embarrassing. (*Cut to motley crew of protestors*) I'm supposed to be a gay man . . . having all this wild, promiscuous sex with thousands of partners! You know how many men I've slept with?

Dad: Geez, son—

Amos: Three! . . . where are my thousands? Where are my discos, and my parties, and my sad and pathetic and lonely life? And what's going to happen when we have the baby? . . . I feel like my life is rushing by. It's completely out of control.

Dad: Now you're back in familiar territory. . . . Listen, I know just what you're feeling. I remember it like it was yesterday. (*They embrace*)

Next thing you know, Amos is out of the tree house, helping his mom out of the limo, jumping in the back seat to get changed with Andy, and walking up the steps to the community center, family in tow. But the scene is complicated, moving back and forth between the desire to understand this moment as essentially a "human" (read: heterosexual) one in which the father can provide moral leadership and guidance, and thus relieve himself of this bigotry, and one in which the son speaks of the paradoxes of this particular moment in gay life. Indeed, the dialogue explicitly notes this, playing up the father's discomfort with the "gay talk" and foregrounding his desire to see the son's ambivalence through hetero eyes.

Nevertheless, the son's gay talk is itself problematic. Admittedly, he addresses the strangeness of having a gay wedding amidst the Defense of Marriage Act and bemoans his assimilated status—a discourse we rarely see in popular culture, so eager are we to assert an uncomplicated desire to assimilate. But the upper-class hubris is deeply galling, as his references for having "made it" are much more about achieving economic status than equal rights and are, of course, unavailable to many Americans—gay or straight. Indeed, the first segment—the one with the most overt bigotry—is also the only one to depict a working-class context, as if to imply that the move toward liberation (signified by the wedding) is also a move toward a wealthy, home-owning, self-employed, white, bourgeois status.

Is our new *Common Ground* to be found in a rainbow-hued wedding? Courtesy of Photofest.

In addition, Amos references the past through "wild sex," parties, and a "sad and pathetic" life. Now, while this is obviously humorous and said tongue-in-cheek, when placed in the context of Amos's clear "purity" it serves to further that victorious narrative in which gays have moved beyond the "excess" that disallowed them access to the American Dream. Indeed, Amos does not climb down from the tree house and head for some gay Valhalla of bars and boys, but walks bravely into the arms of his beloved and the embrace of his family and friends.

The final scene is similarly contradictory, offering up both a tentative critique of the marriage/assimilation route while also reaffirming it through the language of love and the power of the marital couple to transform the world around them. At the end of the scene, narrator Johnny turns around to see the gay characters from the previous segments nodding and smiling happily, putting even more weight to the final words of the wedding vow soliloquy:

> Amos: What the hell are we doing here? . . . I know that we didn't get here alone. We owe our lives to the generations of gays and lesbians that struggled before us. Some of whom gave up their freedom, others of whom gave up their very lives. I also know that it's up to us to do our very best to carry the next generation to where they need to be. Is this it? Is *this* equality? I don't know. I guess we have to trust that if what we've built here together can inspire this gathering, then we can't be too far off the mark. I love you Andy, and I am nothing if not yours.

Here Amos invokes the gay movement (something we rarely see in popular culture) and questions the current political situation (is this equality?) but then turns it back around to the couple's love as inspiration.

Thus it is not at all clear that, say, same-sex marriages will present a *fundamental* challenge to the institution of marriage or that gay parents will construct truly new ways of raising children. Is it possible that the creation of gay families through marriage (or commitment ceremonies) and the raising of children is the *least* challenging aspect of gay and lesbian life? Is the formation of gay families the nail in the assimilationist coffin, linking gays irrevocably with mainstream heterosexuality? Or do these moves shake up heterosexual dominance like nothing else, permanently altering the very definitions of family? These are, as we social scientists like to say, empirical questions. But the argument that gay marriage, for example, will *necessarily* alter (sexist, heterosexist) marriage as we know it seems far-fetched. Have the Log Cabinites altered the GOP? If gays marry from within the dominant heterosexual frameworks—invoking dangerous ideologies of familialism, faith, and fidelity—the prospect of internal combustion fizzles out.

Nine   MOM, I'VE GOT SOME-
THING TO TELL YOU:
THE COMING-OUT
STORY IN THE AGE
OF VISIBILITY

I f the wedding scene is the quintessential heterosexual epiphany, then coming-out stories are the gay community's Bildungsroman, our claim to fame, our climactic trope. While coming-out stories take many forms (youthful coming out, coming out of a marriage, coming out at midlife) and have many different locales (the workplace, the family, friendship networks, school), the one that primarily occupies me here is perhaps the iconic one of a gay youth revealing his or her identity to an astonished family. Coming out into the family of origin is often the first story gays tell each other, often the opening line in a date come-on. It's our "come here often?" Nevertheless, the very meaning of "coming out" has shifted throughout history. George Chauncey, in his pioneering book on gay life in pre–World War II New York, argues that "gay people in the prewar years . . . did not speak of *coming out of* what we call the gay closet, but rather of *coming out into* what they called 'homosexual society,' or the 'gay world,' a world neither so small nor so isolated, nor, often, so hidden as 'closet' implies." From an earlier sense of coming out into this gay world or community (and being "brought out" sexually by another), it has in more recent years taken on a more individualistic tone, as in "announcing one's homosexuality to straight friends and family. The critical audience to which one can come out had shifted from the gay world to the straight world."[1] This is important to remember, as we look at some contemporary versions of the "coming-out" story. Chauncey may indeed be correct in asserting that the tales we tell now are more often than not ones centered on a "personal" revelation to an individual, typically a heterosexual individual. It is interesting to ponder how different these stories might be if the audience was somewhat different, if that older sense of coming out *into* was strengthened and reinvigorated, so that gay youth could say to their parents, "You're not losing a heterosexual child, you're gaining a fabulous gay community!" But it remains the case that most of our current media reckonings of "coming out" are familial ones, marked by trauma and melodrama, often devoid of that exhilaration derived from entrance into that small band of lovers.

The very place of family is often a fraught one for lesbians and gay men. While the larger social world offers few sites of freedom for gays, the family is all too often the site of the most outrageous rejection and brutality. For so many lesbians and gays, the family is not only the first place where they experienced homophobia but the place where they felt most betrayed, most alone, most violated. Like battered women beaten by those who pledge their love, the rejection of gay people by their families is one of our ugliest social secrets. Some of the saddest stories gay people tell are the stories of family—remaining in the closet for fear of rejection, being kicked out of the home, being told you are no longer a son/daughter, being kept away from other kids, being beaten, being told you are sick, telling your mother it is not "her fault," being disinherited, being shunned.

How different is this story now? In this new age of visibility do gay youth tell stories unfettered by the secrecy and invisibility of earlier times? Are those different stories finding their way into popular culture? A persistent question raised by this research is thus a generational one. Logic would lead us to believe these are much better times, that gay youth coming out in the context of a world in which gay images abound must have it easier than us older folks did. Of course, social exclusion, denigration, and violence still remain a part of daily life for gay teens, as groups like the Gay, Lesbian, and Straight Education Network catalogue. Homophobic remarks have hardly disappeared (in one report, 97 percent of students in public high schools reported regularly hearing homophobic remarks), teachers and administrators are still reluctant to include gay-positive curriculum and training for staff, and suicide rates and rates of anti-gay violence remain alarmingly high, as does the percentage of homeless youth who self-identify as gay. Parents still kick kids out of the home, abuse them, call them names, even as gay PTAs pop up.

Yet the *cultural* world in which these realities persist has changed. When we announced to our parents that we were gay, we had little to show for it. For our parents, gayness was perceived (if it was perceived at all) as disease, as affliction, as willfully throwing ourselves into the abyss of a sort of subcultural hell where no light shined and dark alleyways prevailed. Even when less dramatic, surely it is the case that previous generations were unable to point anguished parents to cultural images (or support groups) that would validate their enmeshment in American society. Our cultural invisibility only magnified the sense of difference and gave family members little space for imagining a happy and healthy life.

So what does it mean, now, for young people to speak of their desires and identities in a world of Ellens and Wills, of out corporate leaders and gay dads, of public rituals of commitment and RuPaul, where a media version of gay identity is hard to avoid by even the most recalcitrant parents? This is not to say that parents can't be willfully blind to the sexuality of their children, but it is the case that one has to work much harder to remain closed off from images of lesbians and gays. For a parent to pick up a newspaper, watch a sitcom, go to the movies is to be confronted with representations of gays, even as that still remains a small part of overall cultural output.

As I have said earlier, it would be foolish to think this doesn't change things, and even more foolish to think times aren't better, even as we challenge these media abrogations of our lives. But it is not at all clear to me that it is easier—or really that much different—to come out now. Two anecdotes tell different sides of this contradictory story. Not long ago, I was speaking to an organization that works with gay youth. On the panel with me was a young high school student, a seventeen-year-old who had come out and organized a gay-straight alliance at her school and become an activist for gay rights within the teen community. She told of watching Ellen come out on TV, joined by her parents, and how that television moment aided her in her own negotiations with her parents. These new times *mattered* for her. The combination of cultural visibility and political resources such as national and local gay youth groups created a *space,* helped create a young woman unusually up-front and empowered.

On the other hand, I had a more painful moment not too long ago where a colleague called me up to reveal to me his sexuality and get my advice about coming out—both in the workplace and with family. He was a bit older than I, partnered for over fifteen years, and had been in the closet his entire life, revealing little to friends and coworkers over the course of a twenty-year association with the university. The conversation was disconcerting, not only for the obvious pain and confusion of the colleague, but for the way in which the conversation felt like a throwback to another time. The visibility seemed to affect him negligibly, and the impetus for coming out now seemed more about being worn down by so many years of the closet than about a recognition of a changed social and cultural world. All his fears—of ruining his career, of losing friends and family, of being ostracized and marginalized—could have been ripped from a tortured pulp novel of the '50s or from the tales of our elders. How do we account for these differences? Obviously, individual life experiences, perspectives, politics contribute to the differing tales, as does the simple truth of the variety in gay experience and self-understanding. And the different ages of these two clearly frame their experiences within specific generational paradigms. But I also see the second story as a cautionary tale, warning us of taking the young woman's truth as the only extant one. Indeed, for all the evidence of newly empowered gay youth, thousands more still tell all-too-familiar stories of alienation, disaffection rejection, isolation, shame. This current cultural moment holds together these seemingly dissonant moments. Older stories still circulate in new times.

The coming-out process—and the coming-out stories told in our films and TV programs—remain a staple of our collective consciousness. Indeed, I see one sign of progress in the receding of these narratives. When we have a television program that features already out gay men (*Will & Grace*), we move, I think, in a very important direction towards a more substantive reckoning with gay life and gay identity. The coming-out story has its purpose, and for many people the move from the closet to a space of openness remains the fundamental marker in their lives. The coming-out story can reveal the damage wrought by homophobia, as it exposes viewers to the pain and internalized homophobia that renders life inward and curled up upon itself. It can open the eyes of heterosexuals to the necessity of coming out. But coming-out stories are problematic too, for they all too often focus more on heterosexual reaction and response than the self-affirmation of the gay person. Anguished parents and hostile "friends" are the staple of these stories, and, while that tells a sad truth about our experiences, it also serves to move the focus on to the struggle of the parents to "understand" their gay child and learn to "accept" them for "who they are." In the process, gayness still remains something to be "accepted" and "explained" while a heterosexual coming of age requires little explanation or acceptance.

In addition, as many gay theorists have noted, coming-out stories often create new kinds of fictions, corralling a messy and chaotic sexuality into a "before and after" narrative that belies the complicated and constructed nature of sexual desire and sexual identity. In popular culture, coming-out narratives often serve conservative ends, reinforcing beliefs in the "essential" and unchangeable nature of sexuality rather than elaborating a more nuanced tale of the circuitous and bumpy ride of sexual desire. These kinds of coming-out stories can boost tolerance for gay identity (because it's seen as inescapable and inevitable) as it simultaneously reinforces the hetero/homo divide, effectively pushing away unnerving questions of choice and ignoring the instability of the very categories of homo and hetero.

"I WAS EXACTLY WHO I WAS MEANT TO BE"

A much advertised Lifetime television movie of 2000, *The Truth About Jane,* reveals in all its messy confusion the troubled nature of the coming-out narrative. At once a poignant lesbian Bildungsroman and a melodramatic soap opera of familial rejection, *The Truth About Jane* surprises with its almost retro quality of parental horror. Narrated by the daughter's voice-over, the movie doubles as a coming-out story and a mother/daughter passion play, featuring a stereotypical controlling, "over-involved," nonworking mother and a benign good old boy of a father. Taking us quickly through the early years—where we witness said over-involved mother presiding over her daughter's life—we light on to the moment in question, when Jane is sixteen, beginning high school and beginning to reckon with her sexuality. Like so many framings of lesbian sexuality (curiously, gay male sexuality is rarely framed this way), Jane's desire for women is first introduced as an absence of desire for men. As the cute new boy in school approaches her in the lunchroom, Jane's catty girlfriends ooh and ah, and see Jane's lack of interest as a sign of arrested development. When the new girl in town sits next to Jane in her English class, our heroine is immediately smitten. The voice-over reveals all: "Why wasn't I like my friends? Why wasn't I like everyone else? Why couldn't I just like a boy named Ned? I was in trouble. Big, big trouble. I had a crush on a girl."

In these early scenes, trouble has not yet hit the household. Indeed, the scenes of loving mother/daughter interactions are paired with the more typically romantic scenes of the two girls getting closer and spending more and more time together. Interspersed with these are scenes at a diner where the mother, Janice, meets for regular lunches with two old friends—Jimmy, a black gay man (played by RuPaul—not in drag), and Beth, a single white woman. Throughout the movie, they serve as sounding board and conscience, reminding Janice of her supposedly more progressive past and moving in and out of the family orbit as the drama of coming out takes its course.

As the relationship progresses, we learn more about the object of Jane's affection. Taylor is tough, straight-talking—adult (she boldly introduces herself to people with a strong handshake and a direct look).

But Taylor is also from the wrong side of the tracks. After Taylor misses several days of school, Jane goes to her house to check up on her. The house is the opposite of Jane's assiduously suburban, bourgeois house with ample front porch and formal dining room. Taylor lives in an isolated rancher, bleak and barren. And inside is an alcoholic mother who beats her daughter and blames her for her failed marriage. So our lesbian—the one who "brings out" our heroine—is marked as one who comes from a dysfunctional and abusive family.

Nevertheless, Jane is hooked, and when they finally kiss both girls seem equally invested. Jane's internal voice-over asks all the questions ("Is this a phase? Was I gay?") and the confusions are increased after the two have sex. While we don't see them making love, the romantic milieu of candles and gentle kisses and Jane's nervousness make this a lovely rendering of a first-time sexual encounter. Jane, of course, freaks out a bit the next day and tells Taylor that "what happened was a mistake . . . because it isn't normal." Taylor stomps off and Jane is left alone, devastated by the absence of Taylor and the recognition of her own internal deceit. Jane gets more withdrawn at home, her parents get more concerned, and Jane is able to reunite with Taylor.

But the joy of reconciliation is quickly shattered. When Jane's little brother catches the girls kissing, a chain of events is set off that sets the stage for the second half of the movie in which the family drama of coming out takes center stage. Throughout the movie, Jane's voice-over serves to tell the story but, more importantly, to present the most positive rendering of gay identity in the narrative, as when Jane tells us that "when I said it was a phase, it wasn't. I was gay. With or without Taylor. I knew it deep down for a long time. But what my mother didn't know is that I was exactly who I was meant to be, whether she liked it or not." Thankfully, what we do not get in this film is a desperate attempt by Jane to deny her sexuality. While she is in turmoil through much of the movie, the anguish is clearly produced by parental rejection and by the pain of first love.

When Mom gets an anonymous phone call outing Jane as a lesbian, the coming-out plot kicks into high gear, with Jane obviously dying to reveal the truth but being reasonably put off by her parents' obvious horror at the thought of gayness: "I wanted so badly to tell the truth but I was so afraid of losing my parents. I couldn't speak. I made myself sick." In anguish over agreeing to her parents' fiction (we were just practicing kissing), Jane reveals all to mom's gay friend Jimmy, whose support consists of telling her to get a thick skin. And this is when one begins to wonder if anything has really changed. While a film like this is important and appears at first glance to be earnestly anti-homophobic, embracing its lesbian heroine and gently chiding the parents for their rejection, on a deeper level it sends quite retro messages about "acceptance" and tolerance that never challenge homophobia in any meaningful way and that certainly never celebrate gay identity. Coming out is still represented as heartache and anguish. Yes, the anguish is produced at least in part by hurtful parents and peers (and *that* part certainly rings true!), but never is an alternative vision of celebration and embrace offered. Given that Jane is not totally tokenized—that there is another lesbian and an out gay man in the narrative—it is even more disturbing that no character presents a challenge to the version of gay life as hard, painful, to be avoided if at all possible. For example, mom gets angry at Jimmy for his refusal to divulge Jane's "secret," and confronts him with the "truth" of his hard life and her desire to "spare" her daughter. His response is only a reactive one ("Don't judge my life . . .") and not one that in any way challenges the dominant theme of this film (and so many others) that stress the melodramatic rendering of gayness as constant battle against loneliness and despair. I was reminded of the scene between Ellen and therapist Oprah when Ellen finally realizes her sexual identity. She complains to Oprah that no one ever says, "Congratulations, you're gay," as a way to indicate how poorly society treats gay people. Oprah then does so, and the rest of series enacted much of that congratulatory ethos. Perhaps that's why it was canceled.

As Jane begins to get hassled at school ("We were about to reenact 'The Children's Hour' . . .") and home life gets more tense, she finally takes the plunge and, after a knock-down with her teasing brother ("Dyke!"), she tells her parents that "it's not just gossip. I lied to the two of you because I was afraid. Afraid that you'd hate me, afraid that you'd throw me out. I did kiss Taylor and I think I'm in love with her." As the parents throw every cliché available ("But she's a girl . . . you don't know what you're saying . . . you're only sixteen . . . it's just a phase . . .") the following dialogue ensues:

> Jane: If you could just see it through my eyes. To have someone you care about care about you, and they make you feel not so alone in this world. Does it really matter who the person is?
> Mom: Of course it matters.
> Jane: Why? Why? And since when do you hate gay people? Jimmy's been your friend for ever and he's gay?
> Mom: He's not my daughter!

Mom and Dad walk out and leave a weeping Jane in the living room. Here, coming out is framed around a theme of loneliness. Again, no "positive" rendering of "the life" but rather a plea by a daughter who only wants some modicum of care in a world in which she, somehow, feels so alone. The anti-homophobic discourse of a film like this is reduced to a live and let live philosophy: she's our daughter, we have to support her. No one refutes that it is an awful life; as the good father says, "I don't want my child to be gay. But she's our daughter, and we have to find a way to help her through this." Of course, they send her to the requisite shrink and things start to get even worse in the family and, in addition, Mom begins to break off relations with Beth and Jimmy, who urge more "acceptance" than Mom can handle. As Jane acts out (going to clubs late at night, drinking, etc.) she is grounded by her parents and, to make matters worse, gets summarily dumped by cavalier Taylor, who finds that it's "getting out of control. It's not worth it." Jane is devastated, but is somewhat buoyed by the aid of her teacher, Miss Walcott, who comes out to her. Again, what role models: Jimmy tells her to get a thick skin, Miss Walcott is in the closet, Taylor is a victimized toughie who dumps her at the first moment of difficulty. Finally, there is some gay context depicted in representations. But the context is this.

When Jane gets suspended at school for fighting with someone who gay baits her, her parents decide to send her away to boarding school. While Jane recognizes the homophobia of the students and her mother ("Why do you care what they say? You're just like them . . ."), the homophobia goes otherwise unpunished and unnoticed. Where is the gay teacher? In the closet. But not for long, as Jane accidentally outs her to her parents. Mom then runs off to the school, threatening to go to the school board if the evil lesbian teacher (who is a beautiful, very feminine blonde) doesn't stay away from her daughter. Again, no challenge from the teacher until Jane shows up at her door that night, in total despair and threatening to kill herself. Miss Walcott pays a visit to the parents (who never invite her into the house), and this is her "challenge" to the homophobia that has driven their daughter to such lengths: "I understand that I may repulse you. But I also understand Jane's pain. The pain of having people hate you not based on you but based on what I think we have little control over. Jane's only crime is that she loves differently than you do. And you don't have to understand it, or even agree with it, but unless you try to, you're going to lose her forever." Gay love is here referenced through a language of repulsion, pain, crime, loss. The repulsion of the straight for the gay is treated as an unfortunate but understandable part of life, but Jane's parents must understand their daughter—or accept her—not out of any moral and ethical imperative but rather because they might lose her if they don't; indeed, the teacher follows her plea by bringing up Jane's suicide talk, and it is this revelation—

In *The Truth About Jane,* vicious homophobia melts into benign acceptance with the help of a 12-stepping parents' support group and a closeted teacher. Where's the pride? Courtesy of Photofest.

and the fear of loss—that finally motivates homophobic mom to reach out to "accept" her gay daughter.

The reconciliation of mother and daughter is then framed around acceptance, fear of loss, and the continuation of disapproval. When Mom finally—reluctantly—attends a PFLAG meeting, she is greeted by a woman who declaims, "Hi, welcome to PFLAG. I'm Dorothy and my son is gay." The depiction of PFLAG as a carbon copy of AA meetings is disturbing and perplexing. The podium revelations ("I'm Sally, and my daughter is a lesbian . . .") followed by applause for the brave truth-teller, replicates AA ("Hi, I'm John and I'm an alcoholic . . .") and thus perpetuates an image of gayness as illness, as affliction. While Mom keeps muddling along ("I'm going as fast as I can . . .") the moment of truth occurs at a gay pride rally in town, which Mom claims she is not ready to attend. While Jane is accompanied by the rest of the family (including Jimmy and Beth—brought back into the family fold now that mom's getting rehabilitated), she remains disappointed by Mom's absence. Again, the "PFLAG Moms" (and where are the dads?) are the stars of the show, getting huge applause for their twelve-step one-liners. Of course, Mom does show up and Jane's voice-over lets us know that she "was so proud of how well she had grown up." On the Web site Lifetime set up for the movie, the language is one of acceptance and tolerance, and the justification is that "these days, homosexuality is not considered to be an illness nor a lifestyle 'choice,' but rather, it is believed to be biologically determined."[2] While the depictions of parental homophobia and young love are affecting and depressingly realistic, the resolution depends on a '90s discourse that mixes liberal acceptance with biological determinism and legitimated revulsion.

Other contemporary narratives of coming out make sure to keep the family in play, allowing for an "acceptable" amount of disgust while at the same time ensuring that the family not be shattered by the news. When teen Jack comes out on *Dawson's Creek* he is at first greeted with hostility by a difficult father but, through the support of straight friends he is able to make amends with him and reunite. *Dawson's Creek,* it seems, wants to have it both ways. On the one hand, the coming out shows the homophobia of his classmates, but on the other hand his best friends—and the ones that are narratively central—are uniformly supportive and helpful. The young man is assuredly an anti-stereotype: typically masculine, a football star, sought after by girls. While he is depicted eventually "accepting" his homosexuality, it is not without the very clear message that he wished it weren't so. In one episode, Jack tries to avoid his father's questions, but when he finally does get asked he confronts his father, who tells him, "You are not gay!" Jack reveals all and continues to say that "as hard as you've tried to stamp it out and to ignore it . . . I have tried harder . . . I have tried harder than you to be quiet and forget—and not bother my family with my problems. But, I can't try anymore, because it hurts. I'm sorry, Dad . . . Andie, I'm sorry . . . I don't want to be going through this, but I am." When young Jack finally gets up the nerve to kiss the object of his desire, he is stunned to find out that he has reunited with his ex. Back home, he finds solace with a newly understanding Dad, who bonds with him around the pain and suffering of gay romance. Bemoaning his fate ("I didn't ask for this!") Jack challenges his father to reject him, but Dad comes through ("No more than I asked for a gay son . . . but I'm sure glad I got one . . .") as Jack collapses in tears. Still, coming out is presented as an unfortunate problem. These days, it is often depicted as less traumatic than in previous years, yet the possibility of representing the acquisition of gay identity as a positive, joyful embrace is still just wishful thinking.

Another addition in recent years has been the "questioning" youth whose flirtation with homosexuality provides a frisson of difference without shaking up the entire sitcom structure. So in the popular teen series *Party of Five,* lead character Julia gets interested in a lesbian teacher after emerging from an abusive heterosexual relationship. The linkage of lesbianism with abuse by men is a tried and true staple of popular fiction and has not disappeared in this "modern" age. Nevertheless, it remains only a flirtation and Julia returns to heterosexuality, this time one hopes without the abuse.

For older folks, coming out still remains a more tortuous process, at least in the world of popular images. In an episode of the critically acclaimed series, *The Practice*, a cop with crucial evidence in a case is challenged in court. He has a secret—the secret is that he is under care by a psychiatrist because he is gay and has been unable to tell his wife and kids for years. While the entire team works to protect his secret, the ethics of his remaining in the closet never is broached. His adamant refusal to come out, and the support of the space of the closet by the rest of the cast, coupled with the linking of homosexuality to medical care (the psychiatrist), creates an episode that seems remarkably retro for such a putatively "cutting edge" series. What does it mean that in the year 2000 the revelation of gayness is metaphorically treated as deadly disease, worthy of psychiatric treatment, whose revelation will bring dishonor and ruin to its "carrier?" The heterosexual woman steps in to "protect" him, but what is she protecting him from? Homophobia? Truthtelling? Gayness itself? Paired with another plotline about a judge coming to terms with his own self-deception, the episode turns internalized homophobia into a problem with truthfulness, thus helping to maintain the strength of the closet through an invisibility of straight acts of discrimination and violence.

In film, coming out seems no longer much of a story to tell, which is itself an interesting phenomenon. In both mainstream and independent film, the story of the already-gay has trumped the tortured tale of the becoming-gay. Particularly for young men, the genre of the "group of gay male friends" is beginning to emerge, with the recent addition of *The Broken Hearts Club* and Showtime's *Queer as Folk*. Even in narratives of youth, such as *The Incredibly True Adventures of Two Girls in Love,* or *Better Than Chocolate,* the coming-out story is relegated to a sideline, while the focus is much more on the youthful passion itself. Often, in films like *Get Real* and *The Incredibly True Adventures,* one young person is already out and has come to terms with his/her sexuality. When films do focus on coming out—such as the hit film *In & Out*—high comedy prevails and the feel-good message downplays both homophobia and gay self-awareness.

Interestingly, coming-out stories differ according to gender. In *Queer as Folk* and *The Broken Hearts Club,* our newbies emerge into a world of clubs and gay friends (although friends might be too strong a word here!). When young lesbians emerge, the frame is often more intimate and dyadic, with the narrative focusing much more on "falling in love" with one particular person than on entering into a group of like-minded people. Even in *The Truth About Jane,* while we glimpse scenes at a club, a larger gay community or group of friends is absent. Lesbian coming out is thus typically configured as "I happened to fall in love with a woman" or titillating experiment. In the sexy but pointless *It's a Girl Thing,* gorgeous blondes Elle MacPherson and Kate Capshaw go at it gracefully when heretofore straight Lauren (Elle) finds herself mysteriously attracted to the bisexual, prototypical "free spirit" Casey (Kate). The gay world that is depicted trades on stereotypes of tough-looking unattractive dykes, making it much easier to counterpose these two women as elegant exceptions—not gay really, but just two girls who happened to fall in love with each other.

ONCE MORE, WITH FEELING: COMING OUT, AGAIN

While the coming-out narrative may have indeed receded in recent years (and I see this as a significant sign of progress), it can also crop up in some new and interesting ways. On a recent episode of *Will & Grace,* the gang meet up at a restaurant and, while waiting for a table, pull in a stray woman weeping over her boyfriend's lack of interest ("Join our little circle of love and dysfunction . . ."). At once, they recognize the problem: boyfriend is gay. Over champagne, they recount the story of Will and Grace in order to enlighten said young thing and get her to face reality and befriend her "friend of Dorothy" (a phrase meaning "gay" to those in the know). As Jack says, "I think you need to hear a little story about when these two were dating or, as I like to call it, when Mary met Sally." The pathos of the typical coming-out narrative is upturned in numerous ways. In the first place, Will's self-understanding as gay is seen through multiple (humorous) perspectives—through the eyes of Grace, who loves him and feels rejected; through the eyes of already out (but younger) Jack, who adores him from not very afar and who serves as his gay guide; and through the eyes of Will himself, whose turmoil seems much more about losing his dearest friend than about self-loathing and internalized homophobia. Karen's continuous interruptions—with her polymorphously perverse story of her own misspent youth (which includes a hilarious walk-on by Martina Navratilova as her lover)—serve to further assure us of the camp quality of this tale. The point here is not the typical one of self-discovery, internal struggle, familial rejection, reconciliation. Rather, they all talk the talk to let their sad, deluded sister walk the walk with them: their storytelling is about speaking queerly, throwing down the signs (if only she would see them!) so that, when all is said and done, she can befriend her homoman the way Grace so lovingly did.

When she still doesn't get it (and here the heterosexual is outsider), Karen finally lets her have it: "Oh cripes honey, let me give it to you in a nut-shell. Your boyfriend's a big, flaming, feather-wearing, man-kissing, disco-dancing, Vermont-living, Christina Aguilara-loving, Mykonos-going—honey, take it on home . . . ," and, with this cue, Jack lets her know that "Tom's queer, dear."

In the end, a queer community seems to peek through—nobody emerges very straight and all but one can read the signs (and she might well learn). An individual, coming-out-as-coming-of-age tale gets re-worked as a queer, bitchy, gotta-have-friends riff on community.

Ten

IT TAKES A LESBIAN
VILLAGE TO RAISE A
CHILD: PARENTING
POSSIBILITIES

I'm driving my daughter and her friend to kindergarten one morning, doing that car-pooling thing with another family. The kids tend to play elaborate games in the back seat, from "pediatric endocrinologist" (my daughter has diabetes) to Spanish-speaking denizens of a happening disco (they go to a bilingual school). For some reason, this morning they were writing down the names of their "family" on brightly colored pads of paper, intently focused on both the declaration of each name and the elaborate calligraphy that goes for youthful spelling. My daughter's friend quickly jotted down her names: Mommy, Daddy, Annie. But Emma's list began like this: Emma, Mommy, Bubbe, Marcia (my partner at the time), Annie (my dearest friend—and an ex—and also Emma's legal guardian), Annie's Lisa (her partner of ten-plus years), Ara (another dear friend and ex), Ara's Stephanie (ditto, sans the ex part), Tanta Lisa (my single-parent sister), Daniel (her adopted son), Diane (another old friend), Ruben (her husband), Arturo (their son), Uncle Shalom (the ex-husband of my estranged sister), Joey and Sammy (his sons), Larry and Mary (more friends), Amy (an old girlfriend and single mom), Ariel (her daughter). My daughter was still writing as we pulled up to the school.

Nothing evokes emotions like the term "family." Always a politicized term, it was raised to new heights (or lows!) by Dan Quayle's tirade against sitcom character Murphy Brown's single motherhood. Quayle's rant—and its aftermath—was but one moment in a larger campaign to make "family values" the new litmus test for political viability. Like so many sound bite phrases, this one encoded much as it worked its way through the cultural landscape. Clearly, and most explicitly, it was an attack on single mothers with special venom reserved for "feminist" single mothers by choice (Murphy) and "dependent" poor, black, teenage single mothers. Family values was thus used as a term to vilify those who challenged—either directly or indirectly—the dominance and desirability of the father-headed, nuclear family.

It is no coincidence that the contemporary "family values" debate emerges in the context of growing discussion and examination of the multiplicity of family forms. In an era when both the feminist and the gay movements have challenged the centrality and desirability of the heterosexual nuclear family (by the ongoing revelations of child abuse, incest, wife battering, etc., as well as through the exposure of more mundane forms of inequity and domination), the phrase "family values" emerges as the catch-all term that attempts to set up a great and impenetrable dividing line between virtuous traditionalists and hedonistic experimenters.

But "family values" was not restricted to its obvious anti-feminist manifestations. It also became a code word for a much more broad-based attack on family diversity and individual self-expression. The deeming of gays and lesbians as "anti-family" is nothing new in the history of homophobia. Indeed, both religious and nonreligious justifications for discrimination have often been based on the assumption that lesbian and gay "lifestyles" threaten the sanctity of the nuclear family by proposing and practicing a sexuality not centered on reproduction. In addition, heterosexual fears of gay "recruitment" ("they want our children") have always been used to whip up anti-gay hysteria. Alongside the fear of "recruitment" has been the mistaken belief that lesbian and gay parents are more likely to produce gay children or foist their gay identity upon their progeny. Indeed, this has been a persistent sore point for more liberal supporters of gay rights who believe that—while it may be unjust—children of gay parents suffer unnecessarily for the choices of their parents. In this view, a critique of homophobia exists alongside a condemnation of "selfish" parents who knowingly expose children to a world of discrimination and prejudice. Whether liberal or outright reactionary, straight folks have always had trouble when the words "gay" and "children" are linked.

It should come as no surprise, then, that some of the most interesting mainstream films discussed in the previous section concern family and its redefinition. The family is both fault line and detonation device, both the place where a resistant culture throws down the gauntlet and the explosive moment of catalytic change. Indeed, "family" is the cultural backdrop for so much of our representational life that marking it out for special attention is in some senses an exercise in futility, as family life and familial discourses frame much of our popular culture. The visibility of the gay family has been plagued by some of the same problems we have seen in relation to film, television, and political discourse, plagued by the vacillation between the depiction of gay families as heterosexual clones and gay families as encroaching, exotic threats. Thus, like so much this book attempts to chart, gay family life too is marked by the frustrating sense of simultaneous victory and retrenchment. For every city or company that grants domestic partner benefits, many others avoid the issue assiduously. For every successful custody suit, there seem to be two defeats. For every parent who is able to successfully "adopt" her or his nonbiological child, others are endlessly delayed or deferred. And, needless to say, it takes great financial resources to be able to access even these tenuous legal avenues.

Nonetheless, gay parents are now a visible, present force to be reckoned with, forming organizations, support groups, participating in PTAs and Little Leagues. There are organizations such as the twelve-year-old Center Kids—based out of NYC's Lesbian and Gay Community Center—which now has a roster of over 2,000 families. Newsletters such as *The Family Next Door* and alternative insemination clinics such as Boston's Fenway have proliferated, as gay parents develop into a recognizable social grouping replete with kiddie camps, gay family cruises, Maybe Baby classes, lesbian Lamaze, and the like. The current "gayby boom" seems to be the result of a confluence of factors: the availability of sperm banks and other reproductive technologies, the growth of the lesbian and gay movement, and the emergence of couples and individuals who never were "in" the closet and never had to extricate themselves from straight relationships, families, marriages.

Let's be clear, lesbians and gays have always had children. What we are witnessing now, though, is the growing phenomena of lesbians and, to a lesser extent, gay men, having children *as gay people,* outside of the conventions of heterosexuality and marriage. Again, this is not brand-new, there have always been gay people who have been out enough—and brave enough—to live their lives the way they wanted to, including having children. But for many lesbians and gays, certainly those of the pre-Stonewall era, gayness itself seemed to close off the possibility of having children. Gayness seemed so outside of the realm of family that not being able to have children appeared the inevitable price to pay for a life on the margins. In earlier times, then, most gay people had children within the contexts of heterosexual relationships, relationships in which they often hid their desires and led painful double lives. They may have raised those children as heterosexuals, only later (sometimes) to come out of the closet and attempt to renegotiate their relationships within the context of their new gay identity. In story after story of older gays, one of the constant refrains has to do with children and family. For many gays, the stress of coming out to parents was exacerbated by a recognition that the parent would not only be experiencing the loss of the presumed heterosexual son/daughter, but of the prospect of grandchildren as well. Parents often report this as one of their biggest fears upon hearing that their child is gay: assuming that gayness disenables reproduction.

Earlier, more pathologizing renderings of homosexuality clearly marked gays as bad candidates for parenthood. If gayness was thought of as arrested development (as in much of psychoanalytic theory), then how could gays be parents? If gayness was thought of as inherited disease, then it might be transferred to progeny. If gayness was understood as predatory and inclined toward conversion, then kids would be forced into "the life" by their recruiting parents. There were no cultural role models, no familial portraits of gays and lesbians, no inkling in the vast social landscape that it could be done.

And just as gay weddings were met with the Defense of Marriage Act, so too have gay parents been met with increasing attacks and roadblocks. The National Center for Lesbian Rights, Lambda Legal Defense Fund, and other gay legal organizations regularly defend mothers and fathers in custody cases, around visitation rights, and in second-parent adoptions. While it is true that sexual orientation in and of itself is less and less a reason to deny custody, the practice still goes on daily with judges around the country. As of 1995, eight state supreme courts have ruled that a gay parent should not automatically be denied custody, but five have ruled the opposite. Roughly half the states have moved toward not making sexual orientation a per se bar to custody, but the District of Columbia is the only jurisdiction in the country that has actually passed a law that says sexual orientation is not "dispositive" in awarding custody. A number of other states have said as much through the courts, but others continue to routinely use sexual orientation as a factor in determining custody, visitation, and adoption, particularly in the South. Gay women are frequently denied access to alternative insemination and both lesbians and gay men are routinely turned down in attempts to foster and adopt.

Victories are often fleeting and can be reversed at a moment's notice. For example, the supreme court of Missouri reversed a landmark court of appeals decision which had overturned "eighteen years of previous Missouri decisions holding that a lesbian or gay parent is automatically unfit to have custody."[1] A similar overturn of an appeals court ruling for the lesbian mother was enacted by a supreme court in Alabama which "made no attempt to conceal its bias against the mother . . . stating that '[the lesbian mother] has chosen to expose the child continuously to a lifestyle that is neither legal in this state, nor moral in the eyes of most of its citizens.'"[2] And, in 2000, the state superior court of Pennsylvania ended the practice of second-parent adoptions in fourteen counties that had been going on for years, proving the important point that victories won can be easily reversed.

On the other hand, positive rulings persist, such as the landmark Maryland case in which gay legal eagles Lambda successfully won a "permanent end to the restrictions on Glenn Boswell's visitation with his two children."[3] Indeed, the Maryland court went even further, arguing that "the need for a factual finding of harm to the child requires that the court focus on evidence-based factors and not on stereotypical presumptions of future harm."[4] Then again, 1999 was ushered in with two states (Arkansas and Utah) adopting "regulations specifically preventing gays and lesbians from becoming foster parents or adopting children,"[5] and bills have been introduced in many more states attempting to prohibit fostering, adoptions, or both. In addition, "courts in New York and Virginia have dealt serious blows to adoptions by lesbian and gay parents, leading both advocates and opponents to say that the legal climate seems to be growing inhospitable to such adoptions."[6] A recent ruling in California gives gay and lesbian parents the same tax benefits given to unmarried heterosexuals with children, effectively making the nonbiological gay parent the "head of household" for tax purposes.[7] Every day brings with it new victories and new defeats, and many of these rulings highlight the difficulty in "thinking" gay families through the lens of a heterosexual, nuclear family.

Indeed, as gays now increasingly build families as open and proud gay people, new issues have arisen that have challenged the courts and society itself to rethink the very terms of "family." One of the most important new developments has been that of second-parent or co-parent adoptions, in which the nonbiological same-sex partner adopts the child. These new moves are not without their detractors; organizations such as the conservative Family Research Council have been active in denouncing second-parent adoptions as chipping away at the heterosexual two-parent model. "It's parental malpractice," says Robert Knight of the conservative Family Research Council. "This is an attempt to hijack the moral capital of the mom-and-dad family. Children need moms and dads. They don't need two moms or two dads." When lesbians and gays do gain access to essentials such as second-parent adoptions, they generally do so "in a complex and expensive two-step process, in which first one parent is allowed to adopt and then the second can petition for joint rights." But a landmark 1997 New Jersey decision allows both parents to adopt together, sharing equally the legal rights and responsibilities. This becomes, of course, "a signal from the state that a gay couple can act as a family unit. More critically, it could determine a child's fate if something happened to one parent. In addition, married couples tend to have an advantage over single people in seeking adoption rights. With New Jersey law now allowing gays as well as unmarried heterosexual couples equal adoption rights, the automatic advantage of married couples would disappear."[8] Of course, victories like these are quickly denounced, by the likes of the Family Research Council, as "a victory for homosexual activism and a defeat for children already bruised in life and in need of an intact, committed husband-and-wife family."[9]

AND A WHITE PICKET FENCE: SELLING GAY SAMENESS

Of course, one would expect the right to see gay parenting as the ultimate horror show. If gays can stake claim to that hallowed ground of (presumed) heterosexuality, then the whole edifice of so-called "family values" becomes shaky. So it comes as little surprise that the site of gay parenting is a heady one for anti-gay fulminations. But, as I have argued throughout this book, the new discourse of liberal tolerance has, at least in some venues and in some ways, displaced these more openly hostile diatribes. The representations of lesbian and gay parents by the "enlightened" media evinces a form of homophobia that is at once less dramatic and more insidious, focusing as it does on acceptance of gay parents as heterosexual clones. For all the confusion and localism of gay family *rulings and legislation,* dominant themes in our popular culture do emerge. Whether it is marriage or parenting, both well-meaning heterosexuals *and* mainstream gays seem to stress gay sameness to straights. Our relationships, our desires, our patterns of partnering, our parenting styles are again and again presented as replicas of heterosexual patterns, as if gay families exist in a sort of alternate universe that isn't really alternate at all. While odes to family *diversity* abound, real invocations of family *difference* are muted.

The resistance (by both gays and straights) to gay parenting *as different* is chilling. Even in descriptions of such seemingly "different" events such as a gathering of gay parents and their kids (Rainbow Families Conference and Celebration), sameness with hetero families is stressed. A participant in the conference, Deb Kotcher of Minneapolis, claims that "this is an alternative image of what it means to be gay or lesbian, it shows people that we are passionate parents who put our kids first and live pretty much the same way as everyone else."[10] But the irony in this drive for sameness is that these parents are meeting *as* lesbian and gay parents, signifying a recognition of the need for mutual support and the *difference* of gay parenting.

Given heterosexual mistreatment of gay parents, what remains striking are the narratives by both gays and straights that relegate this mistreatment to a sidebar while focusing on the overwhelming "truth" of assimilated sameness. In article after article on, for example, gays with children, the reader is presented with strikingly similar formats. Articles typically go something like this: "Little Katy is playing in her crowded room with her beat-up old dolly and a mass of congealed Play-Doh. She is a bundle of energy, babbling mysterious words, running around the room, occasionally dipping in her bowl of Cheerios, while her parents grin in exasperation and anxiously keep her out of harm's way. She is like every other happy, healthy, willful two-year-old. Except Katy has two mommies." In other words, the parents might be June and June (instead of June and Ward) but—not to worry America—it's all the same anyway. In and of itself, there is nothing so terribly wrong with this: the lives of gay families do indeed often look much the same as the lives of straight families. Kids have to be fed, diapered, bathed, loved, taught, bundled off to school, disciplined, nurtured. Barney rules, wherever you go. Nevertheless, in the context of structural discrimination, things take on a different hue. Katy is—of course—like every other kid. But she is a kid that will have to face homophobic comments (and perhaps worse) from other kids, parents, schoolteachers. She is a kid who will rarely see her life depicted in the textbooks and teaching aides, much less the TV she will endlessly consume. Her parents do not have the same rights as other parents; they can lose jobs, be denied housing, not be promoted. She can even be removed from her parents simply because of their sexual orientation. In addition, it just might be the case that her parents don't *want* their lives to look like that of the Cleavers. Perhaps they want to build *new* kinds of families with *different* kinds of values.

Finally, gay parents are visible and are not (by and large) depicted in popular culture as lurking demons and perverts. What could be wrong with this? When the media make gays "safe" for American cultural consumption, are they not confining gays to a new kind of closet and denying the realities of homophobia? In "reducing" homophobia through assimilation there is a danger of making homosexuality itself invisible again—"straight, with a twist." Aside from the obvious and tendentious attacks by the right, denouncing gay parents as immoral and dangerous to the very concept of family, most reportage is supportive and steers clear of overt bigotry, although they almost always insert a line or two from the likes of Gary Bauer or James Dodson. Like so much of current discourse around lesbians and gays, the dominant liberal ethos does not simply gay bash or rule out of hand the possibility of gays raising happy and healthy children. What these articles do share is an almost identical narrative; indeed, in literally dozens if not hundreds of pieces on gay families, the writers could be interchangeable, such is the continuity of style and substance. Here are some samples:

> The children chatter on about their dreams and plans as their parents look on with pride. Except for the fact that both parents are female, they are much like any other family. Perhaps the most striking thing about this ex-traordinary family is how ordinary they are.[11]

> To look at her, Alanna Gabrielle Handler seems an altogether conventional baby. Just 14 weeks old, she scrunches her tiny face and inspires the usual oohs and ahhs. The nursery in her family's Van Nuys apartment is pastel and girlish and graced with a banner proclaiming, "Welcome Alanna— Grandma and Grandpa." But Alanna is not a typical infant. She was not conceived the traditional way and her parents are not a conventional couple—or should we say trio? No, Alanna is different. She is a tribute to lesbian romance and a product of artificial insemination, a baby whose very existence challenges traditional views of nature and family. And for the gay rights movement, she is a tiny bundle of hope.[12]

> In many ways, Katie Love-Cooksey's world is no different than any other 5-year-old girl's. She has a taste for very feminine things, prefers dresses and Mary Jane shoes to pants and enjoys her Barbie dolls. When she grows up, she wants to be a ballerina.[13]

> Sunshine streams into the kitchen as a small, tow-headed boy and his par-ents bite into breakfast muffins rich with cherries from their backyard or-chard in Cockeysville, Md. There's a whisper of white noise from the room monitor tuned to a sleeping baby. It's a Kodak moment of the '90s: Dad, Daddy and Duncan.[14]

> School's out. Eugene explodes through the door. Homework comes first, but Nintendo has been calling him all day. Danielle storms in starving. Good new, she says, slicing off hunks of cheese. Teacher forgot to give us homework. Jason gets home last, finds Turtle, his stuffed alter ego, and climbs onto his dad's lap for a hug. How was your day? Fine, he signs. They're a pretty typical family, the Serkin-Pooles: Three kids. A split-level house on a cul-de-sac in Bellevue, across Lake Washington from Seattle. A basketball hoop out front. Nintendo on the basement TV. A snooty cat named Ariel. A collection of potato bugs gasping for air in a jar. And two doting dads.[15]

> Four-year-old Trevor wants to touch the ceiling. He leaps, grunts and tries to climb the wall, but soon figures out he's not going to get there on his own. "If you put me on your shoulders, I can touch the ceiling," he tells his dad. Dad is dubious—but a good sport. The shouldering is successful. But the pair are still inches away from their destination. Enter Dad-dy. He

lifts his son easily onto his taller shoulders and raises the little boy's arms. Mission accomplished. Innocent of the social implications of being the adopted son of gay parents, Trevor is quite content to have two fathers. . . . In all but one respect, they are the classic America family. The couple say that despite what stereotypes might suggest about a male child raised by gay men, Trevor is "all boy." He loves trucks, guns, sports and playing in the dirt, and wants to be a policeman.[16]

In 1992 the *Chicago Tribune* did a two-part series on the "growing phenomenon of gay and lesbian parenting" that acknowledged that "while gay and lesbian parents confront legal issues that straight couples take for granted, for the most part their joys and travails in raising children are little different. 'We get up in the morning and get our kids breakfast and get them off to school,' Robinson said. 'We pick them up and take them to tap dance class and football practice. Our issues, our lives are the same as those of any parent.'"[17]

When mainstream narratives aren't extolling the sameness of homosexual family life, they are concerned with how children of gay parents will reckon with their own sexuality. A number of articles raise the issue of whether children raised by gay parents will themselves be gay or otherwise "do worse" than other kids. To counter the hetero fears of a bumper crop of gay kids emerging from the gayby boom, gay researchers have jumped into the fray to argue that children of gay parents are "no worse" off than kids of "normal" parents: "In the largest study of its kind to date, a University of Virginia psychologist has found that children born to or adopted by lesbians are psychologically healthy. The study involved 4–9-year-olds in 37 lesbian families from the Bay Area. Although other studies have indicated that the children of gay parents show normal personal and emotional development, most of the earlier research has focused on children born to heterosexual couples in which either the father or the mother later came out of the closet. The parents in the new study by Charlotte Patterson, an associate professor of psychology, were open lesbians when they had their children."[18] Patterson, one of the pundits in this area, challenges the heterosexual fears "that homosexuals recruit their children to their lifestyle—which, besides being insulting to gays, appears to be empirically false."[19] But this article goes on to challenge the claim that kids raised by gays are no more likely to be themselves gay by indicating that "there is some conflicting evidence: One 1986 study of 34 gay households indicated that the children became homosexual or bisexual 15 percent of the time; and a 1990 study, published in the book, 'Homosexuality and Family Relations,' found that 16 percent of the daughters of lesbian mothers identified themselves as lesbian. Both of these findings might be seen as worst-case scenarios, but other studies come up with figures below 10 percent for children of gays and lesbians."[20] Like many other articles (including those by gay researchers) this kind of discourse implies a "natural" desire to raise children as heterosexual and figures the incidence of gayness in kids raised by gays as a "worst-case scenario." Like the discourse that argues children of single parents fare "as well" as children of two-parent households, it inadvertently lends itself to a reassertion of the centrality and desirability of heterosexuality and dual parenting. It takes a kid, of course, to set us "straight" about gay parenting. An article about same-sex parents focusing on the author Phyllis Burke (*Family Values: Two Moms and Their Son*) features the thoughts of ten-year-old Jenilee Boyd: "At first, she said, she was worried that because her mom was a lesbian, that might make her a lesbian. 'Then I thought, if I am gay, so what, and if not, so what,' she said. 'I think I am being raised differently, but I don't think there's anything wrong with being raised differently. Whoever I become, I become.'"[21]

An interesting article in *Newsweek* picks up on the contradictions expressed in narratives of gay parents. On the one hand, as the article points out, "being social pioneers is never easy" and these lesbian moms face a wide range of discrimination—from neighbors who avoid them, to inappropriate questions, to outright hostility. And this structure of discrimination and the adjustments made to it convince the moms that "their sons are growing up with a profound sense of diversity and tolerance." Yet this recognition of gay difference—and the effect it has on parenting styles and structures—meets up with an equally strong commitment to a belief that "people realize we're not that different." One mom argues that "most Americans haven't come into personal contact with lesbians and gay men . . . and we hope that when they see us, they think, 'They look just like us. They have kids like us. Their kids play with Pokemon just like ours do.'"[22] The linkage of family, children, and marriage couldn't be more explicit, as we are told that, amidst all the discrimination and double standards, "some dreams do come true." One woman reports that "when I was 8 years old . . . I was playing with dolls and thinking what it would be like to be married. I imagined a life like I had now. The difference is I didn't marry Ken. I married Barbie."[23]

NOT THE BRADYS: TALES OF GAYS PARENTS

Gay parents have a strange history in films and television. Typically, since gayness used to be considered de facto singleness, gays (particularly men) have been seen in units of one, set off not only from a community of other gay people but from that which—at least in our culture—signifies "the good life": a family. Earlier renderings of gay parents almost completely conflated the narratives of parenting with those of coming out. So in the infamous TV movie of 1972—*That Certain Summer*—gay divorced dad Doug (Hal Holbrook) is forced to come out to his fourteen-year old son when the obviousness of his relationship with another man (played by Martin Sheen) becomes unavoidable. Self-hating Doug is left bereft of his son and, of course, no intimacy between the men was allowed. Even in *Lianna,* John Sayles's quirky lesbian movie, the conflation of parenting and coming out undercuts the possibility of a meaningful dialogue on gay parenting as a specific and unique mode. The 1978 TV movie with Jane Alexander and Gena Rowlands, *A Question of Love,* frames the custody battle and attendant debates with ex-husbands in the context of a coming out to the eldest son.

The short-lived TV series *Normal, Ohio* moves a bit away from this model. Gay dad William ("Butch") Gamble (played by an increasingly rotund John Goodman) returns to his hometown to reunite with his grown son. Here, parenting and being gay are seen as mutually exclusive. It is wholly unclear why dad has remained so cut off from his son. The implication is that he left the family upon coming out, never to be heard from again until he shows up at his sister's house four years later. While the series seems built around the reuniting of gay dad with straight (and often homophobic) family, Butch seems to do little parenting and is "devised as a happily outspoken, unapologetic gay man who offers no evidence of a gay lover, past or present" and who evinces more "delight in shocking and embarrassing his bigoted father"[24] than in reinventing his family life. As one reviewer notes, "The show does revolve around a gay character, but it seems to be written with a pandering nod to those viewers who are uncomfortable with gayness."[25] While putatively at ease with his homosexuality, Butch can't really bring himself to combat homophobia. He brushes off the remarks of his family with glib asides and, when faced with taunting football fans, he drags his angry son off rather than confront the homophobia. The bigots are airily dismissed and the son's attempts to fight the good fight rebuffed.

In early TV renderings, such as an episode of *Marcus Welby* from 1973, gay parents (usually fathers) are depicted as pathetic sickos who must be cured so as to protect their children. In early film, married gay men were depicted as haunted figures, lurking around gay bars and inviting humiliation and, typically, death. Their gayness was a sign of their betrayal of family, their inability to be meaningful and responsible parents.

Until recently, most renderings of gay parents have shown them as refugees from ill-conceived marriages. In other words, gay parents have been largely depicted as having produced their children in the context of heterosexual relationships and then reckoning with their parenting in the context of their newly out gayness. This remains overwhelmingly the case, and should be no surprise. Certainly, such has indeed been the experience of most gays until recently. In this sense, our popular media is reflecting the actual ways in which the vast majority of gays came into parenthood—through heterosexual relationships. And while this *social* reality has changed, there are still very few *cultural* examples of gays becoming parents in the context of their gayness. Nevertheless, there have been some notable exceptions, from the lesbian mom in *Ellen* to the glam lesbian couple in *If These Walls Could Talk*. Numerous series have featured lesbians attempting parenthood, including the TV producer on *Sisters*, who gets pregnant with the sperm of a friend's husband, and the cop on *NYPD Blue* who befriends goofy Medavoy and gets him to donate sperm as well.

Surprisingly, it was a 1993 ABC after-school special about lesbian mothers (*Other Mothers*) that came close to depicting a gay household not preceded by heterosexuality. Starring the ever-present TV mom Meredith Baxter, and Joanna Cassidy as the biological mother, this TV movie is remarkable in its ability to make the sameness ideology powerful and moving. These moms are perfect, their son is perfect, their home life squeaky clean and bordering on a parody of '50s sitcom life. The parents and kids who harass them come off as silly bigots and the gay family is wholeheartedly embraced as positive and healthy. Of course, this haven is dependent on an aggressive insistence—through visuals, dialogue, actions—that these lesbian moms construct a "normative" household for their heterosexual son. The stage is set even before the opening credits, when young Will is seen playing basketball at his new school, making friends, and returning home to shoot some more hoops in the suburban driveway. He is greeted by one mom, who nags him about his homework, and then by mom number two, who drives up with the groceries and more homework questions. The opening scene thus introduces us to hypernormal Will in a hypernormal home environment. Then the kicker comes to let us know that this is, in fact, no ordinary family. When he tells them not to worry about his homework, Mom number two responds, "Don't worry? We're your parents!"

Like the newspaper articles on gay parents, the structure visually asserts the absolute ordinariness of the family life as a precursor to the introduction of the gay theme. This strategy clearly invites the "sympathy" of the viewer (see, they look just like us, or—really—just like other TV offerings of "normal families"), gaining a certain amount of identification with the moms prior to the introduction of the sexual identity that will, presumably, challenge that identification. Thus, when the harassment of Will and his moms inevitably begins, we are wholly prepared to stand with them, to stand for the moms, to share the position of their brave son who resists the attempts to distance him from the women who raised him.

One of the interesting things about this film is that it actually takes a good fifteen to twenty minutes for us to find out who the biological mom is. In fact, while the film could very easily slip into a determinist position, situating the bio mom as the "real" mom who knows more about her kid, is more attuned to his needs, the film undercuts this possibility by playing it up directly. Toward the end, when Will breaks down and tells them, "I don't want to be different anymore! I'm sick of it!" the two women have an argument in which the bio mom (Linda) pulls rank by saying, "It's not the same for you," in an attempt to get Paula, the nonbiological mom, to acquiesce to her desire to sort of "re-closet" themselves. But the determinism gets firmly stamped down when Paula incredulously asks her, "Is this what it comes down to all these years? Biology?" Clearly, we are meant to identify both women as co-equal partners in the parenting of this boy, a parenting that began when Will was only two, thus effectively removing the heterosexual origins of his birth.

Because it is an after-school special geared toward kids, the focus is on Will and his ability to wrestle with the bigotry and ostracism that comes his way as a result of his family being "different." When the moms attend a school meeting of the "booster club" (Will is an aspiring basketball player), they casually and easily "out" themselves ("I'm Will's other mother . . .") and the idyllic family scene laid out so strongly at the outset begins to unravel. The homophobic booster club president pays them a visit, urging Paula to stay away because the club is limited to "family." When Paula refuses, the homophobia gets stepped up and Will becomes teased, ostracized, cut off from basketball and the coach he worships. The school is no help, and the guidance counselor holds the parents responsible for "forcing" him to deal with these issues.

The question of the movie becomes, then, focused on how Will will respond to peer pressure and deal with the homophobia that is now pervasive. And here the message is mixed. After all is said and done, Will learns the lesson of standing up for equality and insists his mothers come to the basketball game, a game in which he sits on the bench because of his homophobic coach. The film ends with images of the family together—moms proudly in the stands cheering him on, Will standing up to the coach: the lesson has been learned. Indeed, the mothers have transferred their values onto the son, as indicated in one of the previous scenes, late in the film. After Will has had his "I don't want to be different anymore!" blowup, Paula is waiting for him when he comes home. He has just had an emotional conversation with Paula's brother, who has spoken with him about bigotry and fear of difference. Paula comes up to Will's room and sits on the bed with him.

> Paula: You said before that I wanted you to be different. I take no special joy in being different Will. I accept it, in the same way I accept that I have a knack for science, no knack for sports.
> Will: Why are you shoving it in my face?
> Paula: I'm not trying to shove it in your face. But every time I stick up for myself, challenge someone's prejudice, I feel like I'm fighting for all of us.
> Will: Maybe I don't want you to fight for me anymore.
> Paula: I hadn't thought of that.

She leaves the room, stops at the door and tells him how much they both love him. Now, while the comparison of her lesbianism to absence of sports ability is galling, and "no joy in being different" a sad statement, the lesbian mom here is allowed a voice, a voice of strength and protest. And her son's statement that he doesn't want her to fight for him anymore is interesting, given that this moment is followed by the scene where he asks both of them to come to the game. Maybe they have passed on lesbian family values, where the son now takes on the (shared) responsibility of fighting for what is right and just. Maybe they don't need to fight for him anymore because he can now do some of that fighting for them.

This TV movie was thus unusual in many respects. Not only did it depict a healthy and happy lesbian household, but heterosexuality was reduced to the margins. The focus was thus more directly on parenting *as* gay people. In contrast, most TV movies, sitcoms, series, and mainstream films that present gay parents have had as their dramatic focus custody disputes. While vitally important to depict, custody battles—like coming-out stories—focus on the terrifying moment of impact between hetero- and homosexuality. The practice of gay parenting, the attempts to think through alternative structures of care and intimacy, are necessarily reduced to the margins as plots revolve around the epic struggle to keep one's own children.

Of course, these custody stories need to be told and the battles for lesbians and gays to keep their own children remains an ever-present reality. Indeed, the case of Sharon Bottoms —the Virginia woman who lost custody of her son to her own mother—found its way into a 1999 TV movie, *Two Mothers for Zachary*. While obviously sympathetic to the mother and her partner, the show pulls at our heartstrings at the same time that it "degays" the couple. Not only do they have little lesbian context or show any substantive affection toward one another, but they look far "femmer" than the actual couple of Sharon Bottoms and April Wade, and clearly less enmeshed in a lesbian social world.

A more substantive and supportive gay community is depicted in the poignant custody drama *What Makes a Family,* which premiered in January of 2001 starring Brooke Shields and Cherry Jones. Like many of these lesbian custody TV movies, one of the women (in this case Jones) plays the more "experienced" lesbian who initiates the untested object of her affection into "the life." While this may ring true for some of us, rarely are we shown lesbian couples (or singles) whose sexuality is depicted as proactive and chosen, determined less by the love of a good woman than by the constructing of identity and the vicissitudes of desire. And rarely are we shown lesbian couples with children outside of the agonies of custody battles. This TV movie is no different. When the biological mom Sandy (played by Jones) dies after a debilitating illness, Janine (Shields) loses custody to Sandy's parents, only to regain it later with the help of a civil rights lawyer (Whoopie Goldberg) and a crew of supportive friends. Unlike in the Sharon Bottoms TV movie, a gay community *is* shown, replete with a multicultural cast of engaged friends who share in childcare and support Janine's legal struggles.

But this thoughtful drama (albeit with little in the way of sexual intimacy) is an exception, and earlier examples, such as 1978's *A Question of Love* (starring Gena Rowlands and Jane Alexander), are disturbingly similar to the more recent ones (e.g. the Sharon Bottoms story), replete with homophobic parents, custody battles, and bigoted legal system. Fair enough and, sadly, true enough. My concern is rather with the depiction of lesbianism as a "one-off" sort of scenario, an "I fell in love with a girl" narrative that inevitably marginalizes both the women's movement and the gay movement as active participants in the acquisition of lesbian identity. Indeed, in most of these dramas, lesbian identity is an unfortunate occurrence resulting from the chance encounter with romance in the feminine form or, as Linda Rae in *A Question of Love* says, "A person doesn't choose everything in their life. Some things just happen." Where's the joy, the passion, the desire *for*? The lesbian moms in our popular imagination don't want to reinvent family, they just want to be left alone in their determined sameness, "free to be you and me" in a nonthreatening non-nuclear family.

AND BABY MAKES . . . TWO: ONE MOTHER'S STORY

As I entered the growing ranks of lesbian mothers, I was struck by the persistence of heterosexual fear and unease, aware that my way of doing family challenges much they hold dear. Certainly, I want to raise my daughter to believe that families come in many forms, that two parents are not necessary and that couples (or individuals) of one gender may provide all the "role models" needed for healthy development. I try to raise her in a community of like-minded people and, in doing so, help to break the hold that the "Cleaver Family" model still has on our cultural imagination. Even for less politically minded gay parents, the choice to raise a child must entail a challenge to many accepted notions of family life and family formation. Times certainly have changed in this regard, and my experience of lesbian motherhood is, I believe, illustrative of some transformations and issues both between straights and gays and within the gay community itself.

I will never forget the time I brought my daughter—barely four months old—to a Kol Nidre service at the local lesbian and gay synagogue. Dressed in her hippest outfit (leopard print pants and top with matching cap) all eyes were upon her. From the beginning of the service, as we milled about the church (borrowed for the occasion), to the end, schmoozing outside on the steps, I felt suffused—almost overwhelmed—by the warmth and beloved attention that came Emma's way. Now, I could attribute this to her exceptional beauty and charm, but— as a wee infant—her delightful manner had yet to emerge. Something was certainly going on. As hands reached out to softly touch her hair and the line formed for the post-service viewing, I was struck by the delight my community seemed to have in this child. Now most people do coo and chuckle over a cute baby. And god knows my daughter is cute. But the response to Emma seemed much more engaged and deliberate—as if to acknowledge our disenfranchisement from this reproductive option and to celebrate it at long last. An elderly heterosexual couple came up to talk with me, tears in their eyes. Their son had recently died of AIDS— he had been a member of this congregation. They wanted to thank me for bringing Emma, for having Emma. An older lesbian approached me and talked to me about "the old days" when it was simply assumed that gay people did not parent, at least not as gay people. Her regrets were clear, even as she talked about her recent decision to attempt adoption. A thirty-something couple approached me for info, comparing notes on sperm banks and pondering the possibility of play groups in the future. This is only one event among many, and Kol Nidre is already an overweighted holiday, filled as it is with memories of those gone and the mournful tones of the cantor's invocation of Kaddish. But I was to find events like this repeated and repeated over the course of Emma's young life, as she was repeatedly welcomed into the world by a newly awakened gay community. In Provincetown, the lesbian moms banded together on a section of Herring Cove, staking out baby territory amidst the friendly hordes of topless young women. In demonstrations and Pride Days, babies figure prominently, adorned with appropriate bumper stickers affixed to their overburdened strollers. And everywhere, everywhere questions. Because the production of a child through anonymous donor by a single lesbian demanded the production of new discourse. How did you do it? Did you go to a doctor? What sperm bank did you use? Did you tell them you were a lesbian? Did they turn you down? Did you experience hostility or discrimination? How did you pick the donor? What was the hospital scene like? What are you going to tell her? Many of the answers to these questions are like any others around pregnancy and birth— when you strip aside the mystification of it all, it is really a rather animalistic and earthy procedure. But other questions, other discussions were particular to this time and place, to this situation, to lesbians choosing children.

My particular situation is perhaps unique (and perhaps not), but it does raise some important questions for how we think about family. For me, having a child was never about an attempt to replicate heterosexual parenting. Because I came from a fairly progressive family and was raised in an era of possibilities, it frankly never occurred to me that being a lesbian would prevent me from having children. On the contrary, I always assumed I would, always wanted to have children, and was simply waiting for the right time. Unlike with most heterosexual women, nothing could have been more planned. While certainly more and more women are controlling their own reproduction and planning when and if to have children, the deliberation that goes into lesbian motherhood by choice is profound. Not dependent on the "right man" to turn up, lesbians choosing children call their own shots, in a context in which the prospect of a lesbian mother still produces terror, anger, discrimination. So they make the choice with the knowledge of the hardship that will likely ensue.

While many lesbians get the sperm and bring it home to self-inseminate, I chose to have a doctor do the procedure and found myself pregnant on the first try. As my mother says, good thing I'm *not* heterosexual! The experience of pregnancy was physically easy and healthy, emotionally quite strange at times. For it seemed that my pregnancy— and later my child—often made me invisible as a lesbian. Heterosexuals—and some gay people—wrongly assumed I was straight because of the belly pushing out in front or the diaper bag slung over my shoulder. A colleague looked at me quizzically and wondered aloud if I had "intended" to get pregnant. In disbelief I told her I just got drunk and had my way with a bunch of sailors and forgot to use birth control. So unable was she to reckon with my lesbianism and my pregnancy simultaneously, that one had to disappear and since my belly wasn't going anywhere. . . .

I simply didn't fit into her mainstream narrative of parenting. While this type of homophobia increased, other forms relented. As I became more recognizable to my colleagues as a woman (real women have babies, therefore I must be a woman, even if I was a lesbian—not a woman), their discomfort with my homosexuality decreased, but not for the "right" reasons. They were not necessarily dealing with their own homophobia, or heterosexism, or assumptions, or bigotries. It was simply that they now *recognized* me—a pregnant woman—and that familiarity (we have seen/experienced this before) made me more accessible.

This new "tolerance" is problematic; does it help demarcate two separate classes of gay people—those acceptable to straights through their assumption of presumably straight practices, and those unacceptable through their insistence on "doing it their way?" Does it avoid reckoning with the real problem—the homophobia of straights? Indeed, I often feel profoundly misunderstood as a lesbian mother. I am no less radical than I was before Emma. Indeed, I am adamant that my raising a daughter as a single lesbian mother by choice is *different* than heterosexual business as usual. I have no desire to mimic families as we know them—I strive (often unsuccessfully) to create other ways of doing family that are feminist and gay-positive. I don't want my family "compared" to heterosexual nuclear families and I'm angered by well-meaning studies that set out to prove that children of gay parents are "no worse off" than children of straight parents. And I'm not really sure I see my family simply as a benign alternative in a sea of welling diversity. Perhaps I see it in more grandiose terms, as forging intimacy and connection in ways that will enhance the life of the child and the life of those she comes in contact with. For as long as we can remember, "good" families were defined as having at least the following characteristics: two parents of the opposite sex, heterosexual marriage, and children produced out of that marriage. My family is none of that. And by separating parenting from socially enforced rules of partnering, I believe there are possibilities for familial constructions that are less mired in the violence, inequality, and longing that characterize the plight of so many families. Gay parents who choose to have children—in the face of a society that wishes they wouldn't—create the context or framework for a reworking of parenthood and family, a reworking that stresses the importance of choice and that hints at the possibility of new structures of intimacy.

But does that mean that gay parenting is inherently radical, or is shaking up family as we know it? Many of the journalists like to put this spin on it, arguing (as much as journalists argue) that the very formation of gay families with children so jolts our image of "family" that it entails—ipso facto—an alteration to that institution. But I think this position implies a uniformity within the gay community that is simply inaccurate. Now, to some extent, there is a certain truth to this. To be openly gay and raising children in a homophobic culture can never be simply the same as being openly heterosexual and raising children in a culture which celebrates and enforces heterosexuality. It is hard to imagine that any gay parent will not experience discrimination, hatred, avoidance, horror—and these things can't help but shape our lives to some extent. But after that initial shared experience, things begin to get more complicated. Many, many lesbians and gay men raising children want desperately to do it like their straight counterparts. These representations of sameness previously discussed are not simply nefarious heterosexual attempts to tame gay difference. Many gays will and do look admiringly at these images and encourage their production. Others don't think much about gay parenting, and see no particular difference in what they are doing. Others—myself included—want just as desperately to do it differently. We don't want to mimic heterosexual families or traditional gender roles and expectations—indeed, we are very critical of them. So there is a great deal of diversity within the gay community on parenting. If that is the case—and I believe it is—then there is no reason to believe that gays as parents will *necessarily* shake up straights as parents. Let me give an example. I went to a first birthday party recently for a child born to a lesbian couple. There were several other lesbian couples there with their children (I was the only single mother). As my daughter and I walked into the house, I was struck immediately by one thing: the elaborately gendered clothes these children had on. Now it might seem like a trivial thing, but clearly clothes (and toys, and education, and sports . . .) all contribute to the gender socialization of girls and boys. As a lesbian mother, I was acutely aware of this and adamant that my daughter would not be forced into the itchy dresses and tight Mary Janes that were an unfortunate part of my own childhood (and that make little practical sense for stumbling toddlers). But all the little girls were dressed in the most stereotypical "little girl" clothes—while their mothers relaxed in more casual and appropriate attire. It wasn't just the gendered clothes that struck me, but time and time again—in discussions with other lesbian mothers—I marvel at the extent to which their ideas about parenting seem uninformed by either feminism or by their own gay identity.[26] I have repeatedly gotten into arguments with other lesbians who are critical of my choice to be a single mother, invoking a traditional (almost Dan Quaylish) ideology of two parents as necessary and right. I have argued with lesbian mothers over my choice to have an anonymous donor and been dumbfounded by their stubborn insistence on "fatherhood" and knowledge of paternity as some mythic necessity. All this is by way of pointing to the variety of opinion and practice amongst actual gays having children.

This is not just a banal argument for diversity of familial forms, but about advocating models of love, support, and intimacy that actively dethrone the sexual/familial couple and present instead ever-expanding webs of relationships—ex-lovers, their partners or lovers, old friends, blood kin, etc. As Michael Warner and others have persuasively argued, "Straight culture has a lot to learn about the kinds of friendships and intimacies that queer culture has developed, about the complexities of households and parenting arrangements that queers have developed, and about the need for reliance on intimacy outside the family."[27] Indeed, one can see this as a gay gift to the bankrupt models of middle-class white heterosexuality that "tend to isolate couples from their larger families and sometimes from friends—especially if they are ex-lovers."[28]

Anthropologist Kath Weston[29] and others have written convincingly of the ways in which lesbians and gay men—so often disenfranchised from their families of origin—have created "families of choice" that serve many of the personal, emotional, and social functions of more traditional familial formations. Many gay people believe that "families of choice" are at least as valid as traditional marriage structures, and certainly as lasting. In creating vast and intricate networks of friends and lovers, gay people have forged intimacies and connections that often seem more lasting and durable than the often tenuous family of origin. Weston argues that these "families of choice" are not merely replicas of heterosexual families but actually create new forms of mutual responsibility that are outside the more typical—and typically gendered—roles inhabited by women and men in heterosexual families. Jess Wells, a lesbian mom and author of numerous books on gay parenting, argues that "the fluidity in which we live has its downside, surely—lack of rights, the homophobia that drives the refusal to allow us to marry, some wickedly nasty custody battles—but we also must acknowledge that this fluidity has given our culture a tremendous ability to invent better systems, to create better ways to live," including "the idea that perhaps romantic love is not the best foundation for a family."[30] Frank Browning concurs and wonders whether, "by rushing to embrace the standard marriage contract, we could stifle one of the richest and most creative laboratories of family experience."[31]

Obviously, not all gay parents are hetero clones, but those are the only gay parents we see in the news. Truly alternative models of parenting and familial arrangements are largely invisible, although they do crop up here and there in independent films such as *The Incredibly True Adventures of Two Girls in Love* (where the out lesbian teen lives in a nonparental lesbian household) and in mainstream films such as *The Next Best Thing* and

The Object of My Affection. In other films, like *Flawless,* we see a familial construction centered around a drag queen and her younger acolytes. But these images are far outweighed by those of gay families mimicking hetero roles and responsibilities.

In and of itself, and given the context of anti-gay attack, this desire to fit into nuclear family frames is not awful. But it is also not necessarily transformative and, indeed, could serve to keep the brass ring of gay liberation out of reach as we settle for simple acceptance and a ride on the family merry-go-round. Gay parents may or may not shake up the heterosexual family. The real question is this: do they want to?

Gay family issues will, I am convinced, be the last holdout in the battle for gay and lesbian rights. In that sense, the Christian right is right: the creation of gay and lesbian families *does* pose a fundamental challenge to "traditional family values." For if traditional family values is just another way of stating the claim that heterosexual, nuclear families (with Dad bringing home the bacon and Mom cooking it up for him and the kids) is the single "right" form of family, then our families most certainly stir things up. As much as straights and many gays might want to argue that there is "no difference" between the way gays create families and the way heterosexuals do, it seems hard to believe that the structure of exclusion and discrimination that surrounds gay life cannot in some way impact gay family life. Because gays parent and partner in a world brimming with hatred, where they have little legal recourse to fight either overt or covert discrimination, gay families can never be simple replicas of heterosexual families. Here, then, I part company with many gay activists who claim "our" families are no different from heterosexual ones. I argue for the joy and possibility in this very difference—the chance to challenge traditional gender norms (norms that have produced the epidemics of incest, wife battering, child abuse, child neglect) and create healthier varieties of family life. By forming "families of choice" (with or without children), lesbians and gays are bringing much-needed revision and sustenance to an institution in crisis.

It is ironic that one of the coded ways gays have of acknowledging other gays is to ask if they "are family." And in this referencing, we hint at a utopian construction of "families of choice" that is not bound by definitions of blood, of law, of sex, of gender. Instead of asking for inclusion and tolerance, gay families of choice should be providing blueprints for the family homes of the future. As lesbian humorist Kate Clinton says, "Listen, we live in a heterosexual mall. I say, if we are really going to try this experiment, let's give the kids some help. Let's get some gold lamé on those boys and a nice little tool belt on those girls. It's time for the Village People to raise some children." [32]

The season of holidays—Thanksgiving and Hanukkah, Christmas and Kwanzaa—immerses us in the loaded language of family. As Jimmy Stewart exudes familial authority and odes to turkey and togetherness slam up against the shop 'til you drop commercialism of sentiment, one can't help but ponder the images of family that pervade our cultural landscape and map out directions for social inclusion and rejection. No surprise, my holiday family portrait doesn't quite mesh with the wonderful life of homespun heterosexuality.

Let's start with Thanksgiving, even though my daughter thought my turkey was "a little dry." A yenta at age five, my daughter was produced through anonymous donor insemination and is named for Emma Goldman. Not that I want to overburden her with parental expectations. We were joined by my mother—a divorced single mom and proud champion of second-wave feminism (e.g. not Naomi Wolf). PFLAG is too tame for my radical mom, whose idea of a good time is hanging out on (gay) Poodle Beach in Rehoboth with her granddaughter. My godmother came from New York, a Polish Holocaust survivor in her late eighties with a sharp mind and even sharper tongue (she too thought my turkey a bit dry). We were joined by her fifty-something son, saved by his mom during the war only to become disabled by a serious car accident. The two of them have raised his daughter, who couldn't join us this year. To round out the party we had my brother-in-law—a kibbutznik who married one of my sisters, and then divorced her after she found fundamentalism and cut herself off from the family. His two sons—with him during his week of joint custody—dutifully played with their younger cousin and complained about the dry turkey.

The table wouldn't be complete without the requisite lesbian love drama in the form of an old girlfriend, now back in the picture and re-embraced by the confused but always amenable family tribe. She brought along her brother, his wife (okay, we did allow one nuclear family), and their two young children. So much for Thanksgiving.

The next day the girlfriend and I went to a post-Thanksgiving party at the home of another lesbian single mom who is—now stay with me here—the sister of the partner of an old lover of mine. To complicate matters, the aforementioned old lover of mine brought her own (twin) sister, also a lesbian, who brought along her girlfriend. There would end up being two pairs of lesbian sisters at this party. While I used an unknown donor, the hostess chose to reproduce with the help of a dear gay male friend, who maintains the posture of kindly but distant uncle, which works out just fine for everyone. Joining us at the feast of turkey leftovers and Chinese food was the ex of the single mom (the hostess), the tattooed young woman who (platonically) lives with the hostess/single mom and shares in the care of her baby, and a lesbian couple with two kids and a third on the way. Oh yes, the father of the first pair of lesbian sisters was also there, sipping a Bud and bonding with the sportier dykes at the party.

My Hanukkah party brings together my girlfriend, my mother, assorted heterosexual couples acquired through my strange incarnation as lesbian soccer mom, another older heterosexual couple with an adopted daughter from Latin America, my heterosexual older sister (not the religious one) and her adopted son from Russia (she divorced her husband one short year into the marriage and has sole custody of the child), another older single mom of indeterminate sexuality with a homegrown cross-racial adoption, an African-American single mom trying to raise a feminist son, and again my nephews and ex-husband of estranged fundamentalist sister. I thought about inviting my most recent ex and her young daughter but opted for my version of a Norman Rockwell Hanukkah (not that Rockwell covered Hanukkah . . .)

We move on to the millennium bash, held at the Queens home of another old flame of mine and her partner of twelve years. They are busily planning their pregnancy. Joining us is another dear friend of ours and her husband and son (our token nuclear family). An old (male) grad school buddy dropped by, our relationship complicated by the realization that we shared a girlfriend, although not at the same time. There were one or two members of the Five Lesbian Brothers performing troupe, and the Long Island in-laws of the hostess.

These are my family values. Replacing those illusory and archaic bonds of biology with the hard-working and complicated bungee cords of choice. This holiday season, I reveled in the hope that these configurations bring to a family structure so deeply in need of vision and revision. Perhaps in years to come, my daughter will turn on the TV and see not the maudlin fictions of Hollywood heterosexuality but *Happy Holidays with Ellen* or *Ru Paul's Very Merry Kwanzaa* or *I'll Be Coming Out for Christmas*. Until then, we'll continue to live the creative families our best instincts imagine.

PART FIVE   # Money Makes the World Go Round

Be yourself and make it a Bud Light.
—print ad for Budweiser's light beer

The campaign not only illustrates diverse
lifestyles . . . it reflects what's common to all of us:
commitment to a relationship, the importance of
family, and making a house a home.
—IKEA marketing director

We're Here, We're Queer, and We're Not Going
Shopping.
—chant heard during twentieth-anniversary march
commemorating the Stonewall Rebellion

Eleven　　　CONSUMING QUEERS:
ADVERTISING AND THE
GAY MARKET

NICHE MARKETING AND THE QUEEN AS COMMODITY

A friend of mine commented that in recent years the annual Gay Pride marches are more likely to resemble an open-air mall and food court than a political rally and declamation of feisty resistance. Indeed, in my more pessimistic moments it appears as if gay liberation has given way to gay commodification. In doing this research, I have been overwhelmed by the amount of material in the mainstream press extolling the virtues of the gay market. Since about the early '90s, story after story has emerged detailing the ways in which advertisers have honed in on this target group and urged more corporate attention to this "golden" and "untapped" market. From the *New York Times* to the trade journals of the advertising industry itself, gays have been tagged as the new niche market of choice, in an era in which niche marketing is the name of the game. The advertising industry has produced cover stories and in-depth demographic studies detailing the juicy gay market and its enviable buying power and gays themselves have been intimately involved in the proliferation of gay marketing mania, through gay marketing firms and the publication of breathless books extolling gay buying power and brand loyalty.[1]

As a specific targeted group, gays have long been ignored by corporate interests. Seen as either too invisible (how do you market to the closet?), too despised, or too dispersed within the general population, gays have largely escaped the *direct* onslaught of advertising. Companies have long been wary to advertise to a population so demonized, for fear of a backlash and possible boycotts. Surely, this fear still exists and we should in no way underestimate the ways in which "fear of association" still governs decision-making at the profit-centered corporate level. Moves are still tentative and still one-way, with gays consuming "straight" images and products and straights immersed in a world in which their centrality is taken for granted.

But these last ten years of increasing visibility have brought with them fundamental changes in this arena as well, as gays have become specifically targeted *as gays* by corporations eager to capitalize both on the supposedly greater wealth of gays and on the supposedly chic status of (white, bourgeois) gay identity. As cultural critic Alexandra Chasin notes in her thorough book *Selling Out: The Gay and Lesbian Movement Goes to Market,* it is often at the moments in which social movements make significant progress that they "become target markets." Certainly, she is correct in asserting that "citizenship and consumption are related to each other."[2] It should be no surprise that gays—perhaps even more than other minority groups—have been aggressively targeted by capitalist image-makers and goods-peddlers. As historian John D'Emilio convincingly argued in his early essay on "Capitalism and Gay Identity," the development of industrial capitalism enabled the development of explicitly gay *identities* and communities in part because of the growth of a wage-earning class not bound by the family economy and in part because of the expansion of public, urban social spaces of recreation and self-expression.

But the machinery of marketing has now gone into overdrive, and gays are being targeted by advertisers and their corporate backers like never before. This influx of marketing to gays has been predicated on a number of shifts. In the first place, niche marketing has itself become the preeminent strategy of both corporations and the media. No longer content—and no longer able—to mass market in the hopes of touching all, marketing strategies have shifted to a more targeted approach. We see this most dramatically, of course, in television. If TV programming and its attendant advertising was originally organized around a sort of lowest common denominator mentality, the proliferation of cable and second-string networks (e.g. Fox and WB) have forced into play a much different strategy. So now we have entire networks or segments of networks largely addressing a youth market (Fox) or a black market (WB) or a women's market (Lifetime "cable for women," and the newly minted "Oxygen" network). The attempt to "reach everyone" through a sort of bland sameness (assuming a white and heterosexual viewing public) has given way to aggressive targeting of populations deemed either golden in terms of their spending patterns (youth) or untapped in terms of their spending potential and brand loyalty (blacks and gays).

Not only is the new campaign to get gays shopping (as if we needed help!) motivated by a more general trend in niche marketing, it is obviously emerging in the context of increasing gay visibility, political power, and social inclusion. If gays are now visible in American popular culture, it should come as no surprise that gays should become visible in that vast and omnipresent world of advertising. And just as we have found that images in other forms of popular culture seem to vacillate between a depiction of gays as exotic and alluring others and a depiction of gays as heterosexual clones, so too do advertising images sell contradictory images depicting gays as hypersexualized and hyperchic arbiters of style at the same time that they are shown as having the same needs as heterosexuals (for financial security, familial happiness, etc.).

This advertising mania takes many forms. On the one hand, we have witnessed a huge increase in targeted, niche marketing, where gay consumers are being actively courted by companies no longer reluctant to be identified with gays, at least for the purpose of purchase. Companies may advertise in the gay press with gay-specific imagery, or may simply copy heterosexually themed ads into gay publications, without alteration. On the other hand, we also have gay imagery—a gay aesthetic if you will—being introduced into heterosexual venues in order to use gay iconography to sell products to heterosexuals, so "at the same time marketers are going after gay consumers, gay imagery is spreading into mainstream advertising. Androgyny and sexual ambiguity are all over fashion and liquor ads."[3] In addition, gays themselves have increasingly gone the entrepreneurial route (the subject of the next chapter), creating companies and services that purport to be gay-owned and -operated, allowing gays to, perhaps, believe that the "patronage of gay-owned businesses, circulation of gay dollars, profit by gay entrepreneurs is tantamount to improvement in the quality of life for gay men and lesbians."[4]

The most explicit discourse of gay marketing is to be found, not surprisingly, in the trade press. Here, the language is straight and to the point: gays have been identified as a potentially lucrative market, a market that has generally been unrecognized, and one that can be cultivated. As usual, the admen themselves put it most succinctly, as does Andrew Isen, president of WinMark Concepts, Inc., when he asserts, "If I were a General Motors, I'd target the lesbian market in a heartbeat. Just stop being so petrified, because it will make you money. This is not a referendum on lesbianism. This is a bottom-line business decision."[5] Given this truth—that marketing to gays is a business decision (with confusing political ramifications), it should come as no surprise that the world of the marketplace promotes a view of gays as largely male, extremely wealthy, overwhelmingly white, and ready to spend their disposable wealth with admirable brand loyalty.

To many, of course, this is precisely the problem. The expansion of an advertising world to include carefree, wealthy white men can, like the similar images on TV and in film—further marginalize those already deemed outside the range of marketing categories: the poor, people of color, the gender noncomformist. For many gay critics, the increased targeting of gays as a market is further evidence of the nail in the coffin of gay uniqueness and a selling out of the more radical potential of the gay movement. Many gay activists argue that gays have not become more accepted or integrated or liberated in this postmodern era; rather, gays have become the newest commodity darlings—both as the subjects and objects of intensive advertising campaigns. For many, this aggressive marketing to gays does indeed spell trouble. Advertising, as we all know, doesn't just sell products, but also—and perhaps more importantly— sells a way of life, a set of values and common beliefs, including "the idea that emancipation could be achieved through the market."[6] And, because advertisements depict a world of wealthy white gays (mostly men) with buff bodies and prodigious bank accounts, heterosexuals can become convinced that these men are representative and that, therefore, discrimination must be a thing of the past.

One of the most ambiguous signs of American integration is the advertisement. Does gay inclusion in advertising signal, finally, full integration into American culture, the realization that gays exist to be both addressed and imagined in the heady world of advertising imagery? Or does gay inclusion in the Madison Avenue hype machine signal nothing more than the restlessness of American capitalism, its need to endlessly discover new sites to mine, new images to circulate? Once shunned by Madison Avenue, what happens when gender-bending boys and androgynous girls slip between the pages of fashion magazines and are plastered on the wasteland of America's billboards? Is Daniel Harris right when he wonders whether " in enlisting the help of Madison Avenue in the cause of gay rights, gay rights may in fact be enlisted in the cause of Madison Avenue"?[7]

Lesbian author and critic Sarah Schulman is critical of this "niche marketing" to gays as an "all import, no export" relationship. "Gay products," she says, "are not being sold to straight people. Straight people are not going and buying books with lesbian protagonists. *Gay* people are being sold straight products. We're being niche-marketed products from companies who don't put any money back into the community, and often don't even have equitable benefit policies for their gay and lesbian employees."[8] For many, then, the niche marketing is rather sinister, selling products and services to gays without transforming corporate practices or otherwise supporting the gay community. As Amy Gluckman and Betsy Reed argue in their article "The Gay Marketing Moment," "It is not as if liberation has suddenly become the bottom line for many of those peddling glamorous images of lesbians, bisexuals, and gay men. Marketers, who make it a rule to tolerate their markets, have had a revelation. The profits to be reaped from treating gay men and lesbians as a trend-setting consumer group finally outweigh the financial risks of inflaming right-wing hate."[9]

In this reading, niche marketing becomes yet another sign of the thin and exploitative nature of the new gay visibility, using gay "difference" to sell products without evincing any substantive engagement in the movement for gay rights. As Ara Wilson, anthropologist and professor of Women's Studies argues: "I think that the logic of niche-marketing, the logic of selling right now, is that you sell to precise markets like, for example, the gay market. The logic of a lot of marketing right now is in fact a kind of liberality. Rather than saying everything's the same, everybody drinks Coca-Cola or everybody drives the same Ford, the idea is that you are different but we're pitching it to your difference. And therefore difference itself is part of marketing right now, and I think in there is homoeroticism or homosexuality."[10]

One indication of the remarkable shift—and its attendant problems—can be found in the data on gay publications. Edward Alwood, Rodger Streitmatter, and others have written of the uneven development of the gay press and have pointed to the challenges faced as gay publications go glossy and gay issues increasingly turn up in the mainstream press. While the gay press was never simply an unambiguously progressive organ for social change, the links to the actual actions and practices of gay community groups and social spaces seemed palpable. Now, however, the publishing industry has caught on to the wave of gay visibility with flashy and slick new gay publications such as *Out* and *Curve,* replete with ads from major corporations and companies. Even old stalwart the *Advocate* has a new look and a new financial picture. Since 1990 its advertising revenue has increased by over 100 percent.[11] Once almost wholly shunned by mainstream advertisers, gay magazines and newspapers are now becoming glossier and more well-funded through advertising dollars, although magazines geared to women remain marginal and comparatively under-advertised. Mulryan/Nash, a (now defunct) agency that produces an annual report on the gay press and focuses on marketing to gays and lesbians, claims that "advertising spending in publications aimed at gay and lesbian consumers rose for a fourth consecutive year. The survey . . . found that spending from July 1, 1997, through June 30, 1998, rose 20.2 percent, to $120.4 million, compared with $100.2 million in the period a year earlier. The study, which surveyed 152 local and national newspapers and magazines, showed that the largest increases by category came in employment recruiting, up 233.3 percent, and electronics, up 200 percent."[12]

Not only did ad spending surge, but relative to other types of publications, "the 20+ percent growth rate for advertising in the Gay Press represents the fastest-growing category for which such information is available. Advertising targeted to Blacks is the only other category with double-digit growth between 1997 and 1998 (and the only category that includes Broadcast media)."[13] Indeed, "Gay publications continue to outdistance both mainstream newspapers and magazines in advertising revenue growth. According to the Newspaper Association of America, mainstream newspapers have grown only 5.6 percent year-to-date, while mainstream magazines have experienced a 9 percent increase in ad revenue, according to American Demographics magazine. This year's revenue estimates of gay publications are based on a sample of 152 publications, up from 138 in 1997."[14] Circulation increased across the board, but most dramatically in national magazines, which increased in number themselves to a 1998 total of 13. This net increase doesn't, however, reflect accurately enough the reality of 48 new titles and 34 closings.[15]

While advertising itself continues to pick up in the gay press, circulation hasn't jumped to epic proportions and there has even been some decline, such as in glossies *Out* and *Genre*. The local press is truly the place of most growth, as it increasingly churns out newspapers and magazines niche-marketed to an increasingly segmented gay population, with local papers targeting not a supposedly generic "gay" audience but black gays, Hispanic gays, bar-oriented gays, urban lesbians, etc.[16] Local newspapers are growing both in size and stature; Los Angeles and Chicago each now have ten gay publications, where previously they had only three.[17] As new magazines proliferate they clean up their act, removing references to explicit sex and direct marketing, thus potentially cutting off a portion of the gay population in the search for an amenable environment for corporate advertising. In addition, the proliferation of local publications may indeed follow the logic of niche marketing and concern themselves more with establishing marketing constituencies than creating alliances and coalitions. During the attempt to sell *Out* magazine in 1999, president and editorial director Henry E. Scott revealed that "we're repositioning *Out* as a magazines for affluent, style-conscious gay men, so we intended to shed some of the less affluent or style-oriented readers. It is my feeling, in much the same way *Martha Stewart Living* was developed into an extremely successful multimedia brand, the same can be done with *Out*, targeted to the gay market.'"[18] Is a gay *Popular Mechanics* far off?

The upshot of this is that, assuredly, the national gay press no longer serves the function of public meeting space that it, arguably, did in earlier times. As the magazines go glossy and court big corporations, "movement" reporting and debate takes a second place to fashion spreads and entertainment gossip. The gay press almost seems to believe the conceit that entertainment gossip *is* the movement. Many national magazines read like a gay *Entertainment Weekly* and are less and less distinguishable from hetero "lifestyle" magazines. With the nationals moving in this (homogenized) direction and the locals moving in an increasingly fragmented direction with group-specific niche marketing, it becomes more difficult to find a space where a national, contentious, multicultural gay public life can be formed and reformed.

The changes in the wedding industry provide cogent examples of the recent marketing trend. Not known for its cutting-edge, trend-setting style, this industry has taken on the paraphernalia of commitment ceremonies and added "gay wedding" to its repertoire. In the language of business, gay weddings are understood as "specialty weddings" like "a Jewish wedding or an African-American wedding."[19] Conceived under the rubric of diversity (which apparently means anything other than a white, gentile, heterosexual couple), gay weddings receive attention at industry meetings and are included in industry guidelines and promotional materials. The largest invitations company even includes gay-themed invitations in its card choices, and in some areas where gays are highly visible, hotels host commitment ceremony expos to show off their wares.[20]

WE'RE HERE, WE'RE QUEER, WE'RE RICH: THE MYTH OF GAY WEALTH

In the rush to claim the gay market as the '90s answer to the declining fortunes of the yuppie, new myths and stereotypes have been created. Analysts assert the desirability of the gay market as an endless fount of bourgeois white men without children, pulling in big bucks and spending it freely. This picture is obviously incomplete: if gays really *are* everywhere then it means that gays are rich and poor, black and white, male and female, with children and without them. This stereotype of the free-spending homo about town has been artfully used by anti-gay activists to stir up animosity toward those "rich queers" who have "so much more" than regular folks. Indeed, the anti-gay referenda movements rely on just such a notion of gay wealth and success when they attack gay rights as "special rights" and adamantly refuse the civil rights analogy.

Gay marketing firms have themselves become part of this wave, to no small amount of controversy. When gay marketing firms released data suggesting an untapped market of wealthier than average gay Americans, eager to spend their disposable income, other gays reacted with suspicion. Gay economist M. V. Lee Badgett released a "counter-study" which indicated a population no different in wealth than the average heterosexual one. In a report entitled "Income Inflation: The Myth of Affluence Among Gay, Lesbian and Bisexual Americans," released by NGLTF, Badgett surveys seven other studies, including the 1998 update of the 1990 U.S. census and the General Social Survey, and concludes that "gay, lesbian, bisexual, and transgendered persons are not, as a class, richer than heterosexuals. In some cases, in fact, we appear to earn less than comparable heterosexuals."[21] Surprisingly, this has been reported (albeit not too widely) in the popular press itself, as this article indicates:

> Makers of upscale products from expensive liquors to designer clothing have for years devised gay marketing strategies based on one common assumption: Gays typically earn more money than their heterosexual counterparts. But that stereotype is a fallacy, says a report to be released today by the National Gay and Lesbian Task Force and an influential economics professor at the University of Massachusetts at Amherst. The report, 'Income Inflation: The Myth of Affluence Among Gay, Lesbian and Bisexual Americans,' concludes that most marketing studies have mistakenly focused on upscale gays and do not accurately reflect the gay population. The study is certain to surprise marketers nationwide who long presumed that gays are perfect targets for many upscale products. Marketers estimate gays and lesbians account for 3% to 6% of the U.S. population and pack an annual spending wallop of $99 billion to $198 billion.[22]

Because the USA Today report ends on the myth ("annual spending wallop"), prospective advertisers are made aware of the "income inflation" only to have it reinforced in the closing sentence. Indeed, the article goes on to quote Teresa Kanode of Diesel Jeans, regular advertisers in the gay media, who claims, "I don't believe it (and) even if it's true, we won't change the way we market."[23] Indeed, the myth continues fairly unabated, with reports claiming that "over 78 percent of gay and lesbian Americans have college degrees, with gay males averaging an annual income of $54,325 and gay females averaging $45,927."[24] Occasionally, serious journals reveal the myth of gay wealth, and correctly point out that it is "promoted simultaneously by gay activists seeking to attract corporate sponsorship and by social conservatives aiming to exaggerate homosexuals' special-interest power."[25]

Many gays themselves, eager to assert gay inclusion, hold fast to the myth of gay wealth and join in the chorus of voices crying "sell to me!" Most influential have been the gay marketing and research firms, as well as gay business types such as Grant Lukenbill, whose 1995 book *Untold Millions: Positioning Your Business for the Gay and Lesbian Consumer Revolution* is oft cited and reputed to be influential in business decision-making. While acknowledging the problem in deriving data from a limited pool of self-identified gay men who read style-centered gay magazines, some argue that the debate on gay wealth misses the point, which is that gay consumers *are* a niche characterized less by affluence per se than by more discretionary income and more disposable time, largely due to the (supposed) absence of children in the majority of gay households.[26]

Clearly, whether wholly fictional or statistically demonstrable (or somewhere in between), the image of free-spending, brand-loyal gays has captivated public relations firms, animated corporate headquarters, and excited gays themselves. As Brenda Pitts, director of the sports administration program at Florida State University, exults, "We are no longer considered a pariah market. We are potentially lucrative, we are chic and highly loyal to brand marketing."[27] The phenomenal success of the Gay Games helps to prove Pitts's point, with "a 1,200 percent growth in participation from 1982 to 1998" and an estimated $50 million worth of economic impact by 2002.[28] The Gay Games are heavily sponsored, with KLM, Levi's, Avis, Speedo, and others sponsoring the event. Where once they were small-scale events that barely blipped on the cultural radar screen, now they are big-money galas, joining sweaty sports with all the trappings of a an upscale gay Woodstock.

In a CNN "Showbiz Today" special on advertising in the gay press, Harry Taylor, the advertising director of *Out* magazine, claimed that "when I talk about the subscribers and the readers of my publication and you look at the demographics, they're incredibly well-educated— well above average household incomes—obviously a lot more discretionary income because we're not saving—most of us are not saving to put kids through school—we're image conscious, we're brand loyal— it's a marketers dream."[29] The part of the myth that is true, however, and that is skillfully revealed in Badgett's study, is that gender is paramount when addressing issues of gay wealth or its absence. Because women typically earn less than men, and because lesbians tend to support children in comparable numbers to heterosexual women (but without any possible addition of the greater male income), it becomes clear that the lesbian population is hardly at an economic advantage. Because people still tend to think "white male" when they think "gay," the mythology of gay wealth has always meant—essentially—the mythology of white gay male wealth. Indeed, this claim of relative gay wealth largely comes from data gathered on the readers of publications which largely cater to wealthy white males. It should come as no surprise, then, that the "gay marketing moment" primarily centers around the culture and life of gay white men. Lesbians remain largely unaddressed by mainstream advertising (compare the ads in the *Advocate* or *Out* with *Curve*). One report claims that only 27 percent of the advertising in gay publications is aimed at lesbians.[30] Lesbians make the news as chic and titillating, but the reality of both sexism and women's lower income has resulted in marketing that is largely addressed to wealthy white men, or men perceived to be that stereotype. As Danae Clark notes, to be targeted by the ad industry a group must be identifiable, accessible, measurable, and profitable and lesbians don't quite fit as they obviously traverse the categories of race, age, income, etc.[31] Of course, gay men can be found in all categories of race, income, age, etc., as well. Yet the mythology of gay male wealth (and the concomitant assumption that they are even more likely than lesbians to be DINKS—dual-income, no kids) combined with the *reality* of male wealth vis-à-vis female earnings entices advertisers to the gay male market in greater numbers. Even the gushing press descriptions of our ideal consumer reveals the limited range of "gayness" depicted. "Do you recognize this consumer?" asks Diane Cyr of *Catalog Age*. "Upwardly mobile. Professional. Affluent. Urban. Dual income, no kids. No, not that yuppified relic of the '80s. This is today's hottest consumer—and he or she is gay."[32]

OF BUDWEISER BOYS AND AMEX GIRLS

Advertisers seem to have several goals in mind when using gay-themed images. Clearly, advertisers want to tap into the gay market itself—to sell more and more products to a group that purportedly has a great deal of disposable income and brand loyalty. In addition, advertisers want to tap into gayness as an aesthetic, to access "the cachet that *gay* seems to add to certain brands."[33] If gayness has been heralded by the media as the very sign of hipness, then attaching oneself or one's product to that sign can be good business. But because gayness is simultaneously vilified as it is lionized, advertisers can also position themselves as "daring" and "on the edge" by depicting gay-themed images. In some senses, then, advertisers can't lose. They can be hip and daring by embracing gayness as happening lifestyle in a way that (putatively) attracts gay consumers but doesn't threaten heterosexual ones. Irreverence sells.

Advertisers employ a wide range of strategies in order to reach the gay market and, simultaneously, appeal to a heterosexual audience eager to be (at least aesthetically) attached to the allure of gay hipness. The strategy of using coded, homoerotic imagery has been operating for years, but it continues to have currency even in these more open times. Just as a sort of homoerotic aesthetic has been used successfully in films, so too in ads it is both eye-catching and safe at the same time. Primarily a strategy of high-fashion advertising, homoerotic imagery throws a wide net, appealing to gays obviously, but also to straights on a more unconscious level, and to straights eager to appear sophisticated. As Clark notes, "Gay window ads avoid explicit references to heterosexuality by depicting only one individual or same-sexed individuals within the representational frame. In addition, these models bear the signifiers of sexual ambiguity or androgynous style. But 'gayness' remains in the eye of the beholder . . ."[34] Now, clearly, gays have always "queered" popular culture. From the veiled references of a sultry Tony Curtis to the arch remarks of a television "interior decorator," gays have found ways to insert themselves into a culture in which they were largely invisible.

Gays have done that with advertisements as well, clipping pictures of buff boys in a macho sneaker-sale embrace next to strong Nike women imploring their sisters to "just do it." High-fashion advertisements have long been a source of hidden meanings for gay viewers, particularly gay men. But much has changed in recent years. Indeed, it seems that the boys of Madison Avenue have caught on to this gay decoding and have begun to use it with much more deliberation. If gays are gazing longingly at the bare chests and tight buns of Calvin Klein's models (his ads have long relied on homoerotic allure), why not go with the flow, why not lend a hand to this decoding, thus inviting gays and straights alike to be more active and more direct consumers of those very products and those very images? If, as columnist Robin Givhan of the *Washington Post* notes, "the Abercrombie & Fitch quarterly magazine has won a place of honor on the cocktail tables of gay men from Chelsea to the Castro,"[35] why not market these images more directly, drawing these gay male viewers into the orbit of dedicated consumer loyalty? Of course, advertisers are eager to deny the direct marketing ploy, claiming instead that "people are reading into it and projecting their own sexuality on the images"[36] even as they hire noted homoerotic photographers like Bruce Weber to shoot their frolicking boys. So homoerotic (but avowedly straight) imagery has grown or at least been more deliberately cultivated, building off of the gay activity of "cannibalizing" straight images.

But homoerotic imagery also speaks to the more legitimized public engagement of *straights* with gays, as if the new visibility of gays makes them more available for the displays of public desire that permeate advertising imagery. Connecting with homosexuals through gay-themed

Abercrombie boys will be boys,
frolicking ruggedly in a way
that invites straight women,
frat boys, and gay men alike
to gaze longingly. Homoerotic
and coded images are an
advertiser's wet dream—
luring in gay consumers while
not alienating heterosexual
viewers.

The use of double entendres is typical in these "gay vague" ads.

imagery allows heterosexuals access to the (media-constructed) hipness factor. As we have seen in film and television, gayness is often used as a sign of the hipness and openness of heterosexuals. "Getting it" (or getting off on getting it), serves to position the heterosexual onlookers as members of the happening crowd, untainted by tired and stodgy prejudices. As Gluckman and Reed note, "Ads don't feature glamourous gays just to connect with gay consumers, either. Firms placing gay-themed ads are also counting on the ability of attractive gay idols to set trends for straight

PHOTO BY GUY MOON NEW YORK SOHO NEW YORK (212) 254-6774

D&G

DOLCE & GABBANA

434 WEST BROADWAY SOHO NEW YORK
SUNSET PLAZA 8641-43 SUNSET BOULEVARD LOS ANGELES

Dolce and Gabbana are a little more up-front in their homoerotic address.

shoppers—a bet that has already paid off for some. Resplendent in red, RuPaul, the queen of drag and Mac cosmetics model, has inspired hordes of genetic girls to buy the company's lipstick through ads placed primarily in mainstream straight media."[37] As psychologist and advertising consultant Carol Moog says, "RuPaul has managed to create a hip, yet clean image for himself. This is the way for mainstream America to experience the outlandish and do it safely and in a nonthreatening way."[38]

Even the "plus-sized" woman gets queered, as Queen Latifah dances suggestively with a group of women, the lone man conspicuously set off to the side.

Coded messages (or what has been called "gay vague" or "gay window" advertising) target gay consumers without the danger of unduly alienating heterosexuals. Cynthia Cohen, president of Marketplace 2000, a consumer-marketing consulting firm based in Miami, claims that "the good news for many retailers . . . is that going after gay consumers doesn't

RuPaul's dual images allows for an openness of reception that keeps the eyes on the page. Man, woman, gay, straight: the selling of ambiguity.

necessitate any major changes in merchandising." [39] As ad analyst Stuart Elliott argues, "Encrypted ads allow advertisers to speak to gay people in public places or through mainstream publications with less risk of backlash since the symbols or slogans are lost on many heterosexuals. [40]

While the homoerotic ads are often quite encoded (while gays see cute boys evincing same-sex love, heterosexuals have no problem reading those same images as rough and tumble straight lads), other types of encoded ads rely on gay "insider" knowledge to inhabit this dual world. So

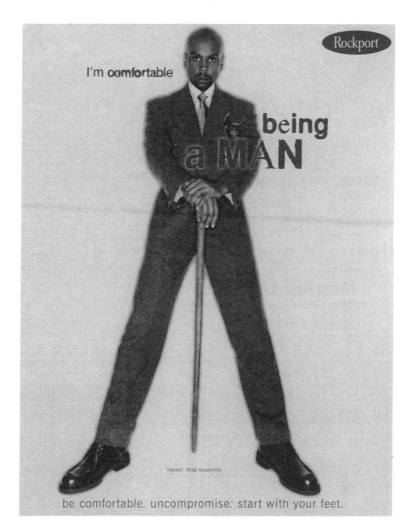

I'm comfortable being a MAN

Rockport

rupaul, drag superstar

be comfortable. uncompromise: start with your feet.

Subaru car ads display bumper stickers with the blue-and-yellow equals sign that is the logo of the gay Human Rights Campaign advocacy group, or have vanity plates that say XENA LVR and P-TOWNIE, which allows gay readers to identify (i.e. the TV show *Xena: Warrior Princess* has a large lesbian following; P-TOWNIE refers to Provincetown, a gay mecca on Cape Cod).[41] "It's sort of like our little secret," says Tim Bennett, marketing services manager at Subaru of America, "It's clever and not offensive, and if you're in the know, you chuckle."[42]

While gay-themed or even vaguely gay ads rarely appear on TV, and what is there tends to be "less overt than what magazine and newspaper

Different Drivers. Different Roads. One Car.

Subaru cars and sport utility vehicles come in all shapes and sizes. But one thing doesn't change. Each one features our popular full-time All-Wheel Driving System for maximum traction and performance. From the comfort and versatility of the unique Forester, to the ruggedness of the Outback, to the get-up-and-go of the 2.5 GT, we think you'll find the right match for your lifestyle. To test drive one of our family of cars, stop by your nearest Subaru dealer, call **1-800-WANT-AWD** or visit our website at **www.subaru.com**.

Subaru supports the community as a national sponsor of the Human Rights Campaign (HRC) and the proud founding sponsor of the Rainbow Endowment. The **Rainbow** benefits community health, civil rights and cultural interests. For more information or to apply, call 1-800-99-RAINBOW.

The Beauty of All-Wheel Drive.

Gay-vague ads like these can be placed in either the gay or straight press. Subaru has made it a point to target the gay audience, particularly lesbians, who are more generally ignored in this rush to niche marketing, and they do so utilizing the noxious idea of biologically determined sexuality.

readers see,"[43] there have been a couple of "gay vague" ads that have provoked speculation. In particular, one Volkswagen ad features "two guys driving around in a VW [who] pick up an old chair off the street. The chair symbolizes the interest of many gay men in home decor, gay marketing experts say. When the driver wipes away a speck of dirt on the

It's Not a Choice.
It's the Way We're Built.

Subaru All-Wheel Driving System.
In every car we make.

Maximum traction, agility and safety. Experience the performance of the Subaru All-Wheel Driving System in the versatility of the Outback, the ruggedness of the Forester and the get-up-and-go of the Legacy GT Limited. To test drive one of our family of cars, stop by your nearest Subaru dealer, call **1-800-WANT-AWD** or visit our Website at **www.subaru.com**.

Subaru supports the community as the proud founding sponsor of the Rainbow Endowment. The **Rainbow** benefits health, civil rights and cultural interests. For more information or to apply, call 1-800-99-RAINBOW.

The Beauty of All-Wheel Drive.

dashboard, they add, that's a reference to the obsessively neat stereotype. The commercial made its debut on the coming-out episode of the TV series 'Ellen,'"[44] although the VW folks claim that they're just "two college guys on a Sunday afternoon with nothing going on."[45] There was also a brief TV ad for Quaker Toasted Oats cereal that featured two suspiciously gay men eating breakfast together (or is it that any men eating breakfast together are suspiciously gay?). Ads like these flirt with gayness in the most hesitant of ways, allowing dual readings from gay and straight viewers. Because gays are still so desperate for everyday images of ourselves in everyday venues of popular culture, even these timid TV ads invite frenzied gay speculation. Of course, more overtly gay TV ads are nonexistent or censored into nonexistence. In "the first Gay-themed television commercial by a beer company . . . viewers of a San Francisco Gay cable program would see winners of a 'Barechested Men Contest' romping in a backyard, including one hunk holding a bottle of Miller's Genuine Draft while he barbeques"[46]—if the ad would have run. While gay access to television ads is, of course, limited (what groups have the money to buy prime-time ad space?), a first was recently made when the Alice B. Toklas Lesbian and Gay Democratic Club of San Francisco ran an ad for mayoral incumbent Willie Brown depicting a gay male couple at home discussing their voting decision.

So advertisers have developed a wide range of strategies for tapping into and maintaining the "gay market," including direct mail. Catalogues, cardpacks, and Internet outreach are particularly appealing to gays because of the privacy they afford the (possibly) closeted consumer. In this manner, companies can reach out to gays in ways that protect the company from scrutiny while also speaking to a population sometimes uncomfortable with the direct address, thus reaping profits while shoring up the closet! In 1994 AT&T directed a huge campaign to gays of about 70,000 brochures; since then corporations have been reaching out to gays with targeted ads ensuring the recipient that she or he will receive acceptance at the hands of the corporate family. Often, these mass mailings promise both "unique treatment" (e.g. you can be out without fear of reprisal or revulsion) and the added incentive of "giving something back" to the community. When the Chubb group of insurance companies contracts with Global Services to provide gay-friendly insurance policies to members of the Gay and Lesbian Victory Fund, they also promise that your business will ensure an annual contribution to the Fund.

This type of outreach borders on another strategy: advertising in the form of sponsorship. Major corporations can kill two birds with one stone by sponsoring a gay event (the Gay Games, AIDS services, film festivals and cultural events), thus achieving product visibility while aligning their company with a "gay-supportive" image. This reached a watershed with the 1994 Gay Games, which found advertisers "expanding their reach into the gay and lesbian markets via event sponsorship. Next month, advertisers including AT&T Corp., Continental Airlines, Hiram Walker & Sons, Miller Brewing Co. and Nora Beverages' Naya Spring Water will connect with the biggest gay and lesbian marketing event of the year."[47] Other companies find that sponsorship produces "brand loyalty": "The 19th San Francisco Gay & Lesbian Film Festival was a shocking experience for Charles Schwab & Co. It wasn't the movies that caught the discount stock brokerage by surprise. It was the response from the gay community to Schwab's $40,000 sponsorship of the event. Schwab had planned to follow up the sponsorship with a direct-mail campaign aimed at festival film goers in the hope of generating a few new accounts. Instead, before the company even had brochures in the mail, gay and lesbian investors had opened new accounts at Schwab with an estimated $10 million in assets."[48]

Many companies attempt to establish a sort of long-term relationship with the gay community through a combination of direct mail, advertising, and event sponsorship. Liquor companies in particular have gone this route, particularly Seagram's, Absolut Vodka, and the Miller Brewing Company. United Airlines did a mailing to gays that detailed their support of gay causes and their corporate gay-friendly policies, as did AT&T and MCI.

Of course, this kind of corporate sponsorship entails numerous risks. For the company, there is the risk of backlash from right-wing activists who counter corporate sponsorship with calls for boycotts and pressure on executives. For gays, there are several risks. Like any minority group, gays risk their independence and autonomy through corporate sponsorship. If, say, Miller Beer sponsors Gay Pride, is there a danger that some of the more "in your face" aspects of gay display will be toned down to assuage anxious corporate sponsors? Unlike the simply homoerotic images, these images trade on a certain insider knowledge that makes them more available to gay spectators and encourages gays to identify more with the products themselves than simply enjoy the aesthetic.

Other campaigns are more direct. And this is perhaps the most dramatic departure from earlier practices. It is one thing to graft a "straight" ad into a gay publication or to entice with vague, ambiguous imagery, or to fly an ad in under the gaydar. But it is quite another to actually create images that attempt to directly address the specificity of the gay consumer. Howard Buford notes that "in the early 90's, it was sufficient to run mainstream advertisements in a gay publication to capture the attention of the market. Today, with more markets vying for the gay consumer dollar, the bar has been raised. Gay consumers now expect advertisers to address them for who they are, directly and openly."[49] Now, granted, we should not forget that this innovation is largely a one-way street: most explicitly "gay" ads are still to be found in explicitly gay publications and only very rarely do they find their way into "mainstream" publications. And "unchanged" ads from major corporations are still the major form of advertising in the gay press. In other words, most ads are still resolutely heterosexual in tone and content, even those placed in the gay press. When we open a gay glossy we still mostly see images of scantily clad hetero

9. GREENWICH VILLAGE, NEW YORK c. 2 MILLION YEARS AGO

Imagine what the world was like 2 million years ago. Before Stonewall. Gay Pride. Or Lea and Kate. It was a time when Naya* Spring Water flowed deep in the Canadian wilderness. Today, Naya still flows. Still pure, still pristine. And still proud contributor to the lesbian and gay community.

NAYA: MADE WHEN THE WORLD WAS STILL PURE.

Both Naya beverages and Clos du Bois wine advertise in the gay press largely through sponsorship of gay events, creating a more generalized identity as "gay positive" companies.

couples frolicking on moonlit beaches, sipping their booze of choice. Do they think we can't see? Clearly, there's no fear of offending gay readers with all that overt, in-your-face heterosexuality. Nevertheless, several campaigns have emerged over the years in which advertisers are producing images with a decidedly queer tilt.

The Banana Republic chain produced a series of ads called "Chosen Families" that depicted explicitly gay family constellations, and Benetton

Those who are with us and
those who have gone.
They have forever enriched
the patterns of our lives.

Celebrate life • Celebrate friendship • Celebrate memories

At Clos du Bois we believe
in celebrating the memory
of friends and family.
That's why we proudly continue
to support The NAMES Project
and The AIDS Memorial Quilt.

www.aidsquilt.org
www.sonoma.com/cdb.html

CLOS DU BOIS

has long had ads both homoerotic but also more explicitly gay, particularly around AIDS issues. Indeed, Benetton was the "first major apparel
retailer to advertise in a gay magazine."[50] High-end designers join exotic
booze in the search for an acceptable gay aesthetic. Dolce & Gabbana featured a series of couples which included both a gay male and a lesbian
couple and Diesel Jeans continues to flirt with both overt and covert gay
images. More often than not, the images are covert, like the Abercrombie
& Fitch boys, working off of a gay aesthetic without explicitly invoking
gay sex, thus allowing heterosexual consumers a position of voyeuristic

It's a beery gay world.

safety while drawing in the gay consumer desperate for any sort of visual recognition. Liquor companies seem the most aggressive when it comes to actually queering their advertising. Disaronna Amaretto features two embracing young women, Amaretto in hand. Clos du Bois wine supports the AIDS quilt (and sells its wine) in a montage of gay families and friends. Alize Red Passion cognac brings us Andre and Jim—two cute boys on the lookout for "a meaningful relationship based on mutual support and understanding." Tuaca liqueur features smoldering women and men searching for same sex-passion in mysterious bars. Bud Light recently chimed in with an image of two men holding hands, with the slogan "be yourself and make it a Bud Light" curling around a rainbowed Bud Light logo, an image that aroused no small amount of right-wing ire. Less explicitly gay imagery is in other Bud Light ads, urging drinkers/readers to "be yourself" or "pour with pride." Numerous others advertise "straight" images (in gay publications) or combine their logo and ad with sponsorship of a gay event, an increasingly attractive way for companies to build brand loyalty without invading the public sphere with overtly gay images. And others continue the insider's "play on words" that make the ads accessible to gay readers but not necessarily readable as gay by heterosexuals.

Financial services have joined in, most notably with American Express's "Travelers Cheques for Two" program that slightly queers the "original" ad by including a signature of same-sex couples in gay magazines and of opposite-sex couples in hetero mags. Others use witty and unmistakable invocations of gay difference to sell the difference of their services. Ads like these acknowledge gays (typically in the form of couples) and market themselves as products and services that pay special attention to "diverse" populations.

This has been a dominant trend, and an interesting one. In these ads, the company attaches itself to an embracing conception of diversity and openness, much in the same way that "incidental gays" in movies tend to impart an air of hip tolerance to heterosexual characters (and, by extension, to those spectators watching the film). The company thus promotes a sort of meta-meaning for itself, beyond the specificity of what the product has to offer. The company offers up diversity and openness per se as that which it sells, thus promoting both an interest in the particular product but also cultivating a large gay identification with the company as a "progressive" one that supports gay causes and encourages a corporate climate of "acceptance."

Like the notorious Virginia Slims campaign which cleverly appropriated the language of liberation (you've come a long way, baby) to target women as potential smokers, much of the advertising to the gay and

The direct address works best for selling booze-induced homolove. The Cuervo ad, like the Subaru ads, plays on gay knowledge and insider language ("we're here, we're queer"). These ads aim to access both multicultural and gay hipness (such as they are), flattering the gay consumer by refusing coded vagueness and instead encoding gay identity. Direct address, yes, but only in gay publications.

Cool girl seeks ex-tomboy (smooth but not too sweet) for girl-power renaissance.

lesbian community uses gay difference to target gays as potential consumers of just about everything. In this process, difference itself changes, becomes refashioned as consumer variable. As critic Alexandra Chasin points out, the marketing of pride strips pride of its history of struggle: "From Miller Beer's 'Celebrate Pride,' to rings sold to commemorate Stonewall that promise that 'Your Pride Will Shine Brighter,' to the title of Shocking Gray's [gay and lesbian mail order] catalog, the word 'pride' has shifted from the name of local marches and parades that constituted the first affirmative moments of collective visibility on the part of gay and

lesbian people, to a pitch word."[51] Or gay conservatism finds voice in car ads, where car maker Subaru insists "It's Not a Choice. It's the Way We're Built," playing up on and reinforcing the belief that gayness is not, in fact, a choice but is "in our genes"—it's the way we're built. Now, whether or not this marketing of corporate openness leads to real openness in corporate policies remains to be seen. Nonetheless, and all cynicism aside, it does seem as if many of these major gay sponsors and advertisers do often have the more progressive corporate policies, such as anti-discrimination inclusion, domestic partnership coverage, etc.

If you've ever come in from the cold, you already know the feeling of Cognac Hennessy

Maison Fondée en 1765

Hennessy
COGNAC

Marketing to gays takes numerous other forms, as well. The tourist industry—both nationally and abroad—has targeted gays as well-heeled travelers who can be counted on to spend big bucks for prime accommodations and "friendly" service. American gays are being targeted by foreign countries eager to get those big gay dollars translated into tourist revenues. Both the U.K. and France have gay-targeted tourist brochures ("See London Inside and Out") and airlines such as Virgin are doing similar marketing techniques. The glossy booklet from the British Tourist

Disaronno Originale.
Italian. Sensual. Warm.

Light A Fire
www.disaronno.com

DISARONNO
ORIGINALE
AMARETTO

Authority is filled with images of same-sex couples frolicking outside the Tower of London and partying in hip clubs in Manchester. Unafraid to be direct, brochures like these sell the country by selling diversity, referencing gay bars, gay tours, gay-friendly hotels, and a general rainbow ambience of Merry Old England. United Airlines sends out a brochure detailing "Some of Our Other Important Routes," which glossily details the airline's commitment to lesbian and gay causes and organizations as well as assuring the gay consumer that "United Airlines has the strongest

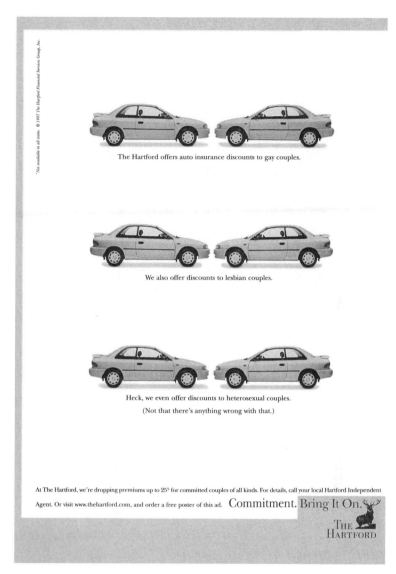

The Hartford offers auto insurance discounts to gay couples.

We also offer discounts to lesbian couples.

Heck, we even offer discounts to heterosexual couples.

(Not that there's anything wrong with that.)

At The Hartford, we're dropping premiums up to 25% for committed couples of all kinds. For details, call your local Hartford Independent Agent. Or visit www.thehartford.com, and order a free poster of this ad. Commitment. Bring It On.

THE HARTFORD

In these "diversity sells" ads, companies (often humorously) align themselves with nondiscriminatory practices. In the ad for Hartford insurance, combinations of pink and blue stand in for the array of couples Hartford serves. In addition, Hartford wittily quotes the Seinfeld phrase "not that there's anything wrong with that" when including *heterosexual* couples in the picture. EDS mirrors the Hartford move by depicting an inclusive world of differently partnered fishies, and Dun & Bradstreet comes right out and tells you that difference "just makes good business sense."

A sea of diversity

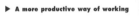
workplace policies among US airlines regarding sexual orientation and HIV/AIDS."

Unlike homoerotic or "gay exotic" imagery, these ads, and similar ads in the financial industry, speak not to some perceived gay difference but rather to gay sameness with straights. Invariably, these ads feature bourgeois-seeming, white couples seeking the "good life" in travel and financial security just like their heterosexual counterparts. In this advertisers' world, gays are affluent, white, and always, always coupled, thus removing the visual threat of wanton single gays searching for sex in all the wrong places.

A piece in the *San Francisco Business Times* sums up quite clearly these different advertising strategies:

> Rex Briggs, project director for Yankelovich Partners talks about what he calls the "psychology of disenfranchisement" that gays and lesbians feel from alienating experiences in today's society ranging from discrimination to hate crimes. Because of that, he said, they are very responsive to advertising that says, "We know who you are and we want to serve your needs." Briggs breaks down advertising to the gay community into several categories. The first is mainstream ads that are simply run in gay publications. Usually these are ads that have a message that translates well into a gay publication. For instance, Saab broke ground as the first automotive manufacturer to advertise in a gay publication early this year [1995] and used its regular ads, which read, "Peel off your inhibitions. Find your own road." A second type of ad is one that would be found in other publications, but has been altered slightly to target gay readers. American Express' 'Checks for Two' campaign in gay publications is identical to ones that run elsewhere, except a close look shows the names on the checks are of two men or two women, rather than a heterosexual couple.
>
> Another approach advertisers take is ads that are specifically about and for gay people. A Kenneth Cole Shoes ad features pink and black shoelaces in the shape of a triangle, a symbol of the gay community. The copy reads, "Shoes shouldn't have to stay in the closet either." Some advertisers choose to run ads in mainstream media that address gay consumers openly. For instance, a television ad for the furniture company IKEA includes a shot of two men shopping for furniture together. Lastly, he said, some ads run in mainstream outlets, but "flies below the 'gaydar'." These ads may play to straight audiences, but have a special appeal to gay consumers. For instance, when Saturn ran a two-page ad in *Out* in May, it featured an ad that ran elsewhere. Although the sexuality of the tuxedoed female engineer who appears in the ad is unknown and never referred to, marketing people point to it as an example of someone with whom lesbian readers would identify.[52]

The attempt to market specifically to gays has not gone unnoticed. Not only are many gays wary of the tentacles of Madison Avenue and corporate America, but conservatives have latched on to gay images in advertising as yet one more sign of a decadent culture. After Jerry Falwell let loose on the poor Teletubbies, he vented his ire on that stalwart of straight-thinking masculinity, Budweiser beer, for daring to depict beer-swigging homos. What ensued is like an object lesson in postmodern politics. Falwell gets mad because Anheuser-Busch hadn't set up a telephone line to receive critical calls, only calls supporting the ad. Falwell

Does it matter

whether he's White?
Or African American?

whether she's Asian?
Or Hispanic?

whether he's Straight?
Or Gay?

Not at Dun & Bradstreet.
We believe people's differences are
our strengths, their ideas our assets.

The infinite potential of the human being—we see it in
everyone who works at Dun & Bradstreet and Moody's
Investors Service. Because we've seen great ideas come
from the most junior person on the team. From a telecom-
muting parent. From people of every religion, culture and
background. It just makes good business sense: a company
where people feel included and valued is a company that
is ready to solve its customers' business challenges. We're
always striving to be a better company to work for, and a
better company to do business with. That's what matters
at The Dun & Bradstreet Corporation.

Visit our Web site at
www.dnbcorp.com
or call 908-665-5854

The Dun & Bradstreet Corporation

then urges his acolytes to call in and complain about the ad. Anheuser-
Busch responds by setting up a line for the opposition and then *gay*
activists start an e-mail campaign urging gays and their supporters to call
in and support the ad. The ads, by the way, were only run in specifically
gay publications.

Companies that advertise to gays, or that have ads on television programs that feature gays (e.g. *Ellen, Will & Grace,* etc.), or that support/
sponsor gay events, or that enact gay-friendly corporate policies, all face

How do you plan for your future together?

When you're ready to plan a future together, who can you trust to understand the financial challenges that gay men and lesbians face?

At American Express Financial Advisors, we offer Domestic Partner Planning℠ services that can help you address issues like protecting assets from unnecessary taxation and getting around restrictions placed on unmarried couples. We offer you the expertise and insight you need to make smarter decisions. So you can take control of your future.

Call 1-800-GET-ADVICE ext. 338 and own your world.
http://www.americanexpress.com/advisors

do more

American Express Financial Advisors offers domestic partner benefits to our lesbian and gay employees worldwide.
©1997 American Express Financial Corporation.

AMERICAN EXPRESS **Financial Advisors**

Ads such as this mirror their heterosexual counterparts, but with slightly different text and images, allying their companies with "inclusive" policies at little cost.

boycotts and attacks by the organized Christian right. While marketing to gays is seemingly a sound financial decision, companies find that it can still have its drawbacks. Thus, contrary to the perception of an all-gay world of images, the corporate moves are still largely in the closet, relegated to the gay press, direct mailing, and other sources at least partially cordoned off to peeping heterosexual eyes.

With just one call to British Airways Holidays, you can effortlessly book your entire London vacation—including flights, hotels, cars, even theatre tickets. With over 600 gay & lesbian pubs, clubs, shops and restaurants, London, the gay capital of Europe, welcomes you with open arms and a spectacular rainbow of choices.

BRITISH AIRWAYS
HOLIDAYS

Call British Airways today at 1-877-436-2081

LONDON

For your FREE gay London vacation planner, call the British Tourist Authority at 1-877-628-6932 or visit us on the web at: www.gaybritain.org/ba

Reaching out to gay travelers with visions of camaraderie and comfort, all to be found in traditional chains such as Hyatt.

Twelve   IF IT'S PINK WE'LL SELL IT: GAY ENTREPRENEURSHIP

Marketing to the more visible and powerful gay audience has now become good business—for straight enterprises as well as gay ones. Not only have heterosexual big businesses begun to court the gay dollar, but gay entrepreneurship has become a boom industry. Gay people have always created their own institutions, but the growth in recent years has indeed been exponential. In the past, bookstores served as community sites and one of the few locations for (struggling) gay businesses. When I came out in Philadelphia in the late '70s, the gay bookstore, along with the gay bar, were my places of reference and often my places of reverence as well. Going to the bookstore seemed less like an act of financial support than a search for a place of affirmation and information. Perhaps we were "buying gay," but I think the patronage of those bookstores felt more like "being gay" in a world in which the spaces for that openness were severely limited.

Now, as it becomes increasingly hard to discern the difference between buying gay and being gay, the gay entrepreneur emerges as a figure to be reckoned with and gay bookstores face an increasingly uncertain future. Faced with competition from the large chain stores and Internet companies that now sell gay books and from the gay start-ups that operate in a more "business-like" fashion, the bookstores are closing at record numbers, particularly those that cater to lesbians. In Washington, D.C., the long-time lesbian bookstore Lammas closed its doors, as has the famed Sisterhood Bookstore in Los Angeles after twenty-seven years. These stores, and many like them, were born in the post-Stonewall fervor of gay activism. For most of the original owners, the bookstores were specifically and deliberately set up as community center/meeting place/ information center. You gathered at the bookstores for demonstrations, pulled chairs together for meetings, came out to yourself and others amidst the stacks.

Many would argue that the time for these places is over, that we now have the community centers we need and, failing that, can now meet in "straight" places that formerly excluded us. Others argue that "some bookshops deserve to go under . . . stores that aren't doing well are those that insist on staying in 1974, where book selling takes a back seat to activism. This is a different era, and these businesses need to operate like bookstores and not community centers."[1] Indeed it is a different era. Everywhere there are gay entrepreneurs, creating flourishing businesses in retailing (selling every form of pink triangle accessory!), travel services, entertainment, financial services, firms that market products for commitment ceremonies, retirement communities, cruise lines—you name it. Aside from the proliferation of products (from rainbow flags to marriage accessories) every possible iteration of merchandising has hit the gay market. There are gay pharmacies, gay greeting card companies, gay video stores. Books advise gays on how to spend their money wisely and queerly and how to start up their own gay-friendly businesses. Indeed, there's even a newsletter called *Quotient*—the newsletter of marketing to gay men and lesbians—and I'm sure that's not the only one! There are gay yellow pages and gay business directories—both nationally and locally. The first national gay and lesbian business expo was in 1994 in Secaucus, NJ, and these are now major events, garnering mega sponsorships and public visibility. And the government is getting into the act. Just recently the Small Business Administration revealed that it will work with the National Association of Gay and Lesbian Community Centers to publicize programs available for small companies.

Gays can purchase products with their "Uncommon Clout" Visa card and access gay-friendly realtors to buy their upscale condos or buy stock in "companies that have gay-supportive policies" through the "Lambda Strategy." Not only are there simply *more* gay services and media institutions, but these forms of gay culture are produced in this new context of visibility. These gay services and gay products reach out to a gay public in a *public* way, still largely through gay venues but more and more seeping into the generalized media.

Ads for gay credit cards use out celebs to merge corporate culture with social giving, luring in lesbian card users with buff bodies and visions of Martina.

Gay businesspeople have been riding the wave of gay visibility in several ways. Most obviously, gays have worked within mainstream companies to promote gay visibility and to move services and products into the gay community. Often, gays within a particular firm either choose themselves or are chosen to head a sort of "gay effort" for that firm. We see this in the case described here, where "the increasing interest among mainstream advertisers in aiming sales pitches at homosexuals has led a major public relations agency to form a unit for marketing communications efforts that address gay men and lesbians. Hill & Knowlton, ranked third among the world's public relations companies in the annual directory published by the J.R. O'Dwyer Company, has begun operating a gay and lesbian specialty group within a group that handle clients in industries like entertainment, food, information technology, sports and travel."[2] In this context, gays work within already established venues to expand the availability of those venues to gay consumers.

This is also evident in the credit card arena, where in 1990 the first gay credit card was launched—the Pride card—issued by Seafirst Bank, a subsidiary of Bank of America. So a major bank works with a gay organization to produce a product or service. In 1995 the Rainbow Card by Travelers Bank (now part of Citigroup) followed suit, and "the involvement of world-renowned tennis star Martina Navratilova as a corporate spokesperson boosted the Rainbow Card's visibility substantially. Navratilova . . . appears in the card's promotional literature, and she also writes a column for a newsletter sent to cardholders."[3] These efforts link largely heterosexual corporate leadership with internal gay employees to develop specific corporate pitches and spin-offs to the gay community. This strategy retains heterosexual control while cultivating the appearance of gay outreach. In many of these strategies, the gay offshoot can be effectively hidden from the public persona that the company projects, thus creating a win/win situation for a company eager to gain access to "gay dollars" but wary of bringing unwanted attention to that effort.

Many gay entrepreneurs have moved from "queering" mainstream heterosexual businesses (e.g. liaisons with the community, heading up gay sections within the industry) to creating gay-owned and targeted businesses themselves. Here, lesbians and gay men (more often gay men) produce their own goods and services from scratch if you will. So, for example, we have the proliferation of direct-marketing appeals and merchandise catalogues such as Shocking Gray where you can buy clothing and housewares from a presumably gay-owned business. Catalogs abound—for housewares, clothing, wedding accessories and commitment rings, and every kind of pink-triangled/rainbow-flagged insignia imaginable. Indeed, the rise in gay entrepreneurship seems to run parallel with the rise of mainstream corporate outreach to gays and lesbians. Following research about gay brand loyalty, gay entrepreneurs have initiated countless products and services designed to bypass corporate outreach in the hopes of creating and sustaining more gay-owned and -operated businesses and services.

Travel companies have been amongst the most successful of entrepreneurial adventures. There is every imaginable gay traveling service, geared to single gays on the lookout for romance, or family tours with like-minded families. Gay travel companies include Toto Tours, Olivia

Cruises, Our Family Abroad, and RSVP Travel, with an estimated "20 companies booking cruises or land packages, often taking over a ship or an entire resort for a week."[4] The travel newsletter *Out & About* premiered in 1992, and another one, *Our World,* started more recently. The well-heeled lesbian can cruise the Aegean with Olivia Cruises[5] and gay men have their pick of national and international cruises. Gay cruise companies now own their own liners. There is even a new venture, "Learning Tours for the Gay Traveler," which is like a sort of pink Smithsonian tour, replete with gay professors lecturing on the resurgence of gay culture in modern China, or the history of homoerotic art in ancient Greece. Travel writers have taken note of this and remarked that "in the last 10 years suppliers and opportunities for travel for homosexual men and women have increased enormously. Some travel experts describe the market as virtually recession-proof, pointing to the pattern among gay couples of two jobs and no children."[6]

> Gay and lesbian travel seems to be out of the closet for good, with tours and cruises for this market increasing in number and visibility. Companies like Cunard and American Airlines are now lending their familiar emblems to targeted sales brochures. The International Gay Travel Association now has 1,000 members, 65 percent of them travel agents, in the estimate of David Alport, the group's vice president, who is also the publisher of the gay travel newsletter Out & About. And last year [1994], for the first time, the Gay Travel Association participated in the convention of the American Society of Travel Agents, held in Lisbon.[7]

These excursions are not without their problems, as gay cruise lines and tours have met with protests at various ports of call and advertising their services still remains a gay-only enterprise. Indeed, one commentator notes that "ABC let Ellen declare she was a lesbian on national television but would not sell 15 seconds of air time to Olivia Cruises & Resorts to advertise lesbian-only cruises on the April 30 show." While these impediments remain, these travel companies seem pretty sturdy. Olivia's "revenue has surged from $1.5 million in 1990 to nearly $6 million in 1996, and most of this year's cruises have been filled to capacity. The Olivia story sums up the state of gay travelers in 1997: They're sought after and yet snubbed."[8]

Gay travel businesses, like many gay enterprises, are built on the assumption of gay unease in overwhelmingly heterosexual environments. Gay enterprises, at least to some extent, depend on the closet, depend on, as Billy Kolber-Stuart, editor of *Out & About,* claims, not wanting to be "one of the 30 fags in the dining room among 3,000 heterosexuals."[9] Gay travel offers both closeted and out gays the opportunity to access resorts and other travel experiences in a safe and gay-friendly environment. In a sense, these services not only depend on the closet, but depend on a sort of marketing of the ghetto or, rather, the creation of bourgeois gay ghettos of affluence amidst the ever-increasing sea of gay integration.

Of course, as with many such ventures, the marketing to gay men as opposed to lesbians is quite different. For the women's travel market, there is a focus on activities, particularly sports, and tie-ins with "alternative" feminist-inspired events like women's music festivals. The gay male cruises and resort trips are, not surprisingly, built much more around partying, sexual adventures, and the lure of bare-chested, washboard-abbed hunks afloat, as the advertising for these different services reveals.

More scholarly marketing endeavors include the proliferation of gay-themed segments within the publishing industry. If African-American women writers such as Toni Morrison and Alice Walker became the literary darlings of '80s culture, perhaps gay writers were their '90s equivalents. Yet, in some ways, the analogy does not hold. While African-American women writers could be—with some contestation—integrated into the canon of exceptional American literature, it has been much more difficult to do that with gay writers. And here the stigma still comes into play: reading a book by a black heterosexual writer doesn't make a white reader black, but reading a book by a gay writer (of any color) immediately raises the "guilt by association" shibboleth that haunts the heterosexual imagination. Nevertheless, the marketing of gay literature continues, with academic presses such as NYU and Columbia producing gay-themed series. Even mainstream venues are getting in on the act, with the Quality Paperback Book Club teaming up with the Book-of-the-Month Club to launch the "Triangle Classics" series of reissues of books such as Rita Mae Brown's *Rubyfruit Jungle*. There is even a series for teenagers put out by Chelsea House Publishers that includes biographies of famous gays in history as well as youth fiction. And now, InSightOut Books initiates an online book club "that knows and understands the joys and challenges of our lives . . . where the diverse needs of the LGBT community are celebrated on common ground: our love of books." Modeled on other specialized book clubs, but even more invested in the Internet than many, InSightOut Books assures you that "now you won't have to rely on gaydar alone to find the best books" or search "through skimpy shelves in the back of bookstores." Of course, the irony is twofold. On the one hand, gay books are no longer relegated to those proverbial back racks and are boldly displayed in most major bookstores (particularly during the month of June—gay pride month). But this kind of advertising almost completely ignores the centrality of gay bookstores while at the same time presenting itself as an online version of the gay bookstore as community center. When you "log on" you can not only access book

Saronged boys and sporty girls find gay cruises just the ticket.

choices but view a calendar of events, commentary on books and politics, interactive bulletin boards, etc. But while a visit to a "real" bookstore is often tantamount to a coming out (I'll never forget the trepidation and anticipation surrounding my first visit), this company has "respect for your privacy" and ensures that "shipping is discrete." So this proudly gay marketing venture tips its hat to the closet even as it explicitly champions gay writers.

While gay entrepreneurs and businesses are taking off, they are also facing a new kind of threat. If once the major obstacle gay businesses faced was homophobia and the closet, perhaps now they are more worried that the mainstreaming of gay and lesbian identities makes of specifically gay businesses an oxymoron. In other words, if gay books can be purchased at Amazon.com or Barnes and Noble, and gays can patronize other services and stores without undue fear of harassment and marginalization, then the need for the "safe" space of gay markets becomes less obvious. While I certainly don't think we're there yet, it does seem possible that the boom in gay businesses could recede as more and more "straight" companies either offer specialized gay services and sections (e.g. travel companies and financial services with a gay representative) or simply make gays with money feel as welcome as any other consumer. Certainly, we see indications of this in the bookstore business, and in the gay publishing industry, with numerous small, local newspapers folding. As one analyst argues, "In large cities the increasing acceptance of gays and lesbians in society has made the 'all-gay' atmosphere less of a commodity . . . decreasing [the] demand for gay-focused businesses." [10]

THE LAVENDER NET

Much of the gay entrepreneurial spirit finds a welcome home on the Internet. This should come as no surprise—the Internet is replacing more and more of our typically public spaces (the bookstore, the community center, the shopping mall) and gay "Netizens" are deemed "affluent and eager to shop." [11] At once meeting place, chat room, pick-up joint, shopping mall, newsroom, these gay Internet sites combine political commitment (or at least some strange new hybrid cyberspace version of it) with corporate sponsorship in ways that challenge our typical understandings of both realms. As is true for much of the Internet, new categories are needed to understand the complexity of our interaction with anonymous others and corporate giants over high-speed lines of communication. The Internet certainly presents new options both for gay entrepreneurs and for their heterosexual counterparts eager to cash in on the "gay market." The anonymity of the Web can serve both interests. Gays can market to gays without the fear some gays may have in, say, attending a public gay event or purchasing an obviously gay magazine at a gay bookstore. For mainstream heterosexually run companies, the anonymity allows them to have a more explicit reach toward the gay community without the same sort of fear, in this case of retribution from right-wing forces witnessing their reach in a more open and public domain. Adam Harris, a research analyst at an information technology consulting firm, claims that "before the Web came along, it would take a very innovative marketing scheme, such as the one Abercrombie & Fitch used, and even that is a little bit risky. But now there's really no risk to advertising to this niche because you have dedicated sections online that are for this community." [12]

By far the largest meeting place for online communities is channeled through the two major "portals," Gay.com and PlanetOut, who "are vying to become the Internet's gay brand name" [13] As of late 1999, PlanetOut had 300,000 subscribers and over 200 advertisers, including major corporations such as United Airlines, Proctor & Gamble, and Citibank. Not only is PlanetOut eager to go public, but it continues to grow, hiring new staff and acquiring new advertisers each year, with the number of employees doubling in six months.[14] The new millennium brings more growth, with approximately 10,000 new member registrations a week.[15] PlanetOut's competition, Gay.com, is no slouch either, featuring ads from corporate giants like IBM, VH1, GM's Saturn, and AT&T's @Home cable Internet service, as well as American Airlines and Neiman Marcus.[16] Of course, inevitably, the two are now set to merge into one gay Internet giant, together boasting more than 1.6 million registered users.[17] PlanetOut has already purchased Liberation Publishers, owners of the *Advocate,* thus indicating that gay businesses follow the same old business rules of merger mania and buyouts. And even more targeted sponsorship occurs, with travel giant American Airlines continuing its outreach to gay consumers through sponsorship of an entire travel area within the Gay.com site.

These sites are becoming "one-stop shopping" sites for gay-related products, including travel, news and information, finance, health, entertainment, and of course shopping.[18] Like most Web sites (e.g. America Online), these gay sites also offer extensive "chat room" opportunities that can provide closeted gays opportunities for community and connection without fear of being "exposed." These Internet sites, and mass marketing to gays in general, have become so significant that the recent big march on Washington—the Millennium March of April 2000—was sponsored by PlanetOut and Gay.com: "The Gay.com Network today announced Gay.com Unity 2000, a free new service that will help promote and organize the Gay and Lesbian Millennium March on Washington. . . . The Gay.com Unity 2000 service will be the first time such a large and diverse community is mobilized online to make a real-world event more effective and enriching. With over 5 million visitors per month, the Gay.com Network is the world's largest gay and lesbian online community."[19]

Gay.com has received record amounts of financing from major sources such as Chase Capital, IDG Ventures, and others, totaling $23 million in 2000, and PlanetOut received just over $16 million for similarly situated sources. Again, the logic of investment in gay sites follows both the logic of the market and uses the mythology of gay wealth as drawing point: "So what appeals to venture capital companies about these gay Internet businesses? For one thing, they're 'niche,' or affinity, portals, which means they have well-developed, loyal audiences who like to spend a lot of time there. . . . Gay people also tend to be more wired, more affluent, and more willing to spend online."[20] Dutifully, this article from the *Advocate* offers a counter-position from economist Lee Badgett, challenging the idea of gay affluence, but the counter-position is dismissed by reference to another canard about gays, that they don't have kids and therefore have more disposable income.

Clearly, affluent incomes are the selling point here and it should therefore come as no surprise that a large number of the gay Web sites deal with financial services of one sort or another. Gay Financial Network (gfn.com) is one of the most successful, announcing recently "that it is partnering with Conseco Annuity Assurance Company and Client Preservation & Marketing, Inc., to offer gays and lesbians a guaranteed return annuity that ties interest earnings to the S&P 500 Index with 100-percent principal protection. James P. Griffin, Conseco Regional Superintendent and member of a Conseco team focusing on national niche marketing, said: 'This is an excellent opportunity for Conseco to be the first company to market an exciting annuity product to the gay and lesbian community, a traditionally underserved group of consumers.'" [21] The Gay Financial Network continues to grow, evidenced by its history-making ad in the *Wall Street Journal* and other magazines and newspapers. Here you have a first: gay companies advertising as openly gay in the mainstream heterosexual press. Walter B. Schubert, the founder, chair, and CEO of gfn.com, stresses that "the most important thing we wanted to get across with this campaign is that we are a financial site targeting gay men and women, and not a gay site with financial content. This is a campaign of inclusion, and one that will touch, educate and also entertain members of the gay and lesbian, as well as the non-gay communities across the country." [22]

While gfn.com, for example, is clearly a business enterprise, it merges its Wall Street desires with gay-activist ones. For example, in October 1999, the president and COO of gfn.com "married" his partner on the "first ever gay wedding cybercast" on another gay site. Over 200,000 people have viewed the wedding and "attended" the cyber ceremony, which was shown on out.com, the website for OUT publishing. While the wedding may not have been a "radical" political act, many of these sites are creating, I think, unique sorts of locations where consumerism, identity politics, gossip, discussion, news, support uneasily coexist. Many see these political inserts as nothing more than window-dressing that gives a sort of legitimacy to what is basically a commercial enterprise. I find that argument quite convincing and think there is much truth in it. Nevertheless, the merger of gay marketing and gay activism is an interesting one, and one that cannot simply be rejected as the sure sign of a corporate takeover of alternative culture. Grant Lukenbill, author of *Smart Spending: The Gay and Lesbian Guide to Socially Responsible Shopping and Investing,* has even developed an indexing system he calls the glvIndex

It's not a choice ...

it's the way we bank.

glbank.com
... G & L Internet Bank

Call **1-888-226-5429** to investigate the security and ease of our website and Internet banking.

FDIC

© 2000 G & L Internet Bank

Again, the play on biological determinism to sell gay banking. Here, gay difference not only matters, it practically compels us to follow the yellow brick road to G & L Bank.

(gay-lesbian values index), which "ranks private companies on a ten-point scale that takes into account whether the company includes sexual orientation in its nondiscrimination policy, has same-sex domestic-partner benefits, and does not support groups that oppose passage of rights protections for gays and lesbians, among other things."[23] Gay.com, for example, includes regular political action "columns" by well-known activists and provides a steady stream of gay-related news and legislative

"You're GAY!!!... Well, I'm feeling quite happy myself."

A first—an openly gay ad in the staid *Wall Street Journal*—but to what effect?

updates. PlanetOut does much of the same. Overlooked Opinions—a gay marketing firm—handed out hundreds of thousands of "event packs" at the 1993 March on Washington that included march route maps and information but also flyers from various firms eager to access the gay market.[24] On an even more perverse note, a number of articles have claimed that "Vermonters profit from equality" and have touted the growing Vermont wedding industry as a sign that a good marriage means good business, and that "the civil unions law is more than good public policy. It's good business."[25] From wedding bands to bed and breakfasts to caterers to romantic country lodges, the civil union law has paid off for gay and gay-friendly proprietors.

On the Gay.com site, they have a section that invites viewers to "meet this month's advertisers." Above the display of the corporate logos, the folks at Gay.com want us to know that "the gay community has always been here, but advertisers and marketers didn't always seem to know that. With more and more high-profile media supporting us, advertisers are taking note and courting our business. They're talking to gay people in gay media, actively and openly. They're supporting us and voting with their wallets. Please support the following advertisers, which are entering the gay market. They're taking unprecedented steps to bring us all closer to a better place in time." And what is that "better place in time"? Is it a world where wealthy white men (who happen to be gay) and their (fewer) wealthier white sisters (who happen to be gay) can become equal partners in consumption with their heterosexual counterparts? And what of those gays—much greater in number—for whom consumption of cruises and designer drinks is hardly the most pressing issue?

While this may seem all for the good, the dangers are of course many. Most obviously, there is the fear of cooptation, the need to tone down, clean up, straighten up gay life and gay identity to fit the corporate mold. But, in addition, I think there is a danger that gays will think that corporate sponsorship is anything other than an attempt to cultivate another market, will believe that—like visibility generally—these corporate sponsors signal a fundamental change in public perceptions and practices. So what is the effect of the marketing of gays on the liberation of gays? Does it signal full citizenship or its evisceration? One thing seems clear to me: gay visibility in the marketplace follows much of the same paradoxical pattern of gay visibility in the rest of the media. Either gays are depicted as chic accouterments, signs of high fashion and savvy consumerism, or as icons of American sameness, feeling—as Grant Lukenbill claims—"all the same emotions about life, God, and country as Americans of heterosexual orientation."[26] Either the drag queen or the tough girl (e.g. Ru Paul and k.d. lang), selling trendy cosmetics, or the happily coupled, suburban, bourgeois, white, asexual duo selling trendy furniture.

In the world of the market, all the gays are men, all the men are white, and all the whites are rich. Even towns like Northampton, MA—always known as a mecca of radical lesbian culture—now become sites for commodity commentary, fueled in part by a 1993 *20/20* special on the town and its lesbian inhabitants. The inevitable focus on the niche most likely to consume freely relegates other gays (women, the poor, minorities, the "excessively" butch or feminine) even further into the shadows.

If advertising—like so much of our popular culture—constructs and makes visible identities and desires (eat this and you'll be satisfied, wear this and you'll find love, drive this and you'll have style), then the parameters of gayness are being drawn very closely as advertisers help to produce the (largely fictional) identity of "gay" as wealthy white man with an eye on fashion and oodles of disposable income. Not only can this feed into the worst sorts of stereotypes about gays, but it can also delude gays into believing in their own inclusion even as that inclusion is simply a business decision. Indeed, this entrepreneurial spirit helps to reinforce the ideology of gayness as "lifestyle": gay clothes, gay travel, gay restaurants, gay resorts, gay lifestyles. As Michael Warner says, "Magazines like *Out* make it possible for large numbers of gay people to . . . feel that they take part in something called 'the gay community' without needing to belong to a political scene."[27] And if gayness gets increasingly defined by the vicissitudes of the market, will we ourselves come to believe those fictions? Will those advertising images of cruise-going, Moët-drinking guppies begin to seep into our national consciousness *as real,* as the truth of gay life? And what of those who aren't targeted by this niche marketing and aren't splashed across the glossy pages of a homoerotic photo spread? How will those gay people understand themselves and their relationship to the national conversation that is advertising imagery?

Alexandra Chasin, writing in the journal *Sojourner,* asks vital questions of this new gay marketability: "What does this market development have to do with the lesbian and gay political movement? Which came first, the movement or the market? Does the market exploit the movement, redirecting resources that would otherwise go to the movement? Or does the market assist the movement by proliferating and normalizing images of gay and lesbian citizens in the media?"[28] Like many other critics, Chasin raises the important point that this advertising (and, one would add, media visibility in general) lacks diversity, so that "the overwhelming majority of this material depicts that 'community' as white, affluent, male, educated, healthy, youngish adults."[29] But would it all be okay if there was more diversity? Is that really the only problem with this visibility, its lack of diversity? Chasin takes to task gay marketing firms such as Mulryan/Nash, Rivendell, and Overlooked Opinions which have misled corporations by "generalizing the results of surveys of gay-publication readers to the 'gay community' nationwide and by using extrapolation techniques that cannot be applied with accuracy to a self-reporting population"[30] and thus overinflating gay wealth and spending patterns.

For all the hype about the "gay market" what's amazing is how little things have actually changed. Gay images are still largely confined to gay ghettos of publishing, unless homoerotic images are used explicitly to tit- illate or to introduce an air of hipness into a product or service. Still, most gay publications feature lower-end ads, with a preponderance of health- related concerns and gay-owned companies and services. Only a few publications, most notably the glossy and vapid *OUT* magazine, feature big-name spreads with a wide variety of companies—from Saturn cars to Evian water to Merit cigarettes. And TV is a veritable heterosexual fantasy- land, with gays effectively banished from hawking the goods of our econ- omy except in the most ambiguous of ways (e.g the VW ad with the two sexually ambiguous men picking up and discarding used furniture). There's no lesbian mom whipping out the Jif and no bubbly group of gay friends grabbing some burgers at McDonald's (and would *this* be a sign of liberation?) While gays are being discussed as if they have practically taken over every facet of popular culture, the reality is of course much different. Even in the bottom-line, profit-centered world of advertising and corporate policy, gays are still seriously marginalized. Gay publica- tions fail regularly and even others are never launched, like Time Inc.'s decision in 1994 not to launch the gay-themed "Tribe." And when new ones are launched, they are more often than not either fashion oriented or niche targeted, like the new gay glossy called *Hero* ("the magazine for the rest of us"), purported to be for "guys in committed relationships, for gay men who want to raise kids, and . . . for people who are single and looking for love and interested in spirituality."[31] Still, the circulation for the two top gay publications is dangerously low. Still, boycotts and threats are heard in corporate headquarters as they weigh the profits to be gained from gay markets against the harassment from the right. And has our own community mistaken commodification for liberation, the right to cruise with whom you want for the right to choose who you love? As marches turn into marketing opportunities, and sponsorship precedes community organizing, are we seeing a troublesome overlap between gay politics and gay markets? Has "marketing asked people to view their own entrance into the marketplace as a corrective for past social alienation,"[32] thus replacing tactics of struggle with targeted consuming? When the largest gay organization raids the corporate world for its leadership and markets a line of "discreet" gay accessories (no need to say "gay"!), have we seen the eclipse of organizing as we know it? The Millennium March on Washington even had its own store in gay-primed Dupont Circle, sell- ing trinkets to fund the march and line the pockets of entrepreneurs. Per- haps that is too grim a picture, but it is inescapable that the inclusion of some gays into some of the world of advertising changes not only advertising but much else as well. Some critics even argue that "the commercialization of homosexuals often involves the active suppression of the gay sensibility, a process by which manufacturers divest us of our subcultural identity."[33]

Controlling our own images and harnessing our selling power to the engine of gay consumerism are necessary and laudable. Nevertheless, as with the other phenomena being discussed, this too holds out certain dangers. As with so much of American culture—always searching for new markets and new regions to exploit—gay media can degenerate into yet another capitalist fashion statement. While it is vital to control our own images and to circulate resources and money within our own communities, gay life stands in danger of becoming another commodity. Robert Bray, program director for the Institute for Alternative Journalism, warns that "the increasing corporatization of Gay American culture is not without pitfalls—ones that become especially evident when examining precisely which Gay people have become visible, rather than the simple quantity of coverage." He argues that "gay and lesbian people have arrived at the right to be marketed to by corporations through the media. And that is a sign of progress. The problem is the other part of the deal. To conform to corporate marketing interests, our identity must conform to a prescribed and rigid identity as a consumer. We are presented as the perfect consumer. In the process, we eliminate those who refuse to conform to that representation."[34] As he points out, "The old defamation is the Andrew Cunanan, Jeffrey Dahmer, serial killer pervert that we've all come to know and oppose in the media. The new defamation is the portrayals of Gays and Lesbians as domesticated, sanitized, primarily white, fairly high economic class, possibly suburbanite. What's defamatory about that is that we can do better. There's a whole range of Gays and Lesbians in the middle of those two types, and we should not just settle for either the old kind or the new kind of defamation."[35]

It may be chic and profitable to be gay these days (in the world of mass images) but we can never believe that this "chicness" is a substitute for, say, a federal anti-discrimination law. There is a real danger that "the politicized consumer quickly degenerates into the consumerized politician, who serves the best interests, not of the gay community, but of the marketers courting this rich new slice of the population."[36] Even worse, it can become all too easy for both gays and straights alike to read this marketing moment (and the new visibility in general) as proof positive of our newly enfranchised place in American culture, as if "the patronage of gay-owned businesses, circulation of gay dollars, profit by gay entrepreneurs is tantamount to improvement in the quality of life for gay men and lesbians."[37] Bray makes the important argument that we "need to shift the focus from media campaigns that are specifically concerned about visibility and countering anti-Gay defamation, and go into the new and uncharted area of media literary . . . teaching us how media can serve us better, how we can make better media, and how we can be better media consumers."[38] Others disagree, and see the normalization as "accurate" and argue that all media is filled with limited depictions of all groups.

There is clearly a new savvy among gays (well, among gays with the financial resources to be entrepreneurs) in relation to media and markets, but it may perhaps be a savvy that leads to the first gay shopping mall rather than the first gay civil rights bill. This was one of the most potent critiques of the controversial Millennium March—that it had become captive to major organizations (HRC) and mega corporations, thus excluding and effacing the contributions and political perspectives of those outside that rubric, such as gays of color, working-class gays, and gays who espouse less mainstream views of sex and identity. True, we can no more be outside the commodity machine than any other group: to turn difference into an object of barter is perhaps the quintessentially American experience. Nevertheless, gays can and should be more thoughtful about the relationship between the culture of commodities and the culture of resistance. But a simple railing against the evils of commodification goes only so far. While we need to point out that this bell of prosperity is only tolling for a few of us, we also need to push at the edges a bit to see how far we can go. Internet sites like PlanetOut and Gay.com, specifically, organize such a seemingly disparate array of offerings—politics, culture, shopping, news—that it is hard to gauge the ways in which they can serve as conduits for more "in the world" activism. Surely, there is every likelihood that the consumerist ethos will trump all others and that the merger of gay activism with gay consumption will produce a movement ever more devoid of a resistant public face. And if these portals lead only to more portals and not to other, embodied gay people, it might just reveal the truth at the heart of the cyber revolution. But I'm not wholly convinced. Perhaps the anonymity of cyberspace will encourage many to come out, find each other, invent political lives. Maybe the chat sites will raise real issues and not just gossip over celebrity shenanigans. It's sometimes hard to know what Alice will find when she falls through the looking glass.

Conclusion BEYOND VISIBILITY
(WELCOME TO OUR
RAINBOW WORLD)

So much change, so little time. Any person reflecting on this period must be struck by the sense of time compression, the feeling of implosion, the experience of living in the eye of the storm. So much seems to have happened, in such a brief period of time. Ending this book seems almost impossible, because every day brings new news, new headlines, new movies, new images, new controversies. Perhaps this is what change means in the age of digitized culture, Internet love, televised history. It is true that other dramatic social and cultural changes have had similar leaps forward; indeed, one need only talk to African-Americans of a certain age (particularly those from the South) to get a sense of what it means to move from a Jim Crow structure of virtual apartheid to at least the appearance of legal equality. Or talk to women of a certain age, who lived lives in which sexual harassment and social second-class citizenship were par for the course. In many ways, of course, this "gay moment" has historical parallels with other social movements, movements that experienced similar catalytic periods of heightened attention and accelerated change. The story I have told here of the explosion of gay visibility is a story with many variants, told in many tongues. While no two movements are identical, few are unique. All movements go through self-defining moments, turnings of the tide, reckoning with internal disputes and external contestations. These dilemmas—of assimilation and its discontents, of co-optation and its temptations, of integration and its disappointments—are familiar to many immersed in the rocky history of movements for social justice. Popular culture is often the site for these debates because mass culture is always in the process of cannibalizing, reusing, appropriating selective aspects of minority and subcultures for its own, uneven, use. In this unequal act of exchange both the minority cultures and the dominant ones are radically altered.

But analogies go only so far. While all movements for social justice and equal rights share much in common, there are several pertinent differences that strike me as significant. In the first place, we cannot overestimate the centrality of the issue of visibility for lesbians and gays. Certainly, all groups have had to reckon with public visibility and part of any movement for equality has been a challenge to be seen in the public eye. Both the civil rights movement and the women's movement struggled— and continue to struggle—to have their constituencies represented fully and fairly in popular culture. And, surely, invisibility has been a problem for these social movements as well, as the recent NAACP crusade to improve television representation of people of color reveals.

But for gays, visibility is wrapped up with identity in a complicated and profound way. Two of the defining experiences for gays—the closet and coming out—speak to the problem of seeing oneself and being seen in a culture in which that simple move into the visible is itself a profoundly troubling act, for the actor and for those seeing the sight. Because we *can* hide, pass, be unknown even to ourselves, dissimulate, aver. Because we can use different pronouns, substitute names, make up spouses and excuses (or excuses for spouses). Because we can choose to think this is not about us, that it's nobody's business, that it's personal. Because being visible—to ourselves, to family, to friends, to coworkers, to anonymous publics—is an act of volition, a willful embrace, a pregnant gesture. Because we must know, somewhere, that the invisibility will not protect us, or will protect us at so great a cost that we lead lives not as full as they could and should be. But the hard truth of this new era of public visibility is this: it will not protect us either. As sociologist Josh Gamson says in his riveting account of the world of tabloid talk shows, "Becoming visible through the commercial media is, for marginalized populations, something like walking a tightrope: dangers await if you fall, some glory if you make it across, and there's not much to keep you in balance."[1]

And this brings me to my second point, another point that moves away from the analogies and locates the specificity of this moment. The gay movement has come into its own at precisely the historical moment in which the brave new world of media saturation, Internet access, nanosecond reporting, and Web organizing have breached the walls of the modern and pushed us all to someplace we can't even begin to define yet. If once there was some space beyond or aside from the swirl of culture and commodity (and culture *as* commodity), spaces of "subculture" for example that existed on a margin largely unknown and unremarked, now precious few of those spaces exist, and if they do exist they soon become grist for the culture machine. Many social theorists have remarked upon this, and pointed out that social movements are irrevocably changed when the mass media (and by this I mean all the myriad ways in which public representation occurs and is circulated) permeate social life to such a degree that referring to nonmediated spaces becomes an exercise in futility. And this is why I think the fundamental question facing us now is not the one that is so consistently offered. That one—"will we assimilate into mainstream, commercial, heterosexual American culture or will we maintain our own distinct subcultural identity?"—is an older question for a time eclipsed.

It's not that real questions of political ideology and strategy aren't embedded in that question, and we will continue to reckon with disputes within the movement around purpose, identity, vision. All one needs to do is to examine even briefly the controversy around the "Millennium March" in which powerful gay groups battled the suspicions of grassroots organizers in a contest about voice, direction, access. This is as it should be. But, still, holding to some binary formation (assimilated vs. unassimilated, commercial vs. "authentic," stereotypes vs. accurate images) misses the point. Indeed, the official Web site for the Millennium March contained within it all the criticism of itself, creating a dialogue of a new sort where opposition, commercialization, radical gestures, and liberal embrace coexist and commingle. The rainbow world is a food court and shopping mall, replete with HRC flags waving brightly above the stadium in tandem with the more familiar American flag, a stadium where we "rocked for equality" with 45,000 others, and watched as corporate sponsors felt our pain and joined our struggle. But the rainbow world is also filled with righteous young queers, whose insistence on the absolute right to visibility has spawned a tidal wave of teen trouble for heterosexual business-as-usual. And the rainbow world is filled with the earnest multiracial families gathered at the Millennium March's Family Garden, making the necessary connections between alternative families and retrograde welfare policies. And it is filled with hundreds of thousands of marchers—mostly white and mostly young—whose desire to be seen, known, respected, valued, brings them to the capital on a sunny April day. And it is filled with their counterparts, whose rejection of gay mediocrity and commercialization renders them no less rainbow, even while that clichéd and overused symbol is disavowed and mocked. We are our own conscience. The contested embrace. The elusive inclusivity. Welcome to our rainbow world.

In the endless circulation of images, where real life and sitcom life merge, where the television show of a homophobic pseudo-doctor (Dr. Laura) gets pilloried by Web-organized activists (StopDrLaura.com) who successfully provoke an "apology" and massive advertiser defections, and today's radical drag queen is tomorrow's cover girl, the visibility of previously marginalized groups cannot be reduced to such linear and simple formulations. The new gay visibility is not a good thing or a bad thing, although some of it is very good and some of it very bad, as I hope I have articulated throughout this book. Are we seeing the gaying of American culture, as supportive heterosexuals (columnist Frank Rich) and optimistic gays (cultural theorist Alexander Doty) would have it? Or is it instead what critic Daniel Mendelsohn has called the "heterosexualization of gay culture," where commodification links all identities to consumer choices? Is this an end of an era or the beginning of a new one? Perhaps this signifies a generational shift that resonates with a "queer" move away from identity politics. Many young gays—both the polymorphous, radical queers who resist definition and the guppies who want to blend in—find the old terms of "identity," "community," and "liberation" tired and narrow. Or, yet again, has gay life simply become, as liberal pundit Anna Quindlen argues, ordinary? Have "the small, incremental ways the world stops seeing differences as threatening" turned "the image of the gay community . . . to one of ordinary people searching for the ordinary ideal: commitment, love, privacy, work, family"?[2] Is gay culture no longer unsettling, has our difference been recuperated? Are we seeing a dramatic and heightened playing out of that old "tension that exists between heterosexual fear of homosexuality and gay culture (and the pleasure they represent) and the equally strong envy of and desire to enjoy that freedom and pleasure?"[3]

One concern many critics have is that the assimilation of explicit and known gayness into mass-mediated culture may spell the death of that uniquely gay contribution to mass culture: camp. If camp was, at least in part, the outsider's way of sending up mainstream culture while at the same time signaling a certain insider's hipness, then what happens to this outrageous sensibility when camp is brought inside, repackaged, and sold to gay and straight consumers alike? Is camp (and its challenge) dead or does "camping" (queering) of mainstream culture bring a new edginess to mass culture, blurring forever those invidious lines of insider/outsider? If queer is no longer coded (or coded so obviously—like Xena!) then what happens to those alternative practices of finding the fag in the haystack, of reading the rainbow in the straightest of stories? These are practices that, for many generations, honed gay identities into finely tuned cultural clue-finders and incipient auteurs. As Creekmur and Doty argue, "There really is no cultural or political 'bottom line' on the use of camp these days. Like other queer reading practices, sometimes it reinscribes queerness on the margins of popular culture, sometimes it questions the notion of a mainstream culture or preferred (read straight, white, middle-class male) cultural readings, while at other times it places queerness at the heart of the popular."[4]

Indeed, as I wrote this book I kept wishing it were simpler, that I could put a stamp on this time and mark it down clearly with a ✓or an ✗, that a simple thumbs up (or thumbs down) would suffice as explanation for an unremitting complexity. When I began this book I had a fairly clear idea of my "positions," even though I was equally committed to the idea of paradox or the contemporary period as, at least, one of rampant confusion. But confusion notwithstanding, I was sure that this explosion of visibility held out at least as much danger as possibility, and my fears of gay assimilation, commodification, depoliticization, and desexualization seemed well-founded.

I feared for our movement, afraid our rage—the rage of the closet, the rage of the unseen, the rage of the despised, the rage of the abject—would be rechanneled into hip aggro so anxious straights could relax and welcome their assimilated gay neighbors into their suburban backyards. Had we all become complacent queens and Subaru-driving dykes, toting our diaper bags and heading to Vermont? I feared that all the daring TV shows, cheeky ad campaigns, and earnest movies would come to supplant the need for substantive social change, and that the cost of public visibility would be civic exclusion. And anyway, I thought, they could and probably would take our TV shows away. How long, I wondered, could we be chic? How soon before the murders once again trumped the sitcoms? And the visibility didn't stop the murders, nor shine much light on those further in the margins—gays of color, working-class gays, not-chic lesbians. As Charles Kaiser argues, in an insightful piece written at the height of the Bush ascendancy and the Ashcroft debate, "despite the huge gains of the gay rights movement during the past 30 years, gay issues remain marginal issues in America. Unless there's a crisis, like Matthew Shepard's brutal murder, or the brouhaha over Bill Clinton's perfectly sensible proposal to allow lesbians and gays to serve openly in the military, the press routinely ignores the subject."[5]

I was furious at the glib assumption that visibility meant the end of oppression, but equally furious at the conviction that visibility was only a smokescreen and that nothing had really changed at all. I was worried about commodification and assimilation, wondering (like many others) if this was the price we had to pay for some modicum of "acceptance." I read those critics—both in the popular press and in the academy—who interpreted this new historical moment as one of transcendence, where gayness no longer mattered and American inclusion had triumphed, and thought them naive and willfully ignorant of the continued reality of oppression, exclusion, and victimization. What new world were they living in, I wondered. Reality-check time. No federal law banning discrimination against lesbians and gays. Anti-gay marriage bills passed in dozens of states. Adoption by gays banned in others. Military still a no-fly zone. Still legal to discriminate, still legitimate to denigrate (see Dr. Laura on this one). But there are paradoxes even in the denigration. When MTV gets stung by gay rights groups for promoting the music of the notoriously homophobic rap star Eminem (whose lyrics include such notable phrases as "My words are like a dagger with a jagged edge / They'll stab you in the head whether you're a fag or a lez / Or the homosex, hermaph or a trans-a-vest / Pants or dress / hate fags? The answer's 'yes' . . ."), the network responds by joining with HRC and others for a year-long "Fight for Your Rights" anti-discrimination campaign, which began with the airing of a film about the death of Matthew Shepard, a panel on anti-gay discrimination, and an eighteen-hour blackout of programming that featured only the names and details of hate crime victims, flashing across the otherwise blank screen. I saw this book as a cautionary tale, warning gays of too quick claims of victory and putting heterosexuals on notice: we are not fooled. A TV show does not a revolution make. We want Ellen and ENDA too.

But a funny thing happened on the way to the gay purgatory I imagined. It's not that the absence of millennial apocalypse has made me overly optimistic, or dulled the edge of criticism into a fake euphoria. Discrimination occurs daily but often is met with different responses than in previous years. When two lesbian lovebirds shared a smooch at Dodger Stadium in LA, they were summarily kicked out by stadium security. But the women threatened to sue, and the team ended up donating five thousand tickets to gay and lesbian groups; the women also got an apology and behind-the-plate seats, and sensitivity training for stadium staff was promised.[6] There does seem reason to hope. Every time I felt cynical or dismayed, depressed that the radical demands of gay liberation were being rapidly swallowed in the tidal wave of visibility, I remembered how it used to be. And while many feel a nostalgia for the old days and, like Daniel Harris, see this period as signaling the death of gay culture, I feel little fondness for the past, although the clarity of purpose is alluring and attractive to those of us muddling through these more confusing times.

While much of the cultural visibility does render gays harmless and innocuous, similar to straights and denuded of politics, sexuality, difference, something else often slips through or past the homogenizing gates of the culture factory. There are moments, indeed, when the ground of heterosexual terra firma begins to rock and quake, not knocking foundations perhaps but shifting things about a bit, insisting on a sort of remapping that leaves little untouched. When Ally relishes a kiss with Ling and then they both assert their desire for the missing male member, we the audience experience a sort of doubling effect. We witness the homophobia of the disavowed kiss, but also wonder at the too eager claims to heterosexuality that our heroines pronounce. When Budweiser boys hold hands in a rainbow world we see ourselves being crassly targeted as a niche market but also recognized as players in the admittedly consumerist game of life. When gays serve as best buddies to lead characters, providing moral centers and handy shoulders, we see ourselves as desexualized accessories to the main event, but also as integrated into the friendship networks and clichéd plots of American film. When our families are touted as functional and happy and identical to heterosexual families, we see the elision of alternative structures of parenting but also the recognition of the importance of communities of care to gay life. When politicians make speeches decrying anti-gay bigotry and then sign the Defense of Marriage Act, we see the craven hypocrisy of poll-driven technocrats but also the realization of gay political might. When corporations include anti-discrimination language and institute domestic partner coverage we understand it might simply be a wise business decision but we also receive real benefits and experience a more hospitable workplace. When even *Newsweek* depicts this moment as "the paradox of gay life in 2000," recognizing that "with every increment of progress in politics, Hollywood and the workplace, there arise new nodes of friction," you know that the range of acceptable public discourse has shifted.

But significant historical moments are rarely simple, and typically resemble a muck-filled mire more than a clear and calm lake. But in the churning, meaning is still discernable, for this new visibility itself redefines what it means to be gay in the twenty-first century. Like it or not, our identities, politics, ways of living and loving will change in the face of a public world in which we are no longer the awkward silent cousins to the main union of an unchallenged heterosexuality. The gaying of American culture. The blurring of lines. The messy mixing up. If the gaying of American culture irrevocably changes gays themselves, now living in a social space of brazen visibility, does it also irrevocably change heterosexuals, no longer able to turn away quite so easily or with such blithe indifference? This is the question I have turned over and over, and the question I find frustratingly difficult to answer. For the obvious response is a resounding yes. How could it not be? The new cultural visibility of gays must make straights both more aware of the realities of gay life and more sympathetic to gay people themselves. Isn't it true that the everyday presence of gays in our social and cultural world—in TV, in films, in ads, in politics, in familial life—helps to create an ease, a familiarity that renders homosexuality less threatening and, ultimately, more acceptable to those formerly mired in bigotry through ignorance? Doesn't the equation visibility = familiarity = acceptance ring true? There is a commonsense truth to this equation that is enticing and, in the face of the present with the past a hard memory, difficult to contest. Now, like never before, "the specter of homosexuality haunts the mainstream imagination in a way that is persistent and unique . . . a placard carried by a lesbian in Manhattan's first Gay Pride March in 1970 said it all: 'We Are Your Worst Fear. We Are Your Best Fantasy.'" [7]

Equations have a firmness, a finality, a singular and linear truth that irks the cultural theorist. We resist that surety, much as we insist on its fundamental inability to tell the whole story or perhaps even to tell a story at all. Surely, some stories, like some equations, are more straightforward than others. Some stories have a firm and unambiguous ending, and characters who embody villainy or heroism with clarity and purpose. But the story of gay visibility contains no such easy equations and is characterized by doublings, reversals, paradoxes, false starts. The story of gay visibility, like all narratives that are solicitous of history and wary of grandiose gestures, is rich with the complications born of social change and the resistance to it. It is a story mindful of the truth that all stories can be rewritten and different endings imagined by authors of varied intent. Some tell the story of gay visibility as a sort of social-movement Bildungsroman, a coming-of-age narrative where the childish antics of gay radicals become supplanted by the grown-up negotiations of straight-laced citizens, hungry for acceptance and willing to accept that as the mark of their maturity. Theirs is a celebratory tale, and one in which the hero triumphs, thus ending the story once and for all. Still others tell the story of gay visibility as a postmodern tale of capitulation and devaluation, a Quentin Tarantino movie where everyone has a price and pop images are recycled as the métier for identity and expression. Theirs is a sad tale, a tale of missed opportunities and false gods. Others, of course, see the story of gay visibility as a morality play, where decadent hedonists face off with righteous defenders in a mighty culture war worthy of

Cecil B. DeMille. Theirs is a story of fire and brimstone, of good and evil, of Sodom and Gomorrah. Still others figure the tale as an epic battle of another kind, of a benighted outcast with a past worthy of a John Ford western or a dark noir thriller, caught between the Scylla of continued oppression (in which the hero still retains his/her outcast allure) and the Charybdis of acceptance and integration (in which the hero finds solace but has lost his/her soul). Beginning, middle, end. Once upon a time. And then.

But I am a child of television, so the story I choose to tell is full of zaps and rewinds, neatly tied-up sitcom segments and the meandering overlays of soap opera torpor. It is a story in which one channel brings enlightened relief and another boring reruns. It is a story in which the mating of fiction and fact produce strange progeny, in which identities blur in the rush to infotain us. In which ghettoization and integration exist on the same frequency. In which we star and are yet secondary. In which we overturn traditions and shore them up twenty-two minutes later. In which we are today's news, as long as that lasts. It is a story being played out now in the most public of ways.

I've always found the sitcom the quintessentially American cultural object. It is at once perfectly banal yet endlessly iterated with meaning. It appears finite yet creeps along in expansionist directions, ceaselessly conquering even as its borders remain intact. It is peopled with rampant stereotypes yet always seems to be slyly upturning them, or at least allowing the knowledge of their fiction to seep through. So perhaps the story of gay visibility reads like a sitcom. Or some tangly, jangly mess of sitcom and soap, where attempts at resolution always appear frail and tenuous, where plots overlap and double back, where time moves exceedingly fast and yet things never seem to change. In its best moments, the sitcom is a structure of infinite possibilities, offering up the appearance of easy progress (in thirty minutes minus commercials) while at the same time depicting familial and social worlds fraying, pulling apart at the seams, ripping ever so slightly at the verities of the family, the citizen, the state. Like Lucy endlessly struggling to escape the boredom of Ricky's paternalistic control and Roseanne chafing at the strictures of working-class penury, the sitcom *contains* dissent and difference, but also displays that containment, makes it visible for all to witness, washes the dirty linen in front of a national audience.

The story of gay visibility is this one of simultaneous containment and display, progress and regress, shattering of old ways and their reassertion. And, like a sitcom, it appears to have a simple beginning, middle, and end, but it is, in fact, endlessly recombinant, returning week after week, showing up in reruns as camp fodder for new generations, and providing spin-offs in new/old directions. The story of gay visibility is thus ongoing and continuous, although never in exactly the same form. The question is not how it will end but rather what forms it will take as it mutates and hip-hops around the cultural marketplace. And here is where I should, I know, impose some narrative cohesion, rescue this story from its tipsy listing, reassure that—after all—Lucy will never escape Ricky's hold. Or that she will manage to sneak past the barricades and run off with Ethel to Lesbos (or at least Brooklyn). I should insist that we celebrate this visibility as at least the prelude to a reworking of American society, if not its main thesis. Or, alternately, bemoan this story as another callous tale of exploitation and avoidance, a cheap airport novel standing in for the great literature we know we can write. But this story is still being written, and we cannot know what lurks beyond visibility, past the sea change, once inside the gates. My sense is the time for dueling narratives is over. Put down your pens, boys. Rest your weary words, girls. Let a thousand sitcoms bloom. The space beyond visibility may be filled with commodified queens and buttoned-down wannabes, but it is also filled with possibilities unimaginable in previous eras. As the gaying of American culture continues on its uneven path, heterosexuals will—I am convinced—come to know themselves differently, to see *their* sexuality in less finite and tandem ways, opening up their sense of family, of place, of intimacy. It is significant, isn't it, that the support groups blossoming in schools all over the country are now called "Gay/Straight Alliances," while in other times heterosexual engagement in gay liberation was an oxymoron. The ideas of intentionality and choice, of equality in difference, of a joyous and messy sexuality, of a steadfast fabulousness that generously branches out—these are just some of the gifts we could bequeath to straights if only, if only.

For gays, the hard work of making ourselves seen *and* known, integrated but not assimilated, same *and* different has just begun. Michael Bronski makes an important point about the distinction between being visible and being public, arguing that being visible is essentially a passive stance while being public "entitles the individual to the rights and responsibilities of citizenship."[8] Ironically, it may be that our new visibility actually mitigates against this kind of citizenship because, once visible, we can be stigmatized, deprived of rights, identified. But remaining in the closet can never be the response to an attenuated visibility. A bland sameness or an exotic otherness are never our only options. That which slips under the borders, through the hedges, between the rock and the hard place always coexists with that egregious impulse to contain and discipline, to tidy up and make neat. These culture wars are more like skirmishes, wars of position and attrition in which the stakes keep changing, morphing like an elusive cybernaut, flitting about only to land someplace beyond definition, beyond fixing. *Que sera, sera, whatever will be will be. The future's not ours to see, que sera sera.* So sang Doris Day, in a kind of '50s benign fatalism that carried with it an acquiescence to the inevitability of the status quo. But now that song is camp, or always was, and the future may in fact be precisely about what we can see and what is revealed when the house lights dim low and that great disco ball drops down.

Notes

CHAPTER ONE

1. David Dunlap, "Gay Images, Once Kept Out, Are Out Big Time," *New York Times,* January 21, 1996, 29.

2. John Dart, "Retreat for Gays, Lesbians Opens," *Los Angeles Times,* April 18, 1998, B1.

3. Don Romesburg, "30 Years Ago Perry Forms MCC," *Advocate,* May 26, 1998, 10.

4. "Co-Media, Inc. to Launch Gay Television Network," PR Newswire, January 16 2001.

5. David France, "Tuning Out Dr. Laura," *Newsweek,* September 18, 2000, 80.

6. Marjorie Williams, "When Cheney Broke Ranks," *Washington Post,* October 13, 2000, A39.

7. Joshua Gamson, "Diversity Follies," *American Prospect* (January 3 2000): 52.

8. Daniel Harris, *The Rise and Fall of Gay Culture* (New York: Hyperion, 1997).

9. Peter Freiberg, "Boy Scout Opposition Continues to Gather Steam," *Washington Blade* (December 8, 2000): 22.

10. Richard Lacayo, "The New Gay Struggle," *Time,* October 26, 1998, 32–36.

11. Michael Bronski, *The Pleasure Principle: Sex, Backlash, and the Struggle for Gay Freedom* (New York: St. Martin's Press, 1998), 234.

12. Personal interview.

13. Personal interview.

14. Personal interview.

15. Andrew Sullivan, "When Plagues End," *New York Times Magazine,* November 10, 1996, 60 (52+).

16. Michael Warner, *The Trouble With Normal: Sex, Politics, and the Ethics of Queer Life* (New York: Free Press, 2000), 60.

17. Personal interview.

18. Richard Goldstein, "Believers Who Brunch," *Village Voice,* October 27– November 2, 1999.

19. Personal interview.

20. Personal interview.

21. Personal interview.

22. Tony Kushner, "Matthew's Passion," *Nation,* November 9, 1998.

23. Independent film is another story altogether and, while not perfect by any stretch of the imagination, it has continued to produce a wider and more complex range of gay representations than its more mainstream Hollywood counterparts.

24. Benjamin Svetkey, "Is Your TV Set Gay?" *Entertainment Weekly,* October 6, 2000, 27.

25. Terry Wilson, "Coming Out from Leading a Double Life; Telling Family, Friends Still a Scary Passage for Gays and Lesbians," *Chicago Tribune,* July 14, 1995, C1.

CHAPTER TWO

1. *Advocate,* March 2, 1999, 15.

2. Rhonda Smith, "Clinton Proclaims June Pride Month," *Washington Blade,* June 18, 1999, 1.

3. Personal interview, 1996.

4. Sean Cahill and Erik Ludwig, "Courting the Vote: The 2000 Presidential Candidates' Positions on Gay, Lesbian, Bisexual and Transgender Issues," Policy Institute of the National Gay and Lesbian Task Force.

5. Rene Sanchez, "'America's Largest Problem' Is Hate, President Tells Gay Group," *Washington Post,* October 3, 1999, A6.

6. Bill Ghent, "Ready for Battle," *Advocate,* December 19, 2000, 30.

7. Richard L. Berke, "Flurry of Anti-Gay Remarks Has G.O.P. Fearing Backlash," *New York Times,* June 30, 1998, A1.

8. Chris Bull, interview with President Bill Clinton, "Triumphs, Trials and Errors," *Advocate,* November 7, 2000, 36.

9. Servicemembers Legal Defense Network.

10. NGLTF Direct Report, March 1998.

11. As quoted by Richard Goldstein, "The Year in Queer," *Village Voice,* December 27–January 2, 2001.

12. NGLTF, "A Plan for Action," September 1999.

13. Chris Poynter, "Kentucky's Gay-Rights Battle," *Courier-Journal,* October 18, 1999, 1A.

14. Editorial, "Gay Rights in California," *New York Times,* October 9, 1999, A16.

15. Michael Ollove, "Voices of People Scorned," *Baltimore Sun,* November 16, 2000, 1E.

16. Carol Ness, "Gains for Gays in U.S. Business: Conference Finds Much Achieved, But Much Left to Do," *San Francisco Examiner,* October 18, 1993, C-1.

17. *Advocate,* November 10, 1998, 18.

18. HRC Press Release, September 7, 1999.

19. Michelle Dally Johnston, "Strange Brew: Coors Taps into Liberal 'Domestic Partner' Benefits, Stunning Its Gay Critics," *Denver Westword,* June 21, 1995.

20. Ibid.

21. Peter Freiberg, "United's Skies Turn Friendlier," *Washington Blade,* August 6, 1999, 1.

22. Ness, "Gains for Gays in U.S. Business."

23. Ibid.

24. Ibid.

25. Art Bain, quoted in Ibid.

26. Ibid.

27. Edward Iwata, "Here's a New One: Corporate America Is at the Vanguard of Gay and Lesbian Rights," *Commercial Appeal,* April 24, 1996, 10B.

28. Brian McGrory, "Gays Face Growing Backlash," *Boston Sunday Globe,* November 28, 1993, 1.

29. Lisa Keen, *Washington Post,* October 31, 1993, C3.

30. Katia Hetter, "Gay Rights Issues Bust Out All Over," *U.S. News & World Report,* October 2, 1995, 71 (71–72).

31. McGrory, "Gays Face Growing Backlash," 1, 20.

32. Mark Sullivan, "Judges Order Scouts to Accept Gays," *Washington Blade,* August 6, 1999, 1.

33. Joan Biskupic, "Court Allows Ban on Gay Rights Laws," *Washington Post,* October 14, 1998, A1.

34. Marla Dickerson, "Christian Group Escalates Boycott against Disney," *Los Angeles Times,* July 2, 1996.

35. Ibid.

36. Reuters, "Disney Boycott Escalated by Baptist Group," *Washington Post,* August 14, 1997, A10.

37. Jonathan Yardley, "The Baptists' Passion Play," *Washington Post,* June 23, 1997.

38. Deborah Fraser, "Gay and Lesbian Groups Targets Hate Speech with TV Ads," All Things Considered, NPR, December 21, 1995, transcript no. 2068-8.

39. Richard L. Berke, "Chasing the Polls on Gay Rights," *New York Times,* August 2, 1998, 3.

40. Carey Goldberg, "Acceptance of Gay Men and Lesbians Is Growing, Study Says," *New York Times,* May 31, 1998, 21.

41. Dan Levy, "Out in America: New Gay Frontiers," *San Francisco Chronicle,* April 28, 1994, A1.

42. Personal interview, 1997.

43. Personal interview.

44. Personal interview.

45. Personal interview.

46. Andrew Sullivan, "When Plagues End," *New York Times Magazine,* November 10, 1996, 56 (52+).

47. Ibid.

48. Ibid.

49. Personal interview.

50. Personal interview.

51. Urvashi Vaid, *Virtual Equality: The Mainstreaming of Gay and Lesbian Liberation* (New York: Anchor Books, 1995).

52. Ibid.

53. Daniel Harris, *The Rise and Fall of Gay Culture* (New York: Hyperion 1997).

54. Doug Ireland, "Rebuilding the Gay Movement," *Nation*, July 12, 1999.

55. Andrew Sullivan, "They've Changed, So They Say," *New York Times*, July 26, 1998, 15.

56. Karen J. Cohen, "Gays in GOP Push Agenda," *Wisconsin State Journal*, October 24, 1993.

CHAPTER THREE

1. There is a wonderful skit on *Mad TV* which depicts a "lost" episode of *Mary Tyler Moore* in which Mary reveals her lesbianism and love for Rhoda.

2. Larry Gross, "What Is Wrong with This Picture? Lesbian Women and Gay Men on Television," in R. Jeffrey Ringer, ed., *Queer Words, Queer Images: Communication and the Construction of Homosexuality* (New York: New York University Press 1994), 146.

3. Joseph Hanania, "Resurgence of Gay Roles on Television," *Los Angeles Times*, November 3, 1994, 12.

4. Mark Hudis, "Gays Back in Prime Time," *Mediaweek* 3, no. 50 (December 13, 1993): 14.

5. Hanania "Resurgence of Gay Roles on Television."

6. Personal interview.

CHAPTER FOUR

1. International Communications Research, telephone survey of 1,003 adults, September 19–22, 1996.

2. Bruce Handy, "He Called Me Ellen Degenerate?" *Time*, April 14, 1997, 86.

3. A. J. Jacobs, "Out?" *Entertainment Weekly*, October 4, 1996, 23 (18–25).

4. Handy, "He Called Me Ellen Degenerate?"

5. Tom Knott, "Did You Hear the News? Ellen Is Still Gay," *Washington Times*, October 23, 1997, C2.

6. Keith Marder, "A Kiss, not The Kiss, on 'Ellen,'" *Daily News of Los Angeles*, September 24, 1997, L7.

7. *TV Guide*, "Cheer and Jeers," May 17–23, 1997.

8. Charles Kaiser, "Valour! Compassion! Laughs!" *New York Times*, December 21, 1997, sec. 2, p. 37, col. 5.

9. Robin Schacht and Greg Varner, "Is Ellen Too Gay?" *Washington Blade*, March 13, 1998.

10. Marder, "A Kiss, not The Kiss."

11. Kaiser, "Valour! Compassion! Laughs!"

12. Ibid.

13. At the end of this episode, Melissa Etheridge shows up in the coffeehouse to have Ellen sign her official forms and get them stamped so that Susan can get her toaster oven.

14. *Larry King Live,* "Homosexuality in American Television," October 16, 1997 (CNN), with guests Betty DeGeneres, Chastity Bono, Jerry Falwell, Barney Frank, Robert Peters.

15. Erika Mil, "It's Not a Secret, but Still Exciting," *New York Times,* April 10, 1997, C1.

16. Ibid.

17. Ibid.

CHAPTER FIVE

1. *Entertainment Weekly,* October 6, 2000.

2. Art Dworken, "TV Goes Gay Crazy!" *National Examiner,* October 24, 2000, 5.

3. Ibid.

4. Kinney Littlefield, "Gay Stereotypes Come Crashing Down on TV as Characters Get 'Real,'" *Arizona Republic,* December 27, 1995, C7.

5. Christopher Jones, "The Point," *Washington Blade,* online edition, September 12, 1997.

6. David Bauder, "TV's Independent Film Channel Running a Gay and Lesbian Film Festival," *Associated Press,* February 9, 2000.

7. A recent *Entertainment Weekly* Gallup poll revealed that 60 percent of 18–29-year-olds say they wouldn't mind seeing a same sex kiss on TV. That statistic should explain why MTV has been somewhat less squeamish about "the kiss." The first version of the pseudo-documentary *The Real World*—about a group of young adults living together in San Francisco—featured regular Pedro Zamora exchanging rings with his boyfriend in a "gay marriage" ceremony. The two men—who are not actors—hold hands and kiss no fewer than seven times in the half-hour cinéma vérité program.

8. Gail Shister, "Gay Alliance Seeks More Characters on Television," *Milwaukee Journal Sentinel,* August 25, 1999, 7.

9. Joshua Gamson, "Diversity Follies," *American Prospect,* January 3, 2000, 52.

10. Eric Gutierrez, "TV's Gay Teenagers Get Real," *Los Angeles Times,* May 10, 1999, F1.

11. David Bauder, "'Dawson's Creek' Gay Character Gets Little Notice So Far," *Atlanta Journal-Constitution,* March 17, 1999, C7.

12. Ken Parish Perkins, "How Deeply Will 'Dawson's Creek' Test Waters with Gay Character?" *Arizona Republic,* March 31, 1999, D5.

13. Ibid.

14. A. J. Jacobs, "When Gay Men Happen to Straight Women," *Entertainment Weekly,* October 23, 1998.

15. Benjamin Svetkey, "Is Your TV Set Gay?" *Entertainment Weekly,* October 6, 2000, 28.

16. Andrew Holleran, "The Alpha Queen," *Gay and Lesbian Review* (summer 2000): 65.

17. Alan Pergament, "Fall Preview: The Television Season Heading into the Year 2000 Offers Some Alarming Trends and Some Thoughtful Shows." *Buffalo News,* September 5, 1999, 24.

18. Gamson, "Diversity Follies," 52.

19. Ibid., 53.

20. Andrea Bernstein, "Commentary on Lack of Gay Sex on Prime Time," *All Things Considered,* NPR, January 18, 1995, transcript no. 1731-7.

21. Epstein, "Prime Time for Gay Youth," 61.

22. Tom Hopkins, "Gays on TV," *Dayton Daily News,* August 20, 1995, 1C.

23. Frank Bruni, "Lip Service: Kiss Between Gays Remains Taboo," *Arizona Republic,* February 16, 1994, D1.

24. Ibid.

25. David Robb, "Family Values Group Urges NBC to Omit Lesbian Kiss from 'Serving in Silence,'" *Baltimore Sun,* January 2, 1995, 7D.

26. Brain Lowry, "Syndicated 'Frasier' Episode Spoofing Dr. Laura Is Pulled," *Los Angeles Times,* November 7, 2000, F2.

27. Joseph Hanania, "Resurgence of Gay Roles on Television," *Los Angeles Times,* November 3, 1994, 12.

28. Joss Whedon, interviewed on *Fresh Air,* NPR, with host David Bianculli, May 9, 2000.

29. Frederic Biddle, "Gays in Prime Time; Network Television Remains Uncomfortable with Homosexuality," *Boston Globe,* December 24, 1995, 25.

30. Ibid.

31. Joanne Ostrow, "Beyond Ellen: Gays Make Headway in Well-Rounded Roles," *Denver Post,* August 3, 1997, E1.

32. John Goodman, "TV Declares Open Season on Gays," *San Francisco Examiner,* September 16, 1999.

33. Richard Goldstein, "Hip Hate," *Images: A Journal of the Gay and Lesbian Alliance against Defamation,* November 2000, 7.

34. Ostrow, "Beyond Ellen."

35. Svetkey "Is Your TV Set Gay?" 26.

36. Ibid.

37. Ibid.

38. Gamson, "Diversity Follies," 53.

39. Corey Creekmur and Alexander Doty, eds., *Out in Culture: Gay, Lesbian, and Queer Essays on Popular Culture* (Durham, NC: Duke University Press, 1995), 393.

40. Paris Barclay, "My Perspective: Color Television," *Advocate,* September 28, 1999, 11.

41. Stuart Elliott, "The Showtime Network Prepares a $10 Million Campaign Blitz for Its 'Queer as Folk' Series," *New York Times,* November 28, 2000, C9.

42. Matthew Gilbert, "Queer as Folk Makes a Convincing Debut," *Boston Globe,* December 1, 2000, F1.

43. Joshua Gamson, "Folktales," *American Prospect,* December 18, 2000,

44. Nancy Franklin, "Unbuttoned," *New Yorker,* January 15, 2001, 94.

45. Gilbert, "Queer as Folk Makes a Convincing Debut."

46. Anthony Tommasina, "Looking for a Breakthrough? You'll Have to Wait," *New York Times,* 38.

47. Phil Rosenthal, "Walls' Talk: Stone Tells of Gay Role in HBO Film" *Chicago Sun-Times,* March 2, 2000, 41.

CHAPTER SIX

1. Richard Corliss, "The Final Frontier; Two New Movies Pose the Question, Can't Hollywood Treat Gays Like Normal People?" *Time,* March 11, 1996, 66.

2. Daniel Harris, *The Rise and Fall of Gay Culture* (New York: Hyperion, 1997), 15.

3. David Ansen, "Gay Films Are a Drag," *Newsweek,* March 18, 1996, 71.

4. Bob Strauss, "Gay Film Roles More Visible, But Honest Portrayals Still Rare," *Plain Dealer,* March 17, 1996, 7J.

5. Larry Kramer, "Why I Hated 'Philadelphia,'" *Los Angeles Times,* January 9, 1994, 29.

6. Richard Corliss, "The Gay Gauntlet," *Time,* February 7, 1994, 62 (62–64).

7. Ansen, "Gay Films Are a Drag."

8. Jim Burke, "'Birdcage' Success Is More about Laughs Than Liberalism," *Boston Herald,* March 14, 1996, 59.

9. Burke, "'Birdcage' Success."

10. Corliss, "The Final Frontier."

11. Ibid.

12. Eric Gutierrez, "Opening Hollywood's Closet," *Los Angeles Times,* March 10, 1996, 4.

13. Ibid.

14. Ansen, "Gay Films Are a Drag."

15. The sort of inverse of the gay-life films is the strange emergence of films such as *Kiss Me Guido* in which gay life and heterosexual life are both hyperbolized and stereotyped and then crash into each other only to find love, brotherly affection, and unity. Here, Frankie (the hunky but sensitive pizza boy from the Bronx) moves in with Warren (the fey and dateless Manhattan fag) because he mistakes an ad looking for a GWM as indicating a "guy with money." After the mistaken identity theme gets worked over, the stereotyped gay guy (with swishy best buddy) and the stereotyped Italian stallion (with macho brother) find friendship and harmony in the end.

16. Jim Moret, "Hollywood Goes Gay with Glut of New Movies," *CNN,* March 11, 1996, Entertainment section, transcript no. 1153-16, 11:21 A.M. ET.

CHAPTER SEVEN

1. James Keller and William Glass, "In & Out: Self-Referentiality and Hollywood's 'Queer' Politics," *Journal of Popular Television and Film* 26, no. 3 (fall 1998): 137 (136–43).

2. Neal Karlen "Ho-hum: The Kiss That Didn't Rock the World," *New York Times,* October 5, 1997.

3. Larry Gross, "Visibility and Its Discontents," *Images* (a publication of the Gay and Lesbian Alliance Against Defamation, 2000): 17.

4. It is vital to note that images of lesbians are not solely a phenomenon of

the gay '90s, but have a rich and complicated history. Indeed, earlier films of the '80s paved the way for the recent wave of representations. *Personal Best, Lianna,* and *Desert Hearts* are three of the films that attempted to reach mainstream audiences with central lesbian characters and lesbian relationships.

5. Edward Guthmann, "Lots of Lesbian Movies Coming Out," *San Francisco Chronicle,* February 25, 1996, 37.

6. Bright quoted in ibid.

7. Charla Krupp, "Can 'Nice' Lesbians Be Good Box Office?" *Glamour,* May 1992, 175.

8. Ibid.

9. Rita Kempley, "'Affection': Two Men and a Barbie," *Washington Post,* April 17, 1998, B4.

10. Ibid.

11. Manohla Dargis, "Getting Past Fabulousness to Real Life," *New York Times,* March 5, 2000, sec. 2, p. 13.

12. The independent films I am discussing here are really those hybrid films that are relatively low budget yet either through distribution or through critical acclaim pick up a larger and more diverse audience than the typical film-festival indie. Obviously there is a whole other world of independent film and video that remains largely outside any mainstream viewing public.

CHAPTER EIGHT

1. The commercialization of marriage is obviously disturbing as well. What does this say about the supposedly "natural" drive to marry, given its relentless marketing? Gays have gotten in on the act as well. Just the other day I received a catalog in the mail for "Family Celebrations," billing itself as "America's First Wedding & Special Occasions Catalog for the Gay and Lesbian Community." Yet the emphasis is clearly on weddings or other such ceremonies, and firmly embedded in a traditional family motif (even the kids' stuff references two mommies or two daddies). Where is the paraphernalia to celebrate single motherhood? Deep and abiding friendships? Political alliances?

2. Fern Shen, "A Same-Sex Couple Married to the Cause," *Washington Post,* September 10, 1996, A4 (A1–4).

3. See particularly my articles on gay marriage and parenting, listed in the bibliography. In addition, the work of Paula Ettelbrick, Nancy Polikoff, and others is helpful. Michael Warner and others critique gay marriage from a radical and feminism perspective.

4. Frank Browning, "Why Marry?" *New York Times,* April 17, 1996.

5. E. J. Graff, "Retying the Knot," *Nation,* June 24, 1996.

6. Carey Goldberg, "Vermont Residents Split over Civil Unions Law," *New York Times,* September 3, 2000.

7. For a full discussion of the "gay marriage debate," see my articles on this subject (listed in the bibliography).

8. A. J. Jacobs, "Out?" *Entertainment Weekly,* October 4, 1996, 22 (18–25).

9. David W. Dunlap, "Gay Images, Once Kept Out, Are Out Big Time," *New York Times,* January 21, 1996, sec. 1, p. 29.

10. Jim Moret, "Newt's Sister Marries 'Friends' Lesbian Stars," *CNN Showbiz Today,* January 17, 1996, transcript no. 1005-3.

11. The construction of gays as congenitally unable to negotiate the vicissitudes of adulthood (read marriage and kids) is a common theme not only in TV neoliberal discourse, but in gay conservative discourse as well. See particularly Andrew Sullivan, ed., *Same-Sex Marriage: Pro and Con* (New York: Vintage, 1997), and Bruce Bawer, ed., *Beyond Queer: Challenging Gay Left Orthodoxy* (New York: Free Press, 1996).

12. Laura Blumenfeld, "Every Girl's Dream," *Washington Post,* November 20, 1996, D1 (D1–D2).

13. Ibid., D2.

14. Deborah Bradley, "Unions: More Gay and Lesbian Couples Are Acknowledging Their Commitment through Ceremonies," *Dallas Morning News,* May 4, 1994, 1C.

15. Jonathan Rauch, "For Better or Worse?" *New Republic,* May 6, 1996, 18.

16. Ibid.

17. Lewin, Ellen. "Weddings without Marriage: Making Sense of Lesbian and Gay Commitment Rituals." In *Queer Families, Queer Politics: Challenging Culture and the State,* edited by Mary Bernstein and Renate Reimann. New York: Columbia University Press, 2001.

18. Bradley "Unions."

19. Catherine Tuerk, "From the Flagpole," 1996.

CHAPTER NINE

1. George Chauncey, *Gay New York: Gender, Urban Culture, and the Makings of the Gay Male World, 1890–1940* (New York: Basic Books, 1994), 7–8.

2. Susan Davis, "A Parent's Perspective: 'Guess What, Mom? I'm Gay,'" "The Truth About Jane" Web site, Lifetime online (www.lifetimetv.com).

CHAPTER TEN

1. *NCLR Newsletter* (fall 1998): 5.

2. Ibid., 6.

3. Beatrice Dohrn, "Bitter Losses, Sweet Victories: A Recipe for Progress," *Lambda Update* (winter 1999): 5.

4. Ibid.

5. Joan Lowy, "Adoptions by Gays Ignite Fights Across U.S.," *Detroit News,* March 7, 1999, A10.

6. David W. Dunlap, "Support for Gay Adoptions Seems to Wane," *New York Times,* May 1, 1995, A13.

7. Reuters, "National News Brief: California Recognizes Tax Right of Gay Parents," *New York Times,* November 4, 2000, A22.

8. Judith Havemann, "N.J. Allows Gays to Jointly Adopt," *Washington Post,* December 18, 1997, A24.

9. Robert Knight, quoted in ibid., A1.

10. Chris Waddington, "Gay Parents Gather to Share Advice, Common Experiences," *Star Tribune* (Minneapolis, MN), February 28, 1999, 1B.

11. Susan Lad, "We Are Family," *News and Record* (Greensboro, NC), August 14, 1995, D1.

12. Scott Harris, "2 Moms or 2 Dads—and a Baby," *Los Angeles Times,* October 20, 1991, A1.

13. Laura A. Kiernan, "Lesbian Couple Thrilled over Adoption Ruling," *Boston Globe,* September 12, 1993, 29.

14. Linell Smith, "Gay Parents Have Typical Worries," *Baltimore Sun,* July 23, 1995, 11E.

15. Sally MacDonald, "Same-Sex Parents Lead Similar Family Life," *Times-Picayune* (New Orleans), July 2, 1995, A6.

16. Claire Loebs, "Gay Partners with Children; Adoption a Challenge in Climate of Intolerance, Legal Ambiguities," *Arizona Republic,* July 27, 1995, C1.

17. Jean Latz Griffin, "The Gay Baby Boom," *Chicago Tribune,* September 3, 1992, C1.

18. David Tuller, "Lesbian Families—Study Shows Healthy Kids," *San Francisco Chronicle,* November 23, 1992, A13.

19. Ibid.

20. Griffin "The Gay Baby Boom."

21. Paul Ben-Itzak, "Same-Sex Parents Struggle for Acceptance in U.S.," *Reuter Library Report,* August 6, 1993.

22. Pat Wingert and Barbara Kantrowitz, "Gay Today: The Family," *Newsweek,* March 20, 2000, 50.

23. Ibid.

24. John Carman, "Goodman Plays It Safe as Gay Guy," *San Francisco Chronicle,* November 1, 2000, D1.

25. Matthew Gilbert, "Fall TV Season," *Boston Globe,* November 1, 2000, C9.

26. When gay power couple Hilary Rosen (head of the Recording Industry Association of America) and Elizabeth Birch (head of HRC) adopted twins, the announcement they sent out coded the babies in pink and blue!

27. Jennifer K. Ruark, interview with Michael Warner, *Chronicle of Higher Education,* February 11, 2000, A21.

28. Frank Browning, "Why Marry?" in *Same-Sex Marriage: Pro and Con,* ed. Andrew Sullivan (New York: Vintage, 1997), 133 (originally in the *New York Times,* April 17, 1996).

29. Kath Weston, *Families We Choose: Lesbians, Gays, Kinship* (New York: Columbia University Press, 1991).

30. Jess Wells, "The Changes Wrought : How Parenting Is Changing Lesbian Culture," in *Homefronts: Controversies in Nontraditional Parenting,* ed. Jess Wells (Los Angeles: Alyson Books, 2000), 94, 96.

31. Frank Browning, "Why Marry?"

32. Kate Clinton, "Kiss Me, Aunt Kate," *Advocate,* June 22, 1999, 101.

CHAPTER ELEVEN

1. See particularly Lance Lukenbill, *Untold Millions: Positioning Your Business for the Gay and Lesbian Consumer Revolution* (New York: HarperCollins, 1995).

2. Alexandra Chasin, *Selling Out: The Gay and Lesbian Movement Goes to Market* (New York: St. Martin's Press, 2000), xvi.

3. Martha Moore, *USA Today,* April 23, 1993, 1B.

4. Chasin, *Selling Out,* 33.

5. Cyndee Miller, "The Ultimate Taboo," *Marketing News TM,* August 14, 1995, 1.

6. Chasin, *Selling Out,* 15.

7. Daniel Harris, *The Rise and Fall of Gay Culture* (New York: Hyperion, 1997), 79.

8. Personal interview.

9. Amy Gluckman and Betsy Reed, "The Gay Marketing Moment," in *Homo-Economics: Capitalism, Community, and Lesbian and Gay Life,* ed. Amy Gluckman and Betsy Reed (New York: Routledge, 1997), 3.

10. Personal interview.

11. CNN, with correspondent Charles Feldman, "Advertising Aimed at the Gay Community Surges," October 7, 1992, transcript no. 200-1.

12. Jane L. Levere, "Gay Publications Gain Ad Spending," *New York Times,* March 4, 1999, C8.

13. Mulryan/Nash, 1998 *Gay Press Report.*

14. "Advertising Spending in Gay Press Increases for the Fourth Straight Year," *Business Wire,* February 22, 1999.

15. Mulryan/Nash, 1998 *Gay Press Report.*

16. Cliff Rothman, "Advertising and Marketing: Gay Regionals Lead Growth in Publishing," *Los Angeles Times,* November 12, 1999, C1.

17. Ibid.

18. Nelson Mui, "Management Buyout Team Envisions a Gay Mega Publishing Brand," *Daily News Record,* Capital Cities Media Inc., April 9, 1999, 8.

19. Phuong Ly, "Industry Embraces Same-Sex Couples," *Washington Post,* February 22, 2000, B3.

20. Ibid.

21. Urvashi Vaid, preface to *Income Inflation: The Myth of Affluence among Gay, Lesbian, and Bisexual Americans,* by M. V. Lee Badgett (New York: A Joint Publication of the Policy Institute of the National Gay and Lesbian Task Force and the Institute for Gay and Lesbian Strategic Studies, 1998), i.

22. Bruce Horovitz, "Report Counters Belief That Gays Earn More," *USA Today,* December 3, 1998, 1B.

23. Ibid.

24. Hadley Pawlak, "New Yellow Pages Directory Finds Market in Gay Community," *Buffalo News,* September 4, 1999, 7A.

25. TZ, "The Myth of Gay Affluence" *American Prospect,* September–October 1999, 14.

26. Howard Buford, "Understanding Gay Consumers," *Gay and Lesbian Review Worldwide* 7, no. 2 (spring 2000): 26

27. Penny Parker, "Ski Resorts Pressed to Diversify," *Denver Post,* March 13, 1999, C1.

28. Ibid.

29. Sherrie Dean, "Showbiz Today," CNN, August 30, 1993, transcript no. 363-4.

30. Ronald Alsop, "In Marketing to Gays, Lesbians Are Often Left Out," *Wall Street Journal,* October 11, 1999, B1.

31. Danae Clark, "Commodity Lesbianism," in *Out in Culture: Gay, Lesbian, and Queer Essays on Popular Culture,* ed. Corey Creekmur and Alexander Doty (Durham, NC: Duke University Press, 1995), 485.

32. Diane Cyr, "The Emerging Gay Market," *Catalog Age* 10, no. 11 (November 1993): 112.

33. Michael Wilke, "A Kiss before Buying," *Advocate,* April 27, 1999, 34 (34–36).

34. Clark, "Commodity Lesbianism," 486.

35. Robin Givhan, "The Fetching Men of Abercrombie & Fitch," *Washington Post,* August 7, 1998, D1.

36. Ibid., D5.

37. Gluckman and Reed "The Gay Marketing Moment," 5.

38. Kevin Goldman, "Baileys Crowns Noted Drag Queen as Pitchperson for New Campaign," *Wall Street Journal,* September 1, 1995, B7.

39. "A New Affluent Target Market Comes Out," *Chain Store Age,* January 1, 1998, 54.

40. Stuart Elliott, "Homosexual Imagery Is Spreading from Print Campaigns to General-Interest TV Programming," *New York Times,* June 30, 1997, D12.

41. Kathy Preble, "Cracking the Gay Market Code," *Tampa Tribune,* July 9, 1999, 2.

42. Ibid.

43. Elliott, "Homosexual Imagery."

44. Preble, "Cracking the Gay Market Code."

45. Elliott, "Homosexual Imagery."

46. Peter Freiberg, "Miller Contemplates Gay TV Ad," *Washington Blade,* July 23, 1999, 12.

47. Riccardo A. Davis, "Markets Game for Gay Events," *Advertising Age,* May 30, 1994, 1S.

48. Daniel S. Levine, "Mainstream Advertisers Start to Discover Gay Market," *San Francisco Business Times,* July 21, 1995, sec. A, p. 5.

49. Buford, "Understanding Gay Consumers," 27.

50. Pat Morgan, "A New Frontier," *Chicago Tribune,* June 3, 1992, sec. 7, p. 21.

51. Chasin, *Selling Out,* 133–34.

52. Levine. "Mainstream Advertisers."

CHAPTER TWELVE

1. Robert L. Pela, "A Different Fight," *Advocate,* August 17, 1999.

2. Stuart Elliott, "Hill & Knowlton Forms a Unit to Direct Public Relations Efforts toward Gay Men and Lesbians," *New York Times,* June 23, 1995, D5.

3. Jason Fargo, "Gay Marketing: A Profitable Niche?" *Credit Card Management,* March 1999.

4. Karla Jay, "Queers Ahoy!" *Village Voice,* September 23–29, 1998.

5. The irony of Olivia Cruises is itself emblematic of the shift in gay identity

and gay life. Begun in the '70s as a women's music production company (and thus on the margins both culturally and financially), Olivia reinvented itself for the visible and upscale '80s and '90s by becoming a luxury cruise and travel company.

6. Betsy Wade, "The Booming Gay Market," *Chicago Tribune,* January 3, 1993, sec. 12.

7. Betsy Wade, "More Options for Gay Travelers," *New York Times,* January 29, 1995, 4.

8. Katia Hetter, "Globe-Trotting in the Gay '90s," *U.S. News & World Report,* June 16, 1997, 69.

9. Jay, "Queers Ahoy!"

10. Mubarak Dahir, "Small Business, Big Trouble" *Advocate,* April 25, 2000.

11. *Interactive PR & Marketing News* 2, no. 26, December 18, 1998.

12. Jennifer Gilbert, "Marketers See Niche Group as Lucrative, No-Risk Target," *Advertising Age,* December 8, 1999.

13. John Schwartz, "Online Gays Become a Market for Advertisers," *Washington Post,* May 22, 1999, E1.

14. "Coming Out," *Advertising Age Interactive Special report Supplement,* November 1, 1999, 40.

15. "PlanetOut Tops One Million Unique Site Visitors," *Business Wire,* February 1, 2000.

16. Jennifer Gilbert, "Ad Spending Booming for Gay-Oriented Sites," *Advertising Age,* December 6, 1999, 58,

17. Andrew Quinn, "Major Gay Online Merger Joins PlanetOut, Gay.com," Reuters (Lycos News), November 15, 2000.

18. Schwartz "Online Gays," E5.

19. *PR Newswire,* April 30, 1999.

20. Jeremy Quittner, "Taking Stock in Ourselves," *Advocate,* July 4, 2000.

21. *PR Newswire,* April 5, 1999.

22. *Business Wire,* February 17, 2000.

23. Jeremy Quittner, "Tempting Gay Employees," *Advocate,* October 24, 2000, 25.

24. Martha Moore, "Courting the Gay Market," *USA Today,* April 23, 1993, 1B.

25. Mubarak Dahir, "Vermonters Profit from Equality," *Advocate,* November 21, 2000.

26. Grant Lukenbill, *Untold Millions: Positioning Your Business for the Gay and Lesbian Consumer Revolution* (New York: Harper Collins, 1995).

27. Michael Warner, *The Trouble with Normal: Sex, Politics, and the Ethics of Queer Life* (New York: Free Press, 2000), 62–63.

28. Alexandra Chasin, "Selling Out: The Gay/Lesbian Market and the Construction of Gender," *Sojourner* 22, no. 10 (June 1997): 14–15.

29. Ibid.

30. Ibid.

31. Dan Savage, "Faithlessly Yours," *OUT,* June 1999, 62.

32. Alexandra Chasin, *Selling Out: The Gay and Lesbian Movement Goes to Market* (New York: St. Martin's Press, 2000), 39.

33. Daniel Harris, *The Rise and Fall of Gay Culture* (New York: Hyperion, 1997), 158.

34. Robert Bray, quoted in Wayne Hoffman, "Mixed Media: Gay People Are More Visible Than Ever Before, but How Do They Look?" *Washington Blade*, November 7, 1997.

35. Ibid.

36. Harris, *The Rise and Fall of Gay Culture*, 79.

37. Chasin, *Selling Out*, 33.

38. Bray, quoted in Hoffman, "Mixed Media."

CONCLUSION

1. Joshua Gamson, *Freaks Talk Back: Tabloid Talk Shows and Sexual Nonconformity* (Chicago: University of Chicago Press, 1998), 214.

2. Anna Quindlen, "The Right to Be Ordinary," *Newsweek*, September 11, 2000, 82.

3. Michael Bronski, *The Pleasure Principle: Sex, Backlash, and the Struggle for Gay Freedom* (New York: St. Martin's, 1998), 2.

4. Corey Creekmur and Alexander Doty, eds., *Out in Culture: Gay, Lesbian, and Queer Essays on Popular Culture* (Durham, NC: Duke University Press, 1995), 5.

5. Charles Kaiser, "What the News Stories Leave Out," *Washington Post*, January 24, 2001, A15.

6. "The Nation," *Advocate*, September 26, 2000, 16.

7. Bronski, *The Pleasure Principle*, 16.

8. Ibid., 183.

Bibliography

Advocate, 2 March 1999, 15.

Advocate, 10 November 1998, 18.

Alexander, Kathey, and Holly Morris. "Gay Activists Plan 'Family' Rally in Cobb." *Atlanta Journal and Constitution*, 14 August 1993.

Alsop, Ronald. "In Marketing to Gays, Lesbians Are Often Left Out." *Wall Street Journal*, 11 October 1999.

Alwood, Edward. *Straight News: Gays, Lesbians, and the News Media.* New York: Columbia University Press, 1996.

Ansen, David. "Gay Films Are a Drag." *Newsweek*, 18 March 1996.

Badgett, M. V. Lee. *Income Inflation: The Myth of Affluence among Gay, Lesbian, and Bisexual Americans.* New York: A Joint Publication of the Policy Institute of the National Gay and Lesbian Task Force and the Institute for Gay and Lesbian Strategic Studies, 1998.

Bauder, David. "'Dawson's Creek' Gay Character Gets Little Notice So Far." *Atlanta Journal and Constitution*, 17 March 1999.

———. "TV's Independent Film Channel Running a Gay and Lesbian Film Festival." *Associated Press*, 9 February 2000.

Bawer, Bruce. *A Place at the Table: The Gay Individual in American Society.* New York: Touchstone Books, 1994.

———, ed. *Beyond Queer: Challenging Gay Left Orthodoxy.* New York: Free Press, 1996.

Berke, Richard L. "Chasing the Polls on Gay Rights." *New York Times*, 2 August 1998.

―――. "Flurry of Anti-Gay Remarks Has G.O.P. Fearing Backlash." *New York Times,* 30 June 1998.

Ben-Iztak, Paul. "Same-Sex Parents Struggle for Acceptance in U.S." *Reuter Library Report,* 6 August 1993.

Bernstein, Andrea. "Commentary on Lack of Gay Sex on Prime Time." *All Things Considered,* NPR, 18 January 1995. Transcript no. 1731-7.

Biddle, Frederic. "Gays in Prime Time; Network Television Remains Uncomfortable with Homosexuality." *Boston Globe,* 24 December 1995.

Biskupic, Joan. "Court Allows Ban on Gay Rights Laws." *Washington Post,* 14 October 1998.

Blumenfeld, Laura. "Every Girl's Dream." *Washington Post,* 20 November 1996.

Bradley, Deborah. "Unions: More Gay and Lesbian Couples Are Acknowledging Their Commitment through Ceremonies." *Dallas Morning News,* 4 May 1994.

Bronski, Michael. *The Pleasure Principle: Sex, Backlash, and the Struggle for Gay Freedom.* New York: St. Martin's Press, 1998.

Browning, Frank. "Why Marry?" In *Same-Sex Marriage: Pro and Con,* edited by Andrew Sullivan, 133. New York: Vintage, 1997 (originally in the *New York Times,* 17 April 1996).

Bruni, Frank. "Lip Service: Kiss between Gays Remains Taboo." *Arizona Republic,* 16 February 1994.

Bull, Chris, and John Gallagher. *Perfect Enemies: The Religious Right, the Gay Movement, and the Politics of the 1990s.* New York: Crown Publishers, 1996.

Burke, Jim. "'Birdcage' Success Is More about Laughs Than Liberalism." *Boston Herald,* 14 March 1996, 59.

Business Wire, 17 February 2000.

―――, "Advertising Spending in Gay Press Increases for the Fourth Straight Year." 22 February 1999.

CNN. With correspondent Charles Feldman. "Advertising Aimed at the Gay Community Surges." 7 October 1992. Transcript no. 200-1.

Cahill, Sean, and Erik Ludwig. "Courting the Vote: The 2000 Presidential Candidates' Positions on Gay, Lesbian, Bisexual, and Transgender Issues." Policy Institute of the National Gay and Lesbian Task Force.

Capsuto, Steven. *Alternate Channels: The Uncensored Story of Gay and Lesbian Images on Radio and Television.* New York: Ballantine Books, 2000.

Carman, John. "Goodman Plays It Safe as Gay Guy." *San Francisco Chronicle,* 1 November 2000.

Chasin, Alexandra. *Selling Out: The Gay and Lesbian Movement Goes to Market.* New York: St. Martin's Press, 2000.

Chauncey, George. *Gay New York: Gender, Urban Culture, and the Making of the Gay Male World, 1890–1940.* New York: Basic Books, 1994.

"Cheers and Jeers." *TV Guide,* 17–23 May 1997.

Clark, Danae. "Commodity Lesbianism." In *Out in Culture: Gay, Lesbian, and Queer Essays on Popular Culture,* edited by Corey Creekmur and Alexander Doty. Durham, NC: Duke University Press, 1995.

Clendinen, Dudley, and Adam Nagourney. *Out For Good: The Struggle to Build a Gay Rights Movement in America.* New York: Simon & Schuster, 1999.

Clinton, Kate. "Kiss Me, Aunt Kate." *Advocate,* 22 June 1999.

Cohen, Karen J. "Gays in GOP Push Agenda." *Wisconsin State Journal,* 24 October 1993.

"Coming Out" *Advertising Age Interactive Special Report Supplement,* 1 November 1999.

Corliss, Richard. "The Gay Gauntlet." *Time,* 7 February 1994.

———. "The Final Frontier; Two New Movies Pose the Question, Can't Hollywood Treat Gays Like Normal People?" *Time,* 11 March 1999.

Cyr, Diane. "The Emerging Gay Market." *Catalog Age* 10, no. 11 (November 1993).

Dally Johnston, Michelle. "Strange Brew: Coors Taps into Liberal 'Domestic Partner' Benefits, Stunning Its Gay Critics." *Denver Westword,* 21 June 1995.

Dargis, Manohla. "Getting Past fabulousness to Real Life." *New York Times,* 5 March 2000.

Dart, John. "Retreat for Gays, Lesbians Opens." *Los Angeles Times,* 18 April 1998.

Davis, Riccardo A. "Markets Game for Gay Events." *Advertising Age,* 30 May 1994.

Dean, Sherrie. "Showbiz Today." CNN, 30 August 1993. Transcript no. 363-4.

D'Emilio, John. "Capitalism and Gay Identity." In *Powers of Desire: The Politics of Sexuality,* edited by Ann Snitow, Christine Stansell, and Sharon Thompson. New York: Monthly Review Press 1983.

Dickerson, Marla. "Christian Group Escalates Boycott Against Disney." *Los Angeles Times,* 2 July 1996.

Dohrn, Beatrice. "Bitter Losses, Sweet Victories: A Recipe for Progress." *Lambda Update* (winter 1999): 5.

Doty, Alexander. *Making Things Perfectly Queer: Interpreting Mass Culture.* Minneapolis: University of Minnesota Press, 1993.

Duberman, Martin, ed. *Queer Representations: Reading Lives, Reading Cultures.* New York: New York University Press, 1997.

Dunlap, David W. "Gay Images, Once Kept Out, Are Out Big Time." *New York Times,* 21 January 1996, 29.

———. "Support for Gay Adoptions Seems to Wane." *New York Times,* 1 May 1995, A13.

Elliott, Stuart. "Hill & Knowlton Forms a Unit to Direct Public Relations Efforts Toward Gay Men and Lesbians." *New York Times,* 23 June 1995, D5.

———. "Homosexual Imagery Is Spreading from Print Campaigns to General-Interest TV Programming." *New York Times,* 30 June 1997, D12.

Epstein, Jeffrey. "Prime Time for Gay Youth." *Advocate,* 27 April 1999, 60.

Ettelbrick, Paula. "Since When Is Marriage a Path to Liberation?" *Out/Look* (fall 1989).

Fargo, Jason. "Gay Marketing: A Profitable Niche?" *Credit Card Management,* March 1999.

Fraser, Deborah. "Gay and Lesbian Groups Targets Hate Speech with TV Ads." *All Things Considered,* NPR, 21 December 1995. Transcript no. 2068-8.

Freiberg, Peter. "Miller Contemplates Gay TV Ad." *Washington Blade,* 23 July 1999.

———. "United's Skies Turn Friendlier." *Washington Blade,* 6 August 1999.

Gamson, Joshua. "Diversity Follies." *American Prospect,* 3 January 3 2000.

———. *Freaks Talk Back: Tabloid Talk Shows and Sexual Nonconformity.* Chicago: University of Chicago Press, 1998.

"Gay Rights in California." Editorial. *New York Times,* 9 October 1999.

Gilbert, Jennifer. "Ad Spending Booming for Gay-Oriented Sites." *Advertising Age,* 6 December 1999.

Givhan, Robin. "The Fetching Men of Abercrombie & Fitch." *Washington Post,* 7 August 1998.

Gluckman, Amy, and Betsy Reed. "The Gay Marketing Moment." In *Homo-Economics: Capitalism, Community, and Lesbian and Gay Life,* edited by Amy Gluckman and Betsy Reed. New York: Routledge, 1997.

Goldberg, Carey. "Acceptance of Gay Men and Lesbians Is Growing, Study Says." *New York Times,* 31 May 1998.

———. "Vermont Residents Split over Civil Unions Law." *New York Times,* 3 September 2000.

Goldstein, Richard. "Believers Who Brunch." *Village Voice,* October 27–November 2 1999.

Goodman, John. "TV Declares Open Season on Gays." *San Francisco Examiner,* 16 September 1999.

Gross, Larry. "Visibility and Its Discontents." *Images* (a publication of the Gay and Lesbian Alliance Against Defamation, 2000).

———. "What Is Wrong with This Picture? Lesbian Women and Gay Men on Television." In *Queer Words, Queer Images: Communication and the Construction of Homosexuality,* edited by R. Jeffrey Ringer. New York: New York University Press, 1994.

Gross, Larry, and James Woods, eds. *The Columbia Reader on Lesbians and Gay Men in Media, Society, and Politics.* New York: Columbia University Press, 1999.

Guthmann, Edward. "Lots of Lesbian Movies Coming Out." *San Francisco Chronicle,* February 1996.

Gutierrez, Eric. "Opening Hollywood's Closet." *Los Angeles Times,* 10 March 1996.

———. "TV's Gay Teenagers Get Real." *Los Angeles Times,* 10 May 1999.

Hanania, Joseph. "Resurgence of Gay Roles on Television." *Los Angeles Times,* 3 November 1994.

Handy, Bruce. "He Called Me Ellen Degenerate?" *Time,* 14 April 1997.

Harris, Daniel. *The Rise and Fall of Gay Culture.* New York: Hyperion, 1997.

Harris, Scott. "2 Moms or 2 Dads—and a Baby." *Los Angeles Times,* 20 October 1991.

Havemann, Judith. "N.J. Allows Gays to Jointly Adopt." *Washington Post,* 18 December 1997.

Hetter, Katia. "Gay Rights Issues Bust Out All Over." *U.S. News & World Report,* 2 October 1995.

———. "Globe-Trotting in the Gay '90s." *U.S. News & World Report,* 16 June 1997.

"Homosexuality in American Television." *Larry King Show,* CNN, 16 October 1997. With guests Betty DeGeneres, Chastity Bono, Jerry Falwell, Barney Frank, Robert Peters.

Hopkins, Tom. "Gays on TV." *Dayton Daily News,* 20 August 1995.

Horovitz, Bruce. "Report Counters Belief That Gays Earn More." *USA Today,* 3 December 1998.

HRC Press Release, 7 September 1999.

Hudis, Mark. "Gays Back in Prime Time." *Mediaweek* 3, no. 50 (13 December 1993).

Interactive PR & Marketing News 2, no. 26. December 18, 1998.

International Communications Research. Telephone survey of 1003 adults, 19–22 September 1996.

Iwata, Edward. "Here's a New One: Corporate America Is at the Vanguard of Gay and Lesbian Rights." *Commercial Appeal*, 24 April 1996, 10B.

Jacobs, A. J. "Out?" *Entertainment Weekly*, October 4, 1996, 22.

———. "When Gay Men Happen to Straight Women," *Entertainment Weekly*, October 23, 1998.

Jay, Karla. "Queers Ahoy!" *Village Voice*, 23–29 September 1998.

Jones, Christopher. "The Point." *Washington Blade*, 12 September 1997, online edition.

Kaiser, Charles. "Valour! Compassion! Laughs!" *New York Times*, 21 December 1997, sec. 2, p. 37, col. 5.

Karlen, Neal. "Ho-hum: The Kiss That Didn't Rock the World." *New York Times*, 5 October 1997.

Keen, Lisa. *Washington Post*, 31 October 1993, C3.

Keller, James, and William Glass, "In & Out: Self-Referentiality and Hollywood's 'Queer' Politics." *Journal of Popular Television and Film* 26, no. 3 (fall 1998): 136–43.

Kempley, Rita. "'Affection': Two Men and a Barbie." *Washington Post*, 17 April 1998, B4.

Kiernan, Laura A. "Lesbian Couple Thrilled Over Adoption Ruling." *Boston Globe*, 12 September 1993, 29.

Knott, Tom. "Did You Hear the News? Ellen Is Still Gay." *Washington Times*, 23 October 1997, C2.

Kramer, Larry. "Why I Hated 'Philadelphia.'" *Los Angeles Times*, 9 January 1994, 29.

Krupp, Charla. "Can 'Nice' Lesbians Be Good Box Office?" *Glamour*, May 1992, 175.

Lacayo, Richard. "The New Gay Struggle." *Time*, 26 October 1998, 32–36.

Lad, Susan. "We Are Family." *News & Record* (Greensboro, NC), 14 August 14 1995, D1.

Latz Griffin, Jean. "The Gay Baby Boom." *Chicago Tribune*, 3 September 1992, C1.

Levere, Jane L. "Gay Publications Gain Ad Spending." *New York Times*, 4 March 1999, C8.

Levine, Daniel S. "Mainstream Advertisers Start to Discover Gay Market." *San Francisco Business Times*, 21 July 1995, A5.

Levy, Dan. "Out in America: New Gay Frontiers." *San Francisco Chronicle*, 28 April 1994, A1.

Lewin, Ellen. "Weddings without Marriage: Making Sense of Lesbian and Gay Commitment Rituals." In *Queer Families, Queer Politics: Challenging Culture and the State,* edited by Mary Bernstein and Renate Reimann. New York: Columbia University Press, 2001.

Littlefield, Kinney. "Gay Stereotypes Come Crashing Down on TV as Characters Get 'Real.'" *Arizona Republic*, 27 December 1995, C7.

Loebs, Claire. "Gay Partners with Children; Adoption a Challenge in Climate of Intolerance, Legal Ambiguities." *Arizona Republic,* 27 July 1995, C1.

Lowy, Joan. "Adoptions by Gays Ignite Fights across U.S." *Detroit News,* 7 March 1999, A10.

Ly, Phuong. "Industry Embraces Same-Sex Couples." *Washington Post,* 22 February 2000, B3.

MacDonald, Sally. "Same-Sex Parents Lead Similar Family Life." *Times-Picayune,* 2 July 1995.

Marder, Keith. "A Kiss, not The Kiss, on 'Ellen.'" *Daily News of Los Angeles,* 24 September 1997.

McGrory, Brian. "Gays Face Growing Backlash." *Boston Sunday Globe,* 28 November 1993.

Mil, Erika. "It's Not a Secret, but Still Exciting." *New York Times,* 10 April 1997.

Miller, Cyndee. "The Ultimate Taboo." *Marketing News TM,* 14 August 1995.

Moore, Martha. "Courting the Gay Market." *USA Today,* 23 April 1993.

Moret, Jim. "Newt's Sister Marries 'Friends' Lesbian Stars." *CNN Showbiz Today,* January 17, 1996. Transcript no. 1005-3.

Morgan, Pat. "A New Frontier." *Chicago Tribune,* 3 June 1992.

Mui, Nelson. "Management Buyout Team Envisions a Gay Mega Publishing Brand." *Daily News Record,* Capital Cities Media Inc., 9 April 1999.

Mulryan/Nash. *Gay Press Report,* 1998.

NCLR Newsletter. Fall 1998 .

Ness, Carol. "Gains for Gays in U.S. Business: Conference Finds Much Achieved, but Much Left to Do." *San Francisco Examiner,* 18 October 1993.

"A New Affluent Target Market Comes Out." *Chain Store Age,* 1 January 1998.

Newsweek, 27 June 1994.

NGLTF. Direct Report, March 1998.

———. "A Plan for Action," September 1999.

———. Press Release. 3 January 2000.

Ostrow, Joanne. "Beyond Ellen: Gays Make Headway in Well-Rounded Roles." *Denver Post,* 3 August 1997.

Page, Clarence. "Same-Sex Marriages Strengthen the Institution, Not Demonize It." *Phoenix Gazette,* 23 May 1996, B5.

Parish Perkins, Ken. "How Deeply Will 'Dawson's Creek' Test Waters with Gay Character?" *Arizona Republic,* 31 March 1999.

Parker, Penny. "Ski Resorts Pressed to Diversify." *Denver Post,* 13 March 1999.

Pawlak, Hadley. "New Yellow Pages Directory Finds Market in Gay Community." *Buffalo News,* 4 September 1999.

Pergament, Alan. "Fall Preview: The Television Season Heading into the Year 2000 Offers Some Alarming Trends and Some Thoughtful Shows." *Buffalo News,* 5 September 1999.

"PlanetOut Tops One Million Unique Site Visitors." *Business Wire,* 1 February 2000.

Polikoff, Nancy. "Marriage as Choice? Since When?" *Gay Community News* 24, nos. 3–4 (winter–spring 1996): 26–27.

Poynter, Chris. "Kentucky's Gay-Rights Battle." *Courier-Journal,* 18 October 1999.

PR Newswire, 5 April 1999.

————, 30 April 1999.

Preble, Kathy. 'Cracking the Gay Market Code." *Tampa Tribune,* 9 July 1999.

Reuters. "Disney Boycott Escalated by Baptist Group." *Washington Post,* 14 August 1999.

————. "National News Brief: California Recognizes Tax Right of Gay Parents." *New York Times,* 4 November 2000.

Robb, David. "Family Values Group Urges NBC to Omit Lesbian Kiss from 'Serving in Silence.'" *Baltimore Sun,* 2 January 1995.

Romesburg, Don. "30 Years Ago Perry Forms MCC." *Advocate,* 26 May 1998.

Rosenthal, Phil. "Walls' Talk: Stone Tells of Gay Role in HBO Film." *Chicago Sun-Times,* 2 March 2000.

Rothman, Cliff. "Advertising and Marketing: Gay Regionals Lead Growth in Publishing." *Los Angeles Times,* 12 November 1999.

Ruark, Jennifer. Interview with Michael Warner. *Chronicle of Higher Education,* 11 February 2000.

Sanchez, Rene. "'America's Largest Problem' Is Hate, President Tells Gay Group." *Washington Post.* 3 October 1999.

Schacht, Robin, and Greg Varner. "Is Ellen Too Gay?" *Washington Blade,* 13 March 1998.

Schwartz, John. "Online Gays Become a Market for Advertisers." *Washington Post,* 22 May 1999.

Seidman, Steven. *Difference Troubles: Queering Social Theory and Sexual Politics.* Cambridge, U.K.: Cambridge University Press, 1997.

Senior, Adriana. "Two New Internet Banks Cater to Gays and Lesbians." *American Banker* 164, no. 198 (14 October 1999).

Servicemembers Legal Defense Network.

Shen, Fern. "A Same-Sex Couple Married to the Cause." *Washington Post,* 10 September 1996.

Shister, Gail. "Gay Alliance Seeks More Characters on Television." *Milwaukee Journal Sentinel,* 25 August 1999.

Smith, Barbara. *The Truth That Never Hurts: Writings on Race, Gender, and Freedom.* New Brunswick: Rutgers University Press, 1998.

Smith, Linell. "Gay Parents Have Typical Worries." *Baltimore Sun,* 23 July 1995.

Strauss, Bob. "Gay Film Roles More Visible, but Honest Portrayals Still Rare," *Plain Dealer,* 17 March 1996.

Streitmatter, Rodger. *Unspeakable: The Rise of the Gay and Lesbian Press in America.* Boston: Faber & Faber, 1995.

Strongheart, Amy Adams Squire. "A Foundation for Same-Sex Marriage." *St. Louis Post-Dispatch,* 10 February 1994, 7B.

Sullivan, Andrew. "They've Changed, So They Say." *New York Times,* 26 July 1998.

————. "When Plagues End." *New York Times Magazine,* 10 November 1996.

————, ed. *Same-Sex Marriage: Pro and Con.* New York: Vintage, 1997.

Sullivan, Mark. "Judges Order Scouts to Accept Gays." *Washington Blade,* 6 August 1999.

Tuller, David. "Lesbian Families—Study Shows Healthy Kids." *San Francisco Chronicle,* 23 November 1992.

TZ. "The Myth of Gay Affluence." *American Prospect,* September–October 1999.

Vaid, Urvashi. Preface to *Income Inflation: The Myth of Affluence among Gay, Lesbian, and Bisexual Americans,* edited by M. V. Lee Badgett. New York: A Joint Publication of the Policy Institute of the National Gay and Lesbian Task Force and the Institute for Gay and Lesbian Strategic Studies, 1998.

———. *Virtual Equality: The Mainstreaming of Gay and Lesbian Liberation.* New York: Anchor Books, 1995.

Waddington, Chris. "Gay Parents Gather to Share Advice, Common Experiences." *Star Tribune* (Minneapolis, MN), 28 February 1999.

Wade, Betsy. "The Booming Gay Market." *Chicago Tribune,* 3 January 1993.

———. "More Options for Gay Travelers." *New York Times,* 29 January 1995.

Walters, Suzanna Danuta. "From Here to Queer: Radical Feminism, Postmodernism, and the Lesbian Menace (or, Why Can't a Woman Be More Like a Fag?)." *Signs* 21, no. 4 (summer 1996): 830–69.

———. "The Gay Next Door (Now in Prime Time)." *Harvard Gay and Lesbian Review* 5, no. 2 (1998).

———. *Material Girls: Making Sense of Feminist Cultural Theory.* Berkeley: University of California Press, 1995.

———. "Sex, Text, and Context: (In)Between Feminism and Cultural Studies." In *Revisioning Gender,* edited by Judith Lorber, Myra Marx Ferree, and Beth Hess. Thousand Oaks, CA: Sage, 1998.

———. "Take My Domestic Partner, Please: Gays and Marriage in the Era of the Visible." In *Queer Families, Queer Politics: Challenging Culture and the State,* edited by Mary Bernstein and Renate Reimann. New York: Columbia University Press, 2001.

———. "Wedding Bells and Baby Carriages: Heterosexuals Imagine Gay Families, Gay Families Imagine Themselves." In *Lines of Narrative: Psychosocial Perspectives,* edited by Molly Andrews et al. London: Routledge, 2001.

Wardlow, Daniel L., ed. *Gays, Lesbians, and Consumer Behavior: Theory, Practice, and Research Issues in Marketing.* New York: Haworth Press, 1996.

Warner, Michael. *Fear of a Queer Planet: Queer Politics and Social Theory.* Minneapolis: University of Minnesota Press, 1993.

———. *The Trouble with Normal: Sex, Politics, and the Ethics of Gay Life:* New York: Free Press, 2000.

Wells, Jess. "The Changes Wrought: How Parenting Is Changing Lesbian Culture." In *Homefronts: Controversies in Nontraditional Parenting,* edited by Jess Wells. Los Angeles: Alyson Books, 2000.

Weston, Kath. *Families We Choose: Lesbians, Gays, Kinship.* New York: Columbia University Press, 1991.

Wilke, Michael. "A Kiss before Buying." *Advocate,* 27 April 1999.

Wilson, Terry. "Coming Out from Leading a Double Life; Telling Family, Friends Still a Scary Passage for Gays and Lesbians." *Chicago Tribune,* 14 July 1995.

Wingert, Pat, and Barbara Kantrowitz. "Gay Today: The Family." *Newsweek* (20 March 2000).

Yardley, Jonathan. "The Baptists' Passion Play." *Washington Post,* 23 June 1997.

Index

AIDS
  and *Angels in America,* 5
  and bringing "on themselves," 76
  and depiction of gays within commu-
    nity, 144
  and *Jeffrey,* 148
  and meaningful representations of gays
    in television, 61
  new organizations relative to, 6
  and new visibility and public debate,
    50
  and *Philadelphia,* 4, 137–40
  public version of, 17
Alda, Alan, 170
Alice B. Toklas Lesbian and Gay Democratic Club of San Francisco, 254
All in the Family (television show), 60, 61
"All the rage," meaning of term, 24
Ally McBeal (television show), 107, 119–
  20, 296
Alport, David, 277
American Beauty (movie), 159–60
American Family Association (AFA),
  45–46
And the Band Played On (television movie),
  103
American Express "Checks for Two"
  campaign, 259, 267
Angels in America (play), 5
Ansen, David, 133
Anti-gay activism
  and backlash against corporations,
    45–46
  and boycotts and attacks from Chris-
    tian right, 114–15, 267
  debate over response to, 52–53
  and gay parenting, 215
  and response of biological argument,
    53
  and response of normalizing, 52–53
  and use of wealth, 241–42
Anti-gay referenda, 43–49
  ballot measures, 43–44
  Oregon anti-gay initiative, 43, 44
  and "special rights" framing of debate,
    44–45
Anti-gay violence
  and checking of behavior in public, 23
  and hate crimes, xvi, 9, 32
  and Matthew Shepard, xvi–xvii, 25,
    294, 295
Anti-sodomy laws, 44

Any Mother's Son (television movie), 103
Apple Computer, 41
Artificial insemination clinics, 212, 213
As Good as It Gets (movie), 108, 146, 150
"Assault on Gay America: The Life and
  Death of Billy Jack" (television documentary), 77
Assimilation, 18–20, 50, 51
  argument for and biological argument
    of gayness, 53–54
  and *Common Ground,* 193–96
  and cooptation, 19–20, 285
  and death of "camp," 293–94
  and drag queens, 142
  and gay entrepreneurship, 285
  of gays into mainstream television,
    112
  and lesbianism and films, 163
  and parenting, 215–19, 221–23, 228
  and *Philadelphia,* 139
  and same-sex marriage, 183–84, 189–
    90, 191
  and tension with "gaying of America,"
    21
  vs. maintenance of distinct subcultural
    identity, 292
  See also Normalizing of gays

Backlash
  against corporations, 45–46, 255
  anti-gay, 9
  and anti-gay initiatives, 47
  and blaming of gays for, 75–76
  See also Anti-gay activism; Christian
    conservatives
Badgett, M. V. Lee, 242, 243, 281–82
Bain, Art, 42
Baldwin, Tammy, 33
Banana Republic "Chosen Families" ads,
  256
Banderas, Antonio, 137
Barclay, Paris, 118
Basic Instinct (movie), 158, 162–63
Bauer, Gary, 216
Bawer, Bruce, 51, 52
Bearse, Amanda, 4
Being John Malkovich (movie), 159
Benetton ads, 256–57
Bennett, Lisa, 3–4
Bennett, Tim, 251
Bennett, William, 180
Berle, Milton, 17

Encoded ads, 245, 249–54
Entertainment Weekly (magazine), 95
Entrepreneurship, gay, 7–8, 273–89
  and activism, 282–84, 286, 289
  and cooptation, 285
  and differences marketing to gays vs.
    lesbians, 278
  and financial services, 282
  and gay bookstores, 273–74, 278–79
  and gay efforts within mainstream
    companies, 275–76
  and gay-lesbian values index, 282–
    83
  and gay-owned and targeted business,
    276
  and Internet, 280–85
  and lack of real change in gay commu-
    nity, 287–89
  and merger mania and buyouts, 281
  and threat of straight companies spe-
    cializing in gay services, 279–80
  and tourism, 276–78, 279
  varieties of, 274
  See also Advertising; Marketing, gay
Eskridge, William, 177, 182, 190
Etheridge, Melissa, 4, 30, 82, 305n13
Everett, Rupert, 156–57, 170–71

Faludi, Susan, 47
Falwell, Jerry, xv, 20, 267
Family (television show), 60, 61
Family, gay, 4, 6, 10, 210–35
  as "anti-family," 211
  and assimilation, 196
  and challenge to nuclear, 211
  and coming out, 198
  and depiction as vacillation between
    normal and exotic, 212
  and difference from straight, 227
  as last holdout in battle for rights,
    230
  and liberal view of sameness to defend,
    215
  as opportunity to create blueprints for
    future, 230
  and politics, 210–11
  and response to AIDS and *Philadelphia*,
    137–38
  and *The Birdcage*, 141
  and *The Next Best Thing*, 170–71
  See also Family of choice; Parents and
    parenting

Family Defense Council, 115
Family Next Door, The (newsletter), 212
Family of choice
  and forms of mutual responsibility,
    229
  and *Object of My Affection*, 168
  as providing blueprints for families of
    future, 230
  and *Queer as Folk*, 123–24
Family Research Council, 115, 189, 214,
  215
"Family values," 38–39, 69
  and feminism, 211
  and gay parenting, 215
  as political litmus test, 210–11
  and same-sex marriage, 181
  and *The Birdcage*, 140–41
Fashion statement, gayness as, 18
  See also "Lesbian chic"
Feinstein, Howard, 136
Feminism and family values, 211
Fierstein, Harvey, 155, 192
Films, 4–5, 131–79
  and "already gay" instead of coming-
    out story, 207–8
  brief history of gay, 131–37
  and depiction of gays in community,
    144–48
  and drag queens and cross-dressing,
    140–44
  and encoded gay content and
    invisibility, 132–33
  and gay content and heterosexual
    audience, 136–37
  and gay parents, 219–20
  and good gays and desexualization and
    loss of community, 150
  and historical development of images
    of lesbians, 307–8n4
  impact of compared with television,
    27, 131
  and "incidental queer," 154–61
  increase in number of films containing
    gay characters, 135
  independent, 173–76, 302n23,
    308n12
  and "lesbian chic," 161–66
  and liberal narrative for the nineties,
    149–76
  and numbers of lesbians few in com-
    parison to gays, 162
  and *Philadelphia*, 137–40

and poor box-office of "gay life" movies, 146–47
and risk of depicting gay characters, 27–28
and self-censorship of gay content, 136–37
and star-crossed lovers and misplaced affections, 166–71
See also Incidental queers; Lesbian chic; *Individual films by name*
Financial services, 282
Flawless (movie), 152–54
Foster children, 213, 214
Fox, Michael J., 98–99, 104
Frank, Barney, 31, 50, 51
Franklin, Nancy, 121
Frasier (television show), 97, 98
Freaks Talk Back (Gamson), 103
Fried Green Tomatoes (movie), 162
Friedman, Jeffrey, 140, 143–44
Friedman, Liz, 101
Friends (television show), 98
and same-sex marriage, 183–85, 186, 192

Gaither, Billy Jack, 77
Gamson, Joshua, 12–13, 103–4, 118, 121, 291
and numbers of gays on television, 111, 112
Garland, Judy, 21
Gay 90's, The: Sex, Power, and Influence (television documentary), 75–76
Gay, Lesbian and Straight Educational Network (GLSEN), xiii
and cataloging of social exclusion and violence, 198
Gay Agenda, The (videotape), 77
Gay and Lesbian Alliance Against Defamation (GLAAD), xv
and Coors Brewing Company, 41
and monitoring of films, 6, 137
and tracking of television through GLAADAlert, 96
Gay and Lesbian Millennium March on Washington, 281, 287, 289, 292
Gay and Lesbian Pride Month, 32
Gay and Lesbian Victory Fund, 254
"Gayby boom," 212
Gay.com, 280–81, 283–84, 285, 289
Gay Financial Network, 282
Gay Games, 7, 8, 243, 254

"Gaying of America," 21, 293, 296, 299
Gay/Lesbian/Bisexual Corporate Letter, 42
Gay man/straight women relationships, 108
"Gay Marketing Moment, The" (Gluckman and Reed), 239
Gay Pride, 255
Gay pride marches, 297
and heterosexual involvement, 48
and March on Washington in April 1993, 47–48
and Millennium March of April 2000, 201, 287, 289, 292
as open-air mall, 235
Gay Pride Month, 102
Gays
as both different and same as heterosexuals, 18
disjunction of cultural and political circumstance of, 22
as last group against whom it is legal to discriminate, 54
as sissy or dandy seen as humorous, 161
survey of general public's acceptance of, 48–49
as unable to be mature enough for marriage or children, 185, 309n11
"Gay/straight alliances," xiii, 299
Gay studies programs, 6
Gay Television Network (GTN), 8
"Gay vague" or coded messages, 245, 249–54, 267
Genre (magazine), 240
Gilbert, Matthew, 123
Gingrich, Candice, 4, 183, 184
Givhan, Robin, 245
GLAAD. *See* Gay and Lesbian Alliance Against Defamation
Glendering, Parris, 40
Gluckman, Amy, 239, 247
Go (movie), 159
Go Fish (movie), 4, 173, 176
Goldberg, Whoopie, 155, 156, 224
Goldstein, Richard, 20
Goldwater, Barry, 38
Good gay
bad gay separation, 76–78
and desexualization and loss of community, 150